PHILIP
MASSINGER

PHILIP MASSINGER

Reproduced from the frontispiece to *Three New Playes* by Philip
Massinger, 1655. The engraving is by T. Cross and the inscription
reads *Vera ac Viva Effigies Phillippi Massinger Gent.*

PHILIP MASSINGER

THE MAN AND THE PLAYWRIGHT

T. A. DUNN

*Lecturer in English at the University College
of Ghana*

PUBLISHED ON BEHALF OF

THE UNIVERSITY COLLEGE OF GHANA

BY

THOMAS NELSON AND SONS LTD

UNIVERSITY COLLEGE OF GHANA
Achimota   Accra   Ghana
London Office
29 Tavistock Square London WC1

THOMAS NELSON AND SONS LTD
Parkside Works Edinburgh 9
36 Park Street London W1
312 Flinders Street Melbourne C1
302–304 Barclays Bank Building
Commissioner and Kruis Streets
Johannesburg

Thomas Nelson and Sons (Canada) Ltd
91–93 Wellington Street West   Toronto 1

Thomas Nelson and Sons
19 East 47th Street New York 17

Société Française d'Editions Nelson
25 rue Henri Barbusse Paris V^e

First published 1957

PREFACE

Little apology is necessary by way of preface to a critical study of Massinger. No full-length, detailed study of the playwright has ever appeared in English. All that we have of what might be called 'book length' is a very brief work by Professor Cruickshank that was published over thirty-five years ago, and this can scarcely now be considered adequate. Even critical essays on Massinger are rare, and comments and asides on the playwright which have appeared in the more general studies of the Jacobean-Caroline period have not usually been notable either for their perspicacity or for the knowledge they reveal of his work. It is in some measure as an attempt to fill this gap that this book has been written.

I have not, however, attempted to claim for Massinger a position or an importance that does not accord with his worth. He is not, it must be admitted, a great, or even always a very good, dramatist. Nevertheless, his plays are of considerable interest as samples of the romantic tragi-comedies that held the stage after the death of Shakespeare. In addition, it must be remembered that Massinger was the principal writer for the public theatres from 1625 to 1640—a fact that in itself argues for his claim to closer examination. Thus the first object of this book has been an examination and appraisal of certain aspects of Massinger's dramatic technique.

Of additional, and perhaps in some respects even greater, interest, however, is the character of Massinger himself; a character that emerges with extraordinary clarity and precision of detail from a reading of his plays. My second object, therefore, has been to reveal or deduce something of the nature of Massinger's mind and character; to attempt as it were, to see Massinger plain. Both of these objects are comprehended in the title of this book.

Perhaps something of the eclipse which Massinger's work has undergone amongst students can be explained by the fact that he is deeply involved in the tangled undergrowth of collaboration which surrounds the Beaumont-Fletcher *corpus*. The reader will find little discussion of such matters here. Many scholars have laboured on the problems of the Jacobean collaborators, and their work forms an extensive literature in itself, embracing studies in Beaumont, Fletcher, Massinger, Field, Shirley, Heywood, and practically every other writer of the period as well as a vast mass of documentary material pertaining to the stage of the times. I have felt, therefore, that to deal adequately with such material would have called for a preliminary volume quite away from my immediate purposes, and that the consideration of such problems here would have confused the reader and obscured the object of my study, Massinger himself. It has seemed to me preferable to approach the Jacobean situation from the other end, and, by considering Massinger in the plays which are definitely his, to make my work absolute as far as he is concerned, but at the same time make it a groundwork to the wider study of the dramatic collaboration of Fletcher and his group by establishing the Massingerian technique and method of approach. It follows, therefore, that the plays with which I am almost solely concerned are the fifteen plays which Massinger wrote on his own.

Of course, in a general critical study of any playwright as prolific as Massinger, it is essential, in order to contain the subject within reasonable bounds, that a certain amount of material should be allowed to go by the board. This is perhaps a rather negative way of saying that I have consciously and deliberately dealt only very briefly with one or two topics which are sometimes considered important in a study of a playwright. My deliberate intention in this respect will be better understood when I say that I consider such topics as jetsam rather than as flotsam. My dismissal of questions of collaboration and attribution has already been explained. Similarly, I have considered that questions of the sources of the plays have already been exhaustively covered by the industrious researches of German scholars at the beginning of this century, and that the more technical aspects of versification are, in Massinger's case, of interest chiefly in connection with problems of collaboration. I have chosen to concentrate chiefly (though by no means exclusively) on matters which have become prominent largely within the last thirty or forty years—such matters as stagecraft, dramatic structure, the dramatist's view of the world, and blank-verse style. I have endeavoured to deal with such matters in ways that, while they have become commoner in studies of Shakespeare, have not yet been applied at all extensively to other writers—and have certainly never been applied to Massinger before. I have also tried to suggest new methods of approach (in particular in respect of matters of style) which may be applied with profit to other Jacobean dramatists. Throughout I have constantly compared and contrasted Massinger with Shakespeare; with Shakespeare, that is to say, both as a yardstick of dramatic excellence whose work is universally known and admired, and as the only other writer of the period with whom Massinger can be fully and fairly contrasted.

The ascertainable facts concerning the life of Massinger form as slight a biography as we possess of any of his contemporaries. Hartley Coleridge spends twelve pages of the introduction to his edition of the plays in bemoaning this dearth of material, and in the process forgets to give us, or misrepresents, some of the facts which are indisputable. In this he is typical of a long succession of writers on Massinger, who, since a dearth of tangible evidence breeds a wealth of conjecture, have each added their own little bit of guess-work to the fabric of the biography, in many cases accepting with an uncritical lack of reserve the statements of earlier writers, and have each contributed towards that process of accretion which culminated in the assertive fantasia of Phelan.[1]

In the general biographical introduction which comprises my first chapter I have tried in the first place to avoid the worst faults of the 'accretional approach' by going back wherever possible (as has not apparently been done before) to the original sources, in book or manuscript, for the verification of my material. In addition, I have explored, as far as has been practicable in the time at my disposal, the likeliest sources of new information. Of course, there must remain many new facts which are still undiscovered, since the wealth of manuscript material available in Britain is only now beginning to yield up its treasures. I have, however, derived a real satisfaction from having personally examined all these sources, both acknow-ledged and unacknowledged. I have, moreover, done something that, so far as I am aware, has not been done since the time of Aubrey: I have gone to Wiltshire and looked for material there, particularly in the collection of the Wiltshire Archaeological and Natural History Society at Devizes. From this quarry I present evidence supporting my contention that the Massingers were a family long established in Wiltshire. In this respect the item concerning the churching of Massinger's mother after his birth has never before been noted in accounts of the playwright's life. These results hardly do justice to long hours of searching through the parish records of Wiltshire and Gloucestershire; but here again I must plead that sources which have not before been examined in this connection have for the first time received adequate treatment. So much for the incontestable facts.

Secondly, I have tried to fill in the story of Massinger's life in the light of the accumulation of modern knowledge, by a re-examination and reassessment of the more conjectural suggestions, both those I have inherited and those I advance as part of my own contribution.

[1] See below, p. 6.

In particular I have taken advantage of the many clues to his life which Massinger has dropped in dedications, prologues, and epilogues, clues which have hitherto been completely ignored by his biographers. This task was long overdue, since, with the exception of a brief chapter in the study by Maurice Chelli, the inferential biography, like the demonstrable, has remained almost untouched during the past seventy years.

It is perhaps not out of place here to make a plea for a full and modern edition of the plays of Massinger. Gifford's edition, which I have had perforce to use, is a remarkable piece of work for its period but is now quite out-of-date and, by modern standards, inadequate. Several of the plays have been published in individual and fairly modern editions (see *Bibliography*) but this is not sufficient. What is required is a complete edition which will give the reader (I am not so concerned for the student of textual or bibliographical matters) a text which he can both study and enjoy and from which the scholar can draw his line-references, similar to those which we now possess for Shakespeare and Ben Jonson. Of course, such an edition would have to be part of a wider plan which embodied an edition of all the 'Beaumont and Fletcher' plays; but until such an edition appears, there must remain much research into this interesting period of the drama which it will be difficult, or even impossible, to carry out.

I should like to acknowledge the kind and generous help given to me by the Trustees of the Carnegie Trust for the Universities of Scotland and the Cross Trust; the assistance rendered by Mr. C. W. Pugh, M.B.E., Honorary Secretary of the Wiltshire Archaeological and Natural History Society, during my visit to Wiltshire; and the courtesy and politeness of many members of Library staffs, in particular those in the Libraries of the University of Edinburgh and the University College of Ghana. I can best acknowledge my debt to other scholars, especially those authors of books on Shakespeare and the Elizabethan-Jacobean period in general, by referring the reader to the bibliography at the end of this book. To those few people who have been most closely associated with me during this work I can only offer my gratitude and thanks, and know that they will appreciate how much I mean by those bare words.

THOMAS DUNN

University College of Ghana.
May 1957.

CONTENTS

★

LIST OF PLAYS

The uncollaborated plays by Massinger with which this book is
chiefly concerned are as follows:

THE BASHFUL LOVER
BELIEVE AS YOU LIST
THE BONDMAN
THE CITY MADAM
THE DUKE OF MILAN
THE EMPEROR OF THE EAST
THE GREAT DUKE OF FLORENCE
THE GUARDIAN
THE MAID OF HONOUR
A NEW WAY TO PAY OLD DEBTS
THE PARLIAMENT OF LOVE
THE PICTURE
THE RENEGADO
THE ROMAN ACTOR
THE UNNATURAL COMBAT

To
A. M. C.

Chapter One
BIOGRAPHY

On the 24th of November, 1583, Philip Massinger was baptised in the parish church of St. Thomas's at Salisbury. The entry in the register reads:

> November, 1583. Philip Messanger, the son of Arthur, baptised the 24th.

Since this entry was recorded in Hoare's *History of Modern Wiltshire* as early as 1843,[1] it is surprising that until quite recently his birthdate has been given tentatively as 1584.

It has been suggested[2] that he was born at Wilton, the seat of the Earl of Pembroke, his father's employer and patron. There is no reason, however, to suppose that he was born anywhere other than in the parish of St. Thomas's. Wilton is indeed only some three miles from Salisbury; but even so, had he been born there it would have been very unusual for him not to be baptised there also, and it was largely a desire to give Massinger a famous and romantic godfather in the person of Sir Philip Sidney that led his biographers to speculate wrongly as to his birthplace. A very brief search through the records of St. Thomas's at once reveals to any interested student not only the baptismal entry but also the further entry under 1583:

> Mr Messenger's wiffe churched the xvi of December, her crisom xiid.[3]

Unless, therefore, some substantial evidence can be produced to the contrary, it must be assumed that Massinger's parents lived in Salisbury itself and that he was born there.

The name of Massinger (usually spelled *Messager* or *Messenger*) is prominent in the records of Gloucester and Gloucestershire. For example, against the north wall of the church at Painswick, six miles south of Gloucester, there are several memorials of a Massinger family.[4] A Thomas Messenger was sheriff and mayor of Gloucester at the beginning of the sixteenth century; in 1553 a William Messenger

---

[1] Sir R. C. Hoare, pp. 619–623. [2] e.g. by H. Coleridge, p. xx.
[3] Printed in *The Chrysom Book of St. Thomas, New Sarum*, ed. E. R. Nevill, (*Wilts. Notes and Queries*, VI, 1908–1910, p. 304).
[4] Article by G. W. Messinger of Boston in *The New England Historical and Genealogical Register*, XIV, pp. 75–76, Boston, 1860.

was a Member of Parliament and afterwards mayor of the city; and the name continues to appear in connection with Gloucester after that date.

It is not necessary, however, to look outside Wiltshire for Massinger's forebears. The name is found in that county from quite early times. It is particularly common in the north, the stretch of country bounded by the triangle which may be imagined as drawn between Swindon, Malmesbury and Cirencester producing many. In 1371 a Thomas Messager was a witness in a case at Swindon.[1] Another Thomas Mesynger was one of the marginal signatories to the deed of surrender of Bradenstoke Priory in 1538–1539[2]; a John Messynger is recorded as being 'of Purton' in 1539[3]; a Thomas Messenger was part-owner of some lands in Cricklade, Chelworth, and Calcote in 1562[4]; an Elizabeth Messenger was married in Purton in 1568,[5] and a John Messenger is mentioned as being of that parish in 1569.[6] Messengers were still in this district in the seventeenth century. Richard and William Messenger were among a number of men who got into trouble for trespassing in Braydon Forest in 1625,[7] and a 'Joane Messenger' married a 'Jeriemia Keyt' at Lea in 1668.[8] A widow, Mary Messenger, was living in Calne in 1695.[9]

Further south, near Marlborough, we have notice of a Richard Massager and his wife, Alice, in 1352.[10] Their descendants, or some of them, seem to have stayed in that district, since from 1638 onwards the name occurs very frequently in the parish records of Preshute (which describe the bearers of the name as being 'of Manton').[11]

Moreover, Massingers appear in Salisbury itself. At the end of the fourteenth and the beginning of the fifteenth centuries Ralph Messenger and his wife Olive were leaseholders of a considerable extent of land near Amesbury.[12] It can safely be assumed that they were the parents, or at least near relations, of the most notable of the early Wiltshire Massingers. This was Walter Messager, who lived in

---

[1] *Abstracts of Wilts. Inquisitiones Post Mortem, Edw. III*, ed. E. Stokes, London, 1914, p. 367.
[2] *Wilts. N. & Q.*, IV, p. 280.
[3] *Musters in Wilts. 30 Men.*, VIII (B.M. TAB 436b.8.(18)).
[4] *A Calendar of Feet of Fines for Wilts*, ed. E. A. Fry (*Wilts. N. & Q., VII*, p. 319).
[5] *Wilts Parish Registers*, ed. W. P. W. Phillimore, VII, 1908, p. 101.
[6] *A Book of Musters in Co. Wilts.*, being an unpublished MS. at Longleat (*Wilts N. & Q.*, II, p. 2).
[7] J. Sadler's MS. *Extracts and Notes on Wiltshire Documents and Genealogy*, The Museum, Devizes, Vol. Bradenstoke-Buttermere, pp. 49–50.
[8] Transcript of *Lea Marriage Register* from a sheet headed 'Mannor of Lea & Cleverton' *Sadler Papers*, The Museum, Devizes, p. 107.
[9] *A Rate Made in August 1695 for the Upkeep of Calne Church*, (*Wilts. Arch. Mag.*, XLVII, 1935–1937, p. 340). [10] *Inquisitiones Post Mortem, Edw. III*, p. 227.
[11] Sadler MS. *Extracts*, Vol. Patney-Rashall, pp. 103, 109, 110, 112.
[12] *Calendar of Antrobus Deeds before 1625*, ed. R. B. Pugh, Devizes, 1947.

Salisbury, at Fisherton Anger. He was a Member of Parliament for Old Sarum in 1427 and again in 1430–1431. He seems to have been a legal man or attorney of sorts and is mentioned in many legal transactions from 1417 to 1460.[1] Before 1428 he married Isabel Saucer, daughter of a prominent Salisbury citizen, and they had only two children, a son, John, who became a priest and was still living towards the end of the century, and a daughter, Ede, who died without issue.[2] It seems fairly certain, therefore, that Philip Massinger was not descended directly from Walter Messager of Salisbury. However, it is not unreasonable to suppose that Walter had brothers. In 1415, for example, a Thomas Messagier occupied a tenement in S. Martin's Street in Salisbury.[3] Certain it is that the family were of considerable position in the town, and when, only a hundred years after Walter, we find Philip's father, Arthur Massinger, not only performing the same sort of legal work as Walter but also possessed of a brother likewise called Walter, a student at the same Oxford college, it would be rash to ignore the probable connection or to seek in Gloucester, as Phelan did,[4] for the dramatist's parentage. Again, had his father come from Gloucester originally and been employed by the Earl of Pembroke, it seems likely that he would have lived at Wilton instead of in Salisbury as the baptismal evidence suggests.

In the baptismal entry, in accordance with custom, the name of the child's mother is not recorded. As far as we are concerned, although the unusually large sum (probably worth about twenty shillings expressed in present-day value) she made as an offering at her churching is indicative of her husband's financial position, she must remain 'Mr Messenger's wiffe', and we have no means of knowing who she was. There is no record of Arthur Massinger's marriage in any of the extant parish registers of Salisbury. The name does not appear under marriages in the extant registers of St. Thomas, St. Martin, St. Edmund, or the Cathedral. These registers are not, of course, complete, but (especially when it is remembered that, as a rule, a man goes to his fiancée's parish to be married) in the absence of any clues pointing in a definite direction, there is little point in looking elsewhere. I have not come across Arthur Massinger's name in any of the many marriage registers I have examined from Wiltshire, Gloucestershire, or London. It

[1] *The Tropenell Cartulary*, the contents of an old Wilts. muniment chest, ed. J. S. Davies, Devizes, 1908, 2 vols. *passim*.
[2] *Antrobus Deeds*, Item 76 (A genealogical tree of the Saucer family).
[3] *Wilts. N. & Q.*, V, 1905–1907, p. 497. See also *Notes and Queries*, Series V, X, p. 465.
[4] For a discussion of Phelan's article, see below, pp. 6–9

should be added that there is no record in Salisbury of any other children born of the marriage.[1]

By reason of his position as an important member of the household of the Earl of Pembroke we know a great deal about Philip's father. In fact, we know a great deal more about the father than we know about the son.

During the seventeenth and eighteenth centuries the idea prevailed that the father's name was Philip. Langbaine, Wood, and Davies give it so. The error arose, as Gifford showed,[2] from the fact that the name is printed as 'Philip' in the dedication to the second (1638) edition of *The Bondman*.[3] This edition, however, is full of mistakes, and in any case the name is given correctly in the first (1624) edition. Davies had persisted in giving the name as Philip in spite of Oldys' correction.[4] It can only be assumed that Oldys is the only one of those older authorities who had seen the first edition of this play.

Arthur Massinger is probably the undergraduate of that name of St. Alban's Hall, Oxford, who graduated B.A. in 1571, was elected a Fellow of Merton College in 1572, and graduated M.A. in 1577.[5] In 1572 there was also a Walter Messenger, presumably a brother of Arthur, who was likewise a student in St. Alban's Hall.[6] That those two men were the father and the uncle of the dramatist is made extremely likely by the fact that when Philip in his turn went up to Oxford he too matriculated at St. Alban's Hall.

In 1578 Sir Humphrey Gilbert sailed on a voyage to 'discover and possess' remote 'heathen lands not actually possessed of any Christian prince or peoples'. This voyage failed of its purpose since, after many difficulties with his crews, Gilbert had finally to abandon it and return to Plymouth, having achieved no more than a brief skirmish with the Spaniards off Cape Verde. Mr. Mark Eccles has pointed out[7] that after Gilbert's first attempt to sail, when some of his company refused to put to sea again, one of the 'asured friends' who continued with him (and the list includes Sir Walter Raleigh) was a certain 'Arthure Messinger, gent'. This is almost certainly the man with whom we are dealing, since of the three Arthur Massingers who are recorded as living in England at that time, he

---

[1] But see the discussion on Phelan's article.   [2] p. xxxvii.
[3] See below, p. 10, for the text of this dedication.
[4] G. Langbaine, *An Account of the English Dramatick Poets*, 1691, copy with MS. notes by W. Oldys in the British Museum (C.28.g.1.). Davies (*Monck Mason*, p. li, footnote) 'cannot guess from what information Oldys . . . gives the Christian name of Arthur to Massinger's father'.
[5] Foster, *Alumni Oxoniensis*, p. 1004.   [6] Ibid., loc. cit.
[7] Letter in *TLS*, 16 July 1931, cf. *C.S.P. Dom. Eliz.*, pp. 126–149.

is the only one for whom we can find definite connections with the nobility and with the courtly circles which planned such ventures.

Arthur Massinger was a servant at Wilton to Henry Herbert, second Earl of Pembroke, and, on the latter's death in 1601, to his son, William, the third Earl, the man who, with his brother, later shared the honour of the dedication of the First Folio of Shakespeare. Numerous writers have been at some pains to make it quite clear that this service was not in any menial capacity. It is hardly necessary to enlarge upon this fact. Arthur Massinger's University qualifications and the business we find him transacting about the court of Queen Elizabeth are sufficient to clear us of any doubts we might have regarding his social status. Langbaine describes him as 'a gentleman belonging to the Earl of Montgomery'.[1] In a letter written by the Bishop of Salisbury to Cecil on 15th April 1596 he is described as 'Mr Messenger, the Earl's solicitor'.[2] He could, perhaps, be best described as house-steward and agent to the Earl, entrusted by him with business of a most confidential and important nature.

There are about a score of references to him in various collections of State Papers and official documents.[3] These references are sufficient to demonstrate the kind of duties he performed and the high trust in which he was held by the Earl. For example, in 1587 Pembroke asked Burghley to grant Arthur the position of Examiner to the Council of the Welsh Marches. In 1590–1591 he had to report to the Privy Council on Pembroke's behalf details concerning a suspected conspiracy involving Sir Henry Berkeley, and this report by Arthur Massinger, comprising some notes 'of Sir Henry Berkeley's manner of dealing', delivered to the Earl at Wilton on 18th April 1591, is now in the British Museum.[4] In this report he describes himself modestly as 'being the most unworthy of many' for the position of one of the deputy lieutenants of Pembroke. Yet he must have proved himself worthy of Pembroke's confidence, for, in 1598, he was engaged in the negotiations for the marriage of Pembroke's son and Burghley's grand-daughter. He journeyed with confidential despatches to present before the Privy Council, with letters to Cecil and to the Queen, and we see him busying himself with his duties

[1] Op. cit., p. 352. It should be noted that Langbaine was wrong in styling Henry Herbert 'Earl of Montgomery'. This title was first conferred upon his second son, Philip, in 1605.

[2] See Eccles, loc. cit., cf. Calendar of MSS. of Marquis of Salisbury.

[3] See, for example, Lansdowne MSS., nos. 63–74 and 77; C.S.P. Dom. Eliz., under dates 28 Mar., 1587; 16 Aug., 1597; 3 Sept., 1597; Cal. of MSS. of Marquis of Salisbury, parts 6, 8, 11, 12; Sidney Papers, II, 93; Acts of the Privy Council, passim. See also, Eccles, loc. cit.; R. H. Ball, Massinger and the House of Pembroke (MLN, XLVI, 1931, pp. 399–400).

[4] Lansdowne, 67–69.

connected with the Council in the Marches, raising levies and receiving monies from the Privy Council. He was Member of Parliament for Weymouth in 1588–1589 and again in 1592–1593, and for Shaftesbury in 1601. There is no record of any of his activities as a M.P. Both his seats were reasonably near to Wilton, and it may be presumed that they were in the control of the Earl of Pembroke.

In an article in *Anglia*[1] Phelan gave an extremely elaborate account of the identity and genealogy of Arthur Massinger, and since this article has never been adequately discussed in seventy years, and since one of Phelan's statements which has a direct bearing on the career of Philip Massinger has been put forward with authority as recently as 1931,[2] it is necessary that the matter should be dealt with here.

Phelan found three Arthur Massingers living in England at the end of the sixteenth century. The first was the Salisbury Arthur, whom we can definitely identify with the father of the playwright. The second was a Gloucester Arthur. This Arthur is identified[3] by a memorial inscription in Gloucester Cathedral to an Ann Massinger, 'wife and widow of Arthur Massinger of this city, Gent., aged 52 years. She departed this life October 21st. 1636. Aetatis suae 70.' Also buried in Gloucester Cathedral is an 'Elisabeth, daughter of Arthur Messinger, Gent., who departed this life A.D. 1665. Aetatis suae 73.' The third Arthur Massinger was one who died in London, and was buried in St. Dunstan in the West, 'out of Shere Lane', on 4th June 1603; his nuncupative Will[4] having been made two days before. In this same church were baptised three daughters of 'Arthur Messenger Esquier'. Susan was baptised on 13th January 1594, Catharine on 23rd December 1596, and Barbara on 3rd January 1599.

According to Phelan, Arthur Massinger was born about 1551 in Gloucester, of a family well known in the town; served the Pembrokes, living both at Wilton and in London[5]; and had a son Philip born in Salisbury in 1583,[6] a daughter Elisabeth born about 1592, and three other daughters born respectively in 1594, 1596, and

---

[1] *The Life of Philip Massinger*, Anglia, II, 1879.
[2] The nuncupative Will of the London Arthur Massinger has been presented by Eccles (loc. cit.) as that of Philip's father.
[3] Phelan is here quoting the article by G. W. Messinger (see above, p. 4, note 2) in which the latter quotes Sam. Rudder's *New History of Gloucestershire*, Cirencester, 1779, p. 173.
[4] P.C.C., 5. Harte.
[5] The three children baptised in London were baptised during the winter when, presumably, the Pembrokes were in residence there.
[6] Phelan did not know the baptismal entry, and gives Massinger's birth-date as 1584.

1599/1600. He had married his wife, Ann, presumably when she was about sixteen; and after his death and burial in London in 1603 at the age of 52, she had returned to Gloucester and spent the rest of her days there with an unmarried daughter.

There is, of course, a possibility that those three Arthurs are one and the same man, though no one now would present such adventurous and conjectural material with the bland confidence and authority displayed by Phelan. We may indeed exclaim with Mrs. Malaprop: 'You are not like Cerberus, three gentlemen at once, are you?';[1] and sympathise with Furnivall when he protests.[2] However attractive I find the idea of the three men being one, I can only agree with Furnivall when he states: 'The fair presumption is, that the three men are three distinct persons, with three distinct families. At least, they must be so treated until they can be proved to be identical.'[3]

In a reply to Furnivall, Phelan attempted to support his contentions,[4] but he merely succeeded in showing them to be still more suppositious. He repeats the categorical statements of his first article, and demonstrates the dubiousness of his arithmetic when he states that Ann Massinger must have been 'about nineteen' when she married Arthur. I have already corrected this error without comment in a previous paragraph. However, there are one or two remarks which may be made before leaving Phelan's article.

These three men cannot be proved to be different. Nor, it might be added, can they be proved to be the same. The discovery of the name of the wife of either the Salisbury Arthur or the London Arthur would be probably the best and most easily-found evidence. The baptismal and churching entries do not give a name to the Salisbury Arthur's wife. The Will does not give a name to the London Arthur's wife, although she is named as legatee. Were the name of either discovered, then there might be a positive argument for or against part at least of Phelan's case.

In the comparison of the Gloucester with the London Arthurs the following points must be noted. Apart from the inscription in the cathedral, I have so far found no record of the activities of any Arthur Massinger in Gloucester during the period. He does not seem to have died or been buried there; in fact, his widow's memorial inscription, giving the gratuitous information that he was 'aged 52 years', is perhaps a little unusual and would seem to suggest that he was buried elsewhere. The birth-dates of the daughter

[1] *The Rivals*, IV, ii.
[2] F. J. Furnivall, *A Couple of Protests* (*Anglia*, II, 1879, p. 504).
[3] pp. 505–506.   [4] In *Anglia*, III, 1880, p. 361.

buried in Gloucester and of the three girls baptised in London fit together neatly and accord with what we know Ann's age to have been. Thus far, then, the facts do not preclude the identity of these two Arthurs. But the London Arthur had a brother called Richard who, according to the Will, was standing by his death-bed in 1603, and there is no record of any Richard Massinger in Gloucester. In addition, the memorial inscription says that Arthur Massinger was 'of this city' (i.e. of Gloucester) and it seems unlikely that either the London or the Salisbury Arthurs should be so described. It would also seem reasonable to assume either that Ann Massinger was a native of Gloucester or that her husband had a house there; otherwise she would not have settled down and eventually been buried there. The London Arthur, we know, had a house in the parish of St. Dunstan's in the West; and it would seem natural for his widow to stay on there in London, especially since she had a brother-in-law already living in the city, to say nothing (if we add the third Arthur Massinger) of a son who was reaching an age where he would have to make his own way in the world. It is also perhaps interesting, if we take the families of the Gloucester and the London Arthurs together, to notice that out of four daughters none is called after her mother.

If we compare the Gloucester and the Salisbury Arthurs, we may note that, while there are no such close correspondences between them as there are between the Gloucester and London families, there is also an absence of negative evidence. The Salisbury Arthur might have been born in Gloucester and married a girl in that city. The question is open; and the only fact that does not quite accord with this identification is the gap of nearly ten years between the birth-dates of Philip and Elisabeth.

We have the same gap to account for if we attempt to combine all three Arthurs, with the added difficulty that we have to explain why Ann Massinger, who had a son when she was seventeen or thereabouts, had no more children until she was twenty-six and then had four in succession. Unless Arthur Massinger married first Philip's mother, and then after her death a Gloucester woman, there seems no explanation for this gap in childbearing—although, to be sure, there might be children between Philip and Elisabeth whose names have not come down to us. Certainly it is true that, in his post as Examiner to the Council in the Welsh Marches, the Salisbury Arthur may have been in Gloucester often enough. He might even have had a house there and thus been entitled to the description 'of this city'.

But there is no end to the amount of conjecture that can be indulged in on this score. The point to note is that it is conjecture, not
fact as Phelan suggested, and there is not one atom of evidence
linking the three men. I would myself hazard the guess that the
Arthur in Salisbury and the Arthur in Gloucester are quite different
persons; the balance of probability, in my opinion, being swayed
by the fact that there were already families of Massingers in each
city.

However, for the purposes of the biography of Philip Massinger,
the London and the Salisbury Arthurs are the prime consideration.
If they were the same man, then we should have a perfectly reasonable explanation for Philip's leaving Oxford without taking a degree
and not have to resort to the fanciful one of his alienating a hypothetical patron by being converted to Roman Catholicism.[1] The
identification of the London with the Salisbury Arthur seems the
likeliest part of Phelan's case, even if it means allowing for the long
gap between the birth of Philip and the birth of a second child and
endowing Arthur with a brother called Richard who, unlike Walter,
did not attend Oxford. We know that the Salisbury Arthur spent
a great deal of his time in London, and we know that William
Herbert, the third Earl of Pembroke, who succeeded to the title on
the death of his father in 1601, hardly ever left London. These
would have been sufficient reasons for the fact that by 1603 Arthur
Massinger had a permanent residence in the city. There, for want
of evidence (though it is almost certain that positive evidence must
exist somewhere), the matter must rest.

Sufficient has been said of Massinger's family to indicate that his
background was certainly not humble or lowly, as was that of many
of his fellow dramatists. Yet it was not courtly. It was rather that
of the professional class, a vantage-point from which to view both
the Court and the City, a betwixt-and-between position. This factor
of family background, when taken along with the classless, and
consequently 'social-climbing', position of the professional playwright, goes a long way to explain the range of the social interest
and the social preferences and prejudices involved in the plays.
The society presented is that of the Court, even although it is a
sort of bourgeois Court; the City and 'trade' in general are scorned
and the lower classes are very sketchily presented; and the general
impression is of a playwright almost, but not quite, in the upper
classes and resenting his ambiguous position. It is well to remember,
however, that throughout his career Massinger seems to have been

[1] See below, p. 22.

treated with a certain amount of social consideration, as, for example, when he is referred to in Sir Henry Herbert's Office Book as 'Mr.' Massinger, a term of address not commonly used by the Master of the Revels in describing a mere playwright.[1]

Of his childhood there is nothing known without a peradventure. A number of writers have suggested that he received his education as a page in the service of the Countess of Pembroke. Cunningham finds in the plays a great number of allusions to the position and duties of pages. But I cannot think that he was ever in service with the Countess. In the Dedication to *The Bondman* (1624), which is addressed to Philip, Earl of Montgomery, the younger son of his father's patron, Massinger says:

> However I could never arrive at the happiness to be made known to your lordship, yet a desire, born with me, to make a tender of all duties and service to the noble family of the Herberts, descended to me as an inheritance from my dead father, Arthur Massinger. Many years he happily spent in the service of your honourable house, and died a servant to it; leaving his to be ever most glad and ready, to be at the command of all such as derive themselves from his most honoured master, your lordship's most noble father.[2]

Massinger, then, could hardly have been a page in the Pembroke household without having met Philip, especially when it is remembered that they were of an age; and certainly so experienced a writer of wheedling dedications would not have failed to mention the fact that he himself had been in service with his prospective patron's family.

He received his early education, we may assume, in Salisbury, probably at the grammar-school; and during that period he would have plenty of opportunity of observing, but from a distance, both the Pembrokes and the large circle of literary celebrities grouped around the Countess. It is likely that it was while he was in Salisbury that he received his first taste of the theatre through the Earl of Pembroke's Men, who played at Wilton, and in whom naturally both he and his father would take an interest. Hartley Coleridge even goes as far as suggesting that Philip played with them.[3] But it is more likely that merely seeing them gave him an original hankering which was strengthened when he arrived at manhood in the golden days of Elizabethan drama.

Education he did receive, since on the 14th of May, 1602, he

---

[1] *Herbert*, p. 26 and p. 41, '*The Noble Bondman*, written by Philip Messenger, gent'; and p. 54, '*The Guardian*, a play of Mr. Messengers.' The title-page of *The Duke of Milan*, the first of the uncollaborated plays published (1623), describes it as 'written by Philip Massinger Gent.'   [2] Gifford, ii, p. 3.   [3] p. xxiv.

matriculated at St. Alban's Hall, Oxford, styling himself the son of a gentleman—'Sarisburiensis, generosi filius'—and from Salisbury, not, be it noted, from London or Gloucester. What he did at Oxford we do not know. Wood says [1] that he spent more time on poetry and romances than on logic and philosophy; Langbaine says,[2] 'he closely pursued his studies in Alban Hall, for three or four years space'; and what Langbaine says is not contradicted by Oldys. None of those older authorities is at all reliable, though Wood is probably more so than Langbaine since he did at least attempt to find out some of his facts, whereas Langbaine contented himself with his knowledge of books, dedications, and the like, producing in consequence such nonsense as the startling statement that Massinger was born 'in the reign of King Charles the First'!

It is not known how long Massinger was at Oxford, since he left without taking a degree and there is no other evidence of his stay. Chelli states,[3] on what authority I do not know, that he left Oxford in 1608. According to Langbaine, he was at Oxford for 'three or four years space',[4] and Wood says that he was there 'for about four years or more'.[5] Hartley Coleridge suggests[6] that he probably left Oxford in 1606; and this account has been followed by Chambers when he states[7] that Massinger left Oxford without taking a degree in 1606. It is reasonable to suppose that he was financed in his studies by his father, and not by Pembroke. Wood seems to imply that he was supported by Pembroke and that the latter withdrew his help when he discovered that his protégé was spending more of his time on poetry than upon logic and philosophy. At Oxford, Wood says,

'tho' encouraged in his studies by the earl of Pembroke, yet he applied his mind more to poetry and romances for about four years or more, than to logic and philosophy, which he ought to have done, and for that end was patronized.'[8]

It seems hardly likely that the third Earl of Pembroke, a renowned patron of the arts, should have withdrawn his support from a promising lad for such a reason. I can myself see no reason at all why he should not have been supported at the University by his father. Langbaine (admittedly not a good authority) says that Arthur Massinger

'bestowed a liberal education on our author, sending him to the University of Oxford, at eighteen years of Age.'[9]

---

[1] *Athen. Oxon.* (ed. Bliss), II, p. 654. [2] *Account*, p. 352.
[3] *Drame*, p. 43. [4] *Account*, p. 352. [5] *Athen. Oxon.*, II, p. 654.
[6] p. xxxi. [7] *Elizabethan Stage*, III, p. 436. [8] Loc. cit.
[9] Loc. cit.

Certainly, from what we can guess of Arthur Massinger's circumstances, he could well afford to support a son at Oxford. In this connection it is interesting to notice a statement made by Cleremond in *The Parliament of Love* which, presenting a typical attitude of Massinger's to matters of lineage, has a somewhat autobiographical flavour:

> My birth
> Was noble as 'tis ancient, nor let it relish
> Of arrogance, to say my father's care,
> With curiousness and cost, did train me up
> In all those liberal qualities that commend
> A gentleman.[1]

If he were financed by his father, as seems to be natural, then lack of money on Arthur Massinger's death, whenever that occurred, would in a very short time be sufficient reason to force him to give up his studies and seek his fortune in London. Of course, if his father was indeed the man who died in London in 1603, less than a year after Philip had entered Oxford, and if Philip continued in residence until 1606, then he must have received assistance from someone. But it is certain, as seems clear from other evidence that I shall mention later,[2] that he got no help from Pembroke, and it seems only reasonable to suppose that he was supported by some member of his own family—by his mother, or by an uncle.

Little or nothing of the length of his stay at Oxford can be inferred from his work. His knowledge of the classics, although he moves about quite freely in the somewhat restricted space of his allusions to classical mythology and Roman and Greek history, could have been gathered by anyone from a reading of Golding's *Metamorphoses*, North's *Plutarch* or Lodge's *Seneca*, not to mention many other storehouses of classical information. His probable ability to read both French and Spanish is evidence of some learning, but certainly not very much more than would be acquired by any intelligent young man-about-town who had never been at a university, and of course neither Oxford nor Cambridge at that time taught modern languages. As for his dry, legalistic, and argumentative mind, it is a trait of character rather than a demonstration of an academic training. His use of the forms and terms of logic, however, his obvious concern with moral problems as subject for debate and didacticism, and the somewhat 'bookish' inspiration which lies behind much of his view of life and colours his terms of reference, incline me to the opinion that he certainly spent more than a few bare months at Oxford. On

[1] V. i. [2] See below, p. 23.

the other hand, if we remember the wide knowledge of literature and the classics displayed by the self-educated Ben Jonson (or even by Shakespeare, for that matter), we are bound to admit that such evidence may be very deceptive. If he did stay at Oxford for several years, as seems likely, there is no necessity to attach much significance to the fact that he did not take a degree. The possession of a degree did not have then the importance that is attached to it now. It was not an essential preliminary to any profession, except possibly to that of the Church, and Massinger seems to have had too much practical hard-headedness and independence of spirit, in spite of a pronounced interest in matters theological and ecclesiastical, to attach himself to such a calling. It is certainly not necessary to adduce, as Gifford did, a hypothetical conversion to Roman Catholicism as a reason for his leaving Oxford prematurely.

In short, then, there is no documentary evidence at all which gives us any idea of Philip Massinger's life between 1602 when he matriculated at Oxford and 1613 when he was working (or rather, not working, for he was in prison at the time) as one of Henslowe's hacks.

There is, however, one interesting conjecture about this period, made by Meissner.[1] It is that Massinger went to Germany in the company of English comedians who played there under John Greene.

This English company was performing in Graz from February 6th to 20th, 1608, during the celebrations marking the betrothal of the Archduchess Maria Magdalena to the young Cosimo de Medici. In a letter to her brother, describing the performances that had taken place, the Archduchess includes the following piece of information:

> Am Montag von ein[en] Herzog von Florenz, der sich in eines Edelmanns Tochter verliebt hat.

This description, brief as it is, certainly bears a superficial resemblance to Massinger's *The Great Duke of Florence*. I think, however, that Meissner is taking too much for granted when he assumes from this that Massinger must have been one of Greene's company. Massinger's *The Great Duke of Florence* was licensed for the Queen's Men on July 5th, 1627.[2] Internal evidence would suggest that it was written in 1624, that is about the same time as Massinger wrote *The Bondman*, *The Renegado*, and *The Parliament of Love* for the Queen's Men—certainly before the death of James I and after the return

---

[1] *Die Englischen Komoedianten zur Zeit Shakespeares in Oesterreich*, von J. Meissner (Beiträge zur Geschichte der deutschen Litteratur), Wien, 1884, pp. 42–43, 100–102.
[2] *Herbert*, p. 31.

of Charles from his visit to Spain. There are no signs in the play of any other hand than Massinger's, and far from being prentice work it seems to have been rather carefully written. The hold-up in the production of the play can easily be accounted for if we remember the upset following the King's death and the reorganisation of the theatrical companies at this time, the ravages of the plague in 1625, and the return of Massinger, who was writing for the Queen's Men for a year or so before 1625, to the King's Men. In addition, it may be noted that Massinger displays no knowledge of German anywhere in his work, nor does he show any understanding of the German character other than the conventional English view that the Germans were rather stupid men who drank too much.

Miss Janet M. Stochholm, the most recent editor of *The Great Duke of Florence*,[1] has conjectured a link between the German play, the anonymous *A Knack to Know a Knave* (1594) which is certainly one of the sources of Massinger's play, and a lost play, mentioned by Henslowe, on *Cosmo* (1592–1593). She suggests that Greene returned to England in about 1619–1620 on the outbreak of the Thirty Years War; that during this spell in London he became friendly with Massinger, and that it was then that Massinger adapted the play. In view of my later discussion on Massinger's religious faith, it is perhaps interesting to note that Greene was very probably a Roman Catholic. In any case, Greene's company were acting at the court of Saxony in Dresden between June and December, 1626, and among the plays they produced, as well as a play on the Duke of Florence, was 'eine Tragödia von der Märtherin Dorothea', which seems from its title to be a version of Massinger and Dekker's *The Virgin Martyr*. The suggestion is that Greene gave the idea of *The Great Duke of Florence* to Massinger, and took *The Virgin Martyr*, a very attractive play from the theatrical point of view, back to Germany with him. While agreeing that *The Great Duke of Florence* certainly owes something to *A Knack to Know a Knave*, I can see no reason at all for connecting the other two plays, Henslowe's *Cosmo* and Greene's *Herzog von Florenz*, with Massinger, and would certainly affirm that there are no traces of any earlier form or any earlier hand in the play.

On the whole, then, I feel that any connection between Massinger and Greene's company in Germany must be discounted, and until any evidence turns up pointing in some specific direction, what Philip Massinger was doing between the ages of twenty and thirty must remain a matter for our imaginations. The nature of his many

[1] (Th. Ph.D., Bryn Mawr, 1929) Baltimore, 1933.

allusions to soldiering, his minute knowledge of the military craft, and his frequent defence of that despised profession, might suggest that he had some practical experience under arms, but I feel that point cannot be pressed in the absence of anything other than internal evidence. Five years of idling and doing odd jobs about London would fill the gap easily and would be more than sufficient to bring him into Henslowe's grasp.

★

Our first definite sight of Massinger shows him in somewhat miserable circumstances. This is in the famous 'Tripartite Letter', a mendicant epistle, addressed to Henslowe by Daborne, Field and Massinger from prison. (The prison is not known.)

> Mr. Hinchlow
>
> You understand our unfortunate extremitie, and I doe not thincke you so void of christianitie, but that you would throw so much money into the Thames as wee request now of you; rather then endanger so many innocent lives; you know there is xl. more at least to be receaved of you, for the play, wee desire you to lend us vl. of that, which shall be allowed to you without which wee cannot be bayled, nor I play any more till this be dispatch'd, it will loose you xxl. ere the end of the next weeke, beside the hinderance of the next new play, pray Sir consider our Cases with humanitie, and now give us cause to acknowledge you our true freind in time of neede; wee have entreated M. Davison to deliver this note, as well to wittnesse your love as our promises, and allwayes acknowledgment to be ever
>
> Your most thanckfull; and loving freinds,
Nat: Field.
>
> The mony shall be abated out of the mony remayns for the play of Mr Fletcher & ours
>
> Rob: Daborne.
>
> I have ever founde you a true lovinge freinde to mee & in soe small a suite it beeinge honest I hope you will not faile us.
>
> Philip Massinger.

The letter is addressed, 'To our most loving friend, Mr Philip Hinchlow, esquire, These.'[1]

If we forgo the sorrowful headshakes which biographers are wont to give on presenting this letter (after all, debt and imprisonment were almost the common lot of Elizabethan and Jacobean playwrights), there are one or two facts about Massinger's life which

---

[1] See W. W. Greg, *Henslowe Papers*, Article 68. The transcript given by Gifford (p. xlix) is most inaccurate. There is also a photograph of this letter in Cruickshank's *Philip Massinger*, opp. p. 4.

emerge.[1] The letter shows that by 1613, ten years before any play was licensed under his name as sole author, he was established as a writer for Henslowe, working with Daborne and Field, and, as Daborne's note suggests, with Fletcher also. During this period he was engaged in the melancholy and unremunerative task of collaborating with other authors and in cobbling and writing new scenes for old plays. He was poor, as all such writers were poor, and the undertone of poverty and complaint which runs through all his plays and begging dedications had already been sounded. On the occasion of the imprisonment, presumably for debt, Henslowe, according to a receipt signed by Davison, lent them the money asked for. But two years later two of the trio at least were still impoverished, still in the clutches of the astute businessman of the theatre, for on the 4th July, 1615, Massinger and Daborne gave a joint bond to him for £3.

Henslowe's manner of dealing with his writers and the poverty in which they lived are demonstrated in a remarkable series of letters to him by Daborne.[2] In one of them, probably written in 1613 or 1614, Massinger is mentioned:

> SIR, I did thinke I deservd as much mony as Mr Messenger, although knowinge your great disbursments I forbour to urdge you beyond your own pleasure; but my occasions press me so neerly, that I cannot but expect this reasonable curtesy, consydering I pay you half my earnings in the play besyds my continuall labor and chrdge imployd only for you; which if it prove not proffitable now, you shall see I will give you honnest satisfaction for the utmost farthinge I owe yow, and take another course. Whearfore this being my last, I beseech you way my great occation this once, and make up my mony even with Mr Messengers, which is to let me have xs. more. I am sure I shall deserv it, and you can never doe me a tymelyer curtesy, resting at your commaund.
>
> ROBT. DABORNE.[3]

Massinger must have served a hard apprenticeship, living on advances and the favour of Henslowe, and dependent upon the charity of influential friends. Apprenticeship he did serve, and the veil which covers this period of collaboration and hack-work covers also a deal of labour, during which his verse, his technique, and his stagecraft developed. When the period of the plays of undisputed and one-man authorship came in the 1620's his style had crystallised

---

[1] It might be added that the letter also shows that Massinger spelled his name with an 'a'. The participial phrase, 'it beeinge honest', is a typical Massingerian interpolation, cf. below, Chap. VI, *passim*.

[2] Printed by Swaen, *Anglia*, XX, 1897–1898.

[3] *Anglia*, XX, p. 171.

and was mature, showing the firm touch of the experienced and long-trained craftsman.

How he managed to survive during this period on what he earned by working for the players will never be known, but a hint is given in the dedications to several of the printed plays. The Dedicatory Epistle to *The Unnatural Combat*, for example, addressed to 'My Much Honoured Friend, Anthony Sentleger, of Oakham in Kent, Esq.,' runs:

> SIR, That the patronage of trifles, in this kind, hath long since rendered dedications and inscriptions obsolete and out of fashion, I perfectly understand, and cannot but ingenuously confess that I, walking in the same path, may be truly argued by you of weakness or wilful error: but the reasons and defences for the tender of my service in this way to you are so just, that I cannot (in my thankfulness for so many favours received) but be ambitious to publish them. Your noble father, Sir Warham Sentleger (whose remarkable virtues must be ever remembered), being while he lived a master for his pleasure in poetry, feared not to hold converse with divers whose necessitous fortunes made it their profession, among which, by the clemency of his judgment, I was not in the last place admitted. You (the heir of his honour and estate) inherited his good inclinations to men of my poor quality, of which I cannot give any ampler testimony, than by my free and glad profession of it to the world. Besides (and it was not the least encouragement to me) many of eminence, and the best of such, who disdained not to take notice of me, have not thought themselves disparaged, I dare not say honoured, to be celebrated the patrons of my humble studies. In the first file of which, I am confident, you shall have no cause to blush to find your name written. I present you with this old tragedy, without prologue or epilogue, it being composed in a time (and that too, peradventure, as knowing as this) when such by-ornaments were not advanced above the fabric of the whole work. Accept it, I beseech you, as it is, and continue your favour to the author,
>
> Your servant,
PHILIP MASSINGER.[1]

This epistle, then, written in 1639, the last year of his life, suggests not only that Massinger was already indebted to the St. Legers, father and son, and to numerous other patrons, but also that he was hopeful of continuing patronage. In other words, at the end of his long career he had not succeeded in gaining a competence. Significant, too, is the description of 'divers whose necessitous fortunes' made playwriting their profession, which implies that writers were driven to their trade merely by want. One would never, for example,

---

[1] Gifford, i, p. 125.

find a lawyer describing his profession thus. But in spite of the implication that Massinger considered that he was made for worthier things, we must remember that playwrights, in the seventeenth century at least, were ever a mendicant crew, knowing only beggary, never luxury, and rarely comfort; and in view of Massinger's frequent expression of the serious purpose of his calling perhaps we must not conclude too much from his depreciatory comment in this one case. Nevertheless, he does speak of 'men of my poor quality', thus acknowledging himself one with all other playwrights, in poverty as in profession.[1]

The phrase occurs again in a dedication which gives us the name of another man who had been Massinger's patron. This is the Dedicatory Epistle to *The Great Duke of Florence*, addressed in a less comradely, more submissive way than that to *The Unnatural Combat*, to 'The truly honoured, and my noble Favourer, Sir Robert Wiseman, Knt., of Thorrel's-Hall in Essex':

> SIR, As I dare not be ungrateful for the many benefits you have heretofore conferred upon me, so I have just reason to fear that my attempting this way to make satisfaction (in some measure) for so due a debt, will further engage me. The most able in my poor quality have made use of Dedications in this nature, to make the world take notice (as far as in them lay) who and what they were that gave supportment and protection to their studies, being more willing to publish the doer than receive a benefit in a corner. For myself, I will freely, and with a zealous thankfulness, acknowledge, that for many years I had but faintly subsisted, if I had not often tasted of your bounty . . .[2]

In two other dedications Massinger took the liberty of combining the names of more than one friend. Thus, *The Roman Actor* is addressed to 'My much honoured and most true Friends', Sir Philip Knyvet, Sir Thomas Jay (the poet[3]), and Mr. Thomas Bellingham, and Massinger says:

> How much I acknowledge myself bound for your so many and extraordinary favours conferred upon me, as far as it is in my power, posterity shall take notice: I were most unworthy of such noble friends, if I should not, with all thankfulness, profess and own them. In the composition of this Tragedy you were my only supporters, and it being now by your principal encouragement to be turned into the world, it cannot walk safer than under your protection. It hath been happy in the suffrage of some learned and judicious gentlemen when it was presented, nor shall they find cause, I hope, in the perusal, to repent them

---

[1] See below, p. 51, for further discussion of this phrase.
[2] 1636. Gifford, ii, p. 429.   [3] See below, p. 39.

of their good opinion of it. . . . I ever held it the most perfect birth of my Minerva; and therefore in justice offer it to those that have best deserved of me; who, I hope, in their courteous acceptance will render it worth their receiving, and ever, in their gentle construction of my imperfections, believe they may at their pleasure dispose of him, that is wholly and sincerely

devoted to their service,

PHILIP MASSINGER.[1]

And in the dedication to *The Maid of Honour*, Massinger gives reasons for bracketing his two patrons, Sir Francis Foljambe[2] and Sir Thomas Bland:

> That you have been, and continued so for many years, since you vouchsafed to own me, patrons to me and my despised studies, I cannot but with all humble thankfulness acknowledge: and living, as you have done, inseparable in your friendship, . . . I held it as impertinent as absurd, in the presentment of my service in this kind, to divide you. A free confession of a debt in a meaner man is the amplest satisfaction to his superiors; and I heartily wish, that the world may take notice, and from myself, that I had not to this time subsisted, but that I was supported by your frequent courtesies and favours.[3]

It is convenient to mention the other dedicatory epistles here. None of them, with the exception of that to *The Bondman*, from which I have already quoted,[4] contains the biographical juice which I have squeezed from those I have just been discussing. These dedications comprise: *The Duke of Milan* (1623), addressed to Lady Katherine Stanhope[5]; *The Renegado* (1630), addressed to George Harding, twelfth Lord Berkeley; *The Picture* (1630), addressed to the 'Noble Society of the Inner Temple'; *The Emperor of the East* (1632), addressed to John, Lord Mohun; and *A New Way to Pay Old Debts* (1633), addressed to Robert, Earl of Carnarvon, the Catholic son-in-law to Philip, Earl of Pembroke and Montgomery.[6] In every case so far the dates I have given are the dates of publication, not the dates of the writing of the play.

The dedication of *The Emperor of the East* is perhaps of interest.

---

[1] 1629. Gifford, ii, p. 329.
[2] There is a short poem addressed by Massinger to Foljambe on this occasion. See facsimile, Gifford, iv, p. 592 (Copy, B.M. Addit., 1854–1875, 28.655 ff., 194b).
[3] 1632. Gifford, iii, p. 3.   [4] See above, p. 10.
[5] There is a poem addressed to her by Massinger (presumably on this occasion) in a seventeenth-century MS. in the library of Trinity College, Dublin (G.2.21, pp. 557–559). It is entitled, 'A New yeares Guift presented to my Lady and M:rs the then Lady Katherine Stanhop now Countesse of Chesterfield. By Phill: Messinger.' It is printed by Grosart, *Engl. Studien*, XXVI, and by A. H. Cruickshank, *Philip Massinger*, Appendix XVII, pp. 208–211.
[6] See below, p. 50.

After some fifteen or sixteen highly-flourished lines of conventional address to Lord Mohun, Massinger goes on to say:

> My worthy friend, Mr. Aston Cockayne, your nephew, to my extra-ordinary content, delivered to me that your lordship, at your vacant hours, sometimes vouchsafed to peruse such trifles of mine as have passed the press, and not alone warranted them in your gentle suffrage, but disdained not to bestow a remembrance of your love and intended favour to me.[1]

This dedication is chiefly interesting for the evidence it provides, from Massinger's side, of a friendship between him and Cokaine; whereas the unsupported statement of the latter, who was perhaps somewhat prone to claim an excessive acquaintance with the poets, might not be sufficient.[2] The remaining dedications are complimentary addresses or formal appeals for assistance and 'protection', and since, as Dr. Johnson said, 'The known style of a dedication is flattery'[3], they are rather courtly flourishes than expressions of genuine feeling. Thus Massinger could address Lady Katherine Stanhope in 1623 in almost the same terms as he used ten years later in addressing the Earl of Carnarvon.[4]

The patrons, then, whom we know for certain, from statements in the dedications, gave Massinger some assistance are:

Thomas Bellingham	Sir Philip Knyvet[6]
Sir Thomas Bland	John, Lord Mohun
Aston Cokaine	Anthony St. Leger
(probably)[5]	(later Sir Anthony)
Sir Francis Foljambe	Sir Warham St. Leger
Sir Thomas Jay	Sir Robert Wiseman

And if we add the numerous members of the Inner Temple whom Massinger mentions but does not name in the dedication to *The Picture*, and remember how often 'frequent bounties' are mentioned, it will be realised how large a part of Massinger's income must have been made up of such gratuities—and that in days when a man could be passing rich with a great deal less than 'forty pounds a year'.

---

[1] Gifford, iii, pp. 242–243.   [2] See below, pp. 45–46.

[3] Boswell, *Tour to the Hebrides*, 4 Oct., 1773.

[4] Cf. Gifford, i, p. 235, and iii, p. 491.

[5] Cokaine was not knighted until 1641.

[6] Cf. B.M. Harl. MS. 6918 (fol. 52r. to 54r.), which is a poem of 138 lines, entitled *The Virgin's Character* and signed 'P. M.' From line 35 it is apparent that it was addressed to 'Knevets first daughter' (i.e. Dorothy Knyvet, born 1611) and the context makes it likely that it was written some time in the years 1625–1630 when this girl was unmarried but of a marriageable age. Printed by A. K. McIlwraith, *RES*, IV, 1928, pp. 64–68. The poem is undoubtedly by Massinger.

While none of these men could be called 'grand patrons' of the arts, they were all wealthy men and sincere amateurs. Seven of these men (in addition to an unknown number of members of the Inner Temple) are specifically named by Massinger as his 'friends', and from this we can get an idea of the circles, professional and literary, in which he liked to move. There is no means of knowing how much support he received or on what terms he existed with these men or with the more noble patrons to whom his other plays are dedicated.

The question of Massinger's relationship with the Herberts, however, merits closer and more realistic attention than it has received so far.

Undoubtedly Massinger remembered with affection the establishment of the Herberts at Wilton. In *A New Way to Pay Old Debts* he gives Lord Lovell, the model of noble chivalry, the following speech:

> Nor am I of that harsh and rugged temper
> As some great men are taxed with, who imagine
> They part from the respect due to their honours,
> If they use not all such as follow them,
> Without distinction of their births, like slaves.
> I am not so conditioned: I can make
> A fitting difference between my footboy,
> And a gentleman by want compelled to serve me.[1]

And in *The Bondman*, in whose dedication to the Earl of Montgomery he speaks of the 'many years' that his father had 'happily spent' in the service of the honourable house of Herbert, he makes Marullo say:

> Happy those times
> When lords were styled fathers of families,
> And not imperious masters! When they numbered
> Their servants almost equal with their sons,
> Or one degree beneath them! . . .
>   . . . All things ordered
> With such decorum, as wise lawmakers,
> From each well-governed private house derived
> The perfect model of a commonwealth.[2]

From the information that has been handed down to us we can be sure that this is not merely a flattering description of the *modus vivendi* at Wilton under the second Earl of Pembroke.

In addition, in some of the early uncollaborated plays, notably *The Bondman* and *The Maid of Honour*, Massinger's criticism of Buckingham and of the foreign policy of James I was almost certainly conditioned to a certain extent by his adherence to the party

[1] III. i.   [2] IV. ii.

of opposition, among whom William, the third Earl of Pembroke, figured prominently.[1]

As I have suggested previously, it is not likely that Massinger was supported at Oxford by Pembroke. *A propos* his leaving Oxford, Gifford says that it was 'not . . . on account of the Earl of Pembroke withholding his assistance, for it does not appear that he ever afforded any'[2]; and he goes on to remark,

> Why the earl of Pembroke, the liberal friend and protector of literature in all its branches, neglected a young man to whom his assistance was so necessary, and who, from the acknowledged services of his father, had so many and just claims on it; one, too, who would have done his patronage such singular honour, I have no means of ascertaining: that he was never indebted to it is, I fear, indisputable; since the Poet, of whose character gratitude forms a striking part, while he recurs perpetually to his hereditary obligations to the Herbert family, anxiously avoids all mention of his name.

Gifford then makes the conjecture that this alienation was due to Massinger's having been converted to Roman Catholicism. I discuss this suggestion more fully later,[3] but at the moment it is sufficient to comment that such a conversion would be likely to alienate Massinger just as much from Montgomery, Pembroke's younger brother, and it seems to be a fact that Montgomery did offer Massinger some patronage.

Massinger did, as we now know, approach William Herbert, the third Earl of Pembroke, for assistance. The evidence for this rests in 'a Letter written upon occasion to the Earle of Pembroke Lo: Chamberlaine', a begging poem of which a copy exists in manuscript at Trinity College, Dublin.[4] This poem, written in miserable rhyming couplets, seems to have been composed probably some time in the late 1610's or at least before Massinger had published anything on his own account, since in it he says:

> If the most worthy then, whose pay's but praise
> Or a few spriggs from the now withering bayes
> Grone underneath their wants what hope have I
> Scarce yet allowed one of the Company
> Of better fortune.[5]

And a little later he exclaims, with a very characteristic independence and spirit, after he has stated that he would never write pretty

---

[1] See Chapter V, pp. 172 ff., for a fuller discussion of this matter.
[2] p. xliii.   [3] See below, p. 50.
[4] The same MS. (G.2.21.) as the poem to Lady Katherine Stanhope (see above, p. 19, note 5), pp. 554–557. This MS. is a copy, not in Massinger's own hand. Printed by Grosart, *Engl. Studien.*, XXVI, and by Cruickshank, *Philip Massinger*, pp. 208–211.
[5] Lines 13–17.

poems just to please patrons, and ignore them when they refused
to give any money,

> I would not for a pension or A place
> Part soe with myne owne Candor, lett me rather
> Live poorely on those toyes I would not father
> Not knowne beyond A Player or a Man . . .
> Ere soe grow famous.[1]

He does not, nevertheless, seem to have received any help from
William Herbert. There is no other document which connects him
with the noble Lord; no play is dedicated to him; and he is not
mentioned in the dedication of *The Bondman*.

With William Herbert's younger brother, Philip Herbert, Earl
of Montgomery and later fourth Earl of Pembroke, however,
there is positive evidence of patronage. It is quite clear, from a
passage quoted previously,[2] that Montgomery was not Massinger's
patron before the publication of *The Bondman* in 1624. Doubtless,
however, the anti-Buckingham passages in the play attracted
Montgomery's favourable attention, since Massinger says in the
dedication:

> When it was first acted [i.e. in December, 1623], your lordship's
> liberal suffrage taught others to allow it for current, it having received
> the undoubted stamp of your lordship's allowance.[3]

Perhaps Montgomery sent a gift of money backstage for the author
along with his commendations. This might even have been Massinger's intention from the very first. At any rate, we can be sure that
the similar expression of the 'party-line' in *The Maid of Honour*
would also have a beneficial effect upon Massinger's purse. Montgomery's patronage seems to have continued, since at the beginning
of 1636 we find Massinger sending him a poem, *Sero sed serio*,[4]
condoling with him on the death of his eldest son, Charles, who died
of smallpox in Florence a year and a half after his early marriage.
Apologising for not having offered a poem on the occasion of the
wedding, Massinger says:

> I curs'd my absence then
> That hindered it, and bit my star-cross'd pen,
> Too busy in stage-blanks, and trifling rhyme,
> When such a cause call'd, and so apt a time
> To pay a general debt; mine being more
> Than they could owe, who since, or heretofore,

---

[1] Lines 40–45.   [2] See above, p. 10.   [3] Gifford, ii, p. 3.
[4] B.M. King's Library MSS., 18.A.xx. Printed by Gifford, iv, pp. 596–598.

> Have labour'd with exalted lines to raise
> Brave piles, or rather pyramids of praise
> To Pembroke and his family.[1]

The 'Pembroke' mentioned here is, of course, Massinger's patron, who had succeeded to the title on the death of his brother in 1630. It might be added that the poem is addressed to 'the Right Honourable my most singular good Lord and Patron, Philip Earl of Pembroke and Montgomery'. Even if we consider that Massinger's omitting to raise a 'hymenaeal song' at the marriage of Charles, Lord Herbert, was a somewhat tactless error on his part, it must be admitted that there is ample evidence here that he was in fact quite considerably beholden financially to Pembroke. We can, then, safely assume that the 'patron' referred to in the Prologue to the revision of *A Very Woman* (licensed 1634) was also Pembroke:

> By command,
> He undertook this task, nor could it stand
> With his low fortune to refuse to do
> What by his patron he was called unto.[2]

And there is no reason at all to doubt the statement of Aubrey that Pembroke paid Massinger a pension of twenty or thirty pounds a year.[3] Although Aubrey was described by Wood as 'magotie-headed', he was a Wiltshireman and did go to considerable trouble to find out about his subjects, and it seems highly probable that what he has to say on this point is quite correct.

★

After this examination of Massinger's patrons, it is now necessary to return to the main stream of Massinger's life, and to where we left him in Henslowe's workshop.

To this period of drudgery belong certain plays in which Massinger's hand has been traced, plays in which he collaborated with Fletcher and others, or which he revised. Many of these plays were ultimately published in the Beaumont and Fletcher Folio of 1647 and others were published separately. None of these plays, collaborations and revisions alike, produced over a considerable number of years, is credited to his pen in editions published during his lifetime, with the exception of *The Virgin Martyr* (pub. 1622) under his name and Dekker's, and *The Fatal Dowry* (pub. 1632) in which his initials are coupled with those of Field. In addition, two plays are attributed to him in editions published after his death: *A Very*

---

[1] Lines 5–13.   [2] Gifford, iv, p. 239.
[3] *Natural History of Wiltshire*, ed. J. Britton, 1847, II, iii, p. 91.

Woman (pub. 1655), a Massinger revision of a Fletcher play, and *The Old Law* (pub. 1657), in which, although published under the names of Massinger, Middleton, and Rowley, there is barely a trace of Massinger's hand.

To summarise the situation briefly as regards Massinger's total output: there are twelve plays extant in which his hand can be traced as a collaborator; eleven plays in which he was probably no more than a reviser; and fifteen plays which he wrote alone. In addition, there are attributed to him, either in Herbert's Office Book or in Warburton's List, fifteen plays of which we can no longer find any trace. Some may be revisions or known to us under other titles; some may be lost; and some (in the case of Warburton's List at any rate[1]) may never have existed. In all, as near as can be estimated, Massinger had to do with some fifty-three plays in (at a generous estimate) thirty years of work for the theatre. From these figures it will be seen that Massinger, though perhaps not so industrious as Heywood, was certainly among the more industrious of the playwrights.

As I have already explained,[2] I do not intend to go in detail into the question of this work of collaboration and revision, involving as it does a large proportion of the Jacobean dramatic output.[3] Although Massinger's hand is probably the easiest of all Jacobean playwrights' to detect, a full consideration of the problems of Jacobean dramatic and theatrical collaboration would have led me very far away from those issues which are my main concern. Nevertheless, the very bulk of the work that he did in collaboration or revision must be recognised. Writing a part of a play meant being paid for only part of a play, and revising another man's play was to be only one-tenth an author; both of which facts must have profoundly affected both Massinger's way of life and his style.

Although Massinger's hand is fairly easy to detect, the evidence we have for his collaborating with other playwrights, in particular for his collaboration with Fletcher, is not confined to internal evidence of style and versification. From the Tripartite Letter we might quite reasonably deduce that as early as 1613 Massinger was already engaged in such work. He himself probably makes an admission to this effect in the poem to the third Earl of Pembroke which I have already quoted:

> lett me rather
> Live poorely on those toyes I would not father . . .

---

[1] See W. W. Greg, 'The Bakings of Betsy', *Library*, 3rd Series, II, 1911, pp. 225–259.
[2] *Preface*, pp. v–vi.
[3] For convenience a list of collaborated plays is given in Appendix I, p. 267.

And in a poem prefacing the first edition (1636) of *The Great Duke of Florence*, George Donne remarks to Massinger that poetry would have

> Withered into a dullness of despair,
> Had not thy later labour (heir
> Unto a former industry) made known
> This work, which thou mayst call thine own.[1]

But it is to Massinger's friend, Aston Cokaine, that we have to turn for confirmation of the partnership of Massinger and Fletcher. In a 'poetical' epistle addressed to his cousin, Charles Cotton, Cokaine says:

> I wonder (Cousin) that you would permit
> So great an injury to Fletcher's wit,
> Your friend and old Companion, that his fame
> Should be divided to another's name.
> If Beaumont had writ those plays, it had been
> Against his merits a detracting Sin,
> Had they been attributed also to
> *Fletcher.* They were two wits, and friends, and who
> Robs from the one to glorifie the other,
> Of these great memories is a partial Lover.
> Had *Beaumont* lived when this edition came
> Forth, and beheld his ever living name
> Before Plays that he never writ, how he
> Had frown'd and blush'd at such Impiety?
> His own Renown no such Addition needs
> To have a Fame sprung from anothers deedes.
> And my good friend Old *Philip Massinger*
> With *Fletcher* writ in some that we see there. . . .[2]

And in another poem, addressed to Humphrey Moseley and Humphrey Robinson, publishers of the Beaumont and Fletcher Folio, he says:

> In the large book of Playes you late did print
> (In *Beaumonts* and in Fletchers name) why in't
> Did you not justice? give to each his due?
> For *Beaumont* (of those many) writ in few:
> And Massinger in other few; the Main
> Being sole Issues of sweet Fletchers brain.
> But how came I (you ask) so much to know?
> Fletchers chief bosome-friend inform'd me so.
> I'th'next impression therefore justice do,

---

[1] Gifford, i, p. clvii.
[2] *Small Poems of Divers Sorts*, London, 1658, Letters to Divers Persons, No. 7.

And print their old ones in one volume too:
For *Beaumonts* works, and *Fletchers* should come forth
With all the right belonging to their worth.[1]

In the Folio of 1647 there are actually eight plays in which evidence suggests very strongly that Massinger collaborated—*The Beggar's Bush, The Custom of the Country, The False One, The Knight of Malta, The Little French Lawyer, The Prophetess, The Queen of Corinth* and *The Spanish Curate*—and another seven in which his hand can be traced, probably as a reviser—*The Coxcomb, The Double Marriage, The Fair Maid of the Inn, The Laws of Candy, Love's Cure, The Lovers' Progress,* and *The Sea Voyage.* So it will be seen that Cokaine was doing no more than claiming for Massinger what was his due. It is an open question who is Fletcher's 'chief bosome-friend' referred to by Cokaine. It might have been his cousin, Charles Cotton, whom he addresses in the first poem as if Fletcher were his 'friend and old Companion'. On the other hand, it might have been Philip Massinger, from whom he might have obtained much information about the collaborations. It is not likely that it was Fletcher himself. Cokaine did not know Fletcher, or we can be sure that he would have told us about it at great length.[2] However, it seems certain that Cokaine did know that Massinger had a hand in these plays. It is perhaps rather surprising that James Shirley, who edited the Folio, makes no mention in his introduction, 'To the Reader', of Massinger. Shirley and Massinger could not have been very close friends, otherwise it must be thought that he would have made some recognition of Massinger's share. There is, of course, no need to deduce any close friendship between the two from the prefixing of verses by Shirley to *The Renegado.* In the same year, 1630, Shirley's *The Grateful Servant* appeared with a commendatory poem by Massinger,[3] so the mutual flattery was probably no more than a 'you-scratch-my-back' arrangement.

That Massinger, then, did collaborate and revise is an important biographical fact which may be recognised without going at length into controversial problems of authorship and chronology. Massinger's name first appears in a contemporary attribution on 7th December, 1621, when an entry for 'A tragedy called The Virgin Martir' appeared in the Stationers' Register.[4] Thereafter his biography is largely an account of the production, performance and publication of his plays.

The Virgin Martyr, in all likelihood a revision by Massinger of a

---

[1] Ibid, Epigrams, 2nd Book, 35 (misnumbered for 52, p. 117).
[2] Cf. below, p. 46.   [3] Printed by Gifford, iv, p. 594.   [4] Arber, iv, p. 62.

play by Dekker, was produced, as the title-page of the 1622 edition shows, 'by the servants of His Majesty's Revels', probably at the Red Bull. The other play in which Massinger was an acknowledged collaborator, *The Fatal Dowry*, although not published until 1632, was certainly finished by 1620 (in which year Massinger's partner in the writing, Nathan Field, died) and was also written for the King's Men. The two earliest plays of what might be called the 'accepted' canon, *The Unnatural Combat* (probably written 1620–1621) and *The Duke of Milan* (written before 1623 when it was published) were also produced at the Globe or the Blackfriars. After this Massinger seems to have been writing for the Queen's Men for a year or two. According to what we can gather from Herbert's Office Book, *The Bondman* (licensed December, 1623), *The Renegado* (lic. April, 1624), and *The Parliament of Love* (lic. November, 1624) were all written for this company[1] and produced at the Cockpit, Drury Lane, afterwards called the Phoenix. Three other plays can be fairly confidently assigned to this period of writing for the Queen's Men. *The Great Duke of Florence* (lic. July, 1627) as I have explained previously,[2] was probably written in 1624 or early in 1625. *A New Way to Pay Old Debts*, although it does not appear in Herbert's Office Book, has internal evidence which suggests that it was written in late 1625.[3] *The Maid of Honour*, credited to the Queen's Men on the title-page of the first (1632) edition, also does not appear in the Office Book, at least under that title; although a play called *The Honour of Women* was licensed for the King's Men in 1628. However the play's most recent editor[4] has little hesitation in assigning it to the same period as *The Great Duke of Florence*.

The earliest plays which Massinger wrote on his own might therefore be placed in the following tentative order of writing:

1620: *The Unnatural Combat*	(Pub. 1639)
1621: *The Duke of Milan*	(Pub. 1623)
Mid-1623: *The Bondman*	(Pub. 1624)
Early 1624: *The Renegado*	(Pub. 1630)
Mid-1624: *The Parliament of Love*	(Pub. 1805)[5]
Late 1624: *The Great Duke of Florence*	(Pub. 1636)
Early 1625: *The Maid of Honour*	(Pub. 1632)
Late 1625: *A New Way to Pay Old Debts*	(Pub. 1633)

[1] The history of the theatrical companies at this time is very confused, and it is impossible from the evidence we now have to decide which of Massinger's plays written during this period were written for the Lady Elizabeth's Company (latterly known as the Queen of Bohemia's) and which for Queen Henrietta's. While the latter company was not quite a continuation of the former, the manager, Beeston, formed a strong link between the two. On this, see *Bentley*, p. 219.   [2] See above, pp. 13–14.

[3] Professor A. K. McIlwraith has half-heartedly suggested an earlier dating (On the date of *A New Way to Pay Old Debts*, MLR, XXVIII, 1933, p. 431).

[4] Eva A. W. Bryne, *The Maid of Honour* (Th. Bryn Mawr), London, 1927.

[5] By Gifford, vol. ii.

While this list cannot be said to be authoritative, it is based on my own personal opinion reached after a study of the opinions of the most recent editors of the plays. It forms in any case a reasonable and practicable basis for a study of the plays, and as such will be used throughout the rest of this book.

Why Massinger went over to the Queen's Company in or about 1623 can only be guessed. Probably as an ambitious author who had just written two plays without the help of a collaborator, he altered his allegiance as a result of an attractive offer from Beeston. The King's Company, after all, would not worry very much since they still had Fletcher writing for them. It is easier to see why he returned to the King's in 1626. The reorganisation of the theatrical companies following the death of James I and the consequent general post in which most of the playwrights seem to have been indulging around 1625–1626, coupled with the death of Fletcher in the plague of 1625, are satisfactory enough reasons. In addition, the return to the Blackfriars from the Cockpit would mark, if anything, an upward step professionally. In any case, from 11th October, 1626, when *The Roman Actor* was licensed,[1] all Massinger's own plays, as well as very probably some at least of his revisions of Fletcher's work, were written for the King's Men and produced either at the Globe or at the Blackfriars.

The plays with which Massinger can be associated in this period of writing for the King's Men during the last fourteen years of his life can be tabulated as follows:

Suggested Dating	Title	Licensed	Published
Early 1626	The City Madam	25 May 1632	1658–9
Mid-1626	The Roman Actor	11 Oct. 1626	1629
Early 1627	The Judge	6 June 1627	Lost
Early 1628	The Honour of Women	6 May 1628	— [2]
Early 1629	The Picture	8 June 1629	1630
Mid-1629	Minerva's Sacrifice	3 Nov. 1629	Lost
Late 1630	Believe As You List	(Rejected 11 Jan. 1631)[3]	
		7 May 1631	1848
Early 1631	The Emperor of the East	11 Mar. 1631	1632
Early 1631	The Unfortunate Piety	13 June 1631	Lost
Mid-1633	The Guardian	31 Oct. 1633	1655
Early 1634	The Tragedy of Cleander	7 May 1634	Lost
Early 1634	A Very Woman (a revision)	6 June 1634	1655
Late 1634	The Orator	10 Jan. 1635	Lost
Early 1636	The Bashful Lover	9 May 1636	1655
Early 1638	The King and the Subject	5 June 1638	Lost
	(The Tyrant ?)	(after reformation)	
Mid-1639	Alexius, or The Chaste Lover	25 Sept. 1639	Lost
Late 1639	The Fair Anchoress of Pausilippo	26 Jan. 1640	Lost

[1] *Herbert*, p. 31.

[2] This play is included (although Herbert does not attribute it to Massinger) since many scholars have equated it with *The Maid of Honour*. See above, p. 28, and below, p. 30.

[3] See below, pp. 43–44.

Of this list, as may be seen by the publication dates, eight plays have survived. Seven of these eight are by Massinger alone, and the remaining play, *A Very Woman*, is a revision of a Fletcher play. What has happened to the remaining nine plays we do not know, and there is little point in entering here into the complex arguments which surround this question. It should be noted, however, that some of the titles may merely indicate 'reformation' of early plays. Thus Fleay has suggested that *The Judge* is an alteration of *The Fatal Dowry*[1]; that *Minerva's Sacrifice* was an alteration of *The Queen of Corinth*[2]; that *The Unfortunate Piety* was an alteration of *The Double Marriage*[3]; that *Cleander* was an alteration of *The Lovers' Progress*[4]; and that *The Orator* was an alteration of *The Elder Brother*.[5] The whole matter is additionally complicated by certain 'blocking entries' under double titles (some of which seem to represent two different plays) made in the Stationers' Register by Humphrey Moseley in September, 1653,[6] and by Warburton's famous (and perhaps spurious) 'List' of the plays in his possession which had been destroyed by his cook. The bibliographical tangle is almost impossible to resolve. In connection with the above list, however, it may be stated that *The Honour of Women* is almost certainly not *The Maid of Honour* but a play by Richard Brome, Jonson's servant, called *The Love-sick Maid*[7]; and the play called *The King and the Subject*, of which Herbert gives us a sample,[8] can probably be equated with *The Tyrant*, a play which was entered in the Stationers' Register on 29th June, 1660, appears in Warburton's List, was sold at his sale in 1759, but has since disappeared.[9] I can see no reason myself why all the other plays which have been lost should not be original plays by Massinger, rather than, as Fleay suggests, mere revisions. But with the example of *A Very Woman* before us, credited to Massinger by Herbert, published posthumously as Massinger's, and yet patently largely Fletcher's work, it is impossible to generalise on this score. If any of this group of plays are to be dismissed as 'reformations', I would personally conjecture that *Minerva's Sacrifice* (the title is very unlike Massinger) and *The Unfortunate Piety* (again on account of the title and for a reason I shall have occasion to mention later) should be the only ones. The other missing plays at least *sound* genuine (for what that hazard is worth), and their dates seem to accord well with Massinger's rate of production.

[1] *BCED*, i, pp. 208, 223. [2] Ibid., i, pp. 32, 206.
[3] Ibid., i, pp. 210–211, 225. [4] Ibid., i, p. 219; ii, p. 156.
[5] Ibid., i, p. 228. [6] See *Herbert, passim*.
[7] *Herbert*, p. 32, under date 9 February, 1629.
[8] See below, p. 44. Cf. Heywood's *The Royal King and the Loyal Subject*. The coincidence of titles may be significant. [9] *Herbert*, p. 38, note 2.

It will be noticed that I have placed *The City Madam* first in the sequence, although it was not licensed until 1632. The most recent editor of the play, Mr. Rudolf Kirk,[1] produces convincing evidence from within the play that it was written probably not later than 1626. I find his argument reasonable, and for me the dating of this play as early as 1626 has the great advantage of bringing it immediately after *A New Way to Pay Old Debts*, a play to which it has very close affinities in style, tone, and spirit. Of course, *The City Madam* may have received some alterations before the 1632 licensing, but if so there is little evidence of this in the play as we have it now. In addition, the percentage of run-on lines in the play accords well with the period of *The Roman Actor*,[2] not with the later date. The 1632 licensing was probably merely a regularising of an irregular state of affairs.

The foregoing paragraphs, which have done little more than skim the surface from what is in effect a large field of study in its own right, are sufficient to set in their chronological and theatrical context the plays with which I shall be chiefly dealing in this study. It will be seen that, especially when we allow for his early collaborations and his later revisions, Massinger led a reasonably busy life, though perhaps not busier than Fletcher's, and that, even allowing for a certain amount of revisionary work, his rate of production seems to have fallen off a little during the last eight or nine years of his life. Doubtless, like most writers, he wrote no more than was necessary to keep himself comfortably, and it must always be remembered that he was probably also receiving assistance from Pembroke. Fletcher was dead, and his position was reasonably secure.

However, Massinger's career was not without its checks. The most important of these seems to have come in the two years preceding 1633. In that year, in the Prologue to *The Guardian*, there is a mention of two plays which had failed on the stage:

> After twice putting forth to sea, his fame
> Shipwrecked in either, and his once-known name
> In two years silence buried, perhaps lost
> In the general opinion; at our cost
> (A zealous sacrifice to Neptune made

[1] *The City Madam*, Princeton Studies in English 10, Princeton, 1934.
[2] Professor T. W. Baldwin, in his edition of *The Duke of Milan* (Lancaster, Pa., 1918), has presented an interesting table of Massinger's metrical peculiarities showing (among other features) how the percentage of run-on lines in the plays tends to increase. The chronology of the plays in the table is wrong, and much of the data is perhaps open to question, but Baldwin has not noticed that, on his own theory, *The City Madam*, with 39·4 per cent run-on lines is closer to *The Roman Actor* (38·7 per cent) than it is to *Believe As You List* (52·4 per cent).

For good success in his uncertain trade)
Our author weighs up anchors, and once more
Forsaking the security of the shore,
Resolves to prove his fortune.[1]

Two plays, then, had failed, and Massinger had been persuaded to write again only by some financial inducement ('at our cost') offered to him by the players. Even if we allow for some of the conventional modesty and self-depreciation which is common in prologues, this check seems to have been a serious one. The Prologue goes on to say:

He submits
To the grave censure of those abler wits
His weakness; nor dares he profess that when
The critics laugh, he'll laugh at them again.
(Strange self-love in a writer!) He would know
His errors as you find them, and bestow
His future studies to reform from this,
What in another might be judged amiss.
And yet despair not, gentlemen; though he fear
His strengths to please, we hope that you shall hear
Some things so writ, as you may truly say
He hath not quite forgot to make a play,
As 'tis with malice rumoured; his intents
Are fair; and though he want the compliments
Of wide-mouthed promisers, who still engage,
Before their works are brought upon the stage,
Their parasites to proclaim them: this last birth,
Delivered without noise, may yield such mirth,
As, balanced equally, will cry down the boast
Of arrogance, and regain his credit lost.

Massinger, it may be gathered, had been accused of 'arrogance' and 'self-love' by a certain group of critics, among whom must be numbered some other playwright.

The fact that one (at least) of Massinger's plays had not succeeded is supported by a poem by Henry Parker[2] entitled 'To his honoured frend Mr. Phillip Massinger, having not had that just applause for one of his playes which was due to him'. Since Mr. G. Thorn-Drury's book, in which the poem has been printed,[3] is not

---

[1] Gifford, iv, pp. 125-126.
[2] This is probably the Henry Parker (1604-1652) recorded in the *Dictionary of National Biography* as an M.A. (1628), barrister in Lincoln's Inn, and later a parliamentarian and publisher of various controversial pamphlets. Massinger must have had many friends among the young men-about-town who were members of the Inns of Court; indeed, he makes reference to his many legal acquaintances in the dedication of *The Picture* (1630).
[3] *A Little Ark*, 1921.

easily come by, I have taken the liberty of reproducing this poem
in full:

> Canst thou be troubled at the hissing croude?
>> tush: let them stretche theire neckes, and hisse as lowde
> At that which doth transcend their valuacon,
>> as that which is belowe, theire estimacon.
> The moone hath power to worke upon the mayne
>> but is not wrought upon by that againe:
> Soe thou should'st all new votes and passions swaye,
>> but should'st not learne thy selfe howe to obeye:
> What if the gallants like not? What if hee
>> which hath a Clearer judgment censure thee?
> haveing soe ponderous a masse of Fame,
>> one grayne diminisht will not wronge thy name.
> That little stayne, that blur'd the rosy face
>> of Cytherea, rather added grace
> then spoyl'd her beautie: yet it was a stayne
>> and in a rude aspect had caus'd disdaine
> Soe that dislike which may procure some scorne
>> to meaner witts, may justly thine adorne.
> Besides in sevrall workes of Poetrie
>> 'tis not as 'tis in Nature Symetrie
> For if one play dislike, it doth not cast
>> Dislike upon that play which pleased last.
> If in a fragrant vineyard wee espie
>> one withered grape which wants maturitie,
> Wee do not blame the soyle, or els impute
>> that small defect unto the Noble roote.
> Soe if the raptures of thy sacred muse
>> take us not all alike, 'tis thy Excuse:
> Thy muse is still the same, and fortune maye
>> in all things eether add or take awaye.

Henerie Parker.

It is interesting to consider which were the two plays that failed.
There can, I think, be no doubt that one of them was *The Emperor
of the East*, which was licensed on 11th March, 1631.[1] As has been
convincingly argued by Professor A. K. McIlwraith,[2] this play was
revised extensively by Massinger before its presentation at Court.
The prologue spoken at this performance at Court is extant, and
makes it quite clear that the play had failed when it first appeared.
After a humble address to the King, commending the play to him

---

[1] *Herbert*, p. 33.
[2] *Did Massinger Revise 'The Emperor of the East'?* (*RES*, V 1929).

as 'fashioned and formed' with the 'best of fancy, judgment, language, art', Massinger goes on to say:

> And yet this poor work suffered by the rage
> And envy of some Catos of the stage:
> Yet still he hopes this Play, which then was seen
> With sores eyes, and condemned out of their spleen,
> May be by you, the supreme judge, set free,
> And raised above the reach of calumny.[1]

The Emperor of the East, then, was definitely one of the two plays mentioned in *The Guardian* prologue as having been a public failure.

It is not quite so easy to determine which was the other failure. *The City Madam*, which was licensed in May 1632, was written and performed long before. Indeed, the argument that *The City Madam* was not produced until the middle of 1632 can be discounted if we take only Massinger's own statement in *The Guardian* prologue that his name had been 'in two years silence buried', without troubling to look for internal evidence for dating the play. The lost play, *The Unfortunate Piety*, gives us another possible claimant for the doubtful distinction. I feel sure, however, that this play was a revision (possibly of *The Double Marriage*, as Fleay suggests), since, judged by his normal rate of output, Massinger would have little time for anything else during the first half of 1631. By March of that year *The Emperor of the East* had been written, and it was probably altered considerably shortly after its first production. *Believe As You List* had been written by January of the same year, and by 7th May had, as the original manuscript shows,[2] been completely rewritten. Massinger would not have had time by the beginning of June to write another brand-new play. In my opinion, then, the second play that failed was *Believe As You List*. It did not finally reach the boards until two months after *The Emperor of the East*. There is, indeed, an allusion to the attack of the critics in the opening of the Prologue to *Believe As You List*, a prologue which was obviously written for the revised version of the play:

> So far our author is from arrogance
> That he craves pardon for his ignorance
> In story.[3]

In *The Guardian* prologue Massinger makes specific mention of two plays as having failed—presumably those two last produced. We

---

[1] Gifford, iii, p. 245.
[2] B.M. MS. Egerton 2828, Tudor Facsimile Texts, London, 1907. The MS. is fully discussed by Professor C. J. Sisson in his edition, Malone Soc. Repr., 1927 and Oxford, 1928. See below, pp. 43–44, and Chapter II, pp. 56–57.   [3] Cunningham, p. 595.

know that *The Emperor of the East* failed, and we know that *Believe As You List* was produced after this. The balance of probability, then, is that it was the second failure.

That this period of criticism, which had serious results in the failures of 1631 and in Massinger's subsequent silence until 1633, was still rankling in his mind three years later is shown by the prologue to *The Bashful Lover* (1636). In this he adopts a pseudo-humble tone of voice, and turns round upon his detractors the accusations they had earlier levelled at him:

> This from our author, far from all offence
> To abler writers, or the audience
> Met here to judge his poem. He, by me,
> Presents his service with such modesty
> As well becomes his weakness. 'Tis no crime,
> He hopes, as we do, in this curious time,
> To be a little diffident, when we are
> To please so many with one bill of fare.
> Let others, building on their merit, say
> You're in the wrong, if you move not that way
> Which they prescribe you; as you were bound to learn
> Their maxims, but uncapable to discern
> 'Twixt truth and falsehood. Our's had rather be
> Censured by some for too much obsequy,
> Than taxed of self opinion.[1]

This meek tone is also obvious in the only other prologue which has survived from the period following *The Guardian*, that to *A Very Woman* (1634), in which the author 'with becoming modesty (for in this kind he ne'er was bold)', defends himself for adapting an old play.

Massinger had, however, already been the object of an attack before *The Emperor of the East*. In the first prologue to the play, given at the performance at the Blackfriars, we read:

> But that imperious custom warrants it,
> Our author with much willingness would omit
> This preface to his new work. He hath found
> (And suffered for't) many are apt to wound
> His credit in this kind: and whether he
> Express himself fearful, or peremptory,
> He cannot 'scape their censures who delight
> To misapply whatever he shall write.
> 'Tis his hard fate.[2]

---

[1] Gifford, iv, p. 353. [2] Ibid., iii, p. 244.

This suggests that something Massinger had written in a prologue had given offence. What it was we do not know. *The Judge* is lost, and there are no prologues to either *The Picture* or *The Roman Actor* extant. Possibly the accusation of arrogance had been growing against Massinger since *The Roman Actor* was produced in 1626. We know that he thought highly of this play, since in the Dedication he says that he had 'ever held it the most perfect birth of his Minerva', and it is possible that he said even more to this effect in a now-lost prologue. There was, to be sure, one playwright living in England who would be almost certain to snarl at the extravagant poetic encomiums heaped upon this play on its publication in 1629, but I shall return to him later.

Massinger's troubles with critics in the early 1630's are reflected in statements made in some of the commendatory verses prefixed to those of the plays published during this period. Prefacing *The Emperor of the East,* John Clavell (1603–1642), reprieved highwayman turned author and poet, says:

> Your Muse hath been
> Most bountiful, and I have often seen
> The willing seats receive such as have fed,
> And risen thankful; yet were some misled
> By NICETY, when this fair banquet came,
> (So I allude) their stomachs were to blame,
> Because that excellent, sharp, and poignant sauce,
> Was wanting, they arose without due grace,
> Lo! thus a second time he doth invite you:
> Be your own carvers, and it may delight you.[1]

And that Massinger's detractors, or one of them at least, also indulged in playwriting is perhaps suggested by the poem prefixed to the same play by William Singleton, who describes himself as a 'Kinsman' of Massinger:

> I take not upon trust, nor am I led
> By an implicit faith: what I have read
> With an impartial censure I dare crown
> With a deserved applause, howe'er cried down
> By such whose malice will not let them be
> Equal to any piece limn'd forth by thee.
> Contemn their poor detraction, and still write
> Poems like this, that can endure the light
> And search of abler judgements. This will raise
> Thy name; the others' scandal is thy praise.

---

[1] Gifford, i, p. clxii.

This, oft perused by grave wits, shall live long,
Not die as soon as past the actor's tongue,
The fate of slighter toys.[1]

A hint of the controversy is dropped even earlier by the verses prefixed to the 1630 edition of *The Renegado* by Daniel Lakyn:

'I did ever glory
To behold virtue rich; though cruel Fate
In scornful malice does beat low their state
That best deserve; when others, that but know
Only to scribble, and no more, oft grow
Great in their favours, that would seem to be
Patrons of wit and modest poesy:
Yet, with your abler friends, let me say this,
Many may strive to equal you, but miss
Of your fair scope; this work of yours men may
Throw in the face of envy, and then say
To those, that are in great men's thoughts more blest,
Imitate this, and call that work your best . . .
If I should say more, some may blame me for't.[2]

And a possible quarter from which criticism might come is mentioned by Joseph Taylor (1586?–1653?), the famous actor in the
King's Men and the first to play the part of Paris in *The Roman Actor*,
when, in lines prefacing the 1629 edition of that play, he says:

If that my lines, being placed before thy book,
Could make it sell. . . .
Or could I on some spot o'the court work so,
To make him speak no more than he doth know;
Not borrowing from his flatt'ring flatter'd friend
What to dispraise, or wherefore to commend:
Then, gentle friend, I should not blush to be
Ranked 'mongst those worthy ones which here I see
Ushering this work.[3]

It is tempting to try to name the source from which this criticism
of Massinger and his work sprang. I think it can with reasonable cer-
tainty be ascribed to Ben Jonson and his circle. Jonson was at his
most quarrelsome and pugnacious in 1630, the year after the disastrous failure of *The New Inn*, and the time of his row with Inigo Jones
over the production of the masque, *Chloridia*.

In the material I have so far presented the hints which seem to

[1] Gifford, i, p. clxiii.   [2] Ibid., i, p. clii.
[3] Ibid., i, p. clvi.

point to Jonson as the *fons et origo* for the criticism directed against Massinger may be detailed as follows:

(i) If Massinger's high opinion of *The Roman Actor* did in fact bring down charges of self-esteem and arrogance, Jonson, grown more rigid in classicism with age, was the man most likely to condemn the play for the Shakespearean freedom with which it treats classical history.

(ii) In his condoling poem, Parker speaks both of the 'gallants' and of 'hee which hath a Clearer judgment'.

(iii) *The Emperor of the East*, the Court Prologue tells us, 'suffered by the rage and envy of some Catos of the stage' who saw the play 'with sore eyes, and condemned out of their spleen'. This sounds uncommonly like the Jonson of 1631.

(iv) The prologue to *The Bashful Lover* speaks of other writers who, 'building on their merit, say you're in the wrong if you move not that way which they prescribe you; as you are bound to learn their maxims'. Clavell, in his poem on *The Emperor of the East*, speaks of the play as having offended because of its lack of what he calls 'NICETY'. Presumably by this he means a lack of conformity to a set code or prescribed rules in playmaking. Jonson considered himself the Grand Prescriber in things dramatic and literary for his age.

(v) Lakyn, in his poem on *The Renegado*, written in 1630, speaks of a writer who is 'in great men's thoughts more blest' than Massinger, and who is in receipt of more patronage. That was certainly true of Jonson, who, as well as receiving money from Pembroke, Massinger's own patron, had a considerable official pension and a chief share of the royal patronage.

(vi) The 'flatt'ring flatter'd friend' to the 'spot o'the court' described by Taylor, might be an unflattering description of Jonson in 1629.

Additional evidence comes in 1630, when, in a poem prefixed to *The Renegado*, James Shirley says:

> I must confess I have no public name
> To rescue judgment, no poetic flame
>> To dress thy Muse with praise,
>> And Phoebus his own bays;
> Yet I commend this poem, and dare tell
> The world I liked it well;
>> And if there be
> A tribe who in their wisdoms dare accuse
> This offspring of thy Muse,
>> Let them agree
> Conspire one comedy, and they will say,
> 'Tis easier to commend, than make a play.[1]

[1] Gifford, i, p. cl.

This stanza by Shirley points, if not directly at Jonson himself, at least at that group of writers and courtiers who surrounded him.

Finally, that the trouble, blowing up in 1630, was in some way connected with Jonson, seems to me to be made certain by the suggestions in the solitary poem which ushered in the 1630 edition of *The Picture*. This poem, written by Sir Thomas Jay, a minor society poet of some pretensions but little ability, opens with conventional lines praising the play and the author. Then Jay, for no apparent reason, adopts a more admonishing tone:

> Yet whosoe'er beyond desert commends,
> Errs more by much than he that reprehends;
> For praise misplaced, and honour set upon
> A worthless subject is detraction.
> I cannot sin so here, unless I went
> About to style you only excellent.

Licet. So far so good. But Jay continues:

> Apollo's gifts are not confined alone
> To your dispose, he hath more heirs than one,
> And such as do derive from his blest hand
> A large inheritance in the poets' land,
> As well as you; nor are you, I assure
> Myself, so envious, but you can endure
> To hear their praise, whose worth long since was known
> And justly too preferr'd before your own.
> I know you'd take it for an injury,
> (And 'tis a well-becoming modesty)
> To be parallel'd with Beaumont, or to hear
> Your name by some too partial friend writ near
> Unequall'd Jonson; being men whose fire,
> At distance, and with reverence, you admire.

Thus far the poem may be interpreted either as praise or as a veiled rebuke. There is, however, no mistaking the tone of admonishment contained in the last lines:

> Do so, and you shall find your gain will be
> Much more, by yielding them priority,
> Than with a certainty of loss, to hold
> A foolish competition: 'tis too bold
> A task, and to be shunn'd.[1]

These lines can, I think, be taken as a warning to Massinger—either to 'ca' canny' in some dispute in which he was already engaged or to

---

[1] Gifford, i, pp. clix–clx. Davies (*Monck Mason*, p. cvii, note) is the only previous writer to have remarked on the peculiar tone of this 'eulogy'.

restrain his self-vaunting. They certainly seem to have a purpose quite divorced from their task of commending *The Picture*.

If Jonson had been challenged or provoked in any way, he would certainly have made his opponent smart. He was the only rival of Massinger with sufficient authority and a large enough claque to have had *The Emperor of the East* hissed off the stage. Neither Heywood nor Dekker would have troubled to chide, and both were in general more inclined to praise. Marston had long abandoned the stage. Shirley, as we have seen, was ranged on Massinger's side, and both he and John Ford (also a writer of commendatory poems on Massinger's plays[1]) were still at the beginning of such estimation as they were to enjoy. And there is no other regular and professional playwright, as distinct from the occasional and amateur ones, to be accounted for. So by a process of elimination we come back to Jonson.

It may be urged that Jonson does not mention Massinger by name anywhere in his plays, non-dramatic verse, or in his prose. On the other hand, many of Jonson's shafts were without label, not because they were shot into the air, but because his contemporaries and in particular his initiates knew perfectly well for whom they were meant. I have, however, not been able to detect any such references —though a sarcastic remark in *The Staple of News* (1625) may be a hit at the Fletcher–Massinger method of manufacturing characters.[2] But in any case, Jonson was so liberal in his censure (and we must suppose that his oral censure was even more extensive than his written) that Massinger, one of the leading dramatists of the day, is very unlikely to have escaped. I have felt compelled, by the evidence I have been able to collect, to come to the conclusion that the disgruntled Jonson was indeed the instigator of a sort of anti-Massinger *Flüsterndpropaganda*.

Massinger himself mentions Jonson only once by name. This is in the poem addressed to William, the third Earl of Pembroke, the patron of Jonson's library:

> I know
> That Johnson much of what he has does owe
> To you and to your familie, and is never
> Slow to professe it.[3]

But it would be unwise to read a sly dig into these lines, since, after quoting other instances of patronage, Massinger goes on to say,

> Those are Presidents [i.e. 'precedents']
> I cite wth reverence.[4]

---

[1] Though it is just possible that these verses were not written by the playwright but by one of the other Fords of whom we have notice at this time.

[2] Quoted below, Chap. IV, p. 134.

[3] *Dublin MS*, lines 49–52.   [4] Ibid., lines 63–64.

It was suggested by Davies[1] that Massinger fell foul of Jonson long before 1630. In 1623, a certain 'W. B.' prefixed verses to the first edition of *The Duke of Milan* which might be interpreted as containing an attack on Jonson. Calling Massinger's play a 'Work', W. B. says:

> I am snapt already, and may go my way;
> The poet-critic's come; I hear him say
> This youth's mistook, the author's work's a play.
>
> He could not miss it, he will straight appear
> At such a bait; 'twas laid on purpose there,
> To take the vermin, and I have him here.
>
> Sirrah! you will be nibbling; a small bit,
> A syllable, when you're in the hungry fit,
> Will serve to stay the stomach of your wit.
>
> Fool, knave, what worse, for worse cannot deprave thee;
> And were the devil now instantly to have thee,
> Thou canst not instance such a work to save thee,
>
> 'Mongst all the ballets which thou dost compose,
> And what thou stylest thy Poems, ill as those,
> And void of rhyme and reason, thy worse prose:
>
> Yet, like a rude jack-sauce in poesy,
> With thoughts unblest, and hand unmannerly,
> Ravishing branches from Apollo's tree;
>
> Thou mak'st a garland, for thy touch unfit,
> And boldly deck'st thy pig-brain'd sconce with it,
> As if it were the supreme head of wit.
>
> The blameless Muses blush; who not allow
> That reverend order to each vulgar brow,
> Whose sinful touch profanes the holy bough.
>
> Hence, shallow prophet, and admire the strain
> Of thine own pen, or thy poor cope-mate's vein;
> This piece too curious is for thy coarse brain.[2]

And in the following year, at the end of his poem commending *The Bondman*, the same writer says:

> in the way of poetry, now-a-days,
> Of all that are call'd works, the best are plays.[3]

---

[1] *Monck Mason*, p. xcix, note.   [2] Gifford, i, p. cxlvii.   [3] Ibid., i, p. cl.

It seems to me, however, that far from being a criticism of Jonson, these verses could just as easily be interpreted as being a check to Jonson's opponents who had derided him for calling his plays *Works*. At any rate, as the 'rude jack-sauce' is specifically described as a poet and prose-writer, not a dramatist, the odds are rather against Jonson's being the object of the attack. Moreover, I think it is unlikely that Massinger would have allowed the first published play from his own unaided hand to go forth with a gratuitous insult to the powerful Jonson in the forefront.

My own tentative suggestion is that the poet criticised by W. B. may have been George Wither. He had drawn a very unflattering picture of Jonson and his tavern-cronies in *Abuses Stript and Whipt*; and for that and perhaps for later offences Jonson pilloried him as Chronomastix in *Time Vindicated* (performed 19th January, 1623). Wither was garrulous and indiscreet. He had twice landed himself in prison, the first time for the ostensibly general satire in *Abuses Stript and Whipt* and the second for offence given either by *Wither's Motto* (1621) or his *Juvenilia* (1622). It is possible that the second imprisonment was referred to in *The Duke of Milan* itself when in Act III, scene ii, the Prison Officer who has whipped the toadying Graccho says:

> I have had a fellow
> That could endite, forsooth, and make fine metres
> To tinkle in the ears of ignorant madams,
> That, for defaming of great men, was sent me
> Threadbare and lousy, and in three days after,
> Discharged by another that set him on, I have seen him
> Cap a pié gallant, and his stripes washed off
> With oil of angels.

Wither fits the picture we may deduce from W. B. exactly. He was very self-assured and conscious of his own merit. His poems had been surreptitiously published in 1620, under the title, *The Workes of Master George Wither, of Lincolns-Inne, Gentleman*, etc., and so qualify him still further for consideration in this respect. Satirised by Jonson, made the butt of Massinger's sally, Wither was fair game for anyone who would hit him (not that, in his uninspired way, he was incapable of reply), and he seems to be the likeliest target for W. B.'s poem.

That W. B. was not, as suggested by Davies,[1] William Browne of Tavistock necessarily follows, if Wither was W. B.'s target. For Browne and Wither, the Willy and the Roget of *The Shepherd's Hunting*, were close friends and collaborators. The lines in question and

---

[1] *Monck Mason*, p. xcix, note.

the lines signed 'W. B.' before *The Bondman* were included by Gordon Goodwin in his edition of Browne,[1] but with the comment that they 'have been also assigned to William Basse'.[2] It seems to me unlikely that they were written by Basse.[3] It may be remarked that the initials 'W. B.' are attached to several publications in the second, third, and fourth decades of the seventeenth century, and there are many other writers bearing names which would yield these same initials.

The diligent enquiries of Professor A. K. McIlwraith have, in fact, revealed another 'W. B.', who is known to have been a friend of Massinger's. This is 'William Bagnall of London, gent', so named in a Chancery Bill in the Public Records Office dated 6th November, 1624, in which he is coupled with Massinger as fellow plaintiff.[4] All that we know of Bagnall is that he did write verses. He contributed a commendatory poem to Barkstead's *Mirrha, the Mother of Adonis* (1617), and the induction to *Certaine selected Psalmes of David*, an item in a Crane transcript in the Bodleian,[5] is signed by him. Significantly enough, the next item in this manuscript, a poem of 206 lines on the 1625 plague, entitled *London's Lamentable Estate* and signed with the initials 'Ph. M.', may be by Massinger.[6] The definite coupling of this William Bagnall with Massinger shortly after the publication of *The Duke of Milan* and *The Bondman* makes it very probable that he was indeed the 'W. B.' of the commendatory poems.

★

Of course, Massinger had his brushes with the official censorship as well as with the unofficial. On 11th January, 1631, a licence was refused for *Believe As You List*, Sir Henry Herbert recording the matter in his Office Book thus:

> This day being the 11 of Janu. 1630(-1), I did refuse to allow of a play of Messinger's because itt did contain dangerous matter, as the deposing of Sebastian King of Portugal, by Philip the (Second,) and ther being a peace sworen twixte the kings of England and Spayne. I had my fee notwithstandinge, which belongs to me for reading itt over, and ought to be brought always with the booke.[7]

---

[1] *The Poems of William Browne of Tavistock.* (Muses Library), 1894, ii, pp. 314–316.
[2] By Gifford, i, p. cxlix, note.
[3] Although R. W. Bond, the editor of Basse (*The Poetical Works of William Basse*, London, 1893), considers they are his work.
[4] Cf. *RES*, IV, 1928, pp. 326–327.
[5] MS. Rawl. poet., 61 (fol. 6r).
[6] Cf. F. P. Wilson, *Library*, VII, 1926, p. 199.   [7] *Herbert*, p. 19.

The play was revised, as the manuscript shows,[1] was resubmitted, and duly received a licence on 7th May.[2]

Eight years later another play by Massinger came under the disapproving eye of no less a person than King Charles himself. Herbert records the trouble as follows:

> Received of Mr. Lowens for my paines about Messinger's play called *The King and the Subject*, 2 June, 1638, 1*l*.0.0.

> The name of *The King and the Subject* is altered,[3] and I allowed the play to bee acted, the reformations most strictly observed, and not otherwise, the 5th of June 1638.

> At Greenwich the 4 of June, Mr. W. Murray, gave mee power from the king to allowe of the play, and tould me that hee would warrant it.

> > Monys? Wee'le rayse supplies what ways we please,
> > And force you to subscribe to blanks, in which
> > We'le mulct you as wee shall thinke fitt. The Caesars
> > In Rome were wise, acknowledginge no lawes
> > But what their swords did ratifye, the wives
> > And daughters of the senators bowinge to
> > Their wills, as deities, &c.

> This is a peece taken out of Phillip Messingers play, called *The King and the Subject*, and entered here for ever to bee remembered by my son and those that cast their eyes on it, in honour of Kinge Charles, my master, who readinge over the play at Newmarket, set his marke upon the place with his owne hand, and in thes words:

> > 'This is too insolent, and to bee changed.'

> Note, that the poett makes it the speech of a king, Don Pedro, king of Spayne, and spoken to his subjects.[4]

The poet who could write such verses at such a time was certainly not lacking in courage; and it might be remarked in passing that they are not the lines of a Catholic Royalist. When it is considered, however, that some of his plays contain political allusions even more pointed than this, it might be thought remarkable that Massinger did not meet with official opposition more often than is recorded.[5]

Massinger seems to have been well liked by his friends. According to Langbaine, 'he was extreamly belov'd by the Poets of that age,

---

[1] See above, p. 34, note 2.   [2] *Herbert*, p. 33.
[3] Possibly to *The Tyrant*. See above, p. 30.   [4] *Herbert*, p. 22.
[5] For a discussion of Massinger's political views, see Chapter V, pp. 163 ff.

and there were few but what took it as an honour to club with him in a play: witness Middleton, Rowley, Field, and Decker . . . nay, further, . . . the ingenious Fletcher'.[1] Langbaine, as I have said before, is not a reliable authority where Massinger is concerned, and collaboration in the Jacobean theatre was a matter of necessity rather than of choice. Nevertheless, there is ample testimony in commendatory poems and dedications of the number of our playwright's friends and of the regard in which they held him. Joseph Taylor the actor, who played Paris in *The Roman Actor*,[2] addresses Massinger as 'his long-known and loved Friend', and says that he (Taylor) writes his poem both to praise a good tragedy and 'to profess our love's antiquity'.[3] W. B., whoever he may be, calls Massinger 'his beloved friend'[4]; and an equally problematical 'T. J.' (Sir Thomas Jay?) calls him 'his dear friend'.[5] To the ubiquitous George Donne he is his 'much-esteem'd friend'[6]; and to Thomas May he is 'his deserving friend'.[7] There is no indication of friendship or of more than a slight acquaintanceship in John Ford's commendatory poems for *The Roman Actor* and *The Great Duke of Florence*. Shirley, too, as I have mentioned before, does not seem to have been very close to Massinger, and addresses him somewhat stiffly as 'my honoured friend' in the verses before *The Renegado*. In return, in his commendation of *The Grateful Servant*, Massinger calls Shirley his 'judicious and learned friend the Author'.[8] Other friends of Massinger whom I have not yet named in this chapter are Thomas Goffe (1591–1629), preacher and tragedian, who addressed some Latin verses to Massinger on the occasion of the publication of *The Roman Actor*; James Smith (1605–1667), churchman and lewd poet, whom Massinger addressed in the heading to a poem,[9] *more Jonsoni*, as 'his son'; and, of course, Fletcher himself. As might be expected, the majority of Massinger's friends were either writers by profession or men-of-letters by inclination.

The most loquacious of these friends is undoubtedly Aston Cokaine (later Sir Aston Cokaine). Cokaine (1608–1684) was a somewhat dissolute litterateur and gentleman-poet, a hanger-on to the fringes of the literary world. He seems to have been inordinately proud of knowing a few poets and writers, and so perhaps his words and their implications should not be relied on too much. He was the type of man who would assume a familiarity or take a liberty in describing such acquaintanceship in order to gratify his vanity. His

[1] *Account*, p. 352.
[2] See *Bentley*, pp. 590–598.
[3] Gifford, i, p. clvi.
[4] Ibid., p. cxlvii.
[5] Ibid., p. cliii.
[6] Ibid., p. clvii.
[7] Ibid., p. cliv.
[8] Ibid., iv, p. 594.
[9] Ibid., p. 595.

scalp-hunting may be gathered from some lines to his cousin, Charles Cotton:

> Donne, Suckling, Randolph, Drayton, Massinger,
> Habbington, Sandy's, May, my Acquaintance were:
> Johnson, Chapman, and Holland I have seen,
> And with them too should have acquainted been.[1]

However, Cokaine does seem to have been on intimate terms with Massinger, and his garrulity is worth much more than the speculations of later writers, none of whom knew Massinger personally.

★

We have no very definite evidence that Massinger had a wife or family. But, according to Aubrey, the pension paid by Pembroke was continued after Massinger's death to his widow. He says, 'his wife dyed at Cardiffe in Wales, to whom the earl of Pembroke payd an annuity'.[2] I feel that this statement is too precise to be ignored, or even disputed. It would, after all, have been unusual if Massinger had not been married. Even if we have no evidence at all, his plays, many of which deal with the relationship between married couples, are not what we should expect from a bachelor. It is Lord Lovell who speaks, but Massinger who has written, the words:

> I know,
> The sum of all that makes a just man happy
> Consists in the well choosing of his wife.[3]

And the dialogue between Sophia and Mathias which opens *The Picture* shows too much understanding of the sort of conversation a man holds with his wife to have been written by a man who never had one. In any case, such speculation being left aside, there is no reason to doubt Aubrey's account. He was a diligent enquirer. He had taken the trouble to visit the house on the Bank-side in which Massinger had lived; and though the visit was admittedly some thirty-odd years after Massinger's death, there was less moving-about of population then than there is today and the information as to the dramatist's having been married or single was just of the kind to be recalled. What the name was of the 'not impossible she', still, of course, is unknown. But one of the panegyrists of *The Emperor of the East*, William Singleton, calls Massinger his 'true Friend and Kinsman'. The name Singleton does not commonly occur in Wiltshire.

---

[1] *Small Poems*, Epigrams, II, p. 99. Cokaine's prefatory verses to *The Emperor of the East* and *The Maid of Honour* are in the same volume (Encomiastic Verses Nos. 2 and 3).
[2] *Brief Lives*, ii, p. 54.   [3] *A New Way to Pay Old Debts*, IV, i.

It is indeed not a common name anywhere. A Hugh Singleton published Spenser's *Shepheards Calender* in 1579, and an Isaac Singleton wrote *The Downfall of Shebna: with an application to the bloudie Gowrie of Scotland* in 1615. I have been unable to trace William Singleton in any of the many registers I have examined, but I throw out the suggestion that his kinship to Massinger may have been by marriage.

As for the possibility of children born to Massinger, Aubrey does not mention any. But such a negative proves nothing either way. Similarly, too much should not be deduced from the fact that Mathias and his wife Sophia in *The Picture* have 'as yet [after many years of marriage] no charge of children' on them. There are in fact no children in any of Massinger's plays, and, so far as *The Picture* in particular is concerned, Mathias's statement was to let Massinger avoid the complications that the existence and appearance of children would have added to the lengthy domestic scenes. On the whole in Elizabethan–Jacobean plays other than Massinger's, children rarely appear gratuitously. If they appear, it is because they contribute to the plot, as in *Richard III* or *The Winter's Tale*, or even *Macbeth*.[1] Frankford and Anne in *A Woman Killed With Kindness*, in order to reinforce the pathos, are endowed by Heywood with 'pretty babes' and he makes much of their existence; but he does not bring them on. The inference I would draw, then, is that Massinger may quite well have had children, though he introduces none in his plays. Certainly, an entry in *The London Magazine* for 4th August, 1762, records the death of 'Miss Henrietta Massinger, a descendant of Massinger, the dramatic poet'.[2] If we are to take this statement at its face value (and there is no reason why we should not), Massinger must have had children. The name is found frequently in London records in the early seventeenth century; but perhaps the likeliest candidates for consideration as Massinger's children are a 'Katheren Messinger' who was married in the church of Allhallows-in-the-Wall on 6th May, 1633,[3] and a 'Thomas Messenger, Gent of St Sepulchres, Widower aged 29' who married a 24-year-old girl called Jane Underwood at St. Peter's, Paul's Wharf, on 24th January, 1636/7.[4] These two names are put forward speculatively out of several I have found in the records as the likeliest to be those of Massinger's own children. I might add that in Wiltshire I found

---

[1] i.e. Macduff's young son. The lack of heirs to Macbeth and Lady Macbeth is a cardinal point in the plot.   [2] Vol. xxxi, p. 449.
[3] *The Registers . . . of Allhallows, London Wall . . . 1559 to 1675*, London, 1878.
[4] *Allegations for Marriage Licences issued by the Bishop of London, 1520–1650*, (Chester and Armytage), London, 1887, ii, p. 306.

that a Mr. Messenger had been Clerk of Works for Salisbury Cathedral until quite recently, a fact which may point to there still being collaterals, if not lineal descendants, of the dramatist in his own birthplace.

★

Massinger died in March 1639/40, and was buried, according to the extant register of the church of St. Saviour (now Southwark Cathedral) on the 18th of that month. The entry reads:

Philip Masenger Strang, in ye church. G—£2. o. o.

and means that he was a stranger to the parish, that he was interred in the church itself, and that the fee for the burial was £2. The fee was considerable, doubtless because of the place of interment. Why, if he lived on the Bank-side, he was considered a stranger to the parish I do not know.

Sir Aston Cokaine has an elegy on the playwright, entitled 'An Epitaph on Mr. John Fletcher, and Mr. Philip Massinger, who lie buried both in one Grave in St. Mary Overie's Church in Southwark'. In this poem Cokaine says:

> In the same Grave *Fletcher* was buried here
> Lies the Stage-Poet Philip Massinger:
> Playes they did write together, were great friends,
> And now one Grave includes them at their ends:
> So whom on earth nothing did part beneath
> Here (in their Fames) they lie, in spight of death.[1]

It should be remarked that 'St Mary Overy's' was the popular name given to St. Saviour's church.

Now, Cokaine was a personal friend of Massinger and was probably present at the funeral, therefore there is no reason for us to doubt his statements on the matter of the burial. In saying that Massinger was buried *in* the church, he is, as the Register entry shows, quite correct. He is also correct in the case of Fletcher, since the entry in the Register says that he, too, was buried 'in the church'. His exaggeration of the friendship between Massinger and Fletcher is perhaps a piece of justifiable poetic licence.

Aubrey and Wood, however, tell a slightly different story of the burial. Aubrey's account is given in an entry under 31st January, 1673:

> This day I searched the register of St. Saviour's, Southwark, by the playhouse then there, vulgo St. Mary's Overy's; and find Philip Massinger buryed March 18th, 1639. I am enformed at the place where he

---

[1] *Small Poems*, Epigrams, I, p. 100.

dyed, which was by the Bankes side neer the then playhouse, that he was buryed about the middle of the Bullhead-churchyard—i.e. that churchyard (for there are four) which is next the Bullhead taverne, from whence it has its denomination. He dyed about the 66th yeare of his age: went to bed well, and dyed suddenly—but not of the plague.[1]

Aubrey should be given priority to his mere repeater, Wood. The latter's account reads:

As for our author Philip Massinger, he made his last exit very suddenly, in his house on the Bank-side in Southwark, near to the then playhouse, for he went to bed well and was dead before morning. Whereupon his body, being accompanied by comedians, was buried about the middle of that churchyard belonging to St. Saviour's church there, commonly called the Bull-head churchyard, that is, in that which joynes to the Bull-head tavern (for there are in all four yards belonging to that church) on the 18 day of March in sixteen hundred and thirty nine.[2]

The statements of Aubrey and Wood are probably reliable as to the manner of Massinger's death, but in view of the Register, they cannot be correct as to the site of the grave.

In my opinion, there can be no doubt that Cokaine's account is to be preferred to that of Aubrey and Wood. I am inclined also to think that he is correct when he says that they were buried in a common grave. That they were both buried actually within the church makes this even more likely. If, for example, Fletcher had been buried in the churchyard it might not be so easy to believe in the common grave, since graves in those days were not purchased in perpetuity but were dug over again as the necessity arose, and after a lapse of fifteen years it might have proved rather difficult to locate Fletcher's grave again. Although Massinger was not such an intimate of Fletcher as Beaumont was, on the occasion of Fletcher's funeral he might very well have given instructions for the disposal of his own body, and it is possible that the large amount charged for his burial was in part due to this request.[3]

★

The question of Massinger's religion is still another biographical detail that will probably never be settled. Gifford was the first to suggest that Massinger was converted to Roman Catholicism while still at Oxford and was in consequence estranged from William, Earl

---

[1] *Brief Lives*, ii, p. 54.   [2] *Athen. Oxon.* (Bliss), ii, p. 654.
[3] We find the 'common grave' idea in *The Duke of Milan*, I. iii:

'I . . . desire,
When you are sated with all earthly glories . . .
. . . That one grave may receive us.'

of Pembroke.[1] He supported his case from the plays, many of which deal in a sympathetic way with Roman Catholic beliefs and practices. I may say at this point that my own close study of the plays inclines me to support Gifford's suggestion, at least in respect of Massinger's Roman Catholic sympathies. At what date Massinger was converted, if he ever was, and with what results to his prospects, I hesitate to say. And I have reserved my discussion of the internal evidence for the possible conversion till a later chapter.[2]

The external evidence is however negligible. Some of his friends were undoubtedly Roman Catholics. But that does not mean much. Shirley was a convert (probably in 1622). Cokaine, if he was perhaps not actually a Roman Catholic himself, at least married a Roman Catholic. And Ben Jonson was a Roman Catholic for a time. The dedication of *A New Way to Pay Old Debts* to the Roman Catholic Earl of Carnarvon signifies, if possible, even less. Carnarvon, besides being a nobleman and hence fair game for dedicators whatever his religion, was ward and later son-in-law of Pembroke, Massinger's patron, who was himself a stout anti-Laudian Protestant and, in the Civil Wars, a Parliamentarian. The instance of the Protestant Pembroke's having the Roman-Catholic Earl of Carnarvon as son-in-law shows how, then as now, friendships were not made or divided by religion, at any rate outside of Puritan and bourgeois circles. It would have been difficult for a man in Massinger's position in and around the theatres, which were all but court-purlieus, not to have had Roman-Catholic friends. The other side of the picture is that the majority of Massinger's friends and patrons were in fact Protestants, including in their number two Anglican clergymen, Goffe and James Smith.

Gifford suggests that Massinger left Oxford without taking a degree because he had 'during his residence at the University, exchanged the religion of his father, for one, at this time, the object of persecution, hatred, and terror'.[3] While agreeing that young men of university age are perhaps more liable to sudden religious conversion than their elders and betters, I can see no reason for making the *locus* of this hypothetical conversion Oxford. The agents of the Counter-Reformation were at that time no more active in Oxford than they were in Cheapside or Aldgate. Anyway, I am sure that had a conversion to Roman Catholicism caused Massinger to leave the university Aubrey and Wood would have had some wind of it.

It was Phelan's idea that the sum spent on Massinger's funeral was

---

[1] *The Duke of Milan*, I, i, pp. xliii–xliv.
[2] See below, Chap. V, pp. 184–191.   [3] i, p. xliii.

so large because it was conducted with Roman Catholic rites.[1] It would be very unlikely that the clergy of St. Saviour's, to say nothing of higher legal and ecclesiastical authorities, would allow such a ceremony. This suggestion may serve as a sample of Phelan's speculative scholarship but it hardly merits further consideration. The £2 recorded in the St. Saviour's Register was not for the funeral but for the burial, and it was high because it was in the church itself (a privileged position) and may have involved some extensive masonry-work or removal and replacement of pews.

★

Massinger's personal attitude to his profession is of some interest in the story of his life. In a passage I have already quoted, addressed to William Herbert, third Earl of Pembroke, he exclaims that sooner than surrender his personal and artistic integrity to the necessity for flattering a patron he would rather

> Live poorely on those toyes I would not father
> Not known beyond a Player or a Man . . .[2]

The use of the word 'toyes' here is no more than a poet's conventional depreciation of his work, equivalent to the word 'trifles' which Massinger similarly uses in describing *The Unnatural Combat*[3] and other of his plays. More interesting is his description of himself as 'a Player and a Man'. It is not safe, however, to assume from this that Massinger was himself an actor. In the dedication to *The Unnatural Combat* he speaks of 'men of my poor quality', and while the word 'quality' is rather specially reserved for the profession of acting,[4] it is clear from the dedication of *The Great Duke of Florence*, in which he speaks of 'the most able in my poor quality', that Massinger uses the word to embrace not only actors but also all those men who wrote for the stage. The self-descriptive phrase might therefore be translated as 'a Playwright and a Man', and it is from these two aspects, the professional and the personal, that I have chosen to consider Massinger throughout this book.

As a playwright, in spite of his complaints of the poverty of his profession and his pessimistic description of 'the dejected spirits of the contemned sons of the Muses',[5] Massinger obviously took himself very seriously and considered his vocation as of some importance.

[1] *Anglia*, II, p. 37.   [2] *Dublin MS*, lines 40–41.
[3] Dedication (Gifford, i, p. 125).
[4] Cf. *N.E.D.* The word is elsewhere used in this special sense by Massinger. Cf. *The Roman Actor*, I, iii: 'In thee as being the chief of thy profession, I do accuse the quality of treason'.   [5] *The Renegado*, Dedication (Gifford, ii, p. 123).

The dedication of *The Roman Actor* displays his serious intent, as well as a certain 'high disdain, from injured sense of merit':

> If the gravity and height of the subject distaste such as are only affected with jigs and ribaldry (as I presume it will), their condemnation of me and my poem, can no way offend me: my reason teaching me, such malicious and ignorant detractors deserve rather contempt than satisfaction.[1]

And the defence of the stage which we find in the same play, although perhaps a little trite, is more than the argument of a man who is merely concerned for his means of livelihood. Nevertheless, his estimate of his own attainments is, in general, modest, although perhaps self-assured. 'Some worke I might frame,' he wrote to the third Earl of Pembroke, 'that should nor wrong my duty nor your Name',[2] and in 1636 he wrote, 'It is above my strength and faculties . . . to rebuild the ruins of demolished poesie'.[3] It is indeed difficult to reconcile what we know of Massinger's modest nature with the accusations of 'self-love' and 'arrogance' which we find surrounding him in 1630. Perhaps it was that, with Fletcher dead and Shirley hardly yet in the full flood of his production, for a brief period he allowed himself to feel, quite justifiably, cock of the theatrical walk. He seems somewhat chastened on his return to the stage in late 1633, and there is perhaps some significance in the fact that after this date, although still only in his early fifties, we find him referring to himself as 'a strange old fellow'[4] and saying that 'he grows old'.[5]

To discover more about Massinger the Man it is to the plays that we have to turn, for it is there that his real biography is written. There, he has revealed his mind, his scale of values, his interest, and his attitude to life and the world, more completely perhaps than do any of his fellow-dramatists in their works.

★

Apart from references in the commendatory verses, there is one critical allusion to Massinger which has come down to us from his lifetime. This has been quoted in accounts of Massinger's life since the time of Langbaine, and the source of the quotation has always been given as some verses entitled 'On the Time-Poets' which appeared in 1656 in *Choyce Drollery*.[6] The whole poem of which

---

[1] Gifford, ii, p. 329.　　　　　　　　[2] *Dublin MS*, lines 65–66.
[3] *The Great Duke of Florence*, Dedication.　　　[4] *The Bashful Lover*, Epilogue.
[5] *The Guardian*, Epilogue. As we have seen, Cokaine speaks of 'Old Philip Massinger' (above, p. 26).
[6] Repr., ed. J. W. Ebsworth, Boston, Lincs., 1876.

these verses form merely a part has now been discovered by Mr. G. C. Moore Smith. They are from an *Elegy on Randolph's Finger* written by William Hemminge, Randolph's school-fellow and friend, and the son of the Hemminge of the First Folio.[1] Randolph's little finger was cut off in a duel somewhere about the years 1630–1632 and Hemminge's humorous elegy can therefore be dated about the same period, that is, to well within Massinger's lifetime. The lines referring to Massinger are:

> Ingenious Shakespeare, Messenger that knowes
> the strength to wright or plott in verse or prose:
> Whose easye pegasus Can Ambell ore
> some threscore Myles of fancye In an hower.[2]

In a commendatory poem which appears before Shakerley Marmion's long narrative of *Cupid and Psyche*, published in 1637, Francis Tuckyr wrote:

> how 'nlike art thou to those,
> That tire out Rime, and Verse, till they trot Prose:
> And ride the Muses Pegasus, poor jade,
> Till he be foundred; and make that their trade:
> And to fill up the sufferings of the beast,
> Foot it themselves three hundred miles at least.
> These have no mercy on the paper rheames,
> But produce *plaies*, as Schole-boys do write theames.

It is tempting to find a connection between these lines and those applied to Massinger in Hemminge's *Elegy*. Certainly the criticism explicit in Tuckyr's lines could with perfect justice be applied to him. If my conjecture is correct then we have a second critical comment, this time an adverse one, coming from within Massinger's lifetime.

Apart from Langbaine's *Account* there is no other seventeenth-century critical comment on Massinger. His name appears among the jury of poets in *The Great Assises holden in Parnassus by Apollo and his Assessors*, an anonymous poem published in 1645,[3] but he is given nothing to say. *Wit and Fancy in a Maze*, an anonymous 'mock romance' published in 1656, contains a description of an imaginary battle between two poetic factions. In the fray Massinger is ranged with the opponents of Jonson—'Shakespear and Fletcher surrounded with their Life-Guards, viz. Goffe, Massinger, Decker, Webster,

---

[1] *William Hemminge's Elegy on Randolph's Finger*, ed. G. C. Moore Smith, Oxford, 1923.
[2] The second line has formerly been given, following *Choyce Drollery*, as 'The strength of Plot to write in verse and prose'. Passage now given in spelling of MS (lines 55–58).
[3] Repr., *Luttrell Reprints*, No. 6, Introd., Hugh Macdonald, Oxford, 1948.

Sucklin, Cartwright, Carew, &c.'. However, the passage, which may wrongly give the reader the idea that Swift owed something to the romance for *The Battle of the Books,* is quite incidental and has no foundation whatever in actual fact, and no serious critical intention beyond the recognised division of the playwrights into the classical school of Jonson and the romantic school of Shakespeare.

The fluctuations in Massinger's reputation since the seventeenth century, covering among other phases a brief revival in the eighteenth century which produced a number of adaptations of the plays and the editions of Coxeter and Monck Mason and a somewhat uncritical enthusiasm provoked in the early nineteenth century by Gifford's edition, are beyond the scope of my book. It can be stated, however, that there has been virtually no important or significant criticism of Massinger during the past thirty years. I do not regard as important or significant the anonymous article which appeared in *The Times Literary Supplement* in 1940 on the occasion of the tercentenary of Massinger's death.[1] It displayed such a complete ignorance and lack of understanding as to call forth a well-deserved rebuke from Professor Clifford Leech.[2] It is my hope to have done something by this study towards asserting Massinger's right to a serious reconsideration, if not as a dramatist of major importance, then at least as one of real interest.

[1] *Philip Massinger, 1583–1640, TLS,* 16 March, 1940.
[2] *TLS,* 23 March, 1940, p. 147.

Chapter Two

PLOTTING

The critics of Massinger's plays from the time of Hemminge have generally praised his skill in plotting. In this, the ordering and presentation of his material in a carefully articulated whole, he has been pronounced pre-eminent. Koeppel praises him in these terms: 'The most striking feature of Massinger's individual art, undoubtedly, is to be found in his great constructive power. The structure of his best plays is admirable in the severity of its lines and in the wise economy shown in the use of his materials . . . Massinger's best plays convey the impression of being well-built and ample halls, in which we move with a feeling of perfect security.'[1] Professor Cruickshank, as the principal of the three features of the plays which he selects for special praise, commends Massinger's 'stagecraft', and his context makes it clear that he means by this word what I would describe more specifically as plotting. 'His command of stagecraft has been universally conceded,' he says, and goes on to describe certain of the plays using such phrases as 'admirably proportioned and dignified', and 'bien charpenté'.[2] Maurice Chelli, a more voluble critic than Cruickshank, says that,

> Massinger est donc un homme à l'esprit duquel le mot *drame* représentait un tout déterminé et cohérent en ses parties, un organisme ou l'équilibre était nécessaire,[3]

and concludes that,

> Une pièce de Massinger, même mauvaise, est méthodique; jusque dans l'extrême romanesque, il nous présente des faits qui se suivent, il prépare un dénouement, il assure un équilibre, il fait œuvre de bon artisan. . . . Massinger était avant tout un esprit d'ordre.[4]

But it must be realised that such praise is purely relative. Admittedly Massinger, compared with, for example, Fletcher, contrives plots which appear structurally sound and solid; and indeed, few of his contemporaries—Shakespeare (if indeed he can be regarded as a contemporary), Ben Jonson, Middleton, and Beaumont being the chief exceptions, with Fletcher, Ford, and Shirley as others on a lower level of skill—can enter into comparison with him on this score at all. In practically all Massinger's contemporaries, other

---

[1] *CHEL*, vi, p. 153.   [2] *Philip Massinger*, p. 26.
[3] *Drame*, p. 183.   [4] Ibid., p. 341.

than those named, plotting is careless and loose, or worse. On the other hand, his plotting appears mechanical and artificial beside the work of dramatists today, operating within the more flexible and naturalistic conventions deriving from Ibsen. Taken, however, in its proper context of the Jacobean theatre, Massinger's plotting is remarkable for its adroit handling of its raw material, improbable, melodramatic, not to say incredible, as much of that was, and its dexterous adaptation of this to the limitations of the prevailing theatrical conventions. In short, for their time and kind, Massinger's plots are very carefully considered and precisely jointed and deserve to the full the praise they have received.

The close dovetailing of his plots and the cold calculation expended on the contraction, expansion, and emphasising of the events is, to be sure, only one result of the care and thought Massinger bestowed on every feature of his dramaturgy. He has left on record that he was conscious of pondering seriously the problems of his craft as a playwright. Thus, in the first (or Blackfriars) prologue to *The Emperor of the East* he says:

> though he cannot glory
> In his invention, (this work being a story
> Of reverend antiquity) he doth hope,
> In the proportion of it, and the scope,
> You may observe some pieces drawn like one
> Of a steadfast hand;[1]

And in the commendatory verse he wrote for Shirley's *The Grateful Servant* (1630) he praises virtues in that play which presumably he would have liked his own work to display. In *The Grateful Servant* he saw

> all so well
> Expressed and ordered, as wise men must say
> It is a grateful poem, a good play.[2]

That is to say, the poetic excellence lay in the expression and the dramatic excellence in the plotting.

Fortunately for the study of his practice there exists a manuscript of one play from which more can be deduced than the printed copies of the others disclose. This is the manuscript of *Believe As You List*,[3] one of the few examples of a holograph play from the seventeenth century. It is regrettable that what the manuscript supplies is not

---

[1] Gifford, iii, p. 244. [2] Gifford, iv, p. 594.
[3] B.M. MS., Egerton 2828, Tudor Facsimile Texts, London, 1907. The MS. is fully discussed by Professor C. J. Sisson in his edition (Malone Soc. Repr., 1927), Oxford, 1928 (see also Sisson, *RES*, 4, Oct. 1925).

the first version of the play. But it is the next best thing, a revision by the author himself before production. In order to meet the objections of Sir Henry Herbert who had refused to license the play as it stood because of its topicality,[1] Massinger transcribed it, altering as he did so the scene from Europe to Africa and Asia (apart from a scene in Sicily), the date from the recent past to classical times, and the characters' names from Portuguese and Spanish to Roman, Greek, and Carthaginian. This manuscript was evidently used as a prompt copy, after it had been carefully edited by the theatre book-keeper or another in the company's employment who altered Massinger's somewhat literary stage-directions in conformity with the actual theatrical arrangements and added notes concerned with the casting and the giving of guidance in the stage-calling of the actors and the properties.

From this manuscript it is clear that Massinger conceived and constructed his play in acts and scenes. That this was a literary rather than a theatrical practice is shown by the fact that the reviser erased all Massinger's act- and scene-headings, merely marking the entrances of the characters and keeping the word *Act* only in the sense of an interval or pause between the separate parts of the play.

This conception and construction of his plays in acts with scene subdivisions may have been a habit acquired during his apprenticeship as a collaborator,[2] a division of labour according to acts being a very likely procedure in collaboration.[3] In fact, an analysis of his plays shows that he relates the several parts of his plots very strictly to a five-act division. His normal practice is to select the five most effective moments in his story and make each supply the highlight of an act. The first act covers the exposition and leads to the initial situation, dilemma, or dramatic paradox from which the rest of the play evolves. The second act is of a bridging kind between the greater tension of the first and third acts. This second act is indeed invariably the quietest and least accented of the five. Nevertheless, it has its own minor climax and it complicates matters by the addition of new threads. In the third act comes as a rule the second most important moment in the play, the action being thereby given

---

[1] *Herbert*, p. 19.

[2] But of course the Horatian injunction as to five acts, neither more nor less (*De Arte Poetica*, 189), and the Senecan precedent, were unquestioned. See J. Dover Wilson, *RES*, 12 Oct. 1927, p. 390): 'The academic tradition [i.e. of writing in acts] seems to have been followed occasionally if not always from the very beginning, in at least one popular London playhouse, viz. the Rose theatre, owned by . . . Henslowe.'

[3] Cf. E. N. S. Thompson, *Elizabethan Dramatic Collaboration* (*Eng. Stud.*, XL, 1909). But see also in this connection Miss O. L. Hatcher, *Fletcher's Habits of Dramatic Collaboration*, (*Anglia*, XXXIII, p. 219), and L. Wann, *The Collaboration of Beaumont, Fletcher and Massinger*, (*Shakespeare Studies*, University of Wisconsin, 1916, Chap. VII).

its final direction; though the actual end is not immediately foreseeable. Act IV is generally like Act II in being mainly a linking one; but always in the course of it there is a considerable amount of business, sometimes in the nature of apparently greater entanglement, but sometimes in a partial resolution. Act V works up to the comprehensive dénouement and grand finale. Thus diagrammatically the line of a Massinger play is:

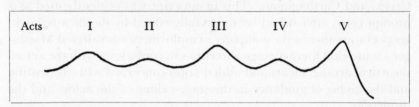

While something like this is the normal disposition, there are plays in which the major climax (and with it the dénouement and conclusion of the main plot interest) falls in the fourth act. These plays can be represented diagrammatically thus:

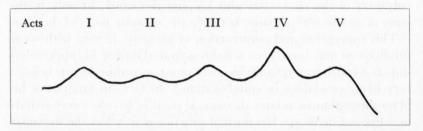

The fifth act of such plays appears rather anticlimactic, but, as I shall show, Massinger always tries to keep back enough to justify the extension into a fifth act with a secondary main climax.

★

A consideration of Massinger's best known play, *A New Way to Pay Old Debts*, will illustrate what I have just said.

In the first act most of the principals are prominently introduced:

(i) Wellborn, the hero, reduced to poverty by his own generosity and prodigality and by the machinations of

(ii) his uncle by marriage, the villainous extortioner Sir Giles Overreach (these two are the focal and moral opposites about which the play rotates);

(iii) Lady Allworth;

(iv) her stepson, young Allworth; and

(v) Justice Greedy, who, though unimportant as an agent, is prominent as a provider of comic relief in a very unsmiling comedy.

The only exception is Marrall, Overreach's unscrupulous clerk; but even he makes at least his appearance and speaks a couple of lines. The characters who do not appear in Act I are dramatically of only secondary importance.

The exposition is pretty well confined to the exhibition of the hero's reduced fortunes. The play is to deal with his restoration and the ruin of his despoiler. The action, therefore, is a counterparted one. From the hero's natural resentment the plot against Overreach begins to take shape. Before the end of Act I, though the spectator is still in ignorance of how it is to proceed, he has seen the hero accepted by Lady Allworth as a welcome guest in spite of his rags and is aware that this is only the first step in a promising scheme of just revenge. But the act also introduces the love of young Allworth for Margaret Overreach, without doing more than stating it through Allworth's confession of it to Wellborn.

Act II brings the anti-Overreach conspiracy well on its way. For Marrall has been deceived by the evidence of his own eyes into believing that Lady Allworth is in love with and intends to marry Wellborn; and this report he carries to the incredulous Overreach. Overreach's brutal beating of Marrall for lying to him, and still more the latter's muttered threats, are a preparation for an unexpected turn later. As the whole action of the play is 'The Tricker Tricked',[1] Massinger has to show Overreach the Machiavel himself in operation. This he does at the beginning of the act with the disclosure of Overreach's ambitions to marry his daughter into the peerage. These two disclosures—young Allworth's love for Margaret Overreach in Act I, and Sir Giles's very different purpose for his daughter in Act II—are leads up to the secondary plot of young Allworth and Margaret which properly begins in Act III.

In Act III Wellborn's scheme so far advances that Overreach, having had similar ocular evidence to Marrall's that Wellborn is in Lady Allworth's very good graces, is eager to be reconciled to his victimised nephew and to lend him money—with, of course, a sinister intention. At the same time the secondary plot of young Allworth and Margaret begins to move with the confession to Lord Lovell and his promise of help; Overreach, in his ambition to marry his daughter to a lord, seizes the chance offered by Lord Lovell's visit to his house, and his very eagerness not only horrifies his

---

[1] For a discussion of the relationship of *A New Way* to *A Trick to Catch the Old One* (1607) by Middleton, see the separate editions of the play listed in the Bibliography.

daughter (in what is perhaps the most powerful scene of the play) but plays into the hands of those determined to frustrate it. Nor does Massinger forget to keep before us Marrall's bitter resentment and longing for an opportunity for revenge and to let us anticipate the match to be made up between Lord Lovell and Lady Allworth.

From this still-developing, multiple situation at the end of Act III, the plot moves towards the resolution, but not an immediate one. In Act IV the lines only converge towards Overreach's complete frustration and defeat. He, indeed, appears to himself to be winning on every front, with his daughter all but married to Lord Lovell and with his nephew enabled to marry Lady Allworth and so provide a richer prey for a second and more drastic fleecing. The audience sees the situation quite otherwise, with Wellborn informed by the vindictive Marrall of a table-turning trickery that will foil Overreach's and with the marriage of his daughter and young Allworth almost completed by his own unwitting furtherance of it. The background plot—admittedly a very minor one—of Lady Allworth and Lord Lovell also progresses uninterruptedly.

Act V is a comprehensive finishing-off. First comes the betrothal of Lady Allworth and Lord Lovell; then the triumph of Wellborn and the discomfiture of Overreach in that direction when the deed upon which he had built his villainy against his nephew proves, by Marrall's agency, to be a letterless and sealless parchment; and finally—the secondary plot *quoad* the hero being the main plot *quoad* the villain—the catastrophic disappointment of Overreach when he hears of his daughter's marriage to Allworth and his apoplectic seizure and collapse.

The six strands of the plot may, therefore, be represented thus :[1]

Acts	I	II	III	IV	V
a	-------------	-------------	-------------	-------------	-------/
b	/··········	·············	-------------	-------------	-------
c		/············	············	-------------	-------
d			/···············	·············	-------/
e			-------------	-------------	-------/
f			/··········	·-----------	--/

a. The rehabilitation of Wellborn and his retaliation on Overreach.
b. Allworth's love for Margaret Overreach and the outwitting of her father.
c. The frustration of Overreach's design to marry Margaret to Lord Lovell.
d. The vengeance of Marrall.
e. The failure of Overreach's machination against Wellborn.
f. The mutual attraction of Lord Lovell and Lady Allworth.

---

[1] In the diagram, dots indicate when a subject has merely been introduced, dashes when it is fully under way.

The six-strand plot gives in retrospect an impression of inevitability. But so to order it that it gives that very impression, and to keep it well-timed and well-proportioned, never disclosing any point too soon, never flagging nor losing the audience's interest, but advancing in a growing complexity and purposefulness to the grand climax in which Sir Giles and the evil he represents are brought to naught—that is a structural feat of which Massinger might well have been proud. Massinger has done more than tell a simple story well: he has told a far-from-simple story surpassingly well.

★

Naturally the first act of a play presents special difficulties and requires special attention. By it the audience has to be put into possession of all the immediately relevant information about the chief characters and their interrelations. In it the motivating situation, the *raison d'être* of the whole play, has to be introduced; and by it the appropriate atmosphere has to be suggested and the right tempo struck. As Professor Allardyce Nicoll says:

> It is a commonplace of dramatic criticism that a successful exposition is the most difficult thing of all to achieve, and the reason of the difficulty lies precisely in the fact that in the exposition the audience has to be provided artistically with such information regarding the characters as is necessary for an understanding of the play. An audience gets bored when information of this kind is provided for it by direct enunciation; unconsciously the spectators feel that here a departure is being made from the sphere of drama, which is action, to the sphere of ordinary narrative.[1]

If Massinger's expositions[2] are never as subtle and masterly as Shakespeare's in *Hamlet* or *Macbeth*, they are never makeshift *protases* like Prospero's address to Miranda in Act I, scene ii, of *The Tempest*.[3] His skill indeed in solving his expository difficulties is uniformly very considerable, and how much is done for the spectator or reader can be to some extent judged by the negative examples of *The Parliament of Love* and *Believe As You List*, in both of which the greater part of the first act is missing. As, in his collaboration with Fletcher and others, Massinger seems frequently to have been assigned the first

---

[1] *The Theory of Drama*, London, 1931, p. 76.

[2] I take Miss U. M. Ellis-Fermor's interpretation of the meaning of this word: '. . . that part of a play which serves to introduce us to the chief characters, to let us grasp the main fact upon which their relations and the subsequent action depend and see the action set going' (*The Jacobean Drama*, 1936, p. 31).

[3] Though the late Sir Arthur Quiller-Couch thought otherwise about this scene (*Tempest*, New Camb. Sh.).

acts as part of his share,[1] it is reasonable to assume that his special competence in dramatic exposition was recognised by his contemporaries.

It is Massinger's frequent practice to begin a play (and indeed most of his later scenes) in the middle of a conversation.[2] The participants in it do not give the impression of just initiating their conversation as they walk on. They are already well launched into it and the audience is plunged right into the middle of it. But the dialogue is so managed that the audience quickly and easily catches up with it. A good example of this naturalistic continuum is the opening of *The City Madam*. The entrants are Sir John Frugal's two apprentices, Goldwire Junior and Tradewell Junior:

> *Gold.* The ship is safe in the Pool then?
> *Trade.* And makes good.
>   In her rich fraught, the name she bears, *The Speedwell*:
>   My master will find it; for, on my certain knowledge,
>   For every hundred that he ventured in her,
>   She hath returned him five.
> *Gold.* And it comes timely;
>   For, besides a payment on the nail for a manor
>   Late purchased by my master, his young daughters
>   Are ripe for marriage.
> *Trade.* Who? Nan and Mall?
> *Gold.* Mistress Anne and Mary, and with some addition,
>   Or 'tis more punishable in our house
>   Than *scandalum magnatum*.
> *Trade.* 'Tis great pity
>   Such a gentleman as my master (for that title
>   His being a citizen cannot take from him)
>   Hath no male heir to inherit his estate,
>   And keep his name alive.
> *Gold.* The want of one
>   Swells my young mistresses, and their madam-mother,
>   With hopes above their birth and scale: their dreams are
>   Of being made countesses; and they take state,
>   As they were such already.

Within these twenty lines we have learned, without the information appearing to be too obviously handed out: that Goldwire and Tradewell are apprentices to a rich and worthy London merchant of good family, Sir John Frugal; and that he is not altogether happy in his marriage, having no son to succeed him and having a haughty

---

[1] But see L. Wann, loc. cit. (above, p. 57, note 3).
[2] See below, Chap. III, pp. 79-80.

wife and two proud and ambitious daughters, Anne and Mary. The next twenty lines just as painlessly make us aware of the ruinous extravagance of Lady Frugal and her daughters, of their aping of court manners, of Sir John's tolerance of all this, and of his brother, Luke, who has been redeemed by Sir John from a debtor's prison and who, although a scholar and a traveller, is treated with contempt by his sister-in-law and nieces as 'an under-prentice or a footman' who sits below the salt. That is, in some forty lines Massinger has provided us with the 'apperceptive mass', to take a term from educational psychology—the minimal information which we must possess before the plot can get going, a plot which is to be a lesson to

> instruct
> Our city dames, whom wealth makes proud, to move
> In their own spheres; and willingly to confess,
> In their habits, manners, and their highest port,
> A distance 'twixt the city and the court.[1]

It only remains for us to meet the principal characters in person (we already know a good deal about them from the apprentices' conversation), and this is done coincidentally with the first moves of the plot. Well before the end of the act the process is complete and the audience *au fait* with the situation and the interrelationships.

An examination along the same lines of the opening of any of the other plays, early or late, will show Massinger pursuing the same technique. The full exposition of a play is not, of course, completed in the first scene. Nevertheless, a first scene is from the expository angle always the most important, and, in his, Massinger comes as near as any playwright can to confining all the expository essentials. What may be called the bearing-lines or *status quo ante actionem* are sketched in swiftly with a few skilful strokes; the interrelationships of character and character, at least in respect of the main plot-interest, are outlined; the immediate domestic background, and, if it is relevant, the larger political one, are indicated, together with the *locus* and the date of the action; and the motif-to-be is insinuated.

It may be useful to illustrate this matter further but more briefly from one or two other plays. Thus *The Renegado* opens, apparently casually, with a brief comic interchange, reminiscent of the more modern playwright's trick of filling in the first few minutes with inconsequential material to let the audience settle down and attune their ears to the actors' voices. But Massinger is not merely putting off time for such a purpose. He sees to it that the *leit-motiv* of the whole play, religion and renegadism, is brought to the front of our

[1] iv. iii.

minds. In this semi-comic passage and in the rest of the not-long first scene we realise that the scene is Tunis and that Vitelli and his man, Gazet, have come there from Venice, ostensibly as merchants, under the direction of Father Francisco, to rescue Vitelli's sister, Paulina, who has been abducted by the piratical Grimaldi, the Renegado of the play's title.

The Duke of Milan opens on a note of broader buffoonery, which, however, is explained before it makes a deeper impression than Massinger needs, by the commentating Tiberio and Stephano as part of a general merry-making. The Court of Milan is celebrating the Duchess Marcelia's birthday in the midst of a political situation fraught with disaster for the Duke of Milan if the King of France, on whose side he has ranged himself, is defeated by the Emperor Charles.

The Unnatural Combat exemplifies a favourite gambit with Massinger—the dropping of the essential initial information by a group of characters waiting either to present or to hear presented a petition to some nobleman or a case to a court of justice, or for some similar purpose. The device is used again, for example, in *The Fatal Dowry*,[1] *The Maid of Honour*, and *The Emperor of the East*.

Generally the expository minima are entrusted to minor characters, possibly because what the great ones are and do is more easily conveyed in the gossip of the not-so-great. But sometimes, as in *The Renegado* and *A New Way to Pay Old Debts*, a principal character is also one of the expositors. In *The Picture* Massinger has a successful exposition by the difficult means of a conversation between two of the principals. By choosing them as the expository agents he denied himself the useful chance of preparing the audience for them by describing them through the mouths of secondary persons. Mathias and Sophia in that play, then, have not only to disclose the initial situation but to reveal at least some traits of their own characters.

So much, then, for the minimal exposition which is largely, if not entirely, covered by the first scene. As the first act proceeds beyond that point and, one after another, the principal characters are introduced (Massinger, as we have seen, is fond of a court, a trial, a pleading scene, or some similar focal point), for some adequate reason the characters pass from being to doing, in the dramatic, not necessarily physical, sense; and the forces of attraction and repulsion, of egoism and reaction thereto, of desire or ambition or revenge, begin to

---

[1] The fact discussed later (p. 66) that this expository passage has got attached to the wrong play is for the moment irrelevant.

gather towards the climax of the first act. Good illustrations of this
are, among others, *A New Way to Pay Old Debts*, *The City Madam*,
The Guardian, *The Great Duke of Florence*, *The Duke of Milan*, and
The Bondman.

But in some plays it is here or hereabouts that Massinger begins
to show defects in his plotting. These defects are almost always due
to his endeavouring to plot in accordance with his moral or thematic
purpose, rather than in accordance with his story. In these defec-
tively plotted plays the thematic purpose and the action are not
properly involuted.

Such a play is *The Roman Actor*, though Massinger pronounced it
in his dedicatory epistle as 'the most perfect birth of my Minerva', an
opinion which his admiring friends seem largely to have shared.
By the end of Act I two *leit-motiven* have been introduced: the nature
of tyranny, manifested in Domitian's desire to be regarded as divine
and above law and in his appropriation of Domitia from her husband
Aelius Lamia; and the value of the actor's profession maintained by
Paris. But there is little or no indication of the direction the action
is likely to take or of the involution of the one *leit-motiv* with the
other. The only link between these and what Massinger intends
to be one of the themes of the play, a tyrant's downfall through a
woman—not, be it noted, through the outraged Lamia's revenge—
occurs in Lamia's prayer at the end of Act I, scene ii:

> . To the gods
> I bend my knees (for tyranny hath banished
> Justice from men), and as they would deserve
> Their altars and our vows, humbly invoke them,
> That this my ravished wife may prove as fatal
> To proud Domitian, and her embraces
> Afford him in the end as little joy
> As wanton Helen brought to him of Troy.

As for the other and more prominent main theme, the actor Paris's
dignity and worth provoking the new Empress's fatal passion for him,
there is neither hint nor preparation for this in the first act. Even in
Act II, which consists of one long and theatrically quite effective
scene illustrating further Domitian's arbitrary will, there are few
seeds of further action sown and the main problem appears to have
been brought no nearer. It is only in Act III that something like
dramatic dovetailing is effected. But even so the play is more episodic
than Massinger's usual skill would lead us to expect. The sequence
is that of a series of striking situations, and the comparative inco-
herence is inevitably worsened by the insetting of three playlets

within the play, even though they have a certain dramatic or thematic relevance.[1] The fact is that Massinger had adopted two conflicting themes which could not easily be co-ordinated. Domitian, the tyrant of arbitrary lust whose uxoriousness to a woman corrupted both by himself and by the imperial dignity leads to his humiliation and ruin, is the initiating or active focus of the play. Paris is only the more passive focus; on the other hand, he is made the more prominent personage—a role obviously designed to give a leading actor a whole string of opportunities. As such, the play has much to offer in the way of histrionic and dramatic variety. But Massinger found it impossible also to make the variety contribute to a unity.

The Fatal Dowry may also be taken to illustrate Massinger's occasional defects in unified plotting, with the proviso that, as this is a play in which Nathan Field had a considerable share, the weaknesses, or some of them, may be due to him, or at least to the dual control. It is unique among the plays of the Massinger canon in being both weak in plotting and unusually strong in characterisation. The view that the strength of the characterisation is due to Field and the weakness of plot due to Massinger has much to recommend it, but the exact nature of the collaboration is of far too doubtful a quantity to apportion the praise or the blame in either respect to either of the writers. Since this is a collaborated play it cannot, it is true, be admitted as an example of Massinger's individual practice, but as an excellent and very obvious example of that failure in plotting I have been describing it is not out of place to mention it here.

The introduction, as I have indicated above, is gripping and powerful. But it introduces only the first part of the play, which may be said to break almost cleanly in two at the end of Act II. The first part is concerned with the reduced estate of Charalois who has nobly impoverished himself to pay his distinguished soldier-father's debts, the appeal to Rochfort whose munificence re-establishes Charalois's fortunes, and the bestowal in marriage on Charalois of Beaumelle, Rochfort's daughter. This is a self-contained and all-but-rounded-off action. It is a play in itself, even though it is more rhetorically than dramatically interesting. The bits that are in excess of the requirements look like accidental intrusions, rather than growing buds. The more dramatic sequel presents the story of a guilty Desdemona (Beaumelle) and Cassio (Novall Junior), a truly honest Iago

[1] I would agree with Professor Cruickshank when (*Philip Massinger*, p. 126) he praises 'the dexterity with which three smaller plays are introduced into the action', but cannot agree when he adds that they are introduced 'without in the least confusing the construction'.

(Romont), and an Othello whose jealousy is only slowly aroused (Charalois). This occupies Acts III and IV and concludes quite as finally as Act V of *Othello*. But Massinger goes on to his fifth act which, while it is admittedly better linked to the fourth than the third is to the second, has a purpose which is more moral than dramatic—to introduce results consequential to those in Act IV which underline the chosen moral that justice should be left to Heaven and that no individual should take the law into his own hands. It is worth pointing out that Nicholas Rowe recognised the break between Acts II and III and economised by beginning his adaptation of the play, *The Fair Penitent* (1703), with Act III.

On the other hand, C. L. Lockert, who is the most recent editor of the play,[1] takes it to be not nearly so disunited as I have suggested. He finds the seeds of the second or middle section in the first, in that Beaumelle, married to Charalois against her will, is unchaste in heart, if not in deed. This, however, is not made clear in Acts I and II. Beaumelle certainly has a serving-maid who talks with a loose freedom, and she has been wooed by Novall Junior before there is any word of her marriage to Charalois. But the passage in which Rochfort offers and Charalois accepts her could leave no impression on the spectator but of her virtue and of her full consent:

Charalois. Fair Beaumelle, can you love me?
Beaumelle. Yes, my lord.[2]

All that is of a sinister note comes in the coda to Act II which begins with the entry of Novall Junior and his friends. Lockert would exonerate Massinger and Field by throwing the flaw back to the story, probably of Spanish origin, from which the plot is taken. But surely if Massinger and Field did find such a flaw, they did not need to take it over into their play. Lockert goes on to justify his authors by the alternative excuse that they could ignore the requirements of unity by presenting their action as 'a cross-section of life'. It is an ingenious explanation. But I can only say that the idea of presenting any action as a 'cross-section of life' is most unlike Massinger or Field or, for that matter, any dramatist till the present day.[3] Massinger and Field seem to have had some realisation of the fissure and to have tried to disguise or remove it. But they did not have much success, and the reader, and probably the spectator, will not find that unifying interaction of part with part which characterises a really well-balanced dramatic machine.

---

[1] Lancaster, Pa., 1918.   [2] II. ii.
[3] Although Ben Jonson, in *Bartholomew Fair*, was perhaps moving towards that idea.

As I have already said, Massinger's usual design is one in which, while each act has its own particular climax, the climax of the total play is in the fifth act and is followed by a swift concluding resolution; but sometimes the climax of the fourth act is the climax of the whole play, the one in the fifth being secondary.

The Duke of Milan is of this latter type. Its fourth act rises to Sforza's murder of his wife, Marcelia, and closes on his swift realisation that she is after all innocent. The whole scene is a theatrical masterpiece, moving, and yet remarkably restrained.[1] Sforza's final cry of anguish could provide one of the most effective tragic endings in English drama and no modern dramatist would ever dream of going beyond it. But Massinger could not leave well alone, ruled as he was by the five-act convention and, what was even more operative, his moral purpose. Sforza must meet his tragic end—be punished for his last as for his earlier sins (not all of which, we discover, have yet been disclosed); and the moral that

> There's no trust
> In a foundation that is built on lust;[2]

must be pointed. So a rather anti-climactic fifth act is inartfully tacked on.[3] To make matters worse (in more senses than one), Massinger introduces what, since he has not made anything like adequate preparation for it, appears to be entirely new action. So we learn that the villainous Francisco, through whose machinations Sforza has killed his wife, was not acting, as we might reasonably have concluded from the earlier scenes, from a motiveless malignity but in revenge for Sforza's betrayal of a sister, Eugenia, who only now makes a very belated appearance. The last scene, adapted rather than imitated from Act V, scene ii, of *The Second Maiden's Tragedy* with its disguises, the painting of the dead Marcelia's face to give an appearance of life, and the device of the poisoned lips, makes a finale which, quite apart from any question of the mere plotting, is to the modern reader ludicrously melodramatic, and appears all the more bathetic after the subtlety of the earlier scenes (e.g. Act II, scene i) between Marcelia and Francisco.

The Roman Actor, already discussed in another relation, provides another grand climax in the fourth, not in the fifth, act and a resulting disintegration in the fifth. By the end of Act IV Paris, after

---

[1] It is not, however, possessed of much poetry (see below, Chap. VI, pp. 239 ff.).

[2] v. ii.

[3] Professor Cruickshank (*Philip Massinger*, p. 136) thought the play 'skilfully constructed', and Professor H. W. Wells, *Elizabethan and Jacobean Playwrights*, New York, 1939, p. 65, says, surprisingly enough, that 'like so many of its author's plays, it tells a simple story uncommonly well'.

whom the play is named and whose first-ranking prominence is un-
questionable, is dead and the Empress Domitia, whose infatuation
for him has led to his death, has been imprisoned by her husband.
But we discover to our amazement in Act V, scene i, that she has
been restored to the Emperor's favour, and we have to jump the
gap as best we may. I suppose that Massinger discovered that he
could not possibly spin out the inescapable fifth act without her,
and the peculiar dichotomy of the plot made it necessary for
Domitian to meet his just end.

The Picture also could very well finish, after some slight re-arrange-
ment, with its fourth act. For all the vital action has ended, and the
remainder of this ridiculous play has to consist of clearing up what
well might have been left to the audience's intelligence; in which
apparently, as I shall have occasion to remark again, Massinger did
not have very high confidence. The uxoriousness of Ladislaus has
been lessened, and all that remains is that the jealousy of Mathias
should be cured, something which, for dramatic effectiveness, would
have been better if more closely coupled to the other incident. As a
result Massinger fills most of his fifth act with mere facile superfluity,
and is forced to stretch his cloth to fit his coat.

The Unnatural Combat rises to a magnificent climax in the first
scene of Act IV. Malefort, a character deliberately invested up to
that point with mystery, first reveals in a soliloquy his incestuous
passion for his daughter, Theocrine, then has a tense interview with
her in which his tortured soul would declare his lust and yet is held
back, and lastly makes a confidant of Montreville. Instead of sweep-
ing straight on to the catastrophe, Massinger introduces in the next
scene an episode of serio-comic semi-buffoonery concerned with the
impecunious Captain Belgarde whom he was using as a means of
praising the military profession and rebuking the ingratitude and
neglect too often meted out to it. But Belgarde's reappearance at
this point involves an abrupt interruption of an intense tragic
ascent. This is a grave example of that fault of 'the mingled drama'
which Dr. Johnson so ably defended for all time. It is an example
of the fault which the wise Doctor himself described when he said
that:

> by this change of scenes the passions are interrupted in their progres-
> sion, and . . . the principal event, being not advanced by a due grada-
> tion of preparatory incidents, wants at last the power to move, which
> constitutes the perfection of dramatick poetry.[1]

[1] *Preface to Shakespeare* (1765) (*Johnson on Shakespeare*, ed. Sir W. Raleigh, London, 1916,
pp. 16–17).

Obviously in this case Massinger uses Belgarde and his affairs merely in order to fill out the play to the required length. He is really a dramatised character-sketch of 'The Discontented Soldier'. His fortunes do not constitute a story and so do not supply a sub-plot.

Massinger, of course, came to play-plotting in the years when the current taste was for the surprise drama of melodramatic tragedy, of comedy, and of tragi-comedy. Surprise and melodrama were not wanting in the drama before Beaumont and Fletcher began, but it might be said that in, for example, *The Spanish Tragedy* or *Antonio's Revenge* the end to which the play moves is inevitable, given the premisses and the characters, as in Shakespeare 'the end of the play is the end of expectation'.[1] Such surprise as there is concerns only the means and often proves surprising more to the characters than to the audience. The characters, even in their most melodramatic decisions, do not run counter to their own natures. Their actions might be highly exceptional, but they do not involve psychological incredibilities. However, in the drama of the Fletcher school to which Massinger belonged, surprise for the audience was more sought after, and the readiest way to achieve it was to make characters run counter to all that they had appeared to be; to make them be swayed by whim or momentary impulse from the bias of their being; to discover suddenly a remote motive; to be converted or perverted by inadequate steps; to be motivated paradoxically and to accept a situation in a way not in accord with their characters.

Credibility is, of course, not something that we are inclined to demand, except in moderation, from our plays, and flaws in credibility or an excess of incredibility show themselves more clearly in an examination of a playwright's legends and characterisation than in an examination of his plot-structure. No one, for example, could hold any brief for the credibility of the legends of *Othello* or *King Lear*. Yet there can come a point in a play in which the weight of accumulated incredibility can topple the most rigid structure. This point, owing to Massinger's enslavement to the drama of surprise, usually comes in the concluding scenes, and while it is not directly a matter of plot-structure it is a result which could have been averted or mitigated by more skilful plotting earlier in the play. Thus, the elaborate theatricality of the final act of *The City Madam* ruins one of the better and more credible of his plays. Sir John Frugal, Sir Maurice Lacy and Mr. Plenty have been received by Luke as American Indians. They promise him untold wealth by magic

---

[1] *Preface to Shakespeare* (1765) (*Johnson on Shakespeare*, ed. Sir W. Raleigh, London, 1916, p. 25).

means if he will deliver two virgins and another woman as sacrifices to the Devil, their master. Luke, who, it must be remembered, is for all his avarice 'a scholar well read and travelled', swallows this balderdash and agrees to hand over Sir John's wife and daughters. A birthday banquet is prepared for him by the 'Indians', supposedly by magic means; and in the course of it a masque of Orpheus and Eurydice is presented; and then he is confronted with what he honestly believes to be the spirits of his servants, his debtors, and others he has wronged. The idea is to move him to repentance for his crimes and his avarice in much the same way as an attempt was made to reform Philargus by the masque of 'The Cure of Avarice' in *The Roman Actor*; and like Philargus, Luke remains unmoved. To pile wonder on wonder it has been contrived that young Lacy and Plenty have taken the place in the frames of their own portraits (Gifford remarks[1] that 'there is some difficulty in understanding the mechanism of this scene'); and the supposed 'spirits' of Lady Frugal and her daughters are introduced, ostensibly to take leave of the portraits of the former suitors and the portrait of Sir John, which, although there is no direct mention of it in the play, was presumably hanging at the back of the room also. On their knees they proclaim their repentance for their earlier presumption. Luke is still unmoved, but says,

> If by your magic art,
> You can give life to these, or bring him hither
> To witness her repentance, I may have,
> Perchance, some feeling of it.[2]

The scene continues:

Sir John.   For your sport
> You shall see a masterpiece. Here's nothing but
> A superficies; colours and no substance.
> Sit still, and to your wonder and amazement,
> I'll give these organs. This the sacrifice
> To make the great work perfect.
>   (*Burns incense, and makes mystical gesticulations. Sir Maurice Lacy and*
>   *Plenty give signs of animation.*)
> *Luke.* Prodigious!
> *Sir John.* Nay, they have life, and motion.
> Descend!
>   (*Sir Maurice Lacy and Plenty descend and come forward.*)
> And for your absent brother—this washed off,
> Against your will you shall know him. (*Discovers himself.*)

Luke is defeated; the fact that his soul is immutably ingrained with

---

[1] iv, p. 115, note.   [2] v. iii.

his wickedness is demonstrated; and he speaks only two more lines before the end of the scene. The audience which, earlier in the play, accepted without question the disguising of the conspirators as Indians, will not be so ready to accept the new-found gullibility with which Luke confronts the pseudo-supernatural staginess of the finale. The element of surprise has undermined and brought tumbling down the carefully planned edifice of the plot.

Again, to mention another example, Camiola's sudden renunciation of the world at the end of *The Maid of Honour*, which admittedly underlines the moral purpose, is sprung on us like a Jack-in-the-box, and appears too much like a cutting of the Gordian knot of the plot's difficulties.

This impression is often given by the endings of many of the other plays. They tend to be too abrupt. While this is perhaps not a matter in which Massinger can be too much blamed, since dramatists from Shakespeare to Shaw have often had difficulty in concluding their plays satisfactorily, it is one which is of importance, since the ending can decide whether the audience leaves the theatre satisfied or dissatisfied. Everything is just huddled away in *The Bashful Lover*, and the audience is left to piece together the story and round off the plot by surmise. And at the end of *The Guardian*, a play which contains more action and still more improbability than the majority, there is too much to clear up, with the result that the dénouement is badly cramped. *The Renegado* finishes with incredible rapidity in a series of short scenes, and is remarkable in that it concludes with only two minor characters and their silent attendants on the stage. Whereas usually there is a full-stage final, this play ends upon a dying fall with Asambeg saying:

> I will hide
> This head among the deserts, or some cave
> Filled with my shame and me; where I alone
> May die without a partner in my moan.

As a 'dying fall' it is quite effective, but it might have been much better if Massinger had brought down his baton more firmly in a full-close.

There remain two plays, not so far mentioned, in which there are flaws due to rather unusual circumstances.

In *The Parliament of Love* Massinger does something which he does not so obviously attempt anywhere else. Normally he handles an action in which, though there may be several threads as in *A New Way to Pay Old Debts*, all of them are subordinated and contributory to a controlling and over-arching main purpose.[1] Only the occasional episodes of (rather stolid) comic relief stand apart; and they do not amount to the status of sub-plots. Moreover, there is normally such close integration in Massinger's plots that the various sub-plots are reciprocally helpful and interacting. But in *The Parliament of Love* there are three plots of equal importance and integrity: the plot of Clarindore and Bellisant, the plot of Novall and Perigot, and the plot of Cleremond and Leonora. The play is not satisfactory, and even Professor Cruickshank, in whose eyes Massinger can do little wrong, seems not to like it. The weakness of course is that the three practically equipollent plots are not closely enough related. The idea of a Court of Love in which all lovers' wrongs are to be adjudged and righted is by itself too loose a link to bind the three stories with three sets of characters into a play. Though the result is an agreeable entertainment, probably the only reason for Massinger's persisting with such recalcitrant material is that he got pleasure from trying the impossible task of making it into a unity. But possibly he had no very high opinion of the finished play, for he never printed it; it may be that it was not very successful when it was produced, or perhaps, having returned to the King's Men, he lost control over the manuscript.

A play we know to have been a failure, *The Emperor of the East*, which is full of talk and disputation but has little real action, leaves a very unsatisfactory impression. It seems in an indefinable way to lack unity of purpose. However, examination of the play shows that this is not due to any real flaw in plotting, but is undoubtedly caused by the fact that, as Professor A. K. McIlwraith has so convincingly argued from textual evidence,[2] the play was originally written as a tragedy and between its failure on the public stage and its presentation at Court was changed into a comedy by the re-writing of the fifth act. Although the play is important for the reflections it utters upon the office of a ruler,[3] it forms indeed a most lamentable comedy.

★

Such an examination of Massinger's play-structure as I have given may seem to give the lie to the common acceptance of his skill as a

---

[1] As Koeppel says (*CHEL*, vi, p. 153), 'The mixture of plots which many of his brother poets preferred . . . seems to have had no attraction for a dramatist whose intellect favoured clearness above all other poetical charms.' Note also that in his collaboration with Fletcher Massinger seems to have concentrated upon the main story and left the sub-plots to his fellow-dramatist. See L. Wann, loc. cit.

[2] *Did Massinger Revise 'The Emperor of the East'?* (*RES*, V, 1929).

[3] See below, Chap. V, pp. 169 ff.

plotter. But that his plotting seems weak when examined in the study is not, of course, to suggest that the weaknesses would always appear obvious in the theatre. Good acting and good direction will go far to mask even major imperfections in any dramatist; and in any case, it is a critical error to get, as it were, at closer grips with any work of art than the artist designed it for. A picture or a statue is painted or carved to be seen only at a certain distance; there are certain mathematical limitations imposed by optical conditions upon the correct viewing distance for a photograph in order that perspective may not be distorted. Likewise a play has the right to be judged in the theatre. The study may be the court of first instance, but the theatre is always the court of appeal. So it is with Massinger. Notwithstanding the account of his plays I have given, it may be said of him with equal justice what Dr. Johnson said of Shakespeare:

> His plan has commonly what *Aristotle* requires, a beginning, a middle, and an end; one event is concatenated with another, and the conclusion follows by easy consequences.[1]

His plays in general are firm and muscular; they move swiftly and develop along a carefully planned route with properly timed and regulated climaxes and dénouements.

Wherever he does most strikingly fail in plotting, it almost always involves a fundamental principle which seems to have governed every aspect of his work, a certain trait in his character which makes it absolutely necessary for him to introduce the moral viewpoint at no matter what cost to anything else. For him, artistic conscience always succumbs to the conscience of the moralist.

Even in the poem on Shirley's *The Grateful Servant* which I quoted at the beginning of this chapter, he places emphasis upon the moral attitude. In Shirley's play, he says, is

no believed defence
To strengthen the bold Atheist's insolence;
No obscene syllable, that may compel
A blush from a chaste maid.

Somewhat similar statements occur throughout his prologues, but even if they did not, his attitude could be superlatively easily deduced from his practice. Every play, for example, has its moral— usually expressed explicitly or implicitly at or near the end of the last act. It may be that jealousy or uxoriousness or unchastity are deadly sins, or that vengeance belongs to God alone, or it may be a

---

[1] *Johnson on Shakespeare*, p. 25.

lesson against pride as shown by the city ladies' courtly ambitions; but whatever the moral is, it is always there.

It is when this moral is imperfectly assimilated to the story that trouble arises. Then Massinger will use every means he can, in plotting and otherwise, to twist an unsuitable story to fit. Thus arise the imperfections I have discussed in *The Roman Actor*, *The Duke of Milan*, *The Picture* and *The City Madam*. In this last play we see the trouble at its very worst. The intended theme or motif, as is clear from the very title of the play, is the just humiliation of the proud women, wife and daughters of the city merchant; but gradually the character of Luke takes charge of the play, and the audience is more interested in his rise and fall than with anything else. It has become the theme of the play, and the attempt made at the end to bring us round to the displaced original theme is clumsy. This confusion as to the theme of *The City Madam* and the similar muddle discussed above in *The Roman Actor* are plotting errors of the profoundest sort, and are entirely due to Massinger's placing a particular moral viewpoint above theatrical and dramatic interest.

Unfortunately, owing to a change in public taste (and not to any inherent unworkability of the plots), it is not possible to see more than a very occasional performance of a Massinger play in the theatre.[1] But it is possible to keep in mind that his are plays written for performance, and to examine them from the point of view of the producer, the actor, and the audience.

---

[1] Productions of *A New Way* can still sometimes be seen. This, in many respects untypical, play has always been a favourite with actor-managers, and, perhaps because of the likeness of Overreach to an unscrupulous business-magnate, it enjoyed great favour in the United States at the turn of the century. I have myself seen a good production by Donald Wolfit and his company. According to Mr. Wolfit, it was not a success with the public.

Chapter Three

STAGECRAFT

In the preceding chapter I showed that Massinger had a stock method of handling his plots. But he carries stock methods much further than that. In his writing of plays he was a slave of habit. There was something inelastic and mechanical in him which made him repeat himself again and again, not only in his plotting but in his stories, his characterisation, his situations, his sentiments, his allusions, his phraseology, and his vocabulary.[1] This self-repetition characterises likewise his stagecraft.

By stagecraft, as something distinct from plotting, I mean the mechanics of the playwright in the management of his stage business: the manipulation of the characters on the stage; the way in which he 'dresses' the stage and groups his characters; the number of persons on the stage at any one time; the management of exits and entrances; the arrangements he makes for casting and for doubling; spectacle; situation; the way in which he uses his dialogue; the assignment of speeches; the use of monologues, soliloquies, asides, interruptions; choral and commenting passages; rhyming couplets as a rhetorical-dramatic device, and so on; in fact, all those features of dramatic handwriting which cannot fairly be grouped under the heading of plotting or plotting-devices on the one hand, or under that of style on the other. I should consider as 'stagecraft' all the purely technical means and conventions which the playwright adopts for the telling of a story in a dramatic form—perhaps for the transfer of a story from a narrative to a dramatic form.

Such mundane, practical matters are all too often ignored by students of our older dramatists, inasmuch as their approach still tends to be from the literary, instead of from the theatrical, angle. This virtual omission of stagecraft from their consideration can largely be attributed to a lack in the critics who have mostly shaped out dramatic criticism—Harley Granville-Barker being a notable exception[1]—of that practical experience of the theatre which only

[1] In this respect, see especially Chap. VII, below, pp. 210 ff.
[2] The work of G. Wilson Knight, a scholar and an experienced actor, in his *Principles of Shakespearean Production* (edition of 1949) is perhaps eclipsed by the general disfavour in which much of his other work is held. Of recent years more interest has been displayed in matters of stagecraft (see Bibliography for works by S. L. Bethell, B. L. Joseph, M. C. Bradbrook, etc.), but it is to be regretted that more men of the theatre, such as Mr. Tyrone Guthrie, have not as yet given us the benefit of their experience in a permanent form.

76

one who has himself acted can have; there are times when ignorance or the ignoring of dramatic mechanics can be a real weakness. After all, it is with such matters that the playwright, having plotted his story, is chiefly and most immediately concerned, and the student of the drama who neglects them misses something vital to a true estimate of an author *as a dramatist*. Perhaps the study of closet-dramas (by which I mean not all plays which for one reason or another have never been acted, but rather plays never intended for the stage) demands no reference to stagecraft. Stagecraft is really an irrelevant consideration with respect to *Prometheus Unbound* or *Manfred* or *Festus*. But a true drama is conceived in terms of the stage, such as that happens to be at the time of the drama's composition. It is a story designed to be taken in by the eye, through the comings, goings, groupings, and action of characters; and by the ear, through dialogue, monologue, soliloquy, and the like—that is, through words spoken by the characters. The narrator's running comments and explanations are not for the dramatist. If he has comments or explanations to make, he has to convey them otherwise than *in propria persona*. It is of the first importance to remember that a true drama is just as much something to be *seen* as something to be *heard*. From that remark it will be gathered that stagecraft has a dual character: the action-mechanics, and the dialogue-mechanics.

As a playwright for a stage which derived from the mediaeval freedoms in respect of action, place, and time, Massinger pays little attention to the so-called unities. The discussion of his plotting, in which he never is concerned with a single uncomplicated plot-thread, will have shown how little attention he pays to the unity of action. As regards the scenic unities, the treatment of which is more a concern of the stagecraftsman, he shifts his scene to suit himself, sometimes over wide areas, as for example in *Believe As You List* which has scenes in Carthage, Bithynia, and Syracuse, and even in plays of less spatial range, such as *The Unnatural Combat*, the actual localities may be many; and he is as liberal as regards time, sometimes keeping to a fairly compact period, as in *A New Way to Pay Old Debts*, but often spreading his action over a number of weeks, as in *The Picture* and *The Parliament of Love*. There is nothing in any way peculiar in all this. It is the common form of the Jacobean–Caroline stage, except in Ben Jonson and in a few plays which by accident or design for once observed the unities.

In respect of many things in stagecraft, of course, Massinger cannot be sharply distinguished from other dramatists, in his own day or indeed at other times. Characters have to be manipulated on the stage pretty much in the same way by all dramatists. And characters must use words to convey statements and their emotional tones in ways which, while they vary not a little from age to age, from Shakespeare to Shaw, from one dramatic convention to another, are nevertheless variable only within limits—the inescapable limits imposed by the nature of drama.

In some ways, the drama, not excepting the most apparently realistic, slice-of-life variety, is a distorting and highly selective mirror. It is largely convention which makes its representation of human action on the stage acceptable or *vraisemblable*. The degree of distortion, or if that word is too strong, adjustment, certainly varies as between different kinds of drama.

But the representation was particularly distorted on the Jacobean–Caroline stage for which Massinger wrote. The fashion was for the more or less romantic melodrama (generally tragi-comic in issue, but not seldom tragic) of what I have called psychological surprise. Such a drama made particular demands on the playwright. Complicated plots necessarily breed complicated stagecraft, and the heightening, or indeed, falsification, of life required all the skill and ingenuity of the dramatist to make the implausible plausible.

★

Entrances and exits deserve more attention than they normally get. The musical composer has to concern himself with something very similar—the introduction of a new subject, the entrance of a new instrument, the resolution of a suspension, and the merging of a solo instrument into a *tutti*. These are musical entrances and exits. Both dramatist and composer have to expend very considerable thought on just such comings and goings if they are to secure their proper effects.

Entrances and exits were by no means easy to manage in the Jacobean–Caroline theatre. It had an open stage, and accordingly (with a minor exception which I shall mention immediately) all the actors had to come 'on' and either go 'off' or be carried 'off'. They could not be left on-stage at the end of a scene or act. Nor could they be already on at the beginning of one, unless they were 'discovered' on the inner stage by the withdrawing of a curtain hiding it. For some reason or other, the dramatists of Massinger's period do not seem to have been very fond of this 'discovery'. Perhaps they avoided it because of the objections of the actors, who may have felt that they could not be heard well when they spoke from the inner stage. Certainly the 'discovering' method lost to the

78

actor the valuable second or two during which, as he walked on, the audience could prepare for his first words.

Massinger did, however, use the device of 'discovering' very skilfully in the unusual opening of scene vi of Act III of *The Guardian*. It opens with a soliloquy by Iolante. According to the stage-direction, she '*is heard speaking behind a curtain*'. When she, heard but still unseen, has finished, '*Enter Severino before the curtain*' in a straightforward walking-on entrance. He has heard the last few words, imagines that the 'poor turtle' is at her prayers, and drawing the curtain, '*discovers Iolante seated, with a rich banquet, and tapers, set forth*'. The technical difficulties of this scene were, of course, easily coped with, since the play was written for indoor performance at the Blackfriars. In a darkened house with candles partly showing their light, the audience's attention was easily held by the opening speech, and one can imagine the rustle of anticipation which ran through the theatre when Severino, the last person Iolante expected or wished to see, entered on the darkened forward stage. In this scene, which shows every sign of having been carefully thought out from a technical point of view, Massinger has managed to make the 'discovering' of Iolante on the inner stage seem not only natural but also dramatically effective.

Of course, few of his scene-openings or entrances are so elaborated as this. As I have noted elsewhere,[1] a great many scenes begin with two or more persons walking on together and already well launched into the theme of a conversation. In *The City Madam*, for example, fourteen of the sixteen scenes in the play begin in this way; in *The Picture* there are eleven openings of this type in seventeen scenes; *The Emperor of the East* has eleven mid-conversation openings in fifteen scenes[2]; and many of the entrances within the scenes of these and all the other plays are likewise made by characters already engaged in speech with one another. Thus, in *A New Way to Pay Old Debts*, of the ten entrances made in the course of the first act, four are made by single characters and, of the remaining six, four are made by characters already engaged in conversation. The device makes for flow and pace and naturalness, and certainly Massinger regularly uses it with effect. Perhaps I might add that while Shakespeare occasionally introduces his characters in this way, it is not nearly so common in him as in Massinger. It is commoner for Shakespeare's characters to come to an action already in process

---

[1] Above, p. 62.

[2] It is not always easy to tell when an entrance is of this nature. I have taken as a criterion in this respect the passage quoted earlier (p. 62) which forms the opening of *The City Madam*, where the nature of the early remarks shows clearly that the conversation has been in progress before the speakers' entrance.

on the stage; whereas Massinger likes to make entering characters bring the action on with them.

Naturally the first entrance of a major character in a play is always prepared for well in advance by discussion on the stage, usually in the early, expository section. We already know something about the characters before we see them; they are made known to us by anticipation. This is perhaps a matter for consideration more properly as an aspect of plotting, and I have in fact already mentioned it in that connexion.[1] More direct, however, and more a matter of elementary stagecraft is the preparation which is frequently made just before a character's entrance, at any point of the play. The entrance is anticipated in the dialogue so that the audience are warned to expect it and are not surprised—though the characters themselves already on the stage frequently are.

At its simplest, the whole scene may be one of expectation of the arrival of an important personage, as in Act I, scene iv, of *The Roman Actor* where the women are gathered together to await the triumphal entry of Domitian to the Capitol, or as in Act I, scene iii, of *The Bondman* where the lords of Syracuse are awaiting in the senate house the arrival of Timoleon.

But the device is frequently used more subtly than that. Very effective is the preparation for the entry of Antiochus near the end of Act I, scene ii, of *Believe As You List*. The audience is aware that Antiochus is still alive; but the merchants, to whom he is about to make his appearance, believe that he has been dead for twenty years. He enters, dramatically, just as they are vociferously wishing that he had not been killed, as they suppose. Again, in *The Maid of Honour*, Act II, scene ii, Adorni soliloquises at some length on his resentment against Fulgentio, his difficulty in attacking him, and his resolve to seize a likely opportunity there and then. At the words,

Ha! 'tis he: my fate
Be ever blessed for't!

Fulgentio enters. Similarly, the entrance of Francisco in *The Duke of Milan*, Act IV, scene ii, is prepared by a long conversation in which Stephano and Tiberio discuss his character. Calandrino, the buffoon in *The Great Duke of Florence*, has an entrance in Act IV, scene i, which is prepared by one of the servants saying,

If we had
Our fellow Calandrino here, to dance
His part, we were perfect.

But examples of such preparation are too numerous in all the plays to

1 See above, p. 63.

quote. [1] They display Massinger as the careful craftsman, considering his audience, and lubricating the movement of his play by a simple technical means.

There is little that is remarkable in the rest of Massinger's entrance-technique. Single characters enter and are recognised and are smoothly drawn into the dialogue; characters enter and interrupt action or enter and overhear matter they are not supposed to hear; characters enter unexpectedly (as does Severino in the passage from *The Guardian* I have discussed above); and groups of characters, as a Court or a royal retinue, enter and the principal takes the chair of state. There is nothing here that was not the common stock of all playwrights—the presence of a character or group of characters is demanded by the plot and he or they have to be on the stage to make his or their particular contribution.

Scene endings and exits (a simpler matter than entrances) may be considered together. Scenes end, of course, when the stage is cleared of characters, this frequently beginning a lapse of time before the action of the following scene or before a change of location. There is nothing particularly individual in Massinger's way of removing his characters from the stage; unless it be that he is fond of taking most of them off in a body and making the one character who is left behind exit on a soliloquy which contains some adumbration of the course of the future action; or making a character exit on an aside which, in a typically Massingerian way, underlines the moral lesson he wishes the closing episode to convey. The soliloquy ending can be illustrated by the two separate soliloquies by Grimaldi and Francisco closing Act IV, scene i, of *The Renegado*, or by Timandra's closing Act V, scene i, of *The Bondman*. As for the aside-exit, *A New Way to Pay Old Debts* supplies two characteristic examples: thus in Act IV, scene ii, Tapwell, who had made an ungrateful return for Wellborn's early prodigality and is rejected when Wellborn's fortunes are restored, goes off-stage with the muttered tag,

Unthankful knaves are ever so rewarded.

And when in Act V, scene i, it comes to Marrall's turn to be dismissed without reward for his disclosure of his knavery which had restored Wellborn and overreached Overreach, he leaves the stage with the words,

This is the haven
False servants still arrive at.

A reader of Massinger's plays will notice how rarely it is that he

[1] Cf. the entrance of Edgar in *King Lear*, I. ii. Edmund names him, 'and pat he comes like the catastrophe of the old comedy'.

uses rhyme. He uses it very occasionally to mark a sentiment within a speech or at the ends of speeches within the scene, but he uses it more frequently, as was the custom of dramatists at the time and earlier, to mark scene- or act-endings. Yet even here he seems a little reluctant to use it. An examination of any of the plays will make this plain. *The Bondman* contains eighteen scenes, but of the nine which end on rhyming couplets, four occur at the ends of acts and two mark the ends of soliloquies as well as the ends of scenes, leaving only three rhymed scene-endings in dialogue; *The Maid of Honour* with seventeen scenes has eight rhymed endings, three of them at the end of acts and three of them marking ends of soliloquies; *The Great Duke of Florence* has eleven scenes, but of the three which have rhymed endings, two are at the ends of acts and one ends a soliloquy. To choose an early play, *The Unnatural Combat*, with twelve scenes, has five which end on a rhyme and four of these are act-endings; and to choose a much later play, *The Guardian* has twenty scenes and only one, the last scene in the play, has a rhymed ending. That is to say, counting all types of ending, whether reinforced by being at the end of an act or a soliloquy or not, Massinger does not seem to have had any rigid rule for ending scenes on a couplet. The only rule which is invariable is that each play should end on a couplet. Yet even so, about one-third of the scenes (this figure holds good for any of the plays) do end on a couplet. So Massinger does seem to have taken *some* account of the convention. It should be remarked that it is not too easy for an actor to round off with a rhyme. To give a couplet its full effect, one has to speak it while still in mid-stage and more or less fronting the audience, not throw it over the shoulder at the last minute before stepping off as is the half-apologetic way in so many modern productions of Shakespeare. There is bound in the circumstances to be a slight hiatus as the actor walks away, which may or may not be filled with applause. In any event, through the awkwardness of the actor, a scene with a couplet-ending often does not snap shut as it should. Nevertheless, on a stage lacking a proscenium curtain there was a great advantage in the rhyming tag to indicate a close firmly and decisively. Massinger seems to have recognised this, and while he does not use this method invariably, he does use it frequently; and, of course, there was one use of the closing couplet that appealed to him; as will be noticed from these examples it is generally of a moral-aphoristic kind:

> Let mountains of afflictions fall on me,
> Their weight is easy, so I set them free.[1]

[1] *The Great Duke of Florence*, IV. i.

> Entreaties fit not me; a man in grace
> May challenge awe and privilege, by his place.[1]

> There cannot be a want of power above,
> To punish murder, and unlawful love.[2]

> Or let mankind, for her fall, boldly swear
> There are no chaste wives now, nor ever were.[3]

Instead of merely rhyming the last two lines of an act, as Shakespeare does, Massinger gives them added weight by turning them into moral comments.

There is one feature of Shakespeare's plays related to stagecraft which is practically absent from Massinger's. That is the 'scenic-descriptive'. It has been said with at least some truth that Shakespeare supplies the scenic deficiencies of his theatre by verbal description. Obvious examples are: Duncan's description of Glamis,

> This castle hath a pleasant seat, the air
> Nimbly and sweetly recommends itself
> Unto our gentle senses;[4]

such passages descriptive of atmospheric circumstance as Puck's,

> For night's swift dragons cut the clouds full fast
> And yonder shines Aurora's harbinger;[5]

or Romeo's,

> Night's candles are burnt out, and jocund day
> Stands tiptoe on the misty mountain tops.[6]

But in Massinger, and indeed in the Fletcherian school as a whole, this verbal description of locale is noticeably lacking—if one excepts such a special case as Fletcher's *Faithful Shepherdess*. No moonlight sleeps upon any of Massinger's banks; the floor of heaven is unpatined. Almost never is the scene directly described. And what is more remarkable is the fact that the atmospheric conditions—heat or cold, freshness or sultriness, sunshine or shade, moonlight or darkness, calm or storm, even the times of the day or night—are rarely indicated or even implied. *The Guardian*, in which much of the action takes place at night, provides practically the only instance, and that because the plot turns on the confusions of identity that occur in the dark. But otherwise the elements take no part in his

---

[1] *Maid of Honour*, II. i.
[2] *Unnatural Combat*, v. ii.
[3] *Roman Actor*, IV. i.
[4] *Macbeth*, I. vi.
[5] *A Midsummer-Night's Dream*, III. ii.
[6] *Romeo and Juliet*, III. v.

plays and contribute not at all to the dramatic effect as they do, say, in *King Lear, Hamlet, Macbeth, The Tempest,* and *As You Like It.*

Massinger's characters are apparently not sensuously aware of the conditions about them and are never heated by the sun or the chase, wet by the rain or by sweat, pleased or disgusted by perfumes or smells, hungry, tired. Their only references to things in nature are by way of simile and metaphor, but never to convey anything about their immediate surroundings. In Massinger's case, familiar as he is with the terms of falconry and venery, as can be seen from Durazzo's elaborate description of the joys of hawking in Act I, scene i, of *The Guardian,* this ignoring of the natural world of his action is undoubtedly partly due to a sensuous aridity in himself; but it is also, as I hinted, partly a defect of his whole school. They were, in this and other things, men of the theatre; and conceiving their plays purely as plays acted on the bare boards and against the routine backcloth of the Blackfriars, the Phoenix, or the Globe, their sensuous imaginations had atrophied. They did not imagine their people living in and responding fully to a conditioning world. Or, to put it in a way more favourable to their aim, they were more concerned with people talking than with people being—with a strictly *ad hoc* existence and activity. This is not less, but more, true of Massinger than perhaps any dramatist of his school.

To such a degree is it true that, except for a minimum of reference to the semi-historical background of most of his plays (purely factual, however, not descriptive or suggestive), it is seldom or never important beyond an irreducible minimum whether a play is set in contemporary London or the Syracuse of Timoleon, the Constantinople of Theodosius II and his sister Pulcheria, or the Nottinghamshire of 1620. Massinger does take some trouble about such things as, the names appropriate to sixteenth-century Italy or Dijon or imperial Rome, the offices of certain characters, the few places mentioned, the oaths used, the coinage, and the like. But beyond that he does not go. It is often not clear from the dialogue where a scene is laid. Of course, many scenes are immediately localised by the static characters, such as house-servants, who appear in them; but many are not, and it must be deduced from all this that Massinger relied upon the property-men and upon costuming to help.

For Massinger's drama is, as I have said, a drama of words. He is essentially the rhetorician-dramatist. From his constant use of the technical terms of rhetoric, such as 'rhetoric' itself, 'solecism', 'argument', 'discourse and reason', 'logic', 'tropes', 'figures', 'elench', 'fallacy' and 'syllogism', it is obvious that he must have studied it

academically—as indeed he would when he was at Oxford. And in
The Unnatural Combat, Act III, scene ii, the witty young Page says,

> I have heard my tutor
> Prove it by logic, that a servant's life
> Was better than his master's;

and thereupon he proceeds to prove it in what is virtually a rhetoric
exercise on a typical rhetorical paradox of the schools:

> Well then; and first to you, sir: you complain
> You serve one lord, but your lord serves a thousand,
> Besides his passions, that are his worst masters;
> You must humour him, and he is bound to sooth
> Every grim sir above him: if he frown,
> For the least neglect you fear to lose your place;
> But if, and with all slavish observation,
> From the minion's self, to the groom of his close-stool,
> He hourly seeks not favour, he is sure
> To be eased of his office, though perhaps he bought it.
> Nay more; that high disposer of all such
> That are subordinate to him, serves and fears
> The fury of the many-headed monster,
> The giddy multitude: and as a horse
> Is still a horse, for all his golden trappings,
> So your men of purchased titles, at their best, are
> But serving-men in rich liveries.

Of course his rhetorical turn is not exactly exceptional. But
whereas Marlowe and Chapman use rhetoric lyrically or in soliloquy,
for its impression on the audience rather than on the other characters, Massinger, who can also do so, uses it more forensically in
dialogue and set speech, to produce an effect on the characters within the play. His is the drama of men and women relating themselves
to and working on men and women by words—conversation, discussion, argument, persuasion, dissuasion, pleading, self-justification,
self-expression, self-concealment, confidences, consultations. It is
the drama of verbal interplay. There is hardly a play without a
pleading or a temptation scene or without an opportunity for a
leading character to urge a case or plead a cause. Again and again—
and this is typical of his bias to rhetoric—he makes the whole play,
not to mention the whole trend of an apparently established character, swing over by means of a character's words. Lady Allworth
is won to acceptance of Wellborn by his verbal persuasion in Act I,
scene iii, of *A New Way to Pay Old Debts*; in Act V, scene iv, of *The
Guardian*, Severino, in his capacity as chief of a gang of banditti, is
persuaded by a ridiculous tale of woe from the disguised King of

Naples to part with all his store of treasure. Examples could be given from every one of the plays of the canon[1]; but the point I wish to make is that it is particularly important in a playwright such as Massinger, whose work is so rhetorical in nature, to pay attention to the aspects of his stagecraft which come under the heading of the technical manipulation of his dialogue, what I called at the beginning of this chapter the 'dialogue-mechanics'.

One of the commonest devices of Massinger's dialogue-mechanics is the aside. He probably uses it more than any other dramatist in English. The number of asides in individual plays varies greatly; from only two in *The Emperor of the East*, five in *The Bashful Lover*, eight in *The Roman Actor*, nine in *The Renegado*, and twelve in each of *The Bondman* and *The Guardian*, it rises to as high as sixteen in *The Picture*, and to twenty-one in *A New Way to Pay Old Debts*. This is a count of the marked asides. There are, of course, many passages in every play of an 'aside' nature which are not so marked,[2] this fact often doubling, or even trebling, the real number of asides in a play. This figure is quite high when it is considered that, according to Professor Baldwin's estimate,[3] a Massinger play has on the average about 650 speeches. It is true that a similar count of some plays selected at random from the work of Beaumont and Fletcher will give very similar figures—*The Knight of the Burning Pestle* has two, *Bonduca* and *The Wild-Goose Chase* have four each, *A King and No King* has eleven, and *The Maid's Tragedy* has thirteen—but the figures cannot really be compared. In the Beaumont and Fletcher plays the asides rarely exceed four or five words in length, and are of a brief ejaculatory type which could quite often be easily dispensed with. Massinger thinks nothing of quite long asides. For example, in *The Unnatural Combat*, Act I, scene i, Malefort has an aside of six lines;

> Thou searcher of men's hearts,
> And sure defender of the innocent,
> (My other crying sins—awhile not looked on)
> If I in this am guilty, strike me dead,
> Or by some unexpected means confirm
> I am accused unjustly![4]

But in general the asides average about three lines in length, as in Wellborn's aside in Act II, scene iii, of *A New Way to Pay Old Debts* where he is commenting on the change of attitude in Marrall now that it seems as if fortune is smiling upon the prodigal:

---

[1] Cf. below, Chap. IV, p. 137.   [2] Cf. below, pp. 88 and 91.
[3] T. W. Baldwin, *The Duke of Milan*, Lancaster, Pa., 1918.
[4] Other examples of long asides are given later in this chapter. See pp. 89-92.

> Is not this a true rogue,
> That, out of mere hope of future cozenage,
> Can turn thus suddenly? 'Tis rank already.

Even three lines is a considerable interruption of the flow of the dialogue; and the whole stage action, as well as the audience, must wait until the characters get these asides out.

Of course, an aside of three or even more lines is manageable enough if, for one reason or another, no stage business or continuity is interrupted. A soliloquy is at its simplest[1] little more than an aside deprived of some of its complications by removing other characters from the stage. However, a comparison with Shakespeare's use of the aside is perhaps profitable here. When, for example, Hamlet ejaculates, 'Wormwood, wormwood,' he is behaving realistically, not conventionally, and far from interrupting the action he is helping it on, speeding it, and making a valid contribution to it, not acting as a sort of vocal programme-note or a mere link to bind *The Murder of Gonzago* to the Court of Elsinore. When, to take an example of a slightly different kind, Macbeth delivers several lengthy asides on his elevation to the Thaneship of Cawdor in Act I, scene iii, of *Macbeth*, Shakespeare is at pains to draw him into the scene by making Banquo remark on his standing 'rapt', and the aside, far from interrupting the action, becomes the action itself. Almost always Shakespeare's asides are in this way really dramatic and integrated. Massinger's seldom are.

There are, of course, two types of aside. An aside may be either a remark made in a stage whisper by the speaker to be heard by one or more characters, or a brief, generally semi-exclamatory, comment made by the speaker to himself. The first type is natural and easily handled, especially when it is made on a fairly full stage when other characters not intended to hear can be engaged in conversation or otherwise occupied.

An example of this occurs in Act V, scene iii, of *The Picture* where Sophia, angry with her husband at his mistrust and attempted betrayal of her, has to greet him in the presence of the King and Queen of Hungary. The Queen and Sophia have kissed on meeting, and as she returns to her place she says to her husband, Mathias,

> Do you hear, sir?
> Without a magical picture, in the touch
> I find your print of close and wanton kisses
> On the queen's lips.

[1] But see below, p. 92.

And he replies,

> Upon your life be silent:—
> And now salute these lords.

Sophia answers,

> Since you will have me,
> You shall see that I am experienced at the game,
> And can play it tightly.

She then turns to greet the courtiers in turn. On a full stage, and
with the bustle of the arrival of the royal party and the interchange
of courtesies, such aside-passages are easily managed.

More difficult examples of this type of aside occur in scenes of
eavesdropping in which an action on the front stage is watched
by one or more characters from behind or above. From time to
time comment is made by the watchers, often at considerable
length. Examples of this are perhaps more common in Massinger
than in other Jacobean dramatists since it is one of his stock situations; but such passages are perhaps too lengthy to quote *in extenso*.
I would, however, instance scene v of Act III of *The Renegado*. Here
Asambeg, the viceroy of Tunis, and Mustapha, a basha of Aleppo,
are watching Donusa and Vitelli, the Christian she is trying to
seduce, from above. The dialogue on the front stage must be
imagined to be flowing quite smoothly; but to the fourteen lines
which Donusa and Vitelli speak while Asambeg and Mustapha are
watching them there are six lines spoken in three asides from above
which they must affect not to hear. In *The Great Duke of Florence*,
Act II, scene iii, Charomonte watches Sanazarro courting Lidia and
makes several comments. (Since he is unaccompanied, his comments
properly belong to the second type of aside.) And there is likewise a
notable example in *A New Way to Pay Old Debts*, Act III, scene ii,
where Sir Giles Overreach attempts to overhear the conversation
between his daughter and Lord Lovell and is interrupted in his
eavesdropping by Justice Greedy's complaining that it is time for
dinner. There are twenty aside lines in this last scene, during which
Lovell and Margaret must be supposed to be talking in low tones in
a corner. But Massinger seems to have tried to make the situation
a little more plausible and realistic[1] by having Lord Lovell say,

> Hah! I heard some noise.[2]

---

[1] Other examples of Massinger's making an aside seem more realistic by having some
character on the stage recognise that something has been said occur in *The Duke of Milan*,
v. i, where Francisco indicates that he has heard Graccho make an aside, and *A New Way*,
ii. iii. Overreach recognises an aside made by Marrall.

[2] None of the examples I have given in this paragraph are marked as asides. Eavesdropping asides seldom are.

The second type of aside, that made by a speaker to himself, is of more doubtful validity. Used with judgement and discretion it can be dramatically effective, as in Hamlet's 'Wormwood, wormwood', for, after all, human beings do comment *sotto voce*. In *The Bondman*, Act V, scene i, for example, Timandra, who loves Leosthenes, listens to Timagoras persuading him that he need not really marry Cleora if he doubts her fidelity, and she murmurs to herself,

This argues for me.

And Gothrio, the Caliban-like servant of Octavio in Act III, scene i, of *The Bashful Lover*, makes quite plausible asides to the 'bottle of immortality' he steals.

But too often the device is resorted to, not for the drama's sake, but for the moral's sake. It becomes a dry and highly artificial convention, used, as underlining was by Queen Victoria and exclamation marks by women generally, as a means of emphasis—the pointing of a marginal finger to a sentiment or information which Massinger wants his audience not to miss:

He begins to waver.	*The Picture*, III. v.
There's a cooling For his hot encounter!	*The Renegado*, III. i.
Here's a second show Of the family of pride!	*The Bondman*, II. ii.
This is but devilish doctrine!	*A New Way*, III. i.

Such asides bear witness to the fact that Massinger never trusts his audience very much,[1] and never leaves anything to chance if he can possibly illuminate the half-obvious with a more obvious comment.

Occasionally in Massinger an aside may be more important and indeed functionally dramatic. For example, in *The Duke of Milan*, Act V, scene i, Graccho enters with an aside:

Now for my whipping!
And if I now outstrip him not, and catch him,
And by a new and strange way too, hereafter
I'll swear there are worms in my brains.

It is an anticipatory aside, to warn the audience of what he is about to do and say. It tells us nothing we do not already know about the speaker, but it helps the action along.

There is a very similar example of the same sort of thing earlier in the play. In the complicated romantic melodrama of psychological surprise, the audience is sometimes, and the characters within

---

[1] See below, p. 98. Jonson, too, as befits another somewhat pedantic moralist-dramatist, is also fond of this sort of commenting aside.

the play are often, deliberately misled as to motive and intention with a view to surprise effects later. So here, in *The Duke of Milan*, the audience has been led to believe in Act III, scene iii, that Francisco's attitude to Marcelia has changed. But as Massinger, despite his loyalty to the drama of surprise, also wants to make sure his audience is properly alive to what is going on, he assigns to Francisco an aside which both corrects any false impression about him and gives a warning or pointer. As he exits, he says,

> It is enough;
> Nay, all I could desire, and will make way
> To my revenge, which shall disperse itself
> On him, on her, and all.

I have mentioned the length of Massinger's asides before, but I have hardly yet dealt fully with the great technical difficulties which the actor must find in delivering such asides when they occur (as they very often do) as integral parts of the dialogue, in the full flight of conversation between one or more characters. It is difficult for us nowadays to imagine just how the actors, both those speaking and those pretending not to hear, behaved. Frequently such asides in Massinger are astonishingly artificial. Consider an example from *The Maid of Honour*, Act IV, scene iv.

The occasion is the presentation by Gonzago of the misrepresented Bertoldo to Aurelia, Duchess of Sienna. She and others are already on the stage, halfway through the scene, waiting for Bertoldo's entrance. As he comes towards her, 'richly habited' and ushered by Gonzago and Adorni, she 'asides' to let us know she is more than favourably impressed by his manly appearance and bearing;

> This is he, sure.
> How soon mine eyes had found him! What a port
> He bears! How well his bravery becomes him!
> A prisoner! Nay, a princely suitor, rather!
> But I'm too sudden.

Gonzago's brief speech which follows is by way of introduction of Bertoldo:

> Madam, 'twas his suit,
> Unsent for, to present his service to you,
> Ere his departure.

Aurelia thereupon has another aside to the same general purpose as before. The following speech by Astutio, who is no friend to Bertoldo,

> The devil, I think, supplies him.
> Ransomed, and thus rich too!

is not marked as an aside but in effect it is one, possibly addressed to his faction on the stage, but certainly supposed not to be audible to Aurelia, Bertoldo, Gonzago, and Adorni. Only now does Aurelia address Bertoldo:

Aurel. You ill deserve
    (*Bertoldo kneeling, kisses her hand.*)
  The favour of our hand—we are not well,
  Give us more air. (*Descends suddenly.*)
Gonz. What sudden qualm is this?
Aurel. —That lifted yours against me.
Bert. Thus, once more,
  I sue for pardon.
Aurel. Sure his lips are poisoned,
  And through these veins force passage to my heart,
  Which is already seized on. (*Aside.*)
Bert. I wait, madam,
  To know what your commands are; my designs
  Exact me in another place.

It will be seen that two of the asides (there are four in 25 lines) contain 33 and 19 words respectively. It is hard to see how such protracted asides, during which the other characters have to be suspended, could be anything but slightly ludicrous. I should add that, so far from the passage from *The Maid of Honour* being exceptional in respect of the asides in it, there are many other passages throughout the plays just as bad; or, if one cannot quite condemn them on this score, they are at the very least very 'difficult' for the actors. It is when we come to consider such passages with the close scrutiny we should have to give them in rehearsal, breaking them up into speeches, even words, and trying to work out just how and from what position an actor should take certain lines and just how every other character on the stage should react, that we really come to grips with the fundamental problems of stagecraft. 'Can such a thing be done?' is the first question the dramatist and then in his turn the actor or producer asks himself. Then he goes on to ask, 'If it is done, will it have the desired effect upon the audience?' When we apply such questions to much of Massinger's aside-technique the answer, for the modern audience certainly, must be in the negative; and most probably the same holds good for the audience of his own day and times,[1] since, although its taste was perhaps artificial, it could never be called naïve.[2] Massinger has carried

[1] Even when it is allowed that the open stage of those times placed actors and audience in more direct rapport one with the other.
[2] Cf. H. S. Bennett, *Shakespeare's Audience*, Proc. Brit. Acad., XXX, 1944.

what, properly handled, could be a useful convention to extremes and the convention breaks down into absurdity in the process.

It is possible to regard the aside, at least as spoken by a character to himself, as a brief soliloquy, or the soliloquy as a glorified aside. But that is rather a superficial equation. The aside is by its nature only incidental or parenthetic. When it occurs it plucks the attention (notionally, only for a moment) off the stage situation as a whole, to which, however, the attention immediately returns when the aside is done. On the other hand, the soliloquy, not merely because of its greater length but because of its very nature, *is* the stage situation for the time being and it demands the undivided attention of the audience. I do not say that a minor character never soliloquises, but on the whole soliloquy is for those who are protagonists or at least characters of some importance dramatically.[1] Just because a character generally soliloquises only when alone on the stage, there is little or no difficulty about the management of such speeches, however artificial the whole convention may be.

Naturally Massinger resorted to it quite often, without being noticeably more given to it than were his contemporaries. His peculiarities in respect of it are not a matter of frequency in use. His most important reason for soliloquy is to make a character tell us something bearing on the course of the future action of himself or others. Here again a comparison with Shakespeare's practice is interesting. Shakespeare often uses the soliloquy, but only occasionally, as in the cases of Edmund and of Iago, to advance the plot. More often it is used as a help to the characterisation which makes us party to the minds and tumultuous souls of his heroes or his villains. Massinger uses the soliloquy less often to reveal character than as a device to speed the action and to explain the motives in gobbets throughout the play. Such soliloquies are that of Francisco in *The Duke of Milan*, Act II, scene i, where, having failed to seduce Marcelia with his lies, he resolves that he must go on with his plans for revenge (for some wrong as yet unspecified); or that of Hortensio at the opening of Act III, scene iii, of *The Bashful Lover*, where he decides that, having failed to make himself worthy of Matilda's love by his success in battle, he will withdraw from the world and live as a simple shepherd. These are prospective soliloquies. They look forward to future action. More retrospective than prospective is the powerful soliloquy of Malefort at the beginning of Act IV, scene i,

---

[1] The characters who soliloquise most in Massinger are those, such as Adorni in *The Maid of Honour*, Hortensio in *The Bashful Lover*, and Malefort in *The Unnatural Combat*, whose motives are most complex and difficult of expression by any other means.

of *The Unnatural Combat*. It dissolves Malefort's mystery and explains his violent capriciousness; but it has of course an anticipatory tendency as well in that the speaker has worked himself into a decision.

Massinger, then, is not given to the musing kind of soliloquy such as Henry VI's at the Battle of Towton,[1] or Henry V's during the night before the Battle of Agincourt[2]; or to the soliloquy of largely character-display alone, such as Justice Overdo's at the beginning of Act II of *Bartholomew Fair*. The character-revelation in Massinger's soliloquies is always only incidental or indeed implicit. If he makes a character muse, it is in order to get across his own moral reflections, not the character's stream of consciousness. For example, Iolante in *The Guardian*, Act III, scene vi, is made to speak about herself as no character would when she says:

> I am full of perplexed thoughts. Imperious blood,
> Thou only art a tyrant; judgement, reason,
> To whatsoever thy edicts proclaim,
> With vassal fear subscribe against themselves . . .
> . . . I, that did deny
> My daughter's youth allowed and lawful pleasures,
> And would not suffer in her those desires
> She sucked in with my milk, now in my waning
> Am scorched and burnt up with libidinous fire
> That must consume my fame.

She is merely Massinger's mouthpiece, and he is emphasising the moral lesson he would teach us by the play and its situations.

So given to edification is he that he will use the soliloquy for casual lessoning. I mean by this for lessons not arising from and reinforcing those of the action. Such is the use of Bertoldo's soliloquy in Act IV, scene iii, of *The Maid of Honour*. He enters reading Seneca and passes to the audience some quite gratuitous moral criticism on Stoicism and suicide (favourite topics of Massinger's[3]). It is true that, when he has disposed of Seneca, Bertoldo goes on to a To-be-or-not-to-be imitation of Hamlet. But though he is in prison, he has not the motive and the cue for passion Hamlet has, and all that he says comes more truly from Massinger's moralistic bias than from his own character or situation. The soliloquy is in fact one of the many extra-dramatic insertions which I discuss in another context,[4] and

---

[1] *Henry VI*, Part 3, ii. v.   [2] *Henry V*, iv. i.

[3] For Massinger and Stoicism, see Chap. V. Other passages in which his condemnation of suicide may be found are: *The Duke of Milan*, i. iii, *The Maid of Honour*, ii. iv, *The Parliament of Love*, iv. ii, *Believe As You List*, iv. ii, and *The Bashful Lover*, ii. vi. See also Cruickshank, *Philip Massinger*, p. 106, footnote.

[4] See below, Chap. V, p. 197.

the audience had to treat it as such. They were no doubt quite ready
to do so. For, after all, one of the secondary functions of the more
literary type of drama in the seventeenth century (a function not
sufficiently recognised today) was to provide miscellaneous ideas and
topics. There would, of course, be no objection lodged by the actor
soliloquising, for any kind of soliloquy is for him an opportunity for
histrionics to be seized and made the most of.

Such is the nature of the soliloquy in Massinger that I have had
perforce to widen my discussion of it beyond mere considerations of
stagecraft. But the purpose of soliloquies in the plays (to speed the
action, to convey information to the audience, to act as a sort of
dramatic shorthand) is not without relevance when we come to consider how they were delivered by the actors. They were regarded by
actors and audience alike as histrionic highlights, special opportunities for the display of the craft of oratory undisturbed by the movement or reaction of other characters. As they are generally delivered
on an empty stage, they tend to come either at the beginning[1] or at
the end[2] of a scene. Even when they come in the middle of a scene,
the stage has generally been emptied to make room for them, and
what follows them, at the entry of others to the soliloquiser, is virtually
a new scene.[3] At the beginning a soliloquy is a prelude to the fugal
dialogue which may follow; at the end it is a subsiding coda.
Rounded off with a rhyming couplet, as it very often is when it forms
the end of a scene, it gives a sense of episodic completeness and may
well mark a pause in the action. From a purely practical point of
view, soliloquies allow the rest of a cast to make any necessary
changes in costume. Such (at least partly) time-making soliloquies
are those by Francisco at the end of scene ii, Act IV, of *The Duke of
Milan*, and by Adorni at the ends of scene iii, Act III, and scene v,
Act IV, of *The Maid of Honour*.

★

The fact that in Massinger dramatic action is more verbal and
psychological than physical springs not from any bent towards the
classical drama and the neo-classic rules, with which like any univer-
sity-bred man of the time he had some acquaintance, but from a
fundamental and individual interest in the verbal manifestation of

---

[1] As, for example, in *Parliament of Love*, III. ii; *Picture*, III. i; *Great Duke of Florence*, II. iii; *City Madam*, III. iii.
[2] *Renegado*, II. v; *Picture*, II. i; *Guardian*, II. iii; *Bondman*, v. i, and IV. iii; *Parliament of Love*, II. ii and IV. ii.
[3] *Renegado*, IV. i; *Bondman*, v. i; *Great Duke of Florence*, III. i; *Picture*, I. i and II. i.

life. Perhaps the period when the aim of dramatists and stage-managers was most directed to the spectacular (even if, by reason of the equipment available, the achievement did not always follow) was the twenty years or so from the late 1580's to about 1610, the glorious heyday of the 'public' theatres, the time which saw Tamburlaine riding in triumph to Persepolis and a thin company,

> with three rusty swords,
> And help of some few foot and half-foot words,
> Fight over York and Lancaster's long jars;[1]

when processions, coronations, dethronements, shipwrecks, mob-scenes, dumb-shows and the like frequently filled the stage—and the pit. But the influence of the contemptuous Ben Jonson on the one hand and of the sophisticated Beaumont and Fletcher on the other, coupled with the move to the greater intimacy of the 'private' theatres, led to appeals less spectacular. This suited Massinger's book perfectly.

It will be noticed in the first place that Massinger rarely has many people on the stage at once, and their presence is hardly ever for visual or spectacular effects. There are no crowd scenes at all. The densest stages (and that does not mean much in his case) are for courts of justice, and they figure more for the forensic opportunities they afford than for their picturesqueness. For instance some notable examples of this kind of scene are Act I, scene ii, of *The Fatal Dowry* and Act I, scene iii, of *The Roman Actor*. As for battles, they are frequently reported, as in *The Duke of Milan*, Act I, scene i, and *The Maid of Honour*, Act II, scene iii. In Act II of *The Bashful Lover*, where the confusions of a battle have a part to play in the plot, Massinger is forced to show some incidents on the field, but only on the periphery; and as the required effects could be produced by no more than the number of speaking characters, they are in no sense spectacular. In only one of the five scenes in this act connected with the battle are there more than four characters on the stage at any one time. Though so many of the plays are court-dramas, the processional and ceremonial side is almost non-existent; it is the private life of the emperors, kings, and grand dukes that is Massinger's more constant concern. Not a few of his plays have deaths *coram populo*, assassinations, sudden death, and fatal duels, as in *The Roman Actor*, *The Duke of Milan* and *The Unnatural Combat*. But unlike Shakespeare in *Hamlet*, *Othello*, *Lear*, or *Antony and Cleopatra*, unlike Webster in *The White Devil* or *The Duchess of Malfi*, Massinger is positively perfunctory in

[1] Jonson, *Every Man in His Humour*, Prologue.

getting them over with the minimum of fuss. Domitian is despatched in *The Roman Actor* very swiftly, and the play ends completely some twenty lines later. When Paris is killed earlier in the play, he exclaims,

> Oh! I am slain in earnest!

and his body is removed after a twenty-five line oration by Domitian explaining the suddenness of his action. Beaumelle in Act IV, scene iv, of *The Fatal Dowry* is stabbed suddenly in the midst of a scene which is a grim parody of a legal trial, and after her death the welter of words and quibbling about the murder continues for most of the rest of the play. It is the words for which the plays exist. The physical action, especially the killings, are mere necessary evils. Such physical action is always telescoped into as little space as possible.

Secondly, it is surprising how much vital action in his plays takes place off-stage. This is often for a good, practical reason. Thus the improbability of the sudden love of Aurelia and Bertoldo in *The Maid of Honour*, Act IV, scene iv, is skilfully masked by removing the principals. When they return, a compact has been concluded between them, the audience having been well conditioned to swallow this by the comments of the other characters marking time on the stage during their absence. This is by no means a solitary instance of Massinger's dodging a difficulty by taking it off-stage. A particularly blatant example occurs in Domitian's surprising forgiveness of his wife which takes place in the interval after Act IV of *The Roman Actor* and is presented to the audience at the beginning of Act V as a *fait accompli*. What has taken place during the act-pause is here a vital, if somewhat awkward, part of the action.

Inevitably, his dramas being what they were in respect of action before the audience, Massinger has a good deal of recourse to the classical *nuntius*-device. The courier in Act I, scene i, of *The Duke of Milan* serves as *nuntius*; but he does it in a bald and purely functional way, not with the expatiation of Queen Gertrude on the death of Ophelia[1] or the bleeding sergeant on the defeat of the Norsemen and Macdonwald, Thane of Cawdor.[2] Amble in *A New Way to Pay Old Debts*, Act II, scene ii, describes the dinner at Lady Allworth's house. And frequently a soliloquist acts the part of *nuntius*. So it is that Hortensio, in Act III, scene iii, of *The Bashful Lover*, describes the reconciliation of Maria and her father, Octavio.

While Massinger uses the *nuntius*, he never uses a preluding or inter-act chorus, as Shakespeare does in *Romeo and Juliet*, *Henry V*, or

---

[1] *Hamlet*, IV. vii.   [2] *Macbeth*, I. ii.

The Winter's Tale—let alone the formal neo-classic chorus which Ben Jonson alone of all the dramatists for the public stage ever ventured to bring on. The need for such informative, imagination-stimulating, or time-bridging devices scarcely concerned Massinger, whose plays are too closely integrated in the events and limited in their range to require them.

But there are certain choral functions, in a broad sense, that he wanted to preserve. For example, there is the function of a confidant to a principal, which the Greek tragic chorus performed to the protagonist, and which Seneca transferred to a character like Medea's nurse in the action proper. The confidant of the Senecan type is a frequent figure in the English drama before Massinger. Such, for example, are Horatio in *Hamlet* and Nerissa in *The Merchant of Venice*; though Shakespeare prefers a confidant like Lady Macbeth and Mercutio, who is more absorbed, as it were, into the action and much less of a mere passive functionary. The confidant who is that and little more also figures in Massinger (as indeed he does in Fletcher), as for example Bellapert to Beaumelle in *The Fatal Dowry*, Beaupré/Calista to Bellisant in *The Parliament of Love*, and Parthenius to Domitian in *The Roman Actor*. But there are plenty of the more active type as well: Marrall to Overreach and young Allworth to Wellborn in *A New Way to Pay Old Debts*, Romont to Charalois and Pontalier to Novall Junior in *The Fatal Dowry*, Timandra to Cleora in *The Bondman*, and Durazzo to Caldoro in *The Guardian*.

Of course in such a drama of moves and counter-moves, motives and counter-motives, of conspiracies, 'close designs and crooked counsels', as Massinger wrote, consultations and the exchange of confidences, half-confidences, and pretended confidences make up a good part of each play. Needless to say, the confidences are often ill-placed, from the point of view of the confider. But in a drama of surprise, however free and offhand a confider tells his story, he is not unlikely to 'keep something to himsel' he darena tell to ony', or that it is expedient for the dramatist of surprise to reserve.

One of the least legitimate of Massinger's dodges in the business of confidences is his not uncommon trick of making the confider entrust part or all of his secret in a whisper unheard by the audience. Thus, in *Believe As You List*, Act IV, scene i, Metellus whispers to Flaminius his plan for working Antiochus to a confession by tempting him with a courtesan; and the audience is kept in the dark. In *A New Way to Pay Old Debts*, Act I, scene iii, Wellborn whispers to Lady Allworth his plan for deceiving Sir Giles Overreach, or at least, his request that she should pretend to be in love with him. Not a small matter to pack into a short whisper! In Act II, scene iii, of the same play the whispering device is managed much more gracefully. Lovell and Margaret are holding a long whispered conversation and Sir Giles is trying to overhear them. But Justice Greedy enters, and by introducing some comic business between Greedy and Sir Giles, Massinger distracts the audience's attention from the whisperers.

The commenting function which belonged to the Greek, not the Latin, tragic chorus is effected by Massinger, as it had been and was by his English predecessors and contemporaries, through the agency of commenting persons. With his distrust of his audience's intelligence, or, if one prefers, his pedantic way of leaving nothing to chance, Massinger makes a more extensive use of such persons than was customary, except perhaps in Ben Jonson. There is always someone, like the Page in *The Unnatural Combat*, Eubulus in *The Emperor of the East*, Gracculo in *The Renegado*, and Calipso in *The Guardian*, who, really for the benefit of the audience, however the dramatic pedagogy is disguised, discusses or remarks on either the plot or what is happening on the stage. Their observations are direct comments on the action; not the oblique comments on life or some great moral or speculative topic which we get from Shakespeare's Jaques or Hamlet or Edmund, but something much more naïve, almost often a sort of incorporation into the dialogue of stage-directions. I have mentioned before in another connection[1] the commentary of Tiberio and Stephano in *The Duke of Milan*, Act I, scene i. These persons are part of the mechanics or stagecraft of the play, almost stage-properties, not real characters or agents at all: they are only there to provide information about what has preceded the action or about what is doing at the moment. To take another example, from *The Guardian*, Act II, scene i, of these commentaries which are found scattered throughout the plays: Calipso says to Iolante on the entrance of Laval,

> Is he not, madam,
> A monsieur in print? What garb was there! O rare!
> Then, how he wears his clothes! And the fashion of them!
> A main assurance that he is within
> All excellent: by this, wise ladies ever
> Make their conjectures.

Sometimes it would appear as if Massinger could not trust his audience to see what is going on before their very eyes. Thus in *The Maid of Honour*, Act I, scene i, after Bertoldo's exhortation to the King of Sicily to wage war on the Duchess of Sienna, some of the courtiers

[1] See above, p. 80.

98

who are standing round remark on what must have been obvious to the youngest groundling, providing that the actors performed adequately:

> *Adorni.* In his looks he seems
> To break ope Janus' temple.
> *Astutio.* How these younglings
> Take fire from him!
> *Adorni.* It works an alteration
> Upon the king.

Surely the audience could see the indecision on the King's face and hear the murmurs of assent from the warmongers. When Shakespeare makes Hamlet interject at the play scene: 'Begin, murderer. Pox! leave thy damnable faces and begin! Come—"the croaking raven doth bellow for revenge",' the comment is not to direct our attention to the grimaces of 'one Lucianus', but to manifest the impatience of Hamlet, himself the croaking raven bellowing for revenge.

Of course, the explanation is simple. Not only did Massinger distrust his audience, but he did not really trust the actors, in spite of his elaborate defence of the quality in *The Roman Actor*. As far as we know, and in spite of Hartley Coleridge's opinion to the contrary, he never acted himself.[1] That may in part account for the periodic and parenthetic syntax of his style,[2] which he admittedly did entrust to the actors but which, if he had once tried himself to put it across in the theatre, he would have realised made very heavy demands on their intelligence and skill. On the other hand, to a man of his pedantic and conscientious nature, it was of prime importance that what he had to say should reach the ears of the auditory without ambiguity (though as I have remarked, the elocutionary difficulties he created for his actors never seem to have occurred to him) and that what he made his actors do should not be missed or go by default on his part. Though naturally modest, he obviously took himself and his playwriting very seriously; and like all solemn people, he did not want what had cost him care and thought to lose its effect. There is nothing of Shakespeare's splendid plethora. Massinger is a dramatic economist: he takes strict account of every penny. His plays are works of deliberation, rather than inspiration. Everything, in his stagecraft as in his plotting, has been carefully worked out so that the moral aim can be unmistakably realised. Such a man, I feel, could never have entrusted the conveyance of his strong convictions and opinions (how strong I try to show in a later chapter[3]) to a company

---

[1] See above, pp. 10 and 51.   [2] See below, Chap. VI.   [3] Chap. V.

of actors, inexperienced boys and semi-literate men, without taking precautions, right down to these prudential minutiae of stagecraft which I have touched on, to make as sure as was humanly possible that the actors 'suited the action to the word, the word to the action' and the audience caught every hint and moral.

In addition to the precautionary comments on the action that I have just been considering, there are also, as I have implied, the moralistic comments—what Aristotle would include under the term of διάνοια. They were not by any means the peculiar province of the chorus in Greek tragedy: indeed Aristotle seems to have regarded διάνοια as rather an element in the dialogue and, he rather confusingly says, in the action.[1] In any case, commentary of this sort with a more or less tenuous or incidental connexion with the action is common in Elizabethan, Jacobean, and Caroline drama, sometimes assigned to persons whose function is that of commentator, otherwise given to any character as the occasion seemed to demand.[2] It goes without saying that such reflections, moral, religious, political, are of the utmost importance in Massinger. The dialogue is largely made up of them, overtly or obliquely. But for fairly obvious reasons, it will be better after this brief mention to reserve them for a fuller discussion in the chapter on his thought.[3]

If Massinger did not trust his actors or see the business of acting quite from the professional point of view, he was not blind to other very practical acting considerations. His casts are never very large, and all his plays seem to have been judiciously cast for a company of some sixteen or seventeen players, including four, or possibly five, who specialised in female impersonation; provided of course that some minor parts were doubled[4] and some of the attendants and servants were not required to speak.[5] The number of allusions made in the plays to the small stature of one or other of the women characters points, as Professor Cruickshank notes,[6] to Massinger's keeping an actual company in mind as he casted.[7] In a more general regard for the fact that boys played the female parts, Massinger may have sometimes conveniently disguised his women as boys (for example, Eugenia in *The Duke of Milan* and Maria in *The Bashful Lover*); but that suggestion can hardly be pressed, since he had inherited the woman-as-man disguise from many dramatic predecessors. On the

---

[1] *Poetics* (ed. Bywater), Chaps. 6 and 19.
[2] Cf. Webster's love of the *sententia*.   [3] Chap. V.
[4] A study of the MS. of *Believe As You List* will show how the playhouse book-keeper has arranged for certain parts to be doubled.
[5] There is an interesting essay on 'mutes' in *Those Nut-Cracking Elizabethans* by W. J. Lawrence, London, 1935.
[6] *Philip Massinger*, App. I.   [7] Cf. Shakespeare.

other hand, he certainly was remembering with a kindly thought an actual performer when he made the epilogue to *The Emperor of The East* an apology for the necessarily youthful actor who had to sustain the role of Theodosius:

> We have reason to be doubtful, whether he,
> On whom (forced to it from necessity)
> The maker did confer his emperor's part,
> Hath given you satisfaction, in his art
> Of action and delivery; 'tis sure truth,
> The burthen was too heavy for his youth
> To undergo:—but, in his will, we know,
> He was not wanting, and shall ever owe,
> With his, our service, if your favours deign
> To give him strength, hereafter to sustain
> A greater weight.[1]

He might just as appropriately have said a word in the proper place for the boys who had to act Beaumelle in *The Fatal Dowry*, Camiola in *The Maid of Honour*, Donusa in *The Renegado*, or Marcelia in *The Duke of Milan*, since his women are frequently complex, or at least anything but straightforward, and are not infrequently morally sophisticated or debased. There is one explicit reference to casting, within an actual play. This is, most suitably, in *The Roman Actor*, where, for some not obvious reason, Domitilla plays the part of Anaxarete in the masque of *Iphis and Anaxarete* in Act III, scene ii. It is explained that she is forced to do this in order to humble her. But, in point of fact, Massinger probably knew that the supply of actors for female parts would not allow him to do anything else.

Massinger does, however, consider the actors inasmuch as he probably distributes his histrionic opportunities among a proportionately larger number of his cast than do Fletcher and Beaumont. Certainly the number of characters, in addition to the protagonist or protagonists of the main plot, who are spot-lighted is remarkably high. Thus in *The Picture*, Mathias and Sophia are the principal characters with Ladislaus and Honoria coming close behind; but there are also what actors would call 'good' parts for Eubulus, the Polonius-like counsellor, Ubaldo and Ricardo, the wild courtiers, and Hilario, Sophia's servant. In *The Parliament of Love* nearly every actor has a good part; and, as far as acting opportunities go, there is little to choose between Bellisant, Leonora, Clarinda, and Lamira, among the women, and Clarindore, Cleremond, Montrose, Perigot, and Novall, among the men, while in addition the parts of Chamont

[1] Gifford, iii, p. 349.

and Dinant are not to be spurned. To take an earlier play: in *The Unnatural Combat*, while Malefort has by far the most important part, Theocrine, Montreville, Belgarde, and Malefort Junior share quite a lot of the limelight with him.

A passing reference must be made here to the frequent use Massinger makes of figures of speech drawn from the theatre. Such figures must, of course, drop naturally from the pen of any dramatist; but in Massinger they are particularly common. Nearly every play will furnish at least one example. In *Believe As You List*, Act III, scene i, Flaminius says,

> I am on the stage,
> And if now, in the scene imposed upon me,
> So full of change—nay, a mere labyrinth
> Of politic windings—I show not myself
> A Protean actor, varying every shape
> With the occasion, it will hardly poise
> The expectation.

The Roman Actor is, naturally enough, full of figures of speech and allusions to things theatrical. But so are many of the other plays which do not have the theatre itself as one of their main themes. There is quite an extended example in *The Parliament of Love*, Act IV, scene iii, where Dinant, the court physician, discusses with Chamont the best way of paying out Perigot and Novall who have been attempting to seduce their wives;

> *Dinant.* . . . I would your lordship
>   Could be a spectator.
> *Chamont.* It is that I aim at:
>   And might I but persuade you to dispense
>   A little with your candour, and consent
>   To make your house the stage, on which we'll act
>   A comic scene; in the pride of all their hopes,
>   We'll show these shallow fools sunk-eyed despair,
>   And triumph in their punishment.
> *Dinant.* My house,
>   Or whatsoever else is mine, shall serve
>   As properties to grace it.

Contemporary theatrical manners are described in *The City Madam*, Act I, scene ii, where among Anne Frugal's marriage demands of Sir Maurice Lacy are:

> A friend at court to place me at a masque;
> The private box ta'en up at a new play,
> For me and my retinue; a fresh habit,

Of fashion never seen before, to draw
The gallants' eyes, that sit on the stage, upon me.[1]

I have already alluded to Massinger's wide distribution of 'good' (in a histrionic sense) matter among his characters. The distribution of his dialogue has to be considered from another angle. In the passage I have already quoted from *The Maid of Honour*, Act I, scene i:

Adorni. In his looks he seems
    To break ope Janus' temple.
Astutio. How these younglings
    Take fire from him!
Adorni. It works an alteration
    Upon the king;

it will be noticed that what is said, though it could easily have been given to one man, is broken up between two speakers and three speeches. This is very typical of Massinger. It is part of his use of 'choral' commentaries. But also he seems to dislike to give longish speeches to minor characters when his principals are on the stage. Perhaps he felt that the speeches of his principals were themselves long enough and that a little variety could be introduced and the tempo quickened if the subsidiary dialogue were broken up. Or perhaps he merely liked to give the characters who were standing around something to say to keep them occupied. Whatever the reason, such passages are almost invariably fragmented between two or more speakers; very often, too, with one speaker running his speech grammatically on from the one before, as in *A New Way to Pay Old Debts*, Act I, scene iii, where the servants comment upon Lady Allworth's reaction to Wellborn's mentioning her 'late noble husband',

Order. How she starts!
Furnace. And hardly can keep finger from the eye,
    To hear him named.

Even when the passage is not of a directly commenting kind, Massinger seems to make it a rule to break it between his minors. Thus in Act II, scene i, of *The Bashful Lover*, in a passage very reminiscent of that in Act II, scene iv, of *Twelfth Night*, in which Viola speaks of her own woes as those of an imaginary sister, Matilda's servants (Beatrice, First Woman, and Second Woman) discuss with her the

---

[1] As some further examples of theatrical allusions or figures in Massinger, see *Guardian*, I. i (Gifford, iv, p. 137), and I. ii (G. iv, p. 148), *Believe As You List*, v. ii (622b), *A New Way*, IV. iii (G. iii, p. 578), *Parliament of Love*, III. iii (G. ii, p. 282), and *Fatal Dowry*, IV. iii (G. iii, p. 441).

disappearance of the page, Ascanio, who later turns out to be a girl disguised as a boy:

> *Beatrice.* An't please your excellence, I have observed him
> Waggishly witty; yet, sometimes, on the sudden,
> He would be very pensive; and then talk
> So feelingly of love, as if he had
> Tasted the bitter sweets of it.
> *First Wom.*   He would tell, too,
> A pretty tale of a sister, that had been
> Deceived by her sweetheart; and then, weeping, swear
> He wondered how men could be false.
> *Second Wom.*   And that
> When he was a knight, he'd be the ladies' champion,
> And travel o'er the world to kill such lovers
> As durst play false with their mistresses.

Undoubtedly all that is said could easily (and just as grammatically) have gone to one speaker. But from the point of view of stagecraft, or rather stage effect, it would have been less effective and a great deal slower in tempo. Nevertheless, the division is a somewhat artificial device when we examine it in the study, an attempt of an uncolloquial dramatist to be colloquial in a pseudo-conversational exchange.

For a similar reason Massinger feels that he has always to break up long harangues and passages of sustained rhetoric with interspersed comments or remarks by the standers-by, which have little dramatic and only a slightly choral function. Massinger loves an occasion for a set speech. But he rarely lets a character run on without a pause or rather a commenting interruption for more than about twenty-five lines. Sforza's speech before the Emperor Charles V in Act III, scene i, of *The Duke of Milan*, for example, is broken by interruptions into four speeches of about twenty-two lines each.[1] One of the longest speeches which occurs in the dialogue of any of Massinger's plays is the famous defence of his profession by Paris in Act I, scene iii, of *The Roman Actor*. It runs to 100 lines in all, but it is broken up into four sections of increasing length by such remarks as this:

> *Aretinus.* Are you on the stage
> You talk so boldly?
>
> *Sura.* There's spirit in this.

---

[1] Speeches in Massinger are rarely longer than this (though this is indeed long enough). Thus the speeches in the dialogue between Francisco and Marcelia earlier in the same play (II. i) seem long, but actually average about 16 lines.

Rusticus. He has put
    The consuls to their whisper.

Latinus. Well pleaded, on my life! I never saw him
    Act an orator's part before.

No doubt Paris was acting an orator's part in the high Roman fashion. Perhaps he also used the stylised gestures which 'developed through the centuries for the specific purpose of swaying all kinds of mixed audiences, many of whose members could not even understand everything they heard'.[1] But, as is clear from his regular practice, Massinger did not rely on the gripping power of an unbroken harangue. He felt compelled to introduce some relief or movement, even if only the movement of interjection, into the comparative immobility of his set speeches. His, as we saw, was a drama of words in any case: he had to give at least the illusion of movement by passing the words from mouth to mouth. The matter is important from the actor's point of view. It is the most difficult thing which an actor can be called on to do on the stage—not to be doing at all and yet to contrive to contribute something in and by silence.

The conclusion is, then, that the thought and care which Massinger, 'the stage-poet' as Sir Aston Cokaine aptly calls him,[2] expended on everything he did is amply evidenced in his stagecraft. Though he can hardly be said to have initiated any new developments, he practised the devices of his day, not haphazardly, but carefully and for the most part competently and skilfully, with respect to the particular kind of polite melodrama in vogue. Shakespeare and Fletcher may be more poetical; but more practical and painstaking they cannot be.

---

[1] B. L. Joseph, *How the Elizabethans Acted Shakespeare, Listener*, 5 Jan., 1950. Cf. Joseph, *Elizabethan Acting*, London, 1951.
[2] *Small Poems*, Epigrams I, 100. 'Epitaph on . . . Fletcher and . . . Massinger'.

Chapter Four

CHARACTERISATION

It is impossible to approach questions of Massinger's characterisation in the way in which Bradley approached Shakespeare's; for, as Coleridge, perhaps the pioneer in this kind of psychological criticism,[1] admitted, 'Massinger's characters have no character'.[2] Critics of the Bradley school looked for naturalness or 'convincingness' of character and went so far as to praise or condemn a work on this score alone, producing such statements as 'The permanent value of a play rests on its characterisation . . . For ultimate convincingness no play can rise above its characterisation.'[3] But it has become more and more recognised that this is certainly not the correct approach to most of our older drama, however proper it may be in respect of modern plays written under the influence of Tchekov. While the criterion of 'convincingness', of truth to life, might hold good for many plays from 1890 onwards and can even produce important results when applied to the exceptional work of Shakespeare,[4] it is definitely misleading when applied indiscriminately to all the dramatists of the Elizabethan and Jacobean period. Characters, after all, as Dr. Johnson seems to have recognised,[5] have no existence apart from the play in which they appear (unless as historical or legendary persons whose characters are already more or less laid down). They are counters moved by the playwright across the chequer-board of his design, beings whose reality is drawn from the action in which he uses them.

It has been demonstrated admirably and in detail by some modern scholars, notably Miss M. C. Bradbrook,[6] that the Elizabethan and Jacobean dramatists worked within a convention in which drama was grounded in action rather than in character, and that their characters largely conformed to a convention of types. Ben Jonson with his 'humours', which are variations on and developments from the

[1] Although, of course, there had been adumbrations and more than adumbrations in the work of Morgann, Whately, William Richardson, and even Johnson.
[2] *Lectures on Shakespeare and the Poets*, ed. Ashe, 1883, p. 405.
[3] G. P. Baker, *Dramatic Technique*, London, 1922.
[4] See, for example, J. I. M. Stewart, *Character and Motive in Shakespeare*, London, 1949.
[5] 'The truth is, that the spectators are always in their senses, and know, from the first act to the last, that the stage is only a stage, and that the players are only players' (*Preface to Shakespeare*, 1765). This awareness of the fundamental artificiality of the drama appears to be a definite hint in this direction.
[6] *Themes and Conventions of Elizabethan Tragedy*, Cambridge, 1935.

Plautine and Terentian categories in accordance with a seventeenth-century satirical purpose, and other practitioners of the comedy of 'humours' are only the more obvious exponents of type characterisation; much of the characterisation outside of the drama of humours also adheres to the type conventions. And the popularity from the last decade of the sixteenth century and earlier, a popularity which lasted for the best part of a century, of character sketches after the Theophrastan model by Overbury, Hall, Earle, and many others, shows that the categorisation of human types was more than a passing fashion. Characterisation by types was in fact a psychological simplification and a methodising of human nature that had a strong appeal for the Renaissance mind. It survived vigorously into the eighteenth century and was in tune with the strong formalising tendencies of that period. However, the increasing diversification of life on the one hand and the increasing awareness of its complexity on the other, have perhaps rendered the present age less ready to accept or to be interested in the neater methods of a simpler age.

But characterisation according to types was even more than a Renaissance habit of mind to the writers practising the drama of surprise, especially to those writing from about 1610 onwards, in whose work the surprise element is particularly prominent. This method of characterisation by types was forced upon them by the nature of the plays they were writing. A play is, after all, a 'narrow plot of ground' when compared, say, with the novel. It will only hold a certain amount of material, and when most of this material is, as in the drama of surprise, incident or action, there is little room left for a characterisation which is naturalistic or convincing. As Dryden said, 'The manners can never be evident where the surprises of fortune take up all the business of the stage, and where the poet is more in pain to tell you what happened to such a man than what he was.'[1]

It is to the drama of surprise that Massinger's plays belong. They belong to a convention where 'variety of incident . . . the romantic interest of situation . . . was aimed at'.[2] Naturally enough in such a drama, the characters tended to become, by necessity, mere agents and, by convenience, mere types. Jonson, who was not of course writing a drama of surprise, carried the method deliberately to an extreme from satiric motives; but it is seen in its normal working in the romantic drama of Beaumont and Fletcher where it has been adopted not consciously or deliberately as in Jonson but rather *faute*

---

[1] Preface to *Troilus and Cressida* from *Dramatic Essays by John Dryden*, 1679 (Everyman Edn. p. 136). [2] G. C. Macaulay, *Beaumont and Fletcher*, *CHEL*, VI, p. 110.

de mieux. In the plays of Beaumont and Fletcher the majority of the characters at least pretend to be real and three-dimensional, but in fact they are often no more than two-dimensional tokens or types. The love-lorn maiden and the romantic young man of Beaumont, the lustful monarch, the Plautine blunt soldier, the witty young gallant and his female partner, of Fletcher are no more real people than Jonson's labelled 'humours'. To say that they are not 'real' people, is not to suggest that they are unnatural, but rather that they have not humanity to spare, and that their minds are unlike the minds of Shakespeare's characters which, as Professor Dover Wilson has reminded us, appear 'to contain many thoughts over and above those which their creator permits the audience to overhear'.[1] They are merely adequate, possessing the low-relief of a frieze as compared with the roundness of Shakespeare's sculptures.

Massinger, however much he owed to Shakespeare in other ways, went mainly to Fletcher for his characterisation. He took over or modified many of the Fletcher types and added some of his own; and almost without exception he rang the changes upon the resulting group of types throughout his dramatic career.

There are, of course, certain corollaries to this proposition of Massinger's characterisation according to types. But I shall postpone a consideration of them until I have illustrated the proposition itself by references to certain of the actual characters. I shall divide them into common-type groups, recognising however that the classes are not self-contained and that some characters combine the features of more than one class.

★

As might be expected of plays which, like those of Fletcher, Shirley and other contemporaries, deal with the relationship of the sexes, with passionate and romantic intrigue, the most common emotion suffered (or perhaps enjoyed) by Massinger's characters is that of jealousy. Consequently the most common Massingerian type is the jealous husband or lover. It is not sufficient, however, to describe such characters simply as *jaloux*. They are more complex than that, and their jealousy is only one manifestation of a particular cast of mind. They are what Chelli describes as *faibles*: 'On peut dire que l'homme faible a été un sujet de prédilection chez Massinger'.[2] But this *faiblesse* is largely in respect of their relations with the opposite sex, since they are often competent men of affairs, like Sforza in *The Duke*

[1] J. Dover Wilson, *Titus Andronicus*, New Cambridge Shakespeare, Cambridge, 1948, Introduction, p. xxvi. [2] *Drame*, p. 270.

of Milan or Charalois in *The Fatal Dowry*, or warriors, like Mathias in *The Picture* or Leosthenes in *The Bondman*.

Their *faiblesse* is, in fact, precisely that of Othello, for they may be bracketed with him as representative of the commonest type of hero in the Elizabethan drama, the man of passion. In the drama, particularly the tragic drama, of our greatest age, as Professor Schücking has said, '. . . the extremely *passionate* individual is chosen for representation, the exhibition of unrestrained passion being the climax of Elizabethan tragedy'.[1] But Sforza, Mathias, Ladislaus, Leosthenes, and Charalois are pale shadows of the great Elizabethan baroque heroes, Othello, Macbeth, Tamburlaine, or Hieronimo. Sexual passion is almost their only dynamic; and, as exemplifying the blurring of the distinction between tragedy and romantic comedy which occurred in the drama of surprise, they appear not only in tragedies, as in *The Duke of Milan* and *The Fatal Dowry*, but also in the tragicomedies, as in *The Picture*, *The Bondman*, and *The Emperor of the East*.[2]

As men of great passion they are often extravagant in their statements about the object of their affection. Thus Sforza, probably the best representative of his type in Massinger, indulges in a typical extravagant outburst in Act I, scene iii, of *The Duke of Milan*:

> Such as are cloyed with those they have embraced,
> May think their wooing done: no night to me
> But is a bridal one, where Hymen lights
> His torches fresh and new; and those delights
> Which are not to be clothed in airy sounds,
> Enjoyed, beget desires as full of heat,
> And jovial fervour, as when first I tasted
> Her virgin fruit—Blest night! and be it numbered
> Amongst those happy ones, in which a blessing
> Was by the full consent of all the stars,
> Conferred upon all mankind.

And even in Act IV, scene iii, when he is at last convinced of Marcelia's adulterous intentions, he can still bestow hyperbolic praise upon her:

> I do believe, had angels sexes,
> The most would be such women and assume
> No other shape when they were to appear
> In their full glory.

---

[1] L. L. Schücking, *The Baroque Character of the Elizabethan Tragic Hero* (Annual Shakespeare Lecture of the British Academy, 1938), Proc. Brit. Acad., XXIV, London, 1938, p. 8.

[2] Though, of course, passionate figures outside tragedy had appeared earlier; for example, in *Measure for Measure*.

As in real life (and this is almost the only occasion that one has to use such a phrase about any of Massinger's characters), the *jaloux* is sometimes fundamentally unsure of himself. In *The Picture*, for example, we are confronted from the outset with a husband (Mathias) who so doubts himself that he can remind his wife that she is of superior lineage and who is conscious of the fact that he has not been able to maintain her in a style befitting her birth.

All these men are excessively uxorious or possessive, doting upon their wives to an almost insane degree, and in Theodosius in *The Emperor of the East* this passion rises to a pitch where he neglects his duties as a ruler. Even Sforza, a man of 'strong judgement', who has been a brave and courageous leader of his people, can be described by one of his courtiers in these terms:

> It is the duchess' birthday . . .
> In which the duke is not his own, but her's:
> Nay, every day, indeed, he is her creature,
> For never man so doted;—but to tell
> The tenth part of his fondness to a stranger,
> Would argue me of fiction.[1]

It is worth noting that in *The Picture* the two attributes, jealousy and uxoriousness, are divided between two characters: Mathias is jealous and Ladislaus is uxorious.

These heroes, in a parallelism to their passionate uxoriousness, tend to be credulous as regards the infidelity of their partners and will believe any absurd story, no matter who produces it. But in this respect Charalois in *The Fatal Dowry* is a notable exception and requires a long time and more than mere allegation to believe that Beaumelle is unfaithful to him. The reason is that in this play the normal situation in which a credulous husband accuses an innocent wife is laid aside, and Beaumelle, unlike Marcelia, Eudocia, Sophia, and Domitia,[2] really is guilty.

As men of passion, Massinger's protagonists are given to sudden and violent action. The murder of Marcelia by Sforza and the execution of Philargus by Domitian in *The Roman Actor* are typical samples of sudden and violent action taken by passionate men. Often indeed, as in the pseudo-judicial murder of Beaumelle in *The Fatal Dowry*, where Charalois forces her father to pronounce her doom in accordance with the laws of justice but in contradiction to the laws of nature, they act outrageously. I cannot, however, quite agree with Professor Cruickshank when he claims that the explanation is that

---

[1] *Duke of Milan*, I. i.
[2] Domitia is, however, at least guilty in intent, see below, p. 114.

'the faults which Massinger loves to portray and censure are such as show themselves in outrageous ways—such as anger, pride, impotence in the Latin sense, uxoriousness, and above all jealousy'.[1] It is rather that the drama of surprise in the Jacobean period, like the melodramatic Senecan drama in the Elizabethan, demanded such outrageous action, and, indeed, demanded characters whose nature was that they should so act. The jealousy and impetuosity of these characters is an outcome of their very natures, wayward and hectic, and it can be remarked that they are as prone to forgiveness (witness Domitian's forgiveness of his wife between Acts IV and V of *The Roman Actor*) or to repentance (witness Sforza's sudden repentance within a minute of murdering Marcelia) as sudden and violent as their actions.

The *jaloux* in Massinger is therefore fundamentally a man of too excessively passionate a nature, prone to violent action or revulsion, possessive and doting, and flamboyant in speech and gestures. He is, in fact, distantly related to Hamlet, or Lear, or Othello, or Macbeth, but he is drawn to a pattern and lacks the essential vitality of his great archetypes. Such characters are, as Chelli suggests, 'visiblement des natures inférieures, on dirait peut-être, des dégénérés,'[2] at best unstable persons and at worst a sort of manic-depressive like Domitian with an emotional graph that is jagged with departures from the norm. As Hazlitt says,

> His impassioned characters are like drunkards or madmen. Their conduct is extreme and outrageous, their motives unaccountable and weak; their misfortunes are without necessity, and their crimes without temptation, to ordinary apprehensions.[3]

It is only fair, however, to remark that Massinger fully realised the weakness of such characters and always arranged for an unfavourable impression of them to be left upon the minds of the audience: Sforza goes mad, Domitian dies a cowardly death, Leosthenes is humiliated in the Senate, and Mathias is mastered by his wife. They even recognise their own faults and pass judgement upon themselves. In Act V, scene i, of *The Bondman*, for example, Leosthenes says,

> 'Tis my fault:
> Distrust of others springs, Timagoras,
> From diffidence in ourselves: but I will strive
> To kill this monster, jealousy.

And Sforza, who has been described by Francisco as 'rash and

---

[1] *Philip Massinger*, p. 72. [2] *Drame*, p. 270.
[3] *Lectures on the Literature of the Age of Elizabeth*, Lecture IV Bohn Edn., 1897, p. 132.

violent',[1] perhaps sums up all these characters as well as himself when, with his dying breath, he says,

My whole life was a frenzy.

Charalois in *The Fatal Dowry* alone of all these men conveys, in spite of his rash action in murdering his wife, the impression of a nobility still greater than his weakness. He alone has had some real justification for his action, and, as he says when he lies fatally wounded, he

dies as he hath lived,
Still constant and unmoved: what's fallen upon me
Is by heaven's will, because I made myself
A judge in my own cause, without their warrant;
But He that lets me know thus much in death,
With all good men—forgive me.

There are no jealous heroines in Massinger. It might be possible to suggest that jealousy is part of the motive of Sophia's renunciation of chastity in *The Picture,* but closer examination will reveal that her motives are not so much jealousy as pride and resentment at her husband's supposed infidelity. The positive right of a woman to be jealous, along with certain other sexual rights, has rarely been recognised in our literature until comparatively modern times. However, although jealousy is not recognised as a feminine motive in Massinger, the woman of passion, as might be expected, does figure considerably in his plays.

His women operate as a rule in a more restricted sphere than his men. They do not, of course, have a profession as the men have. Their sphere of operations is rather the narrow domestic one of the presence-chamber and the boudoir than the wider world of affairs, and, naturally enough, most of them direct their attention and energies towards matters amorous. It is in this relation that we find the female counterpart of the man of passion. She is the passionate woman who falls in love at first sight and sets about seducing the object of her affection as soon as possible. Donusa is suddenly struck with love for Vitelli in *The Bondman,* Domitia with Paris in *The Roman Actor,* Aurelia with Bertoldo in *The Maid of Honour,* and Iolante with Laval in *The Guardian.* Even in *A Very Woman,* written by Fletcher and revised by Massinger, there is the case of Almira who, having rejected the Prince of Tarent as a suitor, falls suddenly in love with him when he is disguised as a slave. Another variety of the same type of woman in violent love, though usually not a character of the first importance, is the woman pursuer of a man who may

---

[1] *The Duke of Milan,* IV. ii.

or may not be a former lover that has rejected her. In *The Bondman*, Statilia is pursuing Leosthenes; in *The Great Duke of Florence*, Fiorinda Duchess of Urbin is pursuing Sanazarro; and in *The Guardian*, Mirtilla is pursuing Adorio. These young women are usually very enterprising and persistent. They remind us of Fletcher's Celia, Oriana, and Alinda.

Massinger's passionate women may be maids, as are Donusa and Aurelia, or matrons, as are Domitia and Iolante. The fact of marriage makes little difference to their passion, and indeed, such is the equivocal morality of his plays (a morality they share with almost all the plays of the late Jacobean convention), there is often a special interest taken in the fact that they are married.

Unlike the man of passion, the woman of passion is most definitely not a *faible*. She is both positive and resourceful, often operating as a *fons et origo* of the action, and she tends to be more active (in a particular sense) than the more passive male who is her goal. This is particularly noticeable in those scenes of sexual tension so favoured by Massinger which usually take the form of a passage in which a man is tempted by a woman. It is indeed quite remarkable how often in the plays there is an episode in which a woman of this type woos, tempts, or seduces her male opposite. Aurelia in *The Maid of Honour*, like her namesake in *The Prophetess*,[1] falls suddenly in love; but Massinger, perhaps in deference to her rank as Duchess of Sienna, takes her and Bertoldo off-stage before the temptation begins.[2] Donusa tempts and seduces the reluctant Vitelli in Act II, scene iv, of *The Renegado*, and in Act IV, scene ii, of *The Roman Actor*, Domitia attempts to overcome the scruples of the actor, Paris. When Paris pretends not to understand what Domitia means she has to come straight to the point:

> Come, you would put on
> A wilful ignorance, and not understand
> What 'tis we point at. Must we in plain language,
> Against the decent modesty of our sex,
> Say that we love thee, love thee to enjoy thee;
> Or that in our desires thou art preferred,
> And Caesar but thy second?

And when he still demurs, this blunt lady goes on,

> You are coy,
> Expecting I should court you. Let mean ladies
> Use prayers and entreaties to their creatures

[1] By Fletcher and Massinger. There is also a wanton Duchess Aurelia in Marston's *The Malcontent* (acted 1601).   [2] See Chap. III, p. 96.

> To rise up instruments to serve their pleasures;
> But for Augusta so to lose herself,
> That holds command o'er Caesar and the world,
> Were poverty of spirit. Thou must—thou shalt:
> The violence of my passion knows no mean,
> And in my punishments, and my rewards,
> I'll use no moderation.

Such scenes of outspoken female sensuality are typical of the behaviour of the woman of passion, and one cannot avoid the suspicion that such characters are introduced into the plays merely to provide an opportunity for such scenes.

Honoria in *The Picture* is a temptress for rather different reasons from her sisters in Massinger's other plays. She attempts in Act III, scene v, to seduce Mathias; but she intends to deny him once he has succumbed and is all the time acting from an ambitious pride to be thought 'the only wonder of the age', an emotion which is passionate in degree with her but not sexual in origin.

The Fatal Dowry, in this as in other respects already noted, presents a difference in the matter of the temptress's guilt. Domitia and Iolante, not to mention Honoria, all of whom are married, do not reach the point of committing adultery in deed, whatever their guilty intention may have been.[1] Beaumelle, however, is in fact an adulteress and continues after marriage the intrigue into which she had seduced Novall Junior before. Though Massinger (and Field, but principally Massinger) have done something to sway our sympathy to her, the nobility of the husband she wrongs makes her offence the greater. It should perhaps be added here that, despite the brevity of the speaking part assigned to her, Beaumelle stands out as one of the most three-dimensional of Massinger's women.

Though the passionate woman is the counterpart of the passionate man in Massinger, the latter is himself generally matched with the woman of virtue. She is the type of woman who appears in almost every one of the plays,[2] typical representatives being Cleora in *The Bondman*, Camiola in *The Maid of Honour*, Eudocia in *The Emperor of the East*, Sophia in *The Picture*, and Bellisant in *The Parliament of Love*. Phrases descriptive of her abound. She is constantly being called 'the only wonder of the age', a 'phoenix', 'unparalleled', ' rare', a 'better angel', 'the excellence of nature'. If she is unmarried she is 'a fair example for noble maids to imitate'; and if she is married, she is likened to 'chaste Penelope'.

---

[1] As Sforza says (*Duke of Milan*, IV. iii), echoing a Senecan sentiment, 'Intent . . . It does include all fact.'

[2] Notable exceptions being *The City Madam* and *The Roman Actor*.

While the woman of virtue is not usually passionate in the ordinary sense, her virtue is in itself often a passion, an idealistic passion. This virtue is, strangely enough, very self-conscious and self-expressive. As Chelli says, 'Si elle se contentait d'un ton un peu moins pompeux, de principes moins sonores, elle nous attacherait davantage'.[1] She is indeed for ever proclaiming her own virtue. For example, Cleora in Act V, scene iii, of *The Bondman* says,

> Since I had ability of speech,
> My tongue has been so much inured of truth,
> I know not how to lie.

And Marcelia, who is very fond of speaking about her 'unspotted honour', when she is accused by Sforza of infidelity and put under guard by him in Act IV, scene iii, of *The Duke of Milan*, does not hesitate to say,

> Which of my virtues,
> My labours, services, and cares to please you,
> For, to a man suspicious and unthankful,
> Without a blush I may be mine own trumpet,
> Invites this barbarous course?

These women are often their own panegyrists, and like the heroines of Fletcher, from whom they derive rather than from those of Beaumont, they show a surprising knowledge of the evils of the flesh which they are resisting so strenuously, and their speech is frequently (to our taste) immodest. When Shakespeare's heroines talk broadly, there can be no doubt that they are chaste women, however free of speech. No one, for example, could suspect the chastity of Beatrice. But there is in Massinger an unhealthy preoccupation with the more smutty side of sexual matters which comes out in the speech of even his chastest heroines, even when they are not trying to be witty or humorous. In fact, some of their remarks smack more of the water-closet or the four-ale bar than of the Court. Marcelia brawls with her sister-in-law and mother-in-law in the manner of a bawdy serving-wench; Honoria, who is as much a woman of virtue as a woman of passion, is extremely forthright in the way in which she attempts (or pretends to attempt) to seduce Mathias; and even Camiola, herself 'the Maid of Honour', is not entirely free from such obscenities in her dealings with the foolish Signor Sylli.

Moreover, the purest of Massinger's good women do not always act in accordance with their high pronouncements, and, being too much taken up with their own virtue, they seldom display much of

[1] *Drame*, p. 275.

the milk of human kindness. So it is that we find Camiola's unkind rejection of the foolish, but harmless, Sylli not in full accord with her character as a good woman, and we feel that the convenient way in which she finally ignores Bertoldo's vows of chastity and ransoms him in order to marry him, while it is a typical 'turn' of the drama of surprise, is a direct contradiction of her advertised virtue.

The virtue of these heroines is, as I have implied, largely concentrated on their chastity. The matrons are pre-eminently faithful: the virgins are resolute in defending their honour and proclaiming their purity. The matrons even insist on the chastity of moderation being practised within the marriage vows. Marcelia, for example, in Act III, scene iii, of *The Duke of Milan* says to her husband,

> Let us love temperately; things violent last not,
> And too much dotage rather argues folly
> Than true affection.

Usually these women are balanced against a jealous husband or lover who wrongly believes that they have been unfaithful. Thus in *The Bondman* Cleora is matched with Leosthenes, and in *The Duke of Milan* Marcelia with Sforza. Chastity and fidelity are confronted with jealousy or unjust suspicion. In plays with tragic endings jealousy in full measure is the motif. Part of Marcelia's tragedy is that she does not realise just how strong are the forces gathering against her nor how deep the jealousy which has been aroused in her husband. Imagining the situation to be less serious than it really is, she meets her husband's jealousy with an angry resentment that seals her own doom. Sometimes, however, Massinger's heroines are confronted merely with a degree of distrust, not amounting to a jealousy of the magnitude and force of Sforza's. This is usual in the comedies, and in them, the suspected ladies, unlike Desdemona, respond vigorously and angrily. Sophia in *The Picture* is the most notable example of a faithful and virtuous wife responding so angrily to her husband's suspicion as to renounce her chastity in a passage in Act III, scene vi, which cannot but strike us as melodramatic and unreal. It is to be noted that Sophia, in common with other of the virtuous heroines, notably Eudocia in *The Emperor of the East*, is not by any means without fault. Both she and Eudocia are proud and haughty women, but their chastity cannot be impugned.

Perhaps the most amazing example of the woman of virtue in Massinger is Bellisant in *The Parliament of Love*. In Act I, scene iv, she is advised by her guardian, Chamont, that in her situation she ought to marry in order to preserve her reputation. When she says that she does not want to marry yet, Chamont answers that she must

in the circumstances lead a retired life and not risk the keeping of
so much company. To this the proud young lady replies with this
surprising speech:

> What proof
> Should I give of my continence, if I lived
> Not seen, nor seeing any? Spartan Helen,
> Corinthian Lais, or Rome's Messaline,
> So mewed up, might have died as they were born,
> By lust untempted: no, it is the glory
> Of chastity to be tempted, tempted home too,
> The honour else is nothing! I would be
> The first example to convince for liars,
> Those poets, that with sharp and bitter rhymes
> Proclaim aloud, that chastity has no being,
> But in a cottage: and so confident
> I am in this to conquer, that I will
> Expose myself to all assaults; see masques,
> And hear bewitching sonnets; change discourse
> With one that, for experience, could teach Ovid
> To write a better way, his *Art of Love*:
> Feed high, and take and give free entertainment,
> Lend Cupid eyes, and new artillery,
> Deny his mother for a deity;
> Yet every burning shot he made at me,
> Meeting with my chaste thoughts, should lose their ardour;
> Which, when I have o'ercome, malicious men
> Must, to their shame, confess it's possible,
> For a young lady (some say fair), at court,
> To keep her virgin honour.

Chamont, presumably a very lenient guardian, gives way tamely:

> May you prosper
> In this great undertaking!

From the very outset this flirtatious project undermines our confidence in the young coquette's very vocal 'virtue'; and little that she
does later can restore it.

The important thing to notice is that a similarly unreal code,
adapted to the exigencies of the plot rather than to character, lies
behind many of the actions of Massinger's virtuous women so that
we find, for example, a devoted wife, on the slightest hint of un-
faithfulness on her husband's part, exclaiming, as Sophia does in
Act III, scene vi, of *The Picture*:

> Chastity,
> Thou only art a name, and I renounce thee!
> I am now a servant to voluptuousness.

We realise that this publicised virtue is a matter of plot-convenience, and indeed is often introduced merely to make possible the titillating spectacle of temptation.

Of course, there are some representatives of this type of heroine whose virtue is not entirely absorbed by chastity. Cleora in *The Bondman*, for example, has moral ideas that take in another ethical area. She is unique among Massinger's heroines in having a long speech expressing reflections on a theme which is strictly not dramatically relevant and which is really the unqualified opinion of the dramatist himself. This is the passage in Act I, scene iii, in which Cleora harangues the Senate on patriotism, a speech which had a very pointed reference to the affairs of England in 1623. Usually Massinger chooses a male character as his mouthpiece for such extra-dramatic matter as this; but by assigning it on this occasion to a woman he not only departs from his normal practice but suffuses the character of Cleora from the outset with a distinguishing colour. Her patriotic fervour gives a peculiar strength and confirmation to her general virtue, much as religious zeal strengthens and distinguishes that of Camiola in *The Maid of Honour*. In a similar way the virtue of Pulcheria, sister of the Emperor Theodosius in *The Emperor of the East*, is not, as it were, orbited by chastity, but is an abstract passion for the general good and a desire to govern wisely and well which provides the motif of the whole play.

As still other representatives of the wholly good heroine in Massinger there are women of a specially rarefied virtue. Such are Lidia in *The Great Duke of Florence* (praised by Professor Cruickshank) and Matilda in *The Bashful Lover* (as much praised by Chelli). To these I would add Theocrine in *The Unnatural Combat* and Paulina in *The Renegado*, at the same time remarking that the dead wife of Duke Cozimo of *The Great Duke of Florence* must have been another such woman. They remind us of Fletcher's Lucina, Evanthe, and Ordelia, so supranormal is the virtue with which Massinger has endowed them. But he has hardly given them any life. Their virtue is mechanical and automatic, not human and a matter of human choice. They are puppets, and, unlike most of Massinger's women, are mere passive functionaries in the plot. The very descriptions of them are remarkable. Matilda, for example, has such beauty that it continually provokes hyperbolic comment; she is divine, she is like the sun or brighter than a comet:

Her beams of beauty made the hill all fire.[1]

[1] *Bashful Lover*, III. ii.

In spite of the beauty of their bodies and of their souls, however, such actions as these women have to perform in give them little or no personality.

Where the woman of virtue is common in Massinger, the corresponding man of virtue is rare, at least in the leading role. I mean the man whose primary concern is the pursuit of a self-conscious virtue-ideal. The nearest Massinger comes to such a type is the virtuously Stoical (but tediously pessimistic) Antiochus, the hero of *Believe As You List*. In general, however, those of Massinger's men, who both fill leading roles and are meant to engage our sympathies, cannot be practising idealists, pure and simple, like his virtuously chaste women, in that they have other involvements. They have parts to play in the wider world of government and war: they have their professions to practise and their official duties to perform. And it is in these external spheres of action, rather than in the more domestic and unofficial domain,[1] that the masculine virtues in which Massinger is interested are to be found.

The heroes whom Massinger wishes us to admire have the public virtues of courage, sensitive honour, candour in word and deed, sense of duty, decision. The noblest of them are all, appropriately, soldiers —in effect, exponents of the knightly virtues. But in addition Massinger's heroes are men of definite competence in their station and office: if their ends are tragic, their *hamartia* is never official ineffectiveness. Thus Sforza is an efficient prince and an able and successful advocate with his sovereign, the Emperor Charles; and Leosthenes is not only a brave warrior but a master of the art of war.

But the good qualities in these characters can be defeated, temporarily or altogether, by passion, violence, and rashness. The overwhelming of virtue by such intemperance provides a tragic interest in *The Duke of Milan* and *The Fatal Dowry*. In plays such as *The Picture*, *The Renegado*, and *The Maid of Honour*, in which the principal male character emerges from the conflict of his good qualities with his passion, the interest lies precisely in the conflict.

Virtue in Massinger's other male characters, that is to say those not protagonists, is either that generalised goodness of such more or less colourless agents as Father Francisco in *The Renegado* or Paulinus in *The Emperor of the East*, or the purely professional merit of the wise and efficient Emperor Charles in *The Duke of Milan*, of the great leader Timoleon in *The Bondman*, of the skilful Surgeon in *The Emperor of the East*, or of the brave soldiers Romont and Pontalier in

---

[1] Male chastity provides only an incidental motif in the resistance (somewhat vacillating) of Mathias in *The Picture* and Vitelli in *The Renegado*.

The Fatal Dowry. Occasionally the virtuous male characters are assigned no real part in the action. They appear in the plays only to give expression to some point of view which Massinger cannot otherwise introduce. Thus Belgarde in *The Unnatural Combat* speaks for the despised ex-servicemen, and Eubulus in *The Emperor of the East* is the voice of criticism of the actions of Theodosius, and perhaps indirectly the voice of criticism of Charles I.[1]

Two characters, not protagonists, but still of great importance in the plot, are of interest while we are considering Massinger's good men, not because their virtue is out of the ordinary, though it is steadfast enough, but because their characters are unusually clearly defined and attractive. The first, Romont in *The Fatal Dowry*, is the truly honest Iago of the play put into the unenviable position of having to make known his suspicions regarding Beaumelle to Charalois, her husband and his friend; and the second is Adorni in *The Maid of Honour*, who is in love with Camiola and has the task of ransoming for her his rival Bertoldo. Both of them are men in awkward situations; and perhaps that is why Massinger has had to go to greater lengths than usual with him to explain their varied motives and emotions, with the result that in them at least he has created characters who remain in our memories.

Other minor male and female characters may be cleared out of the way at the same time, since, for the most part, they have no special features and are as much stage-properties as are tables and chairs. Servants, courtiers, ladies-in-waiting, messengers, pages, and other lesser mortals we expect to be no more than puppets. But there are also in Massinger 'property' kings and rulers, such as Charles VIII in *The Parliament of Love*, and noble relatives, such as Domitilla in *The Roman Actor*.

A few of the minor characters, however, some of them already referred to in other connections, are more clearly defined and tend to arrange themselves into type-groups. For example, the 'blunt soldier', familiar to us from Shakespeare's Faulconbridge, Enobarbus, and Hotspur, and Fletcher's Memnon and Leontius, appears in Belgarde in *The Unnatural Combat* and Pontalier in *The Fatal Dowry*, as well as in the more important roles of Timoleon in *The Bondman*, Romont in *The Fatal Dowry*, Pescara in *The Duke of Milan*, and Gonzago in *The Maid of Honour*. The romantic young lovers, reminiscent of Beaumont and Fletcher's Philaster and Euphrasia or Amintor and Aspatia or of Shakespeare's Lorenzo and Jessica, appear in Young Allworth and Meg Overreach in *A New Way to*

[1] See below, Chap. V, p. 199.

Pay Old Debts and Giovanni and Lidia in *The Great Duke of Florence*. The Polonius-like courtier figures in Eubulus in *The Picture* and Charomonte in *The Great Duke of Florence*. The spurned and revengeful woman who is pursuing her lover is represented by Maria/Ascanio in *The Bashful Lover* and Eugenia in *The Duke of Milan*, and the spurned woman who in disguise has become the servant of her lover's new mistress, by Statilia in *The Bondman* and Beaupré in *The Parliament of Love*. Other types that appear frequently in the plays are: the worldly young man, an active or a reformed rake, such as Adorio in *The Guardian*; the wild courtier, such as Ubaldo and Ricardo in *The Picture*, and Novall and Perigot in *The Parliament of Love*, all corresponding more or less to Fletcher's wits and gallants (Don John, Mirabel, Valentine, Monsieur Thomas), generous and good-hearted and profligate as much from fashion as from vice; the older man of the world, such as Durazzo in *The Guardian*; and the doting lover, such as Hortensio (a minor character, though a major agent) in *The Bashful Lover* and Caldoro in *The Guardian*.

One could go on grouping and re-grouping the minor characters into types under such headings as temperament, circumstances, or even professions; but this would avail us nothing since it is obvious, on the barest reading of the plays, that these characters are just extracted from convenient pigeon-holes.

It is perhaps more interesting to note some types altogether missing from Massinger's list. In view of his own devotion to the theatre and his faith in its moral benefits, it is remarkable that he has no characters that can be regarded as satirical of the puritan opposition. Again, the clergy of any persuasion are, if not unrepresented, rare. Parson Willdo in *A New Way to Pay Old Debts* is hardly on the stage before he is off again, and the same applies to Father Paulo, the *deus ex machina* of *The Maid of Honour*. Much more important is Father Francisco, the Jesuit in *The Renegado*, whose surprisingly sympathetic presentation I shall consider in another chapter and connection. But he is the only cleric of any consequence in a Massinger play. Another notable fact is that there are no really old people, men or women, far less dotards. Nor are there any children. Massinger has a few quite young men and women just past their adolescence. But for the most part his men and women—Wellborn and Lady Allworth in *A New Way to Pay Old Debts* spring to mind immediately—are not merely fully adult but past their first youth. They are in their thirties and forties.

So far I have said nothing of the characters on whom so much of Massinger's reputation is founded, the criminal types, those who are positively evil as distinct from those who are merely weak and over-come by temptation. The chief examples are, of course, Sir Giles Overreach in *A New Way to Pay Old Debts*, Luke Frugal in *The City Madam*, Malefort in *The Unnatural Combat*, and, perhaps, Domitian in *The Roman Actor* (though he partakes more of the characteristics of the man of passion than of the straight criminal), with, on a much lower plane of effectiveness, Flaminius in *Believe As You List*, Francisco in *The Duke of Milan*, Marrall in *A New Way to Pay Old Debts*, and Montreville in *The Unnatural Combat*. All of them, the greater crim-inals and the less, represent slightly different aspects of evil. Over-reach is a ruthless man with an abnormal, inhuman power complex. Luke Frugal is a scheming and self-seeking hypocrite. Francisco is a vindictive and plotting coward. Malefort is the villain hero, not without an impressive strength and even nobility. And Domitian is the despot, sinning, but also sinned against. While they could not be interchanged from play to play as many of the good characters could, there is much that is common to the make-up of them all. They are all positively and consistently evil and all instigate evil actions. They all have, with the exception of Malefort, natures as single-minded as Massinger's good characters, but turned inside-out so to speak so that like Milton's Satan they have made evil their good. They are not the feeble butts of fortune or the helpless victims of an irresistible passion. They are well aware of what they are doing and can give reasons adequate, in their estimation, for their wicked-ness. They have, again with Malefort as an exception and possibly this time Domitian as a partial exception, no mitigating character-istics, any more than Iago or Edmund. They are brought to book by the counter-measures or parallel machinations of others, arousing in us no sympathy and only repulsion and detestation. And all in the end are dismissed or disposed of with punishments which, if sometimes light enough, are always poetically just.

They do, however, vary somewhat within that broader uniformity; and so, although I shall have to glance at them again in connection with the morality-play aspect of Massinger's characterisation, a brief consideration of some of the principals is appropriate here.

Sir Giles Overreach is by far the most famous of Massinger's characters; indeed, except some of Shakespeare's, there is probably no character in the drama of the period so well known and none that has been represented so often on the English stage. While part of this fame is certainly due to the remarkable performances given by Kean and later actors (including several in America) and to the histrionic chances the role offers to those actor-managers who for so long dominated our theatres, there is a *largeness*, an almost portentous enormity, about him which overwhelms the reader or spectator and silences criticism. As Hazlitt says:

> . . . he has strong, robust points about him that repel the impertinence of censure, and he sometimes succeeds in making us stagger in our opinion of his conduct, by throwing off any idle doubts or scruples that might hang upon it in his own mind, 'like dew-drops from the lion's mane'. His steadiness of purpose scarcely stands in need of support from the common sanctions of morality, which he intrepidly breaks through, and he almost conquers our prejudices by the consistent and intrepid manner in which he braves them.[1]

Hazlitt's lengthy and masterly description of Sir Giles has never been surpassed, and it is doubtful if it ever will be. He sees him as,

> . . . a character of obdurate self-will, without fanciful notions or natural affections; one who has no regard to the feelings of others, and who professes an equal disregard to their opinions. He minds nothing but his own ends, and takes the shortest and surest way to them. His understanding is clear sighted and his passions strong-nerved. Sir Giles is no flincher and no hypocrite; and he gains almost as much by the hardihood with which he avows his impudent and sordid designs as others do by their caution in concealing them. He is the demon of selfishness personified; and carves out his way to the objects of his unprincipled avarice and ambition with an arm of steel, that strikes but does not feel the blow it inflicts.[2]

But Hazlitt perhaps over-emphasises the element of avarice in Sir Giles's nature. He is not a conventional miser as is Philargus in *The Roman Actor* or even Shylock or Barabas. He is not niggardly or mean. He is indeed lavish and ostentatious and lives in princely style. As Furnace says in Act II, scene iii:

> To have a usurer that starves himself,
> And wears a cloak of one and twenty years
> On a suit of fourteen groats, bought of the hangman,
> To grow rich, and then purchase, is too common:
> But this sir Giles feeds high, keeps many servants,
> Who must at his command do any outrage;
> Rich in his habit, vast in his expenses;
> Yet he to admiration still increases
> In wealth and lordships.

Sir Giles's lust is not for money in itself but for power; and this last

---

[1] *New Writings by William Hazlitt, Second Series*, collected by P. P. Howe, London 1927, pp. 119-120.   [2] Op. cit., p. 120.

concentrates itself in an ambitious snobbery so tremendous as to shoot beyond the ridiculous:

> All my ambition is to have my daughter
> Right honourable, which my lord can make her:
> And might I live to dance upon my knee
> A young lord Lovell, born by her unto you,
> I write *nil ultra* to my proudest hopes.[1]

The snobbery of Overreach is almost his only understandably human motive, and it is thrown all the more into an incongruous but striking relief by the absolute inhumanity of the rest of his nature. A desire for his daughter's advancement which can make him urge her to let herself be debauched in order to catch Lord Lovell as a husband is actuated by nothing remotely resembling kindness or parental affection. It is all part and parcel of his colossal selfishness. He is in fact, as Hazlitt says, 'the demon of selfishness personified'. We do not, and cannot, have any feeling for him save an awful detestation and disgusted revulsion. It would seem that Massinger has deliberately tried to let no spark of pity kindle in our minds. The contrast with Shakespeare's Shylock, to whom Sir Giles bears a distinct resemblance, is illuminating. Though Shakespeare has sometimes been condemned for the treatment meted out to Shylock, it has only been by those who failed to realise that their resentment was Shakespeare's intention and could only be aroused by some indignity done to dignity. This indignity to Shylock swings some at least of our sympathy over to him, and in so doing—in a sense—diminishes his stature. But at the same time, by making Shylock pitiable Shakespeare has drawn his superhuman malefactor back into the fold of a common humanity. Massinger in my opinion is more chargeable, morally and aesthetically, for keeping Overreach outside of it. He is a monster, undoubtedly impressive, but as lacking as Count Cenci in the 'senses, affections, passions' of even sinful humanity. As he is led away to Bedlam, only one voice can be heard in pity for him: 'O my dear father!'[2] exclaims the daughter he had used as a pawn. But this single phrase is not meant to release any pity in others and is inserted probably to give a little depth to Margaret Overreach's otherwise thin enough part. Sir Giles loses nothing of his monstrous stature thereby. He, the first in literature to be called 'a bold, bad man',[3] never cringes. Like Iago he ends as he begins. But there is this vital difference. *A New Way to Pay Old Debts*, though not nominally a tragedy, is really an example of Aristotle's third

---

[1] iv. i. But see *King Henry VIII*, ii. ii. 44.   [2] v. i.   [3] iv. i.

category of unsatisfactory tragic plots—'an extremely bad man . . . falling from happiness into misery. Such a story,' Aristotle goes on, 'may arouse the human feeling in us, but it will not move us to either pity or fear; pity is occasioned by undeserved misfortune, and fear by that of one like ourselves; so that there will be nothing either piteous or fear-inspiring in the situation.'[1] The 'human feeling' in question is merely a moral satisfaction at poetic justice. On the other hand, important as Iago is and morally satisfied as we may be at his downfall, the play is not his tragedy and our fear and pity are respectively roused and discharged for beings 'like ourselves'. Similarly in *King Lear*, Goneril, Regan, and Edmund do not provide the tragic or impair the pity and fear.

> Dumb yearnings, hidden appetites are ours,
> And they must have their food,

says Wordsworth.[2] So long as the serious drama provides an outlet for our emotions of pity and fear, the monstrosity or inhumanity of a character below the level of the protagonist causes no discomfort. There is, however, this very kind of discomfort in *A New Way to Pay Old Debts*. For nothing can alter the fact that Overreach is the protagonist—the very cynosure and focus of the play. Undoubtedly in his magnificent self-sufficiency and self-consistency he bestrides his narrow world like a colossus. Sane (if sane at any time he can be called) and unremittingly resolute, or mad and unflinchingly unrepentant, he is overwhelmingly impressive.

To move from Sir Giles Overreach to Luke Frugal in *The City Madam* is to descend. Luke has the same heartlessness and lack of feeling for others, but is not drawn on anything like the same impressive scale, and compared with the superhuman and Machiavellian Overreach he appears a petty and mean trickster. It is difficult to know just what gives this impression of meanness since he has many passages of magnificent rhetoric, equal to any given to Overreach; but I suggest that it is caused by two attributes which are lacking in the character of Sir Giles—avarice and hypocrisy. Avarice can sometimes be dignified when it is grandly and imaginatively expressed, as by Barabas in *The Jew of Malta* or even by Sir Epicure Mammon in *The Alchemist*. But, however much Massinger has tried, by means of high-flown rhetoric, as in the soliloquy at the opening of Act III, scene iii, to elevate the avarice of Luke into something tremendous, he does not really succeed in making it

---

[1] *Aristotle on the Art of Poetry*, a Revised Text by I. Bywater, p. 35.
[2] *The Prelude*, Book 5, lines 506–507.

more than the greed of a mean wretch. And this ignobility is doubled by an accompanying base hypocrisy. In short, Luke Frugal is despicable, whereas Overreach is hateful. Professor Cruickshank says that 'Luke in *The City Madam* is perhaps the most skilfully drawn example of a development of character'.[1] This comment is doubtful since all the elements in Luke's character are present from the very beginning of the play, though by his hypocrisy he presents an aspect other than the authentic one. The process in the play is a revelation of character, not a development. He is, in fact, an example of that type of character in sixteenth-seventeenth-century drama who conceals his true nature by a behaviour and speech which make him seem the very opposite of what he really is.[2] Massinger, I feel, has handled him somewhat clumsily, in that he has dropped too few indications of Luke's real nature early in the play. So when his true nature does become apparent, we feel less the wonder proper to the drama of surprise than bewilderment at being misled. The opening of the play would lead us to believe that Luke is the innocent and wronged defender of the down-trodden, the unworthily-treated dependant of his extortionate brother, Sir John, when in reality the very reverse is the case. It is perhaps this play that led Arthur Symons to remark that 'the good or bad person at the end of a play is not always the good or bad person of the beginning'.[3]

Malefort in *The Unnatural Combat*, the most tortured and complex of all Massinger's characters, is more worthy to be placed alongside Overreach. Like Sir Giles, who may have been suggested to Massinger by the infamous Sir Giles Mompesson,[4] Malefort has perhaps an historical prototype in Francesco Cenci. But Malefort's villainy is very different from that of either Overreach or Luke Frugal. Both of these villains are completely single-minded. Not so Malefort. He is a man of mystery through the greater part of the play. It appears eventually that the (at first) unexplained enmity to him of his own son, an enmity the more mysterious because of the high respect and general esteem which Malefort enjoys, is due to Malefort's having poisoned his first wife, the mother of his son, before the action of the play begins in order to be free to marry the lady he had stolen from Montreville. During the action of the play he kills his son, not in error or by accident, but remorselessly and in open combat, to close

---

[1] *Philip Massinger*, p. 73.
[2] Cf. B. L. Joseph, *Elizabethan Acting*, London, 1951, p. 106.
[3] Mermaid Edn. of Massinger, Introd., p. xviii.
[4] For a discussion of the relationship between Overreach and Mompesson, see A. H. Cruickshank, *A New Way to Pay Old Debts*, Oxford, 1926.

the mouth of the sharer of his secret. But also during the action of
the play another protracted mystery is exposed: Malefort's strange
moods and dark hints adumbrate the incestuous passion he has
conceived for Theocrine, his daughter by his second marriage. The
disclosure does not come until the first scene of the fourth act. Until
then we have seen only the effects, not the cause. In spite of his
unnatural crimes, committed or intended, he is not a defiant con-
temner of the laws of God and man. He has a real nobility of bearing
and speech, however tortuous the ways into which his passions have
harried him. He repents in his own harsh way for what he has done:
he is horrified by what he may do, and it is his own resolve to make
this impossible by giving his daughter into the hands of the im-
placable but deceptive Montreville that brings about the deaths of
himself, his daughter, and his victim-victor Montreville. Overreach
is several times denounced as an atheist and so is Luke Frugal; Malefort, on the other hand, like Shakespeare's Claudius or Macbeth, has
religious visitings and compunctions. In Act I, scene i, when he is
wrongly accused of conspiring with his son to harry the state, he
prays thus, very much in character:

> Thou searcher of men's hearts,
> And sure defender of the innocent,
> (My other crying sins—awhile not looked on)
> If I in this am guilty, strike me dead.

And as he dies, he recognises to the full his sin:

> Can any penance expiate my guilt,
> Or can repentance save me?

It is the conflict in him, the war in his members, which makes
Malefort so interesting. Other characters in Massinger also endure
conflict; but in none is the struggle so intense or convincing. If
his state of soul is pathological, it is nevertheless, not like the portentous Overreach's, or, for that matter, like Shelley's Cenci,
inhuman.

In depicting Malefort's conflict Massinger has added many subtle
touches of psychological truth. His interest in his daughter is perhaps aroused by memory of his dead wife. As he says in Act II,
scene iii, in extravagantly passionate terms that remind one of
Sforza's in The Duke of Milan,

> looking on the daughter,
> I feast myself in the imagination
> Of those sweet pleasures, and allowed delights,

> I tasted from the mother, who still lives
> In this her perfect model; for she had
> Such smooth and high-arched brows, such sparkling eyes,
> Whose every glance stored Cupid's empty quiver,
> Such ruby lips,—and such a lovely bloom,
> Disdaining all adulterate aids of art,
> Kept a perpetual spring upon her face,
> As Death himself lamented, being forced
> To blast it with his paleness.

The first awakening of his passion for his daughter is fraught with misgiving:

> I nourish strange thoughts, which I would
> Most willingly destroy.[1]

The direct revelation of his incestuous passion in the soliloquy at the beginning of Act IV, scene i, shows his mind desperately resisting temptation, and although, as Gifford pointed out,[2] the passage is a near-translation from Ovid,[3] Massinger presumably selected it because it expresses so admirably Malefort's dilemma. Right triumphs and he resolves to send his daughter away, but his resolution falters on seeing her.

> I
> Have reason to discern the better way,
> And yet pursue the worse![4]

he cries, and the torment of his soul carries us as sympathetically with him as when the red-handed Macbeth and his fierce wife are startled by the knocking on the gate. That, I think, is the key to the greatness of the character of Malefort. For once Massinger has created a hero, and a villain hero at that, who succeeds in gaining our sympathy. He has taken a dignified criminal, and, by endowing him with the passion of a Sforza, the doting nature of a Theodosius, and the vacillation and moral awareness of a Vitelli or a Mathias, has made a dark, but human, creature more in the style of Webster or Ford than of Beaumont and Fletcher.

Domitian in *The Roman Actor* I have already discussed as a man of passion. His villainy is of a more conventional kind and is drawn from Massinger's historical source.[5] He is a despot of the cruel and lustful type, akin to Fletcher's Valentinian, Antigonus, and Frederick, but for all his evil and his killing of human beings, as he killed flies, 'for sport', he is closer to Sforza, Theodosius, and even Mathias, than to Overreach or Malefort.

[1] III. iii. [2] i, p. 191, footnote. [3] *Metam.*, IX, 456.
[4] IV. i.
[5] See the introduction by W. L. Sandidge to his edition of the play (Princeton Studies in English, 4), Princeton, 1929.

The other bad men in Massinger are in varying degrees less important in the plays in which they figure. The two most villainous are the long-term hypocrites, Francisco in *The Duke of Milan* and Montreville in *The Unnatural Combat*. They belong to the revenger type which had so many avatars, particularly in the Seneca-derived thrillers of the fifteen-nineties and the sixteen-hundreds. In the earlier examples, the bloodiest methods and the direst catastrophes were offered and no questions as to the propriety of revenge asked or suggested. In *Hamlet* the delay in effecting revenge, which delay was at least as old as *The Spanish Tragedy* and probably the *Ur-Hamlet*, was made the more profoundly interesting and moving by being mainly due to the operation of unconscious moral scruples and moral disgust in the mind of the character on whom the 'duty' of revenge had fallen. The Prince of Denmark is by proverbial testimony very much the protagonist of *Hamlet*. That is to say, the revenger is still the principal. But in the seventeenth century, though plays with revengers as protagonists—protagonists with whose violent taking of the law into their own hands our approval is assumed—were written according to the older recipe, two changes became apparent. The one is the moral proscription of the revenger, as for example in Tourneur's *The Atheist's Tragedy*, in *The Revenger's Tragedy* (perhaps also by Tourneur), and, in so far as they contain a revenge motif, Webster's *The Duchess of Malfi* and *The White Devil*. Webster's pair likewise illustrate the other change I have alluded to, the removal of the revenge motif as a foreground interest and so the reduction of the revenger to a role less than that of a protagonist. Such was the variety of revenge play taken over by Massinger and such the diminished stature of his revengers.

Other evil agents in Massinger are: Marrall, who in *A New Way to Pay Old Debts* is the jackal or inferior devil to Overreach; Flaminius, who, similarly, is the obedient instrument of the Roman state in the persecution of Antiochus in *Believe As You List*; and, if he may be mentioned here, Novall Junior, the seminal shadow of Rowe's Lothario, who, in *The Fatal Dowry*, is not much more than a worthless and rakish tempter. There are no such criminal women in Massinger as Fletcher's Lelia, Brunhalt, and Hippolyta (though the last two admittedly appear in plays in which he had at least a revising hand) or Webster's Vittoria. But he has a number of immoral women, such as Corisca in *The Bondman*,[1] in minor capacities of an allegedly comic nature.

[1] Corisca is paralleled closely by Borachia in *A Very Woman*, by Fletcher, revised by Massinger.

Massinger's so-called 'comic' personages are scarcely worth consideration as characters. Certainly they cannot be compared with the nimble and sprightly creatures of Fletcher's plays, or even with the more solid and heavily satirical ones of Jonson's. They are mostly crude clowns and coarse buffoons—a few type-grotesques excepted—and, even more than with similar characters in Shakespeare, one cannot understand how the courtly principals could tolerate their presence on the same stage. It is perhaps significant that in Massinger's most courtly play, his only romantic comedy, *The Great Duke of Florence*, there is a noticeable lack of the lower clowning. Hilario in *The Picture* is a feeble and somewhat nauseating jester if we consider him as an attempt at a Feste or a Touchstone. Signor Sylli in *The Maid of Honour* is a pale shadow of Jonson's Sir Amorous La Foole. We can hardly bring ourselves to laugh at Corisca in *The Bondman* who seduces her own stepson Asotus, or at the bawdy serving-wenches, Calipso in *The Guardian* or Bellapert in *The Fatal Dowry*, any more than we can laugh at Hircius and Spungius who are the foul-minded and foul-mouthed clowns (perhaps by Dekker) of *The Virgin Martyr*. Even the evil tempters of *The Picture*, Ricardo and Uberti, who are severely trounced and become objects of fun and ridicule, almost buffoons, leave an acrid taste in the mouth. When Massinger intends to be humorous he is heavy and lumbering, and the result is very often as obscene without being funny as anything in the drama of his age. Ben Jonson can be as grossly bawdy; but it is obvious that in him this is only the free-spoken robustness and realism of a satirical moralist and that it is caught up and integrated into the broad satirical-moral purpose. When Massinger tries something comparable, as in *A New Way to Pay Old Debts* and *The City Madam*, the results are singularly unsmiling. Elsewhere, as in the scene of the Projectors in *The Emperor of the East*,[1] he introduces scenes of alleged humour, without dramatic relevance but with a satirical-moral aim. On the other hand, in any play he may indulge in merely gratuitous bawdry. It is always stodgy and incapable of raising a laugh, except among those who think any reference whatever to sexual acts or organs are *ipso facto* funny. These heavy-handed and serious endeavours at humour seldom relax for a moment or encourage us to sit back and laugh at and with the minor follies of human nature or the humorous expansion of a richly comic soul. There are no Bottoms or Dogberrys in his world, no Sir Tobys or Sir Johns. But then a true humorist like Shakespeare loves his comic characters. Massinger

[1] I. ii.

does not. Only occasionally does a character make us laugh: the esurient Belgarde once or twice in *The Unnatural Combat*; the not-unsimilar Justice Greedy in *A New Way to Pay Old Debts* (a 'humour' in the Jonsonian sense, offering greater acting opportunities than a mere reading of the play would indicate); and the facetious Durazzo in *The Guardian*. Apart from these, the characters in Massinger who are meant to provide incidental humour are obscene and unfunny buffoons, while those more serious characters who are meant to be sprightly can be just as unfunny and obscene. The conclusion we must inevitably come to is that Massinger was a fundamentally serious man trying to be funny, and resorting, as is the regular resort of those who joke with difficulty, to the standby of the obscene.

★

This examination of Massinger's characterisation by types may, by reason of its detail in the consideration of some of the examples, give the impression that they are 'life-like' characters. Few indeed of them seem to me to attain to individuality, at least to the kind of individuality we find in life, however impressive they may sometimes be. Massinger was not interested in or capable of rendering the infinite varieties and unexpectednesses of life. He had none of what Keats called '*Negative Capability*, that is when a man is capable of being in uncertainties, mysteries, doubts, without any irritable reaching after fact and reason'.[1] He was a born moralist, shaping life to a predetermined end, and a born schematiser of human diversity into categories. Dominated by his moral purpose, he makes the dramatic conflicts in his plays an opposition of passional forces or points of view, not, like Shakespeare, who was intimately concerned with the manifold, various and incalculable soul of man, an opposition of characters or of man to the incalculable Fates. Moreover, whereas even the characters of Shakespeare are opposed (perhaps the less emphatic word 'related' would be better) in all sorts of obliquities, deflexions, and degrees in addition to the occasionally direct and face-to-face, Massinger's opposites are clear-cut and absolute. He begins from an abstract conception of the conflict and uses his schematised characters primarily as mouthpieces of the thesis and antithesis.

This is precisely, as I have already suggested, the method of the morality plays. In them, most obviously in the moralities written

---

[1] To George and Thomas Keats, December 22, 1817 (Colvin, *The Letters of John Keats*, London, 1925, p. 48).

before more secular and pedagogic morals supplied the themes, the conflict was always the same—the conflict of good and evil. That is, of course, a basic antagonism, for human life is polarised to good and evil. And it remains the one recurrent conflict in Massinger. It may be ethically accented, which much more often than not means for him the ethics governing the sexual relation with such aspects as fidelity and infidelity, moderation and excess, uxoriousness and jealousy. Or it may have a political accent, with justice and injustice, freedom and despotism, good government and bad, as the aspects; or else a religious one, with faith and unbelief, conversion and renegadism, self-dedication and worldliness. Within the one play there may be two or more manifestations, crossing or parallel, of the conflict of good and evil. Each of these is made as explicit as the conflict in the morality plays, by their careful presentation and development and usually also by a summarising moral tag or two. No spectator could ever be in doubt what lesson Massinger meant him to carry away—and he always did mean to lesson his audience. Poetic justice is always done: the forces of good prevail; the forces of evil are routed. In the comedies or tragi-comedies this is acceptable enough, if a little too ingenuous. In the tragedies 'the pity of it' is more than a little diminished by Massinger's generally reserving disastrous ends only for those whose *hamartia* is so grave as to forfeit most of our sympathy.[1]

Sometimes, as in *A New Way to Pay Old Debts* and *The City Madam*, the conflict is externalised: the two opposed forces are embodied in two opposed groups. In other plays, the conflict is in part at least internal: the clash is in the protagonist's mind and soul. In such cases it is always a war in the members—a conflict between the reason and the passions. As Chelli says, 'L'homme est susceptible, à peu près également, d'être entraîné par ses appétits et convaincu par la raison.'[2] The characters in whom an internal conflict wages, as for example Vitelli in *The Renegado*, Sforza in *The Duke of Milan*, and above all Malefort in *The Unnatural Combat*, are much the most individual and real of all Massinger's creatures. They have something more like the three-dimensional tension and reverberation of life, something more like its incalculability, as they argue with themselves for and against the dictates of passion or of reason, swaying and vacillating this way and that, strengthened and weakened by their friends and confidants. But always beside the internal conflict in the protagonist, there is an external conflict, or perhaps more than one, exemplified in some active human opposing force of evil.

[1] Paris, in *The Roman Actor*, is an exception.   [2] *Drame*, p. 268.

In *The Duke of Milan* it is the feebly-motivated figure of Francisco; in *The Unnatural Combat* it is Montreville; and in *The Picture* it is the courtiers, Ubaldo and Ricardo. The most obvious manifestation of this conflict, however, though of course not the only one and sometimes only episodic in a broader issue, is a manifestation which is also a characteristic feature of the moralities—a temptation scene. This is not surprising since in such scenes the internal and external conflicts tend to show themselves in their closest juxtaposition. There is indeed scarcely a play of Massinger's in which at least one such scene does not occur: Marrall tempting Wellborn and Overreach his own daughter in *A New Way to Pay Old Debts*; Donusa Vitelli in *The Renegado*; Honoria Mathias and the courtiers Sophia in *The Picture*; Francisco Marcelia in *The Duke of Milan*; and so on. A counterparted situation in which one character, like the Bonus Angelus of the moralities, confirms another character in the right way is also exemplified in Father Francisco's advice to Vitelli in *The Renegado*, in Pulcheria's admonitions to Theodosius in *The Emperor of the East*, in Eubulus's frank statements to Ladislaus in *The Picture*, and elsewhere.

The likeness of Massinger's characterisation to that of the moralities is especially clear in the two plays which come nearest to them in theme and development,[1] *A New Way to Pay Old Debts* and *The City Madam*. The characters here seem even more than usually drawn in blacks and whites. In *A New Way to Pay Old Debts* Overreach is Anti-Christ, the principle of evil personified; and he speaks of himself as a morality character might, but hardly as a real person would:

> I would be worldly wise; for the other wisdom,
> That does prescribe us a well-governed life,
> And to do right to others as ourselves,
> I value not an atom.[2]

His henchman Marrall is Accessory Wickedness, a minor devil; and his hanger-on Justice Greedy is the deadly sin of Gluttony, as conceived in allegorical art and literature for centuries. Similarly in *The City Madam*, Luke Frugal is Hypocrisy; Lady Frugal and her two daughters Anne and Mary respectively Pride, Extravagance, and Vanity[3]; Sir John Frugal Misrepresented Worth, and, in the latter part of the play, Justice Delayed. And without too much

---

[1] *The Virgin Martyr*, which bears closer resemblance to the moralities than any other play of its period, must be excluded as certainly not originating with Massinger.

[2] II. i.

[3] Mr. Plenty significantly observes after a display by the mother and daughters: 'I have read of a house of Pride, now I have found one' (II. ii).

ingenuity we could give names to most or all of the characters comparable to those in the moralities and interludes: New Guise, Now-a-days, Lust and Liking, Honest Recreation, Worldly Shame, Private Wealth, Sensual Appetite.

In Massinger's other plays the morality-like characterisation is perhaps less patent. But it is there, and from time to time, especially in passages in which the moral tension is greatest, the characters tend to shed their variations and disclose their theme in the sense that they become more like personified abstractions and less like complex individuals.

The use of ticket names, on which the possessors of them as in the moralities often pun, is another indication of Massinger's tendency in characterisation. Practically all the persons in *A New Way to Pay Old Debts* and *The City Madam* display ticket-names; and many others in other plays, generally but not always minor figures, are similarly labelled, as for example, Astutio, Signor Sylli, Malefort, Beaufort, Belgarde, Asotus, Philamour, Philargus, Eubulus.

Ben Jonson threw a side-glance at such characters in the exchange between Tattle and Mirth at the end of Act II of *The Staple of News* (1626):

> *Tattle.* . . . I would not give a rush for a Vice, that has not a wooden dagger to snap at everybody he meets.
>
> *Mirth.* That was the old way, gossip, when Iniquity came in like Hokos Pokos, in a juggler's jerkin, with fake skirts, like the knave of clubs; but now they are attired like men and women of the time, the vices male and female.

Massinger's virtues, as well as his vices, are indeed 'attired like men and women of the time'.

The mention of Ben Jonson suggests, as I have indicated before, a parallel nearer in time than the moralities, that of the comedy of 'humours'. In oft-quoted words Jonson defines a 'humour' in his conception:

> . . . thus far
> It may, by metaphor, apply itself
> Unto the general disposition:
> As when some one peculiar quality
> Doth so possess a man, that it doth draw
> All his affects, his spirits, and his powers,
> In their confluxions, all to run one way,
> This may be truly said to be a humour.[1]

Jonson had in mind a didactic-satirical comedy as a stage for the

---

[1] *Every Man Out of His Humour*, Induction.

remedial display of his 'humours', and the actions of his comedies were devised, not as generally in Massinger for the broad inculcation of one or at any rate only a few moral lessons, but to provide as many opportunities as possible for the display of as many 'humours' as possible. When Massinger aims at comic effects, he clearly has Ben Jonson as his master in 'humours'; but these occasions are comparatively rare. And it is important to recognise, as has not been done, that Massinger, whether consciously or not, was mainly a dramatist of serious 'humours'—characters operating in serious plays and not *pour rire*, who were conceived in the same insulating and simplifying way as Ben Jonson's and his own comic 'humours'.

★

Just because Massinger is more intent on directing his actions to a predetermined moral purpose than on 'imitating' life, he never gives his characters a chance to shape the plot. As Brander Matthews says, 'The plots are not the result of the characters, but the work of the playwright.'[1] Professor Cruickshank similarly recognises as 'Massinger's great fault [that] the characters do not develop the plot so much as adjust themselves to its requirements'[2]; and E. C. Morris 'cannot help feeling that the previously prepared outline of the plot was more keenly in his mind than the characters'.[3]

Since his plays are grounded in ideas rather than character, it is not surprising that, as I have already shown, he planned the actions that were to be the vehicles of the ideas very carefully. But he did not therefore *neglect* characterisation. That is not the trouble. On the contrary, he devoted a similar, and indeed, excessive, care to the planning of his characters. But thereby he prevented them from having anything but a very intermittent life. Coleridge wisely remarked that 'the characters (unlike Shakespeare's) do not have a life of their own. They are planned *each by itself*'.[4] They are hewn out of some unmalleable material, inserted into their appropriate niches in a prepared plot, and presented to us complete, instead of growing to life before our eyes, stepping down from their pedestals, and snatching control of the action.

It is this subordination of character to plot (the plot itself being subordinated to moral purpose) that is the root cause of our dissatisfaction with Massinger's characterisation. The improbabilities

---

[1] *Representative English Comedies*, vol. III, New York, 1914, p. 312.
[2] *A New Way to Pay Old Debts*, Introd., p. xvi.
[3] *On the Date and Composition of 'The Old Law'*, PMLA, XVII, 1902.
[4] *Miscell. Crit.*, (Raysor), p. 95.

inherent in the drama of surprise are immediately visited upon the characters, with the result that many of their actions are psychologically incredible. Shakespeare also handled plots involving improbabilities. That Portia's father left his heiress to be disposed of by an elaborate thimble-rigging; that King Lear was ready to divide his kingdom in accordance with oral protestations of love; that Othello proceeded from faith to suspicion, suspicion to assurance and assurance to murder without examining the principal witness for the defence; and that Hermione's existence was kept secret for sixteen years from Leontes—these are improbable. But Shakespeare had such an infallible and intuitive knowledge of the human heart that all the accompanying psychological reactions of the characters are convincing in themselves and make plausible the very improbabilities they enact—or make them not matter, which is just as good. But Massinger was left with surprise plots, far more dependent on surprise than those which Shakespeare normally used, and had not the necessary 'poetical Character',[1] as Keats called the gift, to create the illusion of life.

All this is not to say that characters must be consistent with common experience. Characters in plays seldom are, at least in the poetic and romantic drama. But we have a right to expect them to be self-consistent, even if their consistency is what Aristotle calls being 'consistently inconsistent'.[2] Massinger's characters, however, often are not—not so much the subsidiary characters who in fact are 'flat' and run all too true to type, as the principals. The plays are full of scenes in which the whole direction of a character is suddenly, violently, and for unlikely or inadequate reasons changed. Such abrupt and unexpected changes—lapses from virtue or loyalty, love suddenly supervening on indifference or hate or the converse, precipitate conversions, and hasty repentances—are of course common form in the two hours' traffic of the drama of surprise. But perhaps no dramatist of the time can show as many and as inadequately motivated as Massinger. This is probably what Coleridge meant when he said that in Massinger's characters there seems to be a 'lack of guiding point' and that we 'never know what they are about'.[3]

---

[1] To Richard Woodhouse, October 27, 1818 (Colvin, *Letters*, p. 184): 'As to the poetical Character (I mean that sort, of which, if I am anything, I am a member . . .) it is not itself—for it has no self—It is everything and nothing—It has no character—it enjoys light and shade; it lives in gusto, be it foul or fair, high or low, rich or poor, mean or elevated—It has as much delight in conceiving an Iago as an Imogen. What shocks the virtuous philosopher delights the chameleon poet. It does no harm from its relish of the dark side of things, any more than from its taste for the bright one, because they both end in speculation. A poet is the most unpoetical of anything in existence, because he has no Identity—he is continually in for and filling some other body.'

[2] *Art of Poetry* (Bywater), p. 193.   [3] *Miscell. Crit.* (Raysor), p. 95.

Occasionally, it must be admitted, Massinger can manage such changes very skilfully. In some of his best scenes, as Professor Cruick-shank says, the features are 'change of mood and vacillation of purpose, under the stress of temptation, or due to the conflict of contrary impulses',[1] as, for example, the vacillations of the love-sick Caldoro in Act I, scene i, of *The Guardian* under the abuse of Durazzo, or the subtle changes of mood in Vitelli between religious asceticism and surrender to his mistress throughout *The Renegado*. In admitting this, I cannot however entirely agree with Professor Cruickshank's assertion that Massinger 'sets himself at times to represent growth, or at any rate, change of character. Even Shakespeare seldom tries to do this.'[2] But, again to quote Professor Cruickshank, 'As a rule . . . the changes are too rapid.'[3] Moreover, they are too facile; characters suddenly change from inadequate reasons or on unconvincing evidence. Very often the trouble is that, apart from the exigencies of the surprise drama, Massinger in Professor Cruickshank's excellent phrase 'overvalued the persuasiveness of rhetoric'.[4] That is to say, a character is quickly talked by himself or herself or by another into an entirely different course. From the dozens of examples in the plays I would cite only the following: Lady Allworth's sudden change of attitude to Wellborn in Act I, scene iii, of *A New Way to Pay Old Debts* (all the more unconvincing because Wellborn's rhetoric is a whisper inaudible to the audience); the conversion of Donusa, whose thoughts had not that way tended, by Vitelli in Act IV, scene iii, of *The Renegado*; Aurelia's sudden succumbing to the love-pleas of Bertoldo in Act IV, scene iv, of *The Maid of Honour* and her equally sudden persuasion of herself to surrender him in Act V, scene ii; the devoted Sophia's ridiculous credulity in believing on the mere assertion of two complete strangers the infidelity of her husband in Act III, scene vi, of *The Picture* and her immediate self-persuasion in the same scene to abandon her chastity; and Adorio's inartfully managed change from indifference to love in Act II, scene iii, of *The Guardian* and Iolante's sudden lust for Laval in Act II, scene i, of the same play.

By a directly contrary improbability, Massinger is so shackled by his own plot that once or twice he deliberately refuses to let a character be persuaded by the patent truth and makes him impervious to rhetoric, as when Charalois in Act III, scene i, of *The Fatal Dowry* rejects Romont's well-substantiated allegations against Beaumelle, or when Eudocia in Act III, scene ii, of *The Emperor of the East*

[1] *Philip Massinger*, p. 74.   [2] Ibid., p. 73.   [3] Ibid., p. 74.
[4] Ibid., p. 76. There is an excellent chapter on this feature of the surprise drama in Professor Hardin Craig's *The Enchanted Glass*, Oxford, 1950.

rejects Pulcheria's wise counsels. For incredulity and credulity are equally useful to the dramatist of surprise. As Professor Cruickshank says, 'when people are soon persuaded, the play gets on',[1] and we could add that when the incredulous man is at last convinced the *anagnorisis* is the more overwhelming.

The psychological improbabilities which run all through Massinger's plays and which are not by any means confined to persuadability (or unpersuadability) are as much a convention of the melodrama of surprise as they are a consequence of his limitations in characterisation. Without the improbability of Honoria's stooping to seduce Mathias in *The Picture*, there would be no play at all and so no lesson taught. Grimaldi's reformation in *The Renegado* is not really a development of character, but it is necessary to accept this if we are to accept the play, and we do accept it, just as we accept as reasonable (if the acclaim accorded modern productions is anything to go by) Hermione's long period in hiding in *The Winter's Tale*. But less acceptable is the manipulated psychology that often goes with such scenes. It is difficult, for example, to accept as credible the passages in *The Bashful Lover* where Hortensio is so singularly, and conveniently, incurious about the wrong done to Ascanio by Alonzo. Ascanio, who is a girl disguised as a page, has asked Hortensio in Act II, scene ii, to avenge some unnamed wrong done by Alonzo should the two chance to meet in the battle. Hortensio has not enquired the nature of Alonzo's crime, yet when he meets him upon the field in the next scene he is perfectly prepared to slay him, and risk his own life in so doing, on the mere word of a youth, and, having overcome him in combat, is just as surprisingly prepared, again at Ascanio's request, to let him go free without the slightest hint of a question.

The fact is that there is a quickly reached limit of probability in the matter of surprise; or, to put it otherwise, dramatists who make surprise their chief aim can keep it up only by trespassing into more and more improbability, and their standards of probability are more and more impaired. But Massinger and his audience were not bothered by scruples on this score. He and they judged, not by real life, but by standards drawn from other plays of the same type, as the modern filmgoer judges films only by other films—from standards drawn from within the convention. They had agreed on a convention of dramatic entertainment in which improbable surprises were all part of the game. Renounce them and you renounce the whole convention.

[1] *Philip Massinger*, p. 74.

However, the net effect on a critical modern reader of Massinger's plays, a critic who looks at them from outside the convention, is that he tends to lose all faith in the characters; he cannot see any real individuality in them at all. They almost seem to be, in Caldoro's words in Act IV, scene i, of *The Guardian*,

> the balls of time, tossed to and fro,
> From the plough unto the throne and back again:
> Under the swing of destiny . . .

★

Professor Cruickshank's assertion, which I have quoted before, that Massinger 'sets himself at times to represent growth, or at any rate, change of character . . . even Shakespeare seldom tries to do this' claims for Massinger what probably never entered his head and could only have been made by one who had forgotten the development of such characters as Juliet, Richard II, Prince Hal/ Henry V, Antony, Hamlet, Lear, Macbeth, and Leontes. Massinger's characters are changeable enough. But they do not grow or develop, for they have no independent life. They are glove-puppets held in the grip of a rigid and purposeful puppet-master.

Their only voice is his voice. Except for a few of the grotesques, they all speak the same rhetoric. There is no differentiation of dialogue between the characters: commoners and kings, courtesans and queens, men and women, all speak alike, at the same high oratorical level. The dialogue is in consequence, despite the passions, seductions, conversions, treasons, crimes, and what not, curiously lifeless. It is never spontaneous or colloquial. It is all a sort of verbal emotion recollected in tranquillity—a post-emotional reconstruction of speech, intellectualised and devitalised phraseology in the mouths of lay figures. It is the uniform mannerism of the professional provider of speeches for all occasions.

Massinger was obviously a diligent student of rhetoric. I have already drawn attention[1] to the academic exercise which he introduces into Act III, scene ii, of *The Unnatural Combat* on the thesis that a servant's life is better than his master's, comparable to Milton's Latin exercises in prose and verse. Hence a frequent debate-like quality marks his dialogue. Professor E. C. Morris has noticed that the speeches of Francisco and Marcelia in Act II, scene i, and Act IV, scene ii, of *The Duke of Milan* are what 'two disinterested persons might use if they were debating the opposite sides of the question'.[2]

---

[1] See above, Chap. III, p. 85.   [2] Loc. cit., p. 31.

But he does not realise how pervasive this debating rhetoric is. Chelli comes nearer the whole truth when he says that Massinger's characters 'sont impregnés de raison, raisonnables, et même raisonneurs. Toute conversation avec eux prend le tournure d'un débat, et il faut leur rendre argument pour argument, si l'on ne veut pas se réduire au silence'.[1]

While the dialogue is never just on the bull's eye—never surprises and delights us with unexpected aptness—there are times when it is blatantly inappropriate. The following passage of verse rhetoric, for example, occurs in Act IV, scene ii, of *Believe As You List*:

> . . . I, as your better genius,
> Will lead you, from this place of horror, to
> A paradise of delight, to which compared
> Thessalian Tempe, or that garden, where
> Venus with her revived Adonis spend
> Their pleasant hours, and make from their embraces
> A perpetuity of happiness,
> Deserve not to be named. There, in an arbour,
> Of itself supported o'er a bubbling spring,
> With purple hyacinths and roses covered,
> We will enjoy the sweets of life; nor shall
> Arithmetic sum up the varieties of
> Our amorous dalliance. Our viands such,
> As not alone shall nourish appetite,
> But strengthen our performance. And, when called for,
> The choristers of the air shall give us music:
> And when we slumber, in a pleasant dream
> You shall behold the mountain of vexations
> Which you have heaped upon the Roman tyrants
> In your free resignation of your kingdom,
> And smile at their afflictions.

Taken from its context, the speech might be supposed to be that of a princess to her royal lover. But it is not. It is spoken by a courtesan of the lower sort to the exiled Antiochus. Again, the sophisticated pronouncement on chastity in Act I, scene iv, of *The Parliament of Love*[2] makes Bellisant say about herself what no woman, let alone Bellisant, would conceivably say about herself. Massinger put it into her mouth because he was determined to have it said somehow. Similarly, Sir Giles Overreach in Act IV, scene i, of *A New Way to Pay Old Debts*, as Sir Leslie Stephen pointed out,[3] has to outline his own character as only other people would think about him. 'It is a description of a wicked man from outside.'

---

[1] *Drame*, p. 274.   [2] See above, p. 117.   [3] *Hours in A Library*, ii, pp. 165–167.

Even when the point of view is true enough, Massinger makes his characters talk *about* what they feel rather than express their feelings. The emotion, passion, sentiment, or degree of feeling whatsoever never speaks itself. That is Massinger's great flaw in characterisation. It is true, in Professor Morris's words, that in his plays 'attention to details of plot killed spontaneity . . . besides trying to say what they feel, the characters are burdened with the plot',[1] but even had Massinger not had this didactic-moralistic bias, his rigidly critical attitude to life and somewhat stiff and unbending turn of mind would always have prevented him from relinquishing to his characters the right to speak for themselves.

[1] Loc. cit., p. 32.

Chapter Five

CRITICISM OF LIFE

Massinger himself was certainly aware of the moral purpose of his plays. He always speaks of his art in serious terms, if sometimes with conventionally modest self-depreciation. In the second, or 'Court', Prologue to *The Emperor of the East* he lays emphasis upon his 'grave matter'; and in the Dedicatory Epistle to *The Roman Actor* he writes:

> If the gravity and height of the subject distaste such as are only affected with jigs and ribaldry (as I presume it will), their condemnation of me and my poem, can no way offend me.[1]

He was struck, too, with the moral seriousness and propriety of the dramatic work of one or two of his contemporaries, as his commendatory verses on Shirley's *The Grateful Servant* show. He praised that play because there was in it,

> no believed defence
> To strengthen the bold Atheist's insolence;
> No obscene syllable, that may compel
> A blush from a chaste maid.[2]

That his work was imbued with a didactic purpose, that it was designed more to instruct than to delight, was recognised by his contemporaries. W. B. says in his commendatory poem on *The Duke of Milan*:

> Here may the puny wits themselves direct,
> Here may the wisest find what to affect,
> And kings may learn their proper dialect.[3]

But Massinger's own view of the purpose of his drama is best expressed in the vehement speech he puts into the mouth of Paris in *The Roman Actor*, Act I, scene iii, using an argument which had been brought to the defence of the stage against its detractors since long before Sidney[4]:

> If, to express a man sold to his lusts,
>   . . . can deserve reproof;
> Why are not all your golden principles,

---

[1] Gifford, ii, p. 329.   [2] Ibid., iv, p. 594.   [3] Ibid., i, p. cxlviii.
[4] As in William Bavand's translation, '*A Woorke of . . . Mantuanus touchynge the good orderynge of a common weale* (1559), Bk. V, chap. 8, and Lewis Wager's *Life and Repentance of Marie Magdalene* (pub. 1566, but written earlier). See also the pamphlets following

Writ down by grave philosophers to instruct us
To choose fair virtue for our guide, not pleasure,
Condemned unto the fire? . . .
              Or if desire of honour was the base
On which the building of the Roman empire
Was raised up to this height; if, to inflame
The noble youth with an ambitious heat
T'endure the frosts of danger, nay, of death,
To be thought worthy the triumphal wreath
By glorious undertakings, may deserve
Reward, or favour from the commonwealth;
Actors may put in for as large a share
As all the sects of the philosophers:
They with cold precepts (perhaps seldom read)
Deliver, what an honourable thing
The active virtue is: but does that fire
The blood, or swell the veins with emulation,
To be both good and great, equal to that
Which is presented on our theatres?
                        . . . But, 'tis urged
That we corrupt youth, and traduce superiors.
When do we bring a vice upon the stage
That does go off unpunished? Do we teach,
By the success of wicked undertakings,
Others to tread in their forbidden steps?
We show no arts of Lydian panderism,
Corinthian poisons, Persian flatteries,
But mulcted so in the conclusion, that
Even those spectators that were so inclined,
Go home changed men.

If the sins of great men are shown upon the stage, the fault lies in the great men, not in the actors; and indeed, Massinger implies that both the actors and the playwrights are to be praised for publishing to the world the 'secret crimes' of the great.

That Massinger endeavoured to carry out in practice this theory of the moral purpose of the drama is evident even in the most cursory reading of the plays; and it becomes the more evident the more closely they are examined. I have already indicated how his endeavour to point a moral controlled his plotting[1]; how his desire to

Gosson's *Schoole of Abuse* (1579) in particular Lodge's *Honest Excuses* (1579). Sidney's *Apology* was not published until 1595. Massinger undoubtedly got to know Heywood during the period, 1624–1626, when they were both writing for the Queen's Men, and the chief source for the above passage is Heywood's *Apology for Actors* (1612). Since *The Roman Actor* was written early in 1626, it seems likely that Massinger's ideas on the stage at this time are the product of direct conversation with Heywood.

[1] See Chap. II, p. 74.

impress his own opinions upon his audience affected his dialogue[1]; and how his moral attitude tended to make him draw his characters in blacks and whites.[2]

The plays are not, alas, intended as mere entertainments. In the first place, as I have already had occasion to remark, Massinger is the unswerving champion of poetic justice. It cannot be said of him, as Dr. Johnson said of Shakespeare, that 'he sacrifices virtue to convenience, and is so much more careful to please than to instruct that he seems to write without any moral purpose . . . he makes no just distribution of good or evil, nor is always careful to shew in the virtuous a disapprobation of the wicked; he carries his persons indifferently through right and wrong, and at the close dismisses them without further care, and leaves their examples to operate by chance'.[3] Whether this is true of Shakespeare is not my concern. But I quote it because the very opposite is so palpably true of Massinger. In him virtue triumphs with monotonous regularity over wickedness. That is why he is not capable of truly cathartic tragedy. Most of his tragic protagonists deserve their catastrophes. If they do not all without exception receive condign punishment[4] it is because there is a limit to what even a *Tendenzdramatiker* can do in making an imitation of life illustrate poetic justice. Besides, it may be very reasonably maintained that when Massinger sacrifices the innocent he gets a *quid pro quo* in a more impressive sanction for his moral lesson. It may be good that one good man or woman should die for the good of the moral. In any case, not tragedy but tragicomedy is Massinger's sphere of action. For, to adapt Miss Prism's words in *The Importance of Being Earnest*, 'The good end happily, and the bad unhappily. That is what Tragicomedy means.'

In the second place, each of Massinger's plays has a particular moral area and moves about a particular moral focus. The foci of the fifteen plays Massinger wrote unaided are: the parent-child relationship (*The Unnatural Combat*); jealousy and pride (*The Duke of Milan*); the antithesis of slavery and liberty (*The Bondman*); religious renegadism and conversion (*The Renegado*); the code of courtly love and its 'modern vices' (*The Parliament of Love*); the religious vows of chastity (*The Maid of Honour*); the effect of a lustful nature both upon the state and upon personal relationships (*The Roman Actor*); the moral problems of widowerhood (*The Great Duke of*

---

[1] See Chap. III, p. 93.   [2] See Chap. IV, pp. 131 ff.
[3] *Johnson on Shakespeare*, Preface, 1765, p. 21.
[4] e.g. Antiochus in *Believe As You List*, whose fate is left very vague. (Possibly because Massinger did not know the fate of Antiochus's modern prototype, Sebastian of Portugal.) We may also include in this class such men as Luke Frugal and Sir Giles Overreach.

Florence); the interaction of jealousy and uxoriousness (*The Picture*); the royal office (*The Emperor of the East*); adherence to principle in the face of temptation and torture (*Believe As You List*); hypocrisy and pride (*The City Madam*); wickedness deceived by trickery (*A New Way to Pay Old Debts*); fidelity and honour (*The Guardian*); and virtue endangered (*The Bashful Lover*).

In the third place each play has a specific main lesson which the action is designed to illustrate and drive home.[1] It is usually summed up in one or more moral tags or *pronunciamientos* towards the end of the play:

> May we make use of
> This great example, and learn from it, that
> There cannot be a want of power above,
> To punish murder, and unlawful love!
> > *The Unnatural Combat*

> . . . learn from this example. There's no trust
> In a foundation that is built on lust.
> > *The Duke of Milan*

> He that truly loved
> Should rather bring a sacrifice of service
> Than raze it [i.e. the goodness of his mistress] with the engines of suspicion.
> > *The Bondman*

> . . . we purpose,
> To give encouragement, by reward, to such
> As with their best nerves imitate that old goodness;
> And, with severe correction, to reform
> The modern vices.
> > *The Parliament of Love*

> . . . May she [i.e. Camiola] stand,
> To all posterity, a fair example
> For noble maids to imitate! Since to live
> In wealth and pleasure's common, but to part with
> Such poisoned baits is rare.
> > *The Maid of Honour*

> Good kings are mourned for after life; but ill
> And such as are governed only by their will,
> And not their reason, unlamented fall;
> No good man's tear shed at their funeral.
> > *The Roman Actor*

---

[1] Cf. E. C. Morris, *On the date and composition of 'The Old Law'*, PMLA, XVII, 1902, p. 27: 'There is clearly a didactic purpose'; and S. R. Gardiner, *The Political Element in Massinger*, Contemporary Review, xxviii, p. 495: 'The main intention of his work is moral.'

... to all married men, be this a caution
Which they should duly tender as their life,
Neither to dote too much, nor doubt a wife.

The Picture

May my story
Teach potentates humility, and instruct
Proud monarchs, tho' they govern human things,
A greater power does raise, or pull down, kings.

Believe As You List

... instruct
Our city dames, whom wealth makes proud, to move
In their own spheres; and willingly to confess,
In their habits, manners, and their highest port,
A distance 'twixt the city and the court.

The City Madam

Here is a precedent to teach wicked men,
That when they leave religion, and turn atheists,
Their own abilities leave them.

A New Way to Pay Old Debts

... virtue, in the end,
Is crowned with laurel.

The Bashful Lover

In one or two plays the main lesson is not crystallised in so many words; but it is just as unmistakable. Thus in *The Renegado* the lesson may be summed up as 'Trust in God, and do the right'; in *The Great Duke of Florence* as 'Deception does not pay'; in *The Emperor of the East* as 'If you are a ruler, do not let your passion sway your reason in the carrying-out of your divine office'; and in *The Guardian* as 'Honour and fidelity will always gain their reward'. In some plays there are one or more secondary lessons as well, which may be likewise provided with moral pointers or which, if not so tagged, are equally clearly indicated. Thus, a warning against uxoriousness is given in *The Duke of Milan*, *The Bondman*, *The Roman Actor*, and *The Emperor of the East*, as well as in *The Picture*; the duties of a wife and the obligation of a ruler to accept advice are stressed in *The Emperor of the East*; the reforming virtues of the drama are pointed out in *The Roman Actor* (though the example we are given of these virtues in action show them to be not nearly as efficacious as Massinger would have us believe); that devoted service to a lover will eventually be rewarded is a theme of *The Bondman*, *The Parliament of Love*, *The Great Duke of Florence*, *The Guardian*, and *The Bashful Lover*; that a sexual relationship outside the marriage bond is wrong and sinful is part of the lesson of *The Duke of Milan*, *The Bondman*, *The Renegado*, *The Parliament of Love*, *The Picture*, and *The Guardian*; and so on.

Finally, many of the speeches and much of the dialogue in every play are, as in Racine, in the nature of moral dialectic. Massinger's characters are largely given to moral pros and cons.[1] Besides their more integral moralising, there occur periodically, incidental moral comments on a great variety of issues, grave and important or more everyday and vernacular, such as remind us of the author of *The Rambler*.

What has just been said will need a little subsequent qualification in view of the fact that Massinger's purpose did not always show itself in an end-product which can be accepted as moral and *sans reproche* by modern standards.[2] But it must be emphasised that his own intention in all his works was moralistic; that the didactic ran all through it; that it is all carefully considered for edifying ends, rather than 'inspirational'; and that its content is intellectual-moral rather than emotional. As Chelli says, 'Les meilleures pièces de Massinger, lues isolément, nous frappent déjà comme étant chargées de pensée'.[3] The less good are no less 'chargées de pensée' of a predominantly ethical character. And it is only necessary for us to add the inability of Massinger to take a comic, or in fact neutral, view of life, his fundamental gravity and sense of responsibility, to arrive at that view of the plays which Swinburne expressed in his sonnet on the dramatist:

> . . . sad and wise,
> The spirit of thought that moved thy deeper lays.[4]

★

Varied as is Massinger's moral commentary on life, he concentrated on three main topics: (i) the man-woman relation, (ii) politics, and (iii) religion. Perhaps I may define them more precisely thus:

(i) The relation between man and woman in courtship and in marriage, in attraction and repulsion, in trust and suspicion; and the way in which this one-one relation affects the parties, especially the man, with respect to their intercourse with others, the world of affairs in which their lot is cast, and their spiritual life.

---

[1] Cf. Sir Leslie Stephen, *Hours in a Library*, ii, p. 154: 'Massinger is a man of much real feeling and extraordinary facility of utterance, who finds in his stories convenient occasions for indulging in elaborate didactic utterances upon moral topics.'
[2] See below, pp. 200–201.
[3] *Drame*, p. 307.   [4] *Philip Massinger*, 1882.

(ii) The place of man (or woman) in an ordered society; his political obligations as a ruler or as a subject and his political rights; and his duties as a Christian in the *civitas terrena*.

(iii) The relation of man to God and to an ethical best; and man's religious convictions as permeating and affecting his general conduct.

It may be noted that Massinger's trifocal ethics anticipate in a way Milton's championship of the 'three species of liberty which are essential to the happiness of social life—religious, domestic, and civil',[1] and it will be seen at once that these three topics are closely linked in a nexus of moral obligations—domestic, or (if the word may be used in the comprehensive sense) sexual, obligation, social obligation, and religious obligation, in that ascending order of importance, though not of frequency, in the Massinger canon—and that they are so interwoven as not to be entirely separated the one from the other. Thus, for example, it is impossible to discuss Massinger's idea of kingship in *The Emperor of the East* without at the same time considering how the sexual relation as operative in Theodosius's doting love for, and subsequent jealousy of, Eudocia affects the monarch's performance of his royal duties and without noting the integrated Christian view of life which involves the ruler no less than the ruled. Similarly in *The Bondman* the questions of man's spiritual as well as his physical freedom, of his moral obligations as well as his political rights, of the duties of a wise and just ruler, of the evils of a wicked plutocracy, and of the status of woman in the sexual relationship are all inextricably intertwined; and in *The Maid of Honour*, although religious interests dominate, concerned as the play is with such questions as chastity and the sanctity of holy vows, we also find varying degrees of emphasis laid upon such topics as the duty of a ruler to govern justly, honour in warfare, and that upwelling of passionate desire which can overwhelm justice and reason in a ruler. The triple bond of Massinger's thought comes into all his plays, with the balance adjusted delicately between them so that sometimes the first, sometimes the second, and sometimes the third strand predominates. Thus the sex-relationship is the central topic in *The Picture*, *The Duke of Milan*, and *The Parliament of Love*; the politics of kingship in *The Roman Actor* and *The Emperor of the East*; and religion in *The Renegado* and *The Maid of Honour*; but whatever the main concern of the three in a play, the other two are always more or less strongly underlined. Other topics undoubtedly crop up. Some of them are for their

[1] *Defensio Secunda.*

occasion of great prominence and importance, as for example the high moral value of the drama and the actor in *The Roman Actor*. Some with less emphasis in any one play are nevertheless recurrent in several, as, for example, society's treatment of the ex-soldier, patriotism, duelling, over-indulgence in gaudy raiment, drunkenness, and the demoralising effect of imprisonment. But these secondary topics are after all, when they are not the common subjects of Jacobean and Caroline dramatic satire, only aspects of the primary three.

It is remarkable how consistent Massinger is in the ruling ideas expressed throughout his career. The view of life expressed in *The Duke of Milan*, for example, is very similar to that he expressed twenty years later in *The Bashful Lover*, though in the latter play it is perhaps weakened by feebler subject matter. Certainly the plays of undivided authorship all belong to the last twenty years of Massinger's life, from his late thirties to his late fifties. But the consistency is not merely that of a man set in his ways by the coming of middle life. Massinger was naturally a methodical person; and it is as certain as such things can be, that from the first he consistently held a systematic, coherent, and almost dogmatic philosophy of life. It is indeed much more than a few working principles and a few beliefs strung tenuously together. On the contrary, it is a precise scale of values, a set of four-square principles of action, and an ordered system of clear ideas of right and wrong, which he himself had deliberately chosen, by which he consciously governed the operations of his judgement, and to which he gave considered expression in his plays. Though Chelli makes no real attempt to elaborate or define Massinger's philosophy, he would have agreed with what has just been said. 'À mesure que nous avançons dans la connaissance de son œuvre,' he said, 'certaines séries d'idées se dessinent, formant des systèmes dogmatiques.'[1]

The systematic nature of Massinger's thought does not, of course, make it any easier to outline it. He has left no treatise in which he has expounded his *credo*, and it goes without saying that it has to be extricated or deduced article by article from its bedding or matrix in what are primarily and principally plays.

Massinger's thought can be described broadly as at once realistic, reasonable, and idealistic. It is realistic in that it describes men as they are, or at least as a shrewd and peculiarly unsentimental observer of considerable experience has found them to be in the seventeenth century. This statement is not, in my opinion, at variance

[1] *Drame*, p. 307.

with what I have said on Massinger's defects and limitations in respect of lively characterisation. I am speaking here, not of his characterisation, but of his systematised conclusions on humanity, which make it possible to liken him to Dr. Johnson in *The Rambler*. Johnson himself was a masterly observer of and abstractor from life, though like Massinger he was not very good as a creator of character in action. In taking a balanced view of life Massinger compares more than favourably with most of his dramatic contemporaries. He does not overdo the knavery and folly like Jonson; he does not sentimentalise like Heywood and Dekker; he does not disrealise like Beaumont and Fletcher. Though Massinger's philosophy of life sees men pretty much as they are, it aspires

> . . . with severe correction, to reform
> The modern vices.[1]

Hence it is idealistic, assuming that there is an ideal of human betterment. And finally it is reasonable, in that the ideal it aspires to is not impossible of human attainment.

Like the methodical man he was, and like not a few who have set up as moral philosophers, Massinger starts with a simple, indeed an all-too-simple, notion of the make-up of man. It was drawn proximately from the Romans and ultimately from the Greeks, especially Aristotle, and the cultures of the hellenised East. According to it the 'passions' are part of the baser or animal side of man's nature, prone to make him choose a wrong course of action, if indeed they are not in themselves evil, and they may take possession of the 'will' which is in itself neither good nor bad, higher nor lower; while the higher and more spiritual side of man's nature is the 'reason', which distinguishes him from the beasts and whose almost divine function is to control the passions and lead man to will the right. This basic idea is given explicit expression frequently in the plays. In *The City Madam*, Act I, scene iii, the passions are described as 'rebels unto reason'. In *The Renegado*, Act I, scene i, they are called

> those tyrants which
> We arm against our better part, our reason.

The moral of *The Roman Actor*, given in Act V, scene ii, tells us that,

> Good kings are mourned for after life; but ill,
> And such as are governed only by their will,
> And not their reason, unlamented fall;
> No good man's tear shed at their funeral.

[1] *Parliament of Love*, v. i.

The idea of the conflict between the reason and the passions is admirably expressed by Romont in *The Fatal Dowry*, Act V, scene ii (a passage by Massinger), in these words:

> The glory got
> By overthrowing outward enemies,
> Since strength and fortune are main sharers in it,
> We cannot, but by pieces, call our own:
> But when we conquer our intestine foes,
> Our passions bred within us, and of those
> The most rebellious tyrant, powerful love,
> Our reason suffering us to like no longer
> Than the fair object, being good, deserves it,
> That's a true victory.[1]

There is another fundamental assumption in Massinger's ethics, that of man's free-will. His plays are built on choice: they do not merely show an occasional operation of choice, but they turn on men and women choosing and doing. That is scarcely surprising. For, though the metaphysical and theological discussion of free-will was as old as Plato's *Republic*, certainly all creative literature of the narrative and dramatic kinds was deliberately or instinctively libertarian. It never occurred to the classical dramatists, to the author of *Beowulf* or the mediaeval romances, to Dante, Boccaccio, or Chaucer, to Spenser or Shakespeare, to make their characters anything but free, however much Fate or Wyrd, Chance or the stars operated in the background. Or if it occurred to them as a speculation, it emphatically did not shape their imitations of life.

> Men at some time are masters of their fate:

says Cassius for Shakespeare the dramatist;

> The fault, dear Brutus, is not in our stars,
> But in ourselves, that we are underlings.[2]

And Edmund dismisses in his own terms a hypothesis that Shakespeare had so little use for:

> This is the excellent foppery of the world, that, when we are sick in fortune,—often the surfeit of our own behaviour,—we make guilty of our disasters the sun, the moon, and the stars: as if we were villains by necessity; fools by heavenly compulsion; knaves, thieves, and treachers, by spherical predominance; drunkards, liars, and adulterers, by an enforced obedience of planetary influence; and all that we are evil in,

---

[1] See Chap. IV for more on the conflict between the reason and the passions as it affects Massinger's characterisation. Much more on this whole subject will be found in Lily B. Campbell's *Shakespeare's Tragic Heroes: Slaves of Passion*, Cambridge, 1930.
[2] *Julius Caesar*, I. ii.

by a divine thrusting-on: an admirable evasion of whore-master man, to lay his goatish disposition to the charge of a star![1]

It is certain that Massinger was aware of the problem of reconciling God's foreknowledge with man's free will (the aspect of the general antithesis of liberty and necessity which had been most discussed from the Stoics to St. Augustine and from St. Augustine to Calvin). But he both ignored it in casual reference and built his plays on the choices expressed by his characters.[2]

★

What he calls Massinger's 'feminism' has been treated at some length by Chelli.[3] But writing as he did, in the period from 1907 to 1913, when questions of women's rights were very much in the air, he tended to exaggerate the importance of this feminism in the plays. After all, a country which looked back to the forty-five years of the reign of Queen Elizabeth as to a golden age, and in which there had been recently and still were many great and learned ladies like 'Sidney's sister, Pembroke's mother' and Donne's Countess of Bedford, could hardly be said to be unaware of the general competence of women and of their ability to rank with men in the moral and intellectual spheres. Such a degree of feminism as Massinger exhibits was not out-of-the-ordinary and would not have excited any surprise at the time. If Ben Jonson had what Dr. Johnson attributes to Milton, 'a Turkish contempt for women',[4] he manifested his own idiosyncrasy, not the age's. Shakespeare and Fletcher, Heywood, Webster, and Dekker, to name no others, as well as Massinger, could each be said to be, like Chaucer, 'wemenes friend'.

Certainly there are women in Massinger's plays who are every bit a match for the men in personality: the suddenly decisive and imperial Donusa in *The Renegado*, the high-spirited and independent Camiola in *The Maid of Honour*, or the patriotic and eloquent Cleora in *The Bondman*, and several others. It is Cleora who, when Timoleon

---

[1] *King Lear*, I. ii.
[2] It may be noted that, while problems of free-will and determinism were very much in the air during Massinger's lifetime, English ethical thought proper (as distinct from certain thinkers in the realm of revelational theology and certain extreme theologians who accepted predestination as an article of faith) did not start developing until the seventeenth century, and had hardly dared as yet to face the question squarely. Bacon's ethics in his *Advancement of Learning* (1605) are very lightly sketched, and Hobbes, in whose philosophy there was latent a certain amount of determinism, did not publish *The Leviathan* until 1651. See Sidgwick's *History of Ethics*, Chap. IV, for further information both on this point and on the decline of Aristotelianism in England.
[3] *Drame*, pp. 308 et seq.
[4] *The Life of Milton*.

has failed to infuse some warlike spirit into the cowardly and idly
rich Syracusans, rises to the occasion:

> If a virgin,
> Whose speech was ever yet ushered with fear;
> One knowing modesty and humble silence
> To be the choicest ornaments of our sex,
> In the presence of so many reverend men,
> Struck dumb with terror and astonishment,
> Presume to clothe her thought in vocal sounds
> Let her find pardon;

and upbraids the assembly to some purpose for its lack of honour
and lack of a love of liberty. Of course, not all Massinger's women
are, in the seventeenth-century rather than in the contemporary
sense, viragoes. He has women less dynamic and more gentle and
reserved, as for example, Lidia in *The Great Duke of Florence*, Matilda
in *The Bashful Lover*, and Theocrine in *The Unnatural Combat*. But his
feminism, if we are to call it that, is as apparent at the one end of his
gamut of women as at the other. He takes women seriously; he
presents them fairly (if, as I indicated when dealing with his characterisation, not very life-likely); he assigns to them an important
place in the forefront of his stage and in the development of his
actions; he gives them as rich an intellectual background, as much
power of argument, and as much eloquence as his men. Moreover,
his men all treat his women with outward respect, even if they have
to kill them; and his women, even the courtesans and seducers, are
dignified.

Massinger, however, does poke (rather ponderous) satirical fun at
the Englishwomen of his time. In *The Renegado*, Act I, scene ii, for
example, Donusa has asked Carazie, her eunuch, an English slave,
to describe the status of women in England. He replies:

> . . . women in England
> For the most part, live like queens. Your country ladies
> Have liberty to hawk, to hunt, to feast,
> To give free entertainment to all comers,
> To talk, to kiss; there's no such thing known there
> As an Italian girdle. Your city dame,
> Without leave, wears the breeches, has her husband
> At as much command as her prentice; and, if need be,
> Can make him cuckold by her father's copy.
>
> *Donusa.* But your court lady?
> *Carazie.* She, I assure you, madam,
> Knows nothing but her will; must be allowed
> Her footmen, her caroch, her ushers, pages,

Her doctor, chaplains; and, as I have heard,
They're grown of late so learned, that they maintain
A strange position, which their lords, with all
Their wit, cannot confute.
Donusa.   What's that, I prithee?
Carazie. Marry, that it is not only fit, but lawful,
Your madam there, her much rest and high feeding
Duly considered, should, to ease her husband,
Be allowed a private friend: they have drawn a bill
To this good purpose, and, the next assembly,
Doubt not to pass it.

Such a satirical passage as this, and the presentation in the same vein
of Lady Frugal and her daughters in *The City Madam*, do not, however, invalidate what I have said on Massinger's general attitude to
women and their importance. Some of them are merely coming in
for such comment and rebuke as he metes out to some men.

A married woman, in Massinger's view, has a wifely duty which is
not incompatible with her right as a free individual. This is an
obligation in the feudal sense, a duty to respect and love her husband,
to obey his familial injunctions, to be a faithful spouse, and to behave
towards her husband and others with the conduct of what I have
called 'the woman of virtue'.[1] But her mind is free, or, in the
Prayer-Book paradox, her wifely service is a perfect freedom. For
she owes such conduct as much to herself as to her husband—to the
categorical imperative of marriage. Her husband has a reciprocal
duty to her, to respect her independence of mind and spiritual
liberty, to honour and trust her integrity and virtue, to be himself
faithful and loving. He is not an absolute lord and master, and she
is anything but a shadow, echo, or chattel. Charalois in *The Fatal
Dowry*, for example, imagines that he is entitled to pass judgement
upon his wife's actions and meets his tragic end as a result. Mathias
in *The Picture* is brought severely to task by his wife for doubting her
fidelity. Marcelia in *The Duke of Milan* is a particularly interesting
case. She had trusted Sforza as she thought he had trusted her.
Their matrimonial contract has been one of mutual obligation as
between equal partners. When she thinks that he has sought her
death, she exclaims,

Sforza is false,
False to Marcelia![2]

And when later she learns that a (highly improbable and purely
surprise-melodrama) consideration for her honour had prompted his

[1] See above, Chap. IV.   [2] II. i.

order for her execution in the event of his own death, she indignantly expostulates:

> But that my lord, my Sforza, should esteem
> My life fit only as a page, to wait on
> The various course of his uncertain fortunes;
> Or cherish in himself that sensual hope,
> In death to know me as a wife, afflicts me;
> Nor does his envy less deserve mine anger,
> Which though, such is my love, I would not nourish,
> Will slack the ardour that I had to see him
> Return in safety.[1]

As revealing of Massinger's sense of a woman's right to be herself is Marcelia's question in Act IV, scene ii:

> Was I born
> To observe his humours? or, because he dotes
> Must I run mad?

Just because she adheres so uncompromisingly and, as the event turns out, too rashly to the wifely conviction of her right to object to Sforza's jealousy and will not let her love as a wife govern her pride as a woman, she herself precipitates the violent moment in which the wrought-up Sforza stabs her.

> Oh! I have fooled myself
> Into my grave,[2]

she cries, in a phrase that contains a world of Massingerian meaning. She recognises herself as having contributed to the tragedy. But though she dies, it is Sforza who will be the more severely punished for his more serious lack of trust; and Marcelia goes on from the last quotation to say:

> I only grieve for that
> Which, when you know you've slain an innocent,
> You needs must suffer.

The punishment which falls on Sforza is that which falls on nearly all Massinger's jealous protagonists. Jealousy is a crime against the marriage bond and against reason: it is punished by a loss of reason. Sforza goes mad, and when, in Act V, scene ii, he himself lies poisoned by the revengeful Francisco and dying, he recognises in a last flash of sanity what his crime—not against Francisco for the wrong done before the play opens to his sister, but against his own wife—has been. To his mother's asking him how he feels, he replies,

> Like one
> That learns to know in death what punishment
> Waits on the breach of faith.

[1] III. iii.   [2] IV. iii.

155

This interaction between the sexes on a footing of equality, this mutual obligation of trust and respect is demanded not only from married couples in Massinger's plays. Though the husband-wife relation figures more prominently, in no less than eight of them, the obligation is recognised as being just as strong between unmarried couples, betrothed or lovers, such as Donusa and Vitelli in *The Renegado*, Camiola and Bertoldo in *The Maid of Honour*, and Cleora and Leosthenes in *The Bondman*. Leosthenes, to take an example of a lover who betrays this trust, is so madly jealous that he is eventually rejected by his mistress. As Cleora herself says in Act IV, scene iii:

> A greater injury cannot be offered
> To innocent chastity, than unjust suspicion.

He is supplanted by Marullo/Pisander whose virtue and knightly service as a lover have been proved by his refusing to injure Cleora when she was a captive and at his mercy. In Act V, scene iii, in which both Leosthenes and Marullo plead in open court for Cleora's hand in marriage, Leosthenes loses his temper and again displays his jealous nature. When it comes to Marullo's turn to speak, he says, in refutation of Leosthenes and in sentiments that square perfectly with Massinger's own *ars amatoria*:

> I dare rise up,
> And tell this gay man to his teeth, I never
> Durst doubt her constancy, that, like a rock,
> Beats off temptations, as that mocks the fury
> Of the proud waves; nor, from my jealous fears,
> Question that goodness to which, as an altar
> Of all perfection, he that truly loved
> Should rather bring a sacrifice of service,
> Than raze it with the engines of suspicion:
> Of which, when he can wash an Ethiop white,
> Leosthenes may hope to free himself;
> But till then, never.

Thus, before ever he has revealed his identity as a prince in disguise and not a slave, or disclosed the fact that Leosthenes is already in a sense pre-contracted to Statilia, Marullo has shown himself as worthy of that full obligation of trust which marriage will bring.

Two things should be remarked here. The first is that, except Heywood, none of the sixteenth- or seventeenth-century dramatists so frequently brings the marriage-relationship into the front and middle of his plays. And the second is that Massinger recognised to the full the third of the Prayer-Book's 'causes for which Matrimonie was ordeined', namely, 'for the mutuall societie, helpe, and comfort that the one ought to have of the other, both in prosperitie and adversitie', but does not explicitly or implicitly show any interest in the first, 'for the procreation of children to bee brought up in the feare and nurture of the Lord, and praise of God'.[1] The concentration on the husband-wife relation and the neglect of the family is highly significant.[2]

So far I have been considering the mutual obligation of men and women in marriage and in love and the jealousy or infidelity which disrupts it. All this is the affair only of the two people involved; and breaches of the contract are visited directly and limitedly upon the heads of the contracted parties. But there are situations of great interest to Massinger in which a particular kind of infringement of the man-woman or husband-wife relationship occurs—an infringement which opens horizons far beyond the walls of the private apartments. These are situations in which doting fondness or uxoriousness (of which, to be sure, jealousy is a frequent accompaniment or obverse manifestation) is the core. For, while such uxoriousness makes the doting partner demand too much from the other and can easily pass into a lack of trust that may threaten or even destroy a union, it can also, when the husband is a ruler, disrupt the state. The ruler has a social obligation which, in the Massingerian scheme of things, is higher than the amatory, sexual, or matrimonial, and his devotion to a woman should not take from his duty as a prince. For Massinger any kind of excess was bad; and uxoriousness, besides being excessive, was both a negation of the doter's individuality and a sin of presumption which placed the loved one above common mortality and social obligation.

Massinger shows his interest in such situations in the following plays: *The Emperor of the East, The Picture, The Roman Actor,* and *The Duke of Milan.* It is in the first two that he is most explicit.

The Picture contains in Act I, scene ii, a detailed representation of the state of affairs in a court in which a ruler (Ladislaus) dotes on his wife (Honoria). As the courtier Ubaldo says,

> At this very instant,
> When both his life and crown are at the stake,
> He only studies her content, and when
> She's pleased to show herself, music and masques
> Are with all care and cost provided for her.

And the rest of the scene is almost entirely taken up with a demonstration of Ladislaus's infatuation and with the objections of the wise

[1] I quote these passages from a Prayer-Book of 1630.
[2] But see Chap. I, p. 46.

157

and out-spoken Eubulus. The latter is so outspoken that he can use parabolically the legend of Ninus and Semiramis in expostulation with the king and can address him thus:

> I have no suit to you, nor can you grant one,
> Having no power: you are like me, a subject,
> Her more than serene majesty being present,
> And I must tell you, 'tis ill manners in you,
> Having deposed yourself, to keep your hat on,
> And not stand bare, as we do, being no king,
> But a fellow-subject with us. Gentlemen-ushers,
> It does belong your place, see it reformed;
> He has given away his crown, and cannot challenge
> The privilege of his bonnet.

In the end of the play Ladislaus is lessoned in the putting of his regal duties above his spousal and in the recognition that there must be measure even in love; and Honoria, who is self-willed and exigent, learns the proper sphere of a wife's authority and influence and the impropriety of her husband's aberration.

In *The Emperor of the East,* on the contrary, Massinger makes the young Empress Eudocia refuse the illegitimate exercise, even in a good cause but one outside her sphere, of a power over her husband which his fondness has put in her hands. She replies thus to Pulcheria, the Emperor's managing elder sister, who has been urging her to use her 'saving counsels' as a wife to curb her husband's prodigality:

> Do you think
> Such arrogance, or usurpation rather,
> Of what is proper and peculiar
> To every private husband, and much more
> To him, an emperor, can rank with the obedience
> And duty of a wife? . . . 'cause he loves me
> With a kind impotence, must I tyrannize
> Over his weakness, or abuse the strength
> With which he arms me, to his wrong? or, like
> A prostituted creature, merchandize
> Our mutual delight for hire, or to
> Serve mine own sordid ends?[1]

As in *The Picture,* the ruler, in this case the Emperor Theodosius II, comes to a realisation of how he has transgressed in fondness and neglected his high office. It is possible that under a Byzantine story Massinger was cautiously mirroring the situation, as he saw it from

[1] III. ii.

a distance, at the court of Charles I, whose prodigality and uxoriousness were not unmarked by his more serious-minded subjects.

To sum up what I have so far said as regards the married relationship in Massinger's plays: there is in this relationship a reciprocal obligation; a wife must serve and be faithful to her husband; a husband must trust and honour his wife. But, since a duty to society is higher than the sexual obligation, and the passions must be controlled by reason, a man must not dote upon his wife to the detriment of his capacity for conducting his affairs or performing his social duties, and a wife must know her place and not presume to impose her will upon her husband's in the conduct of affairs.

As regards the sexual act itself Massinger has quite a lot to say. In fact, none of his contemporaries has more; and some of what he says is extremely broad, not to say obscene. But one has to distinguish here between what Massinger permits his men- and women-of-the-world to say, often for so-called 'comic' purposes, and what he puts into their mouths or the mouths of other more appropriate characters in order to express his own proper sentiments. These sentiments in this regard are uncompromising. Thus he takes a strongly condemnatory line on sexual indulgence without the sanction of marriage. This is how Eugenia in *The Duke of Milan*, long before seduced by Sforza, receives the news of Marcelia's death at the hands of her husband Sforza:

> She . . . had discretion
> Not to deliver up her virgin fort,
> Though strait besieged with flatteries, vows, and tears,
> Until the church had made it safe and lawful.
> And had I been the mistress of her judgment
> And constant temper, skilful in the knowledge
> Of man's malicious falsehood, I had never,
> Upon his hell-deep oaths to marry me,
> Given up my fair name, and my maiden honour,
> To his foul lust; nor lived now, being branded
> In the forehead for his whore, the scorn and shame
> Of all good women.[1]

Again, in *The Parliament of Love* even the desire, without the accomplishment, of seduction before marriage is severely condemned.

I confess,

says the now-repentant Cleremond,

> After you promised marriage, nothing wanting
> But a few days expired, to make me happy,

[1] v. i.

> My violent impatience of delay
> Made me presume, and with some amorous force,
> To ask a full fruition of those pleasures
> Which sacred Hymen to the world makes lawful,
> Before his torch was lighted; in this only,
> You justly can accuse me.

But Leonora replies to this not ignoble apology:

> Dar'st thou think
> That this offence can ever find a pardon,
> Unworthy as thou art![1]

Other passages in the plays, and still more the working-out of several plots (including *The Duke of Milan* with its revenge-for-seduction catastrophe, and the similar, though less serious, theme in *The Bashful Lover*), witness to Massinger's regard for pre-marital chastity both for women and for men. Those who have erred, it is true, are sometimes allowed by a marriage *post copulam* to do what they can to restore their virtue. Leosthenes marries Statilia in *The Bondman* after his rejection by Cleora, and Alonzo marries Maria in *The Bashful Lover*. Another seduced lady, Eugenia in *The Duke of Milan*, is committed by the dying Sforza to a convent, because with his death she cannot be made 'an honest woman'. But in spite of such ways of escape from the moral dilemma, ways long-sanctioned by civil and religious custom, Massinger makes it quite clear that the original offence is no less a sin. Those who attempt adultery are no less severely dealt with. Ubaldo and Ricardo in *The Picture* are tricked and made laughing-stocks by Sophia. Perigot and Novall in *The Parliament of Love* are likewise frustrated and punished; and in the same play the sanctity of marriage is preserved by the time-honoured device of making Clarindore sleep with his own wife instead of with Bellisant as he had intended. When adultery has actually been committed, as in *The Fatal Dowry*, a tragic catastrophe follows; and in *The Roman Actor*, though there is technically no adultery, death falls on Domitian for stealing a wife by a forced-on divorce, Domitia for consenting and for her infidelity (in desire if not in deed) to her second husband, and even upon Paris for being the more or less innocent second party to that uncompleted adultery. No, Massinger is no condoner of sexual irregularity, no easy-going admirer of such gay young men and light young ladies as we frequently find in Fletcher.

Within marriage itself, sexual love, according to Massinger, ever

---

[1] *The Parliament of Love*, ii. ii.

true to his μηδὲν ἄγαν, should be indulged with moderation. Thus Marcelia in *The Duke of Milan*, the most signal victim in the plays of immoderate love, talks admonishingly to her husband of

> The pleasures
> That sacred Hymen warrants . . .
> Of which, in troth, you are too great a doter.[1]

And she goes on to say in stronger terms:

> And there is more of beast in it than man.
> Let us love temperately; things violent last not,
> And too much dotage rather argues folly
> Than true affection.

The same insistence on sexual moderation in marriage occurs in *The Picture*, when Mathias, on taking leave of his wife, says,

> We have long enjoyed the sweets of love, and though
> Not to satiety or loathing, yet,
> We must not live such dotards on our pleasures,
> As still to hug them, to the certain loss
> Of profit and preferment.[2]

This same scene, which was commended by Lamb,[3] gives better than any other single passage Massinger's idea of a happy marriage:

> You have been an obedient wife, a right one;
> And to my power, though short of your desert,
> I have been ever an indulgent husband . . .
>   'Tis for thee
> That I turn soldier, and put forth, dearest,
> Upon this sea of action, as a factor,
> To trade for rich materials to adorn
> Thy noble parts, and show them in full lustre.
>   . . . therefore, Sophia,
> In few words know my pleasure, and obey me,
> As you have ever done. To your discretion
> I leave the government of my family,
> And our poor fortunes; and from these command
> Obedience to you, as to myself.

The wife has been dutiful; the husband considerate. Their love has been deep but temperate; and the husband has not neglected his proper duty of providing 'competent means' for his wife and household. But, to recall what has previously been said, it should be

---

[1] III. iii.   [2] I. i.

[3] *Specimens of English Dramatic Poets*, 1808: 'The good sense, rational fondness, and chastised feeling of this dialogue, make it more valuable than many of those scenes in which this writer has attempted a deeper passion and more tragical interest' (Bohn Edn., 1854, p. 364).

noted that, although Mathias and Sophia have been married for years, they have 'as yet no charge of children'.

It is perhaps appropriate to conclude this section of this present chapter by contrasting briefly Massinger and Shakespeare in the matter under discussion. Nearly all Massinger's plays deal in some measure with the premarital, marital, or extra-marital relationship of men and women. They all raise problems which he takes seriously and, indeed, round which the actions of quite a number of the plays rotate. In five (*The Duke of Milan*, *The Picture*, *The Emperor of the East*, *The Roman Actor*, and *The Guardian*, not to mention *The Fatal Dowry*) we are directly concerned with problems of the married relationship; and in four (*The Bondman*, *The Parliament of Love*, *The City Madam*, and *The Great Duke of Florence*) these problems enter indirectly but importantly. That is, in more than half of his plays Massinger is dealing, as one of his prime interests, with the man-woman relationship in marriage; and, of the remaining six plays, four (*The Unnatural Combat*, *The Renegado*, *The Maid of Honour*, and *The Bashful Lover*) deal with the sexual relationship in other respects in which the question of marriage looms large. Shakespeare, on the other hand, does not in general concentrate so exclusively anywhere on the purely sexual relationship. Problems of marriage, for example, are rarely Shakespeare's specific concern, except in *Othello*, and perhaps also in *Cymbeline* and *The Winter's Tale*; though of course they make incidental appearances, sometimes as background matter and sometimes of importance in the foreground, elsewhere, as in *Hamlet*, *Julius Caesar*, *Coriolanus*, *Antony and Cleopatra*, *Macbeth*, *King Lear*, and *Pericles*. However, Shakespeare's treatment of the subject is not, as in Massinger, of a nature which almost excludes everything else, and consequently it is all the more true-to-life. Hence the difference between Shakespeare and Massinger is not, as might appear on casual inspection, in the *amount* of interest, but in the *kind*. Massinger's interest is that of the theorist and social problematist: Shakespeare's is that of the mirrorer of life. As is to be expected of his genius, Shakespeare presents the truer picture. Yet there is something to be said for Massinger. He views marriage in a graver light, with more attention to detail, and with more regard to its social and religious implications. Marriage is to him more than a goal to be attained after which it can be assumed that life will proceed smoothly and happily, more than an uneasy yoke to be borne with good-humoured tolerance. It is a state which has to be maintained with rigour, with perseverance, and according to principles of moral virtue. But it is, nevertheless, a state which is essential to the happiness of man. As Lord Lovell says in *A New Way to Pay Old Debts*:

> I know,
> The sum of all that makes a just man happy
> Consists in the well choosing of his wife.[1]

★

In his political thought Massinger has two main concerns. The first of these is liberty, and the second, which is indissolubly linked with the first, is wise and just government. Inevitably, Massinger sees these, except perhaps in *The Bondman*, in a monarchical field of reference. But there is in him a Whiggism before the Whigs and a foreshadowing of that academic republicanism which crops up in eighteenth-century Whiggism as a sentiment rather than as practical politics and which at last became a doctrine with Tom Paine, Godwin, and Horne Tooke.

Political liberty for Massinger is founded on an ethical conception of the liberty of the individual soul. We have already seen the place of the latter in the private bond of man to wife and wife to man. But it is likewise not to be infringed by the social bond of subject to state or subject to prince. The liberty of the individual soul can be attained only when reason, and consequently right thinking and conduct, prevail in the individual over the baser passions. As we shall see, Massinger maintains, through Timoleon in Act I, scene iii, of *The Bondman*, that only the virtuous deserve freedom. The body may owe a duty to an overlord, but the mind of the good subject is free.

> Though the king may
> Dispose of my life and goods, my mind's my own,

exclaims Camiola in Act II, scene ii, of *The Maid of Honour*; and in Act IV, scene v, she again puts forward the same idea, along with a distinction between a legitimate or just ruler and a tyrant and between even a legitimate ruler's virtues, which rightly demand loyalty, and his vices, which do not:

> 'Twas never read in holy writ, or moral,
> That subjects on their loyalty were obliged
> To love their sovereign's vices; . . .
> Tyrants, not kings,
> By violence, from humble vassals force
> The liberty of their souls.

[1] IV. i.

Cleora, another of Massinger's freedom-loving heroines, considers in Act I, scene iii, of *The Bondman* that this high liberty of soul which can be rated as on a par with honour is worth the surrender of all riches and worldly goods:

> Think you all treasure
> Hid in the bowels of the earth, or shipwrecked
> In Neptune's watery kingdom, can hold weight,
> When liberty and honour fill one scale,
> Triumphant justice sitting on the beam?

The Bondman is, of course, the play above all others in which political liberty is most fully dealt with. The action of the play concerns a rising of the oppressed slaves of Syracuse during the absence of their masters at the war against Carthage. But even before the rising has been hinted at in the play, Timoleon, the Corinthian general who has been called in to take charge of the Syracusan army, gives us in the very first words he speaks on his entrance in the Senate in Act I, scene iii, what is the main issue of the plot:

> I have ever loved
> An equal freedom, and proclaim all such
> As would usurp on others' liberties,
> Rebels to nature, to whose bounteous blessings
> All men lay claim as true legitimate sons:
> But such as have made forfeit of themselves
> By vicious courses, and their birthright lost,
> 'Tis not injustice they are marked for slaves,
> To serve the virtuous.

On the other hand, Marullo, who leads the rising of slaves, speaks with great indignation in Act IV, scene ii, of the treatment the slaves had had to endure from their cruel masters:

> . . . tyranny
> Drew us from our obedience. Happy those times
> When lords were styled fathers of families,
> And not imperious masters! . . .
> Humanity then lodged in the hearts of men,
> And thankful masters carefully provided
> For creatures wanting reason . . .
> . . . but man to man more cruel
> Appoints no end to the suffering of his slave;
> Since pride stepped in and riot, and o'erturned
> This goodly frame of concord, teaching masters
> To glory in the abuse of such as are
> Brought under their command; who, grown unuseful,
> Are less esteemed than beasts.

And in Act II, scene iii, Marullo proclaims in surprisingly democratic terms the natural equality of men:

> Equal Nature fashioned us
> All in one mould. The bear serves not the bear,
> Nor the wolf the wolf; 'twas odds of strength in tyrants,
> That plucked the first link from the golden chain
> With which the Thing of Things bound in the world.
> Why then, since we are taught, by their examples,
> To love our liberty, if not command,
> Should the strong serve the weak, the fair, deformed ones?
> Or such as know the cause of things, pay tribute
> To ignorant fools? All's but the outward gloss,
> And politic form, that does distinguish us.

In *The Bondman*, however, Massinger has found himself in a
dilemma. The egalitarian declaration I have just quoted and the
sympathetic account of the rising of the slaves would seem to demand
that the slaves should be victorious. Yet, because Massinger is an
anti-revolutionary and holds by political stability, the slaves have to
be defeated. He extricates himself from his difficulty by a somewhat
dubious juggling with our sympathies. He glosses over as well as he
can the defeat of the slaves and the consequences thereof to them,
and asks, in the expectation of a favourable answer, whether the
brave citizens of Syracuse who have returned from the foreign war
have done their patriotic duty, vindicated their honour, and justified
their positions as lords and masters. It was the cowardly citizens
who had remained at home that had maltreated their slaves and
suffered defeat in the rising. So the slaves, victorious over the worthless and defeated by the worthy, are dealt with leniently and presumably enjoy thereafter a happier condition and the redress of their
grievances. Just to tie everything up nicely, even the bad stay-at-
homes undergo a reformation as a direct result of the rising.

But otherwise, and despite the ambiguous issue of *The Bondman*,
Massinger holds fast by his love of liberty. It is perhaps significant
that two of his favourite words are 'bondman' and 'bondwoman' and
that they occur repeatedly in almost all the plays in the canon,
always with an explicit or implicit condemnation of slavery or serf-
dom (except when they are used semi-metaphorically to connote the
duty of spouse to spouse or lover to lover).

His insistence on political liberty and his democratic statements on
kingship and the relation between ruler and law led Coleridge to
call him a Whig. 'Massinger,' he said, 'is a decided Whig; Beaumont

and Fletcher high-flying, passive-obedience Tories.'[1] And in another place, speaking of the Elizabethan and Jacobean periods generally, he observed that 'Stage, pulpit, law, fashion—all conspired to enslave the realm. Massinger's plays breathe the opposite spirit.'[2]

Questions about rule and government, and in particular the function and character of the prince or ruler receive special attention from Massinger in *The Roman Actor* and *The Emperor of the East*. But they also get more incidental consideration in a number of other plays, notably *The Maid of Honour*, *The Bondman*, and *The Great Duke of Florence*.

The divine right of kings, which was one of the political commonplaces of the day,[3] is accepted by Massinger, but with his own implications. Kings are divinely called and justified only when they exercise their functions wisely and with justice. A ruler becomes a tyrant whenever he places his personal interests and caprices above the moral law and before the interests of his subjects. Evil rulers, the moral of *The Roman Actor* tells us,

> And such as are governed only by their will,
> And not their reason, unlamented fall.

As Chelli says, 'Le souverain déchoit du moment où il oublie sa mission pour suivre son caprice.'[4]

The Maid of Honour provides a good illustration of momentary or isolated caprice on a ruler's part. King Roberto of Sicily commands Camiola to marry his favourite, Fulgentio. She refuses. Without her knowledge or approval Adorio, who loves her, fights a duel with Fulgentio over the matter. The King then demands an explanation from Camiola and accuses her of setting her man on to murder Fulgentio. This is her protest in reply:

> With your leave, I must not kneel, sir,
> While I reply to this: but thus rise up
> In my defence, and tell you, as a man,
> (Since, when you are unjust, the deity,
> Which you may challenge as a king parts from you)
> 'Twas never read . . .
> That subjects . . . were obliged
> To love their sovereign's vices.[5]

---

[1] *Miscell. Crit.* (Raysor), p. 77. [2] *Ibid.*, p. 85.
[3] On this, see particularly the second and third of Lord Radcliffe's Reith Lectures on *Power and the State*, *The Listener*, 1951, pp. 827–829 and 877–879.
[4] *Drame*, p. 319. [5] IV. v.

And when Roberto in the end admits her innocence of the charge he had made against her, she declares:

> Ay, now you show whose deputy you are:
> If now I bathe your feet with tears, it cannot
> Be censured superstition.

In the last couplet of the scene she sums up the political message of the play:

> Happy are subjects, when the prince is still
> Guided by justice, not his passionate will.

The trouble in *The Maid of Honour* came from an isolated interference of the prince with a subject's liberty of choice as regards marriage, in which sphere the law gave him no authority; but Roberto was otherwise a good ruler, open to argument and ready to admit his mistake. In *The Roman Actor*, on the other hand, Domitian is practically everything that a ruler should not be, arbitrary, unjust, self-willed, capricious, and cruel. For in the mysterious operations of Providence the semi-divine office of ruler sometimes falls to unworthy persons. As Malefort (one of Massinger's bad men, to be sure, but one not without characteristics that his creator respected) says, when called on to drink a health to 'the worthiest of women',

> I will not choose a foreign queen's,
> Nor yet our own, for that would relish of
> Tame flattery; nor do their height of title,
> Or absolute power, confirm their worth and goodness,
> These being heaven's gifts, and frequently conferred
> On such as are beneath them.[1]

Domitian, to return to *The Roman Actor*, is too bad to be reformed like Roberto, and fit only for the extreme punishment of death. It comes to him from a conspiracy of six of his chief victims. The wicked ruler is punished in accordance with the prophecy generally denounced against all such tyrants in Act III, scene i:

> The immortal Powers
> Protect a prince, though sold to impious acts,
> And seem to slumber, till his roaring crimes
> Awake their justice.

The phrasing deserves close attention in view of Chelli's declaration that Massinger is 'anti-tyran, jusque — à le prendre au mot — jusqu'au tyrannicide'.[2] On the contrary, however, the lines just

---

[1] *The Unnatural Combat*, III. iii. [2] *Drame*, p. 319.

quoted are not a simple justification of tyrannicide but an affirmation of faith in the working of the moral law. Indeed, the prophecy goes on to say that the 'immortal Powers',

> looking down,
> And with impartial eyes, on his contempt
> Of all religion and moral goodness,
> They in their secret judgments, do determine
> To leave him to his wickedness, which sinks him,
> When he is most secure.

If Massinger makes a character say:

> I am confident he deserves much more
> That vindicates his country from a tyrant,
> Than he that saves a citizen;[1]

he must not be understood to mean by 'vindicate' 'assassinate'. Rather Massinger's position is covered by the Gospel words, 'It must needs be that offences come; but woe to that man [tyrant and tyrannicide impartially] by whom the offence cometh.'[2] So Domitian—

> . . . was our prince,
> However wicked;[3]

says the tribune who breaks in and arrests the murderers;

> . . . and, in you, this murder,—
> Which whosoe'er succeeds him will revenge:
> Nor will we, that served under his command,
> Consent that such a monster as thyself,
> (For in thy wickedness Augusta's title
> Hath quite forsook thee) thou, that wert the ground
> Of all these mischiefs, shall go hence unpunished.
> Lay hands on her, and drag her to her sentence.—
> We will refer the hearing to the senate,
> Who may at their best leisure censure you.

Thus Massinger recognises that some sort of divinity doth hedge even a wicked prince and implies that tyrannicide is never justifiable. But the same tribune cannot leave us there: he finishes his speech and the play on the distinction between good kings who are mourned after their deaths and the arbitrary and tyrannical who die unlamented:

> He in death hath paid
> For all his cruelties. Here's the difference;
> Good kings are mourned for after life; but ill,

---

[1] *The Roman Actor*, III. i. But the same idea in almost the same words occurs several times in Massinger.   [2] *Matthew* xviii. 7.   [3] v. ii.

> And such as, governed only by their will,
> And not their reason, unlamented fall;
> No good man's tear shed at their funeral.

If Massinger gives surprisingly bold lessons to rulers, that is to say James I and Charles I, he also condemns those of their subjects whose deference was a dangerous incense and sycophancy. In *The Emperor of the East* he actually puts a heartfelt protest into the mouth of the jealousy-tortured Emperor Theodosius himself, the sincerity of which as an expression of Massinger's belief is not impaired by the obvious debt to *Othello* and *The Merchant of Venice*:

> Wherefore pay you
> This adoration to a sinful creature?
> I am flesh and blood as you are, sensible
> Of heat and cold, as much a slave unto
> The tyranny of my passions, as the meanest
> Of my poor subjects. The proud attributes,
> By oil-tongued flattery imposed upon us,
> As sacred, glorious, high, invincible,
> The deputy of heaven, and in that
> Omnipotent, with all false titles else,
> Coined to abuse our frailty, though compounded,
> And by the breath of sycophants applied,
> Cure not the least fit of an ague in us.
> We may give poor men riches, confer honours
> On undeservers, raise, or ruin such
> As are beneath us, and, with this puffed up,
> Ambition would persuade us to forget
> That we are men: but He that sits above us,
> And to whom, at our utmost rate, we are
> But pageant properties, derides our weakness:
> In me, to whom you kneel, 'tis most apparent.
> Can I call back yesterday, with all their aids
> That bow unto my sceptre? or restore
> My mind to that tranquillity and peace
> It then enjoyed?—Can I make Eudocia chaste,
> Or vile Paulinus honest?

There is another equally emphatic rebuke in the same play, administered by Pulcheria to the projectors and other parasites about the Court, who, for their own base ends, flattered the monarch in order to lure him to unjust and arbitrary exactions:

> You roar out,
> All is the king's, his will above his laws;
> And that fit tributes are too gentle yokes
> For his poor subjects: whispering in his ear,

If he would have their fear, no man should dare
To bring a salad from his country garden,
Without the paying gabel; kill a hen,
Without excise: and that if he desire
To have his children or his servants wear
Their heads upon their shoulders, you affirm
In policy 'tis fit the owner should
Pay for them by the poll; or, if the prince want
A present sum, he may command a city
Impossibilities, and for non-performance,
Compel it to submit to any fine
His officers shall impose. Is this the way
To make our emperor happy? can the groans
Of his subjects yield him music? must his threshholds
Be washed with widows' and wronged orphans' tears,
Or his power grow contemptible?[1]

These are two striking passages in view of the period for which they were written. Massinger writes more briefly in the same vein in *The Great Duke of Florence*, Act I, scene i, when the noble and conscientious tutor of Prince Giovanni tells the Duke's secretary that princes

> being men, and not gods, Contarino,
> They can give wealth and titles, but no virtues;
> That is without their power.

The very humanity of the ruler, however, claims for him a larger tolerance in minor matters than ordinary men can expect:

Charomonte.   Are not these
　Strange gambols in the duke!
Alphonse.   Great princes have
　Like meaner men, their weakness.
Hippolito.   And may use it
　Without control or check.
Contarino.   'Tis fit they should;
　Their privilege were less else, than their subjects'![2]

And Massinger realises that, even so, the princely office is no blessing but an exalted servitude:

> Greatness, with private men
> Esteemed a blessing, is to me a curse;
> And we, whom, for our high births, they conclude
> The only freemen, are the only slaves.[3]

[1] I. ii.　　　[2] v. ii.　　　[3] I. i.

In Massinger's plays not only is the ruler isolated from the ordinary run of his subjects, but he is absolutist in his methods.

> We stand not bound to yield account to any,

says Duke Cozimo in Act I, scene iii, of *The Great Duke of Florence*,

> Why we do this or that (the full consent
> Of our subjects being included in our will) . . .

He and other rulers in Massinger have counsellors, some of whom, like Eubulus in *The Picture* and Pulcheria in *The Emperor of the East*, are frank enough in their advice and comments. The good advice of such counsellors is not to be spurned. As Theodosius says in *The Emperor of the East*:

> He never learned
> The right way to command that stopped his ears
> To wise directions;[1]

—a significant and directed remark perhaps, in view of the fact that the play received a special Court performance before Charles and Henrietta Maria. Cozimo also in *The Great Duke of Florence*, Act I, scene ii, expresses the same sentiment:

> We are not grown so proud
> As to disdain familiar conference
> With such as are to counsel and direct us.

But wise council is accepted only because it is wise and for no other reason, the ruler being the judge and exercising his reason in deciding. For his counsellors have no standing as official representatives of a parliament; and there are no intermediaries, except minor executive officers, between the ruler and the ruled. The ruler himself is omnipotent—the great first cause in the state. He reigns and rules. In so far as he considers his subjects' best interests he does so as one obedient to God, but not answerable to men. The ruler, however, ought to hear his people's grievances directly. Theodosius states this kingly duty in Act III, scene ii, of *The Emperor of the East*:

> Since that dread Power by Whom we are, disdains not
> With an open ear to hear petitions from us;
> Easy access in us, His deputies,
> To the meanest of our subjects, is a debt
> Which we stand bound to pay.

And he is shown as graciously hearing an old countryman and receiving from him the simple (but, as it turns out, fateful) gift of an apple. This is, however, one of the few occasions on which a monarch is

[1] I. ii.

171

shown in juxtaposition to his humbler subjects, apart from palace domestics. Otherwise Massinger's rulers live, move, and have their being in a society of nobles, courtiers, favourites, and advisers—no doubt more because of the ingredients and exigencies of the kind of play Massinger was writing, than from any inference as to kingship that he meant his audience to draw.

Such absolutism, then, as I have been illustrating from Massinger makes it hard to accept without serious qualification Coleridge's description of him as 'a democrat'.[1]

To sum up: a king or ruler, in Massinger's politics, has a twofold duty, to God who has created him both man and monarch, and to his subjects; he can carry out this double duty only if he rules, not according to mere man-made law, but according to that Moral Law or Justice which is an attribute of God Himself.[2] If the ruler allows his passions or caprice to rule his reason, he is *ipso facto* a tyrant and sooner or later, unless he repents and reforms, will be brought to book for his evil or foolish actions. The whole duty of a king is to rule his people disinterestedly, wisely, and justly, not with harshness, but with sympathy and with that

> saving mercy
> Which sets off . . .
> A prince, much more than rigour.
> . . . And becomes him,
> When 'tis expressed to such as fell by weakness,
> That being a twin-brother to affection,
> Better than wreaths of conquest.[3]

Massinger's political ideas cannot be left without fuller reference to their bearing on and his allusions to contemporary affairs. Surprisingly enough, except for occasional footnotes in Gifford, the dramatist's relation to political situations under James I and Charles I received no attention till S. R. Gardiner broached it in an article in *The Contemporary Review* for August, 1876.[4] It was his opinion that 'in many of Massinger's plays we have a treatment of the politics of the day so plain and transparent, that anyone who possesses only a slight acquaintance with the history of the reigns of the first two Stuarts can read it at a glance'.[5] One may be permitted to doubt if such a slight acquaintance with the history of the period is as adequate as Gardiner supposed. But undoubtedly the plays

---

[1] *Miscell Crit.*, (Raysor), p. 69.
[2] Cf. *The Bondman*, III. iii: 'Thou art just, Thou all-creating Power!'
[3] *The Roman Actor*, v. iii.
[4] *The Political Element in Massinger*, Repr. *Trans. New Sh. Soc.*, I, 1875–1876.
[5] p. 495.

amply reveal Massinger as a close, thoughtful, and outspoken observer of the first two Stuart kings and their government.

It is perhaps not necessary to go into these matters in great detail here since they have been dealt with at such length by Gardiner. But some comment is certainly called for. Many of the allusions in *The Bondman*, *The Maid of Honour*, and *The Great Duke of Florence*, are directed against George Villiers, Duke of Buckingham, the dissolute and arrogant favourite of Charles. Two quotations will suffice to show how pointed these passages can be.[1] In Act I, scene i, of *The Bondman* he is the prototype of the admiral of the Carthaginian fleet:

> Gisco's their admiral,
> And 'tis our happiness; a raw young fellow,
> One never trained in arms, but rather fashioned
> To tilt with ladies' lips, than crack a lance;
> Ravish a feather from a mistress' fan,
> And wear it as a favour. A steel helmet,
> Made horrid with a glorious plume, will crack
> His woman's neck.

In *The Maid of Honour* he appears on the stage thinly disguised as Fulgentio, favourite of King Roberto of Sicily. In Act I, scene i, he is described as

> A gentleman, yet no lord. He hath some drops
> Of the king's blood running in his veins, derived
> Some ten degrees off. His revenue lies
> In a narrow compass, the king's ear; and yields him
> Every hour a fruitful harvest. Men may talk
> Of three crops in a year in the Fortunate Islands,
> Of profit made by wool; but while there are suitors,
> His sheepshearing, nay, shaving to the quick,
> Is in every quarter of the moon, and constant.
> In the time of trussing a point, he can undo,
> Or make a man: his play or recreation,
> Is to raise this up, or pull down that; and, though
> He never yet took orders, makes more bishops
> In Sicily, than the pope himself.

Gardiner suggests that these anti-Buckingham passages were inserted by Massinger to manifest his adherence to the party of opposition, which included the Herberts. It is, however, perhaps too easy to exaggerate Massinger's partisan tendencies on the strength

---

[1] For other Buckingham allusions, see *Duke of Milan*, IV. i; *Bondman*, I. iii; and *Great Duke of Florence*, I. i, and the two scenes quoted above *passim*. For other direct political allusions, see *Great Duke of Florence*, I. i, II. i; *Renegado*, II. i; *Maid of Honour*, III. iii; and *Emperor of the East*, I. i; and perhaps also *Believe as You List*, *passim* (see Gardiner, loc. cit.).

of a few passages critical of Buckingham. There were, after all, many other people in the period from 1625 to 1627 who were equally critical of Buckingham. I am inclined to think that Massinger owed little political allegiance to the cause of the Herberts, or of anyone else for that matter, but criticised what he saw and condemned what he disapproved of, honestly, as was his custom. He looks at politics as a moralist, not as a politician or a partisan.

In such early plays as *The Bondman*, *The Maid of Honour*, and *The Great Duke of Florence*, his political comment on current affairs was admittedly personal. But after the assassination of Buckingham in 1628, though his commentary has occasional personal applications, it becomes more general and takes up in greater detail than before the question of ruler and ruled. The ruler of course to whom Massinger directed his scrutiny was Charles I. He had already subtly praised him as Prince Giovanni in *The Great Duke of Florence*,[1] especially in the lines in Act I, scene i:

> . . . my noble charge,
> By his sharp wit, and pregnant apprehension,
> Instructing those that teach him; making use,
> Not in a vulgar and pedantic form,
> Of what's read to him, but 'tis straight digested,
> And truly made his own. His grave discourse,
> In one no more indebted unto years,
> Amazes such as hear him: as for knowledge in
> Music, he needs it not, it being born with him;
> All that he speaks being with such grace delivered,
> That it makes perfect harmony. . . .
> And that there may be nothing wanting that
> May render him complete, the sweetness of
> His disposition so wins on all
> Appointed to attend him, that they are
> Rivals, even in the coarsest office, who
> Shall get precedency to do him service;
> Which they esteem a greater happiness,
> Than if they had been fashioned and built up
> To hold command o'er others;

and the joy in London on Charles's return from Spain inspired the account of Giovanni's arrival in Florence in Act III, scene i:

> Being, as you are, received for the heir apparent,
> You are no sooner seen, but wondered at;

---

[1] This play was licensed in 1627, but from internal evidence was almost certainly written before the accession of Charles. See above, Chap. I, p. 13 and p. 28.

> The signiors making it a business to
> Enquire how you have slept; and, as you walk
> The streets of Florence, the glad multitude
> In throngs press but to see you; and, with joy,
> The father, pointing with his finger, tells
> His son, This is the prince, the hopeful prince,
> That must hereafter rule, and you obey him—
> Great ladies beg your picture, and make love
> To that, despairing to enjoy the substance—
> And, but the last night, when 'twas only rumoured
> That you were come to court, as if you had
> By sea past hither from another world,
> What general shouts and acclamations followed!
> The bells rang loud, the bonfires blazed, and such
> As loved not wine, carousing to your health,
> Were drunk, and blushed not at it.

When Charles had been some years on the throne, Massinger wrote *The Emperor of the East* for his monarch 'throned by the west'. The Court Prologue directly addresses it to the King:

> As ever, sir, you lent a gracious ear
> To oppressed innocence, now vouchsafe to hear
> A short petition. At your feet, in me,
> The poet kneels, and to your majesty
> Appeals for justice. What we now present,
> When first conceived, in his vote and intent,
> Was sacred to your pleasure.

The play may seem to us in some ways so critical of Charles that we may wonder how Sir Henry Herbert passed it for performance at all, let alone for performance at Court. Undoubtedly in it Massinger warned Charles against his uxoriousness, prodigality, and lack of grip.[1] But what is clear enough today might well escape Charles's awareness of its similarity to his own circumstances. He probably approved of many of the political *sententiae* as echoing his own conception of his position and took pleasure in the ideal monarch which it presented, not in Theodosius but abstractly, and which he imagined himself to resemble. For in its fundamental principles the play is undeniably royalist and devoted to the throne, and any salty flavour of specific admonishment might well be counteracted and washed away by the patently tragicomic ending. Very different was Charles's attitude in 1638 to a play by Massinger called *The King and the Subject* which is now lost. 'Readinge over the play at Newmarket',

---

[1] See the quotations given above from this play, pp. 169–70, 171.

says Sir Henry Herbert,[1] the King took royal objection to a passage in it, and, 'set his marke upon the place with his owne hand, and in thes words: "This is too insolent, and to bee changed." ' But other things had already changed and the sky had darkened by 1638; and Massinger may have been less discreet in masking cautiously the contemporary application, while Charles himself was probably more aware of public opinion and of the pointedness of such oblique allusiveness. Nevertheless, in spite of his well-intentioned political animadversions, Massinger remained definitely a King's man. Had he lived until the Civil War he would probably have been a member of the conservative group who, after disapproving of many of Charles's actions that brought the War about, fought for him un-hesitatingly as their divinely-appointed ruler. He would have sub-scribed, perhaps more heartily than their author, certainly with a more single-minded royalism, to these words:

> Upon considering all, I think the cause was too good to have been fought for. Men ought to have trusted God—they ought to have trusted the King with the whole matter. The arms of the Church are prayers and tears, the arms of the subject are patience and petitions. The King himself being of so accurate and piercing a judgement would soon have felt where it stuck. For men may spare their pains when Nature is at work, and the world will not go the faster for our driving. Even as his present Majesty's happy Restoration did itself, so all things else happen in their best and proper time, without any heed of our officiousness.[2]

★

It is quite impossible to particularise Massinger's attitude to religion as I have tried to do with the other two recurring topics of his commentary on life. But as far as I can, I shall try to define his elusive but all-pervasive religious prepossession. I deliberately so describe it, for it pervades and interpenetrates all his work and thought. Alone of all the Elizabethan and Jacobean dramatists he displays an almost constant religious bias. His *gravitas* is only equalled by his *pietas* (in the religious sense). 'His view of life,' says Sir Leslie Stephen, 'is not only grave, but has a distinctly religious colouring.'[3]

An examination of the plays, however, reveals no particularly individual religious ideas, nor indeed anything religiously eccentric. Massinger's religion, as far as doctrine goes, was central and ortho-dox. I cannot think that this was a mere playing for safety: it was

---

[1] This passage is given in full in Chap. I, p. 44.
[2] Andrew Marvell, *The Rehearsal Transprosed.*   [3] *Hours in a Library*, II, p. 153.

the result of solid convictions and a natural conservatism. Massinger can be outspoken; but it is with the candour of a traditionalist, never the *empressement* of the innovator. His standpoint in all his plays is that of a morality unquestioned and venerable, and behind all his morality lie the generally unstated but undeniable sanctions of Christianity. His good characters are always devout, even where, as in *The Bondman*, *Believe As You List*, or *The Renegado*, the creed they hold is pagan or Muslim, not Christian. The wicked characters are always presented as breakers of 'the laws of Heaven'.

The play which deals most closely and most representatively with religious issues is *The Renegado*, not of course in such a controversial way as would have brought the jealous authorities of Church and State down on it.[1] It presents, more sophisticatedly than Heywood's not wholly unsimilar *Fair Maid of the West*, the opposition, not of two Christian denominations, but of Christianity and Islam. The Christians are in the right and the Muslims are in the wrong and are, of course, eventually foiled, one of them, Donusa, being (somewhat improbably) converted and Grimaldi the Renegado being reconverted. As the Christians are Italians, there is good reason for making them Roman Catholics. Whether there was another reason in Massinger's own religious adherence I shall discuss later. The fact to notice is that the play might be described as undenominationally Christian. As in the other plays, religion is the crown of Massinger's philosophy, religious duty being paramount above all others. The particular issue here is that of religious versus amatory obligation. Vitelli is torn between his sincere desire to act virtuously and according to Christian principles and his passionate love for the seductive Mohammedan princess Donusa. It is in effect Massinger's frequently refaceted conflict of reason and the passions.

At the very beginning, before Vitelli has seen Donusa or knows of her existence, he is seen being schooled by his *bonus angelus*, Francisco, in the general conquest of the passions.

> O welcome sir!

exclaims Vitelli on seeing Francisco.

> Stay of my steps in this life,
> And guide to all my blessed hopes hereafter.
> What comforts, sir? Have your endeavours prospered?
> Have we tired Fortune's malice with our sufferings?
> Is she at length, after so many frowns,
> Pleased to vouchsafe one cheerful look upon us?[2]

[1] *The Virgin Martyr* must, for my purposes, be ruled out of court since it is impossible to determine how much of its religious element was already present before Massinger came to handle it.   [2] I. i.

In Francisco's reply there is a most fatherly rebuke:

> You give too much to fortune and your passions,
> O'er which a wise man, if religious, triumphs.
> That name fools worship; and those tyrants which
> We arm against our better part, our reason,
> May add, but never take from our afflictions.

Vitelli attempts to excuse himself:

> Sir, as I am a sinful man, I cannot
> But like one suffer.

But Francisco continues in his admonishing vein:

> I exact not from you
> A fortitude insensible of calamity,
> To which the saints themselves have bowed and shown
> They are made of flesh and blood; all that I challenge
> Is manly patience. Will you, that were trained up
> In a religious school, where divine maxims,
> Scorning comparison with moral precepts,
> Were daily taught you, bear your constancy's trial,
> Not like Vitelli, but a village nurse,
> With curses in your mouth, tears in your eyes?—
> How poorly it shows in you.

Of course, such an emphasis on rational control of the passions is to set the tone and prepare the audience.

Thereafter throughout the play Francisco exhorts Vitelli to live the life of a good Christian. Vitelli is indeed seduced by Donusa and sins, not so much through having fallen in love with an infidel as through having succumbed to the temptations of the flesh. Chastity is somehow or other practically equated with the Christian way of life. When Vitelli resists the further allurements of Donusa in Act III, scene v, and rebukes her and condemns himself for the sin they have committed, she asks him,

> Whom do you fear?

And he replies:

> That human frailty I took from my mother,
> That, as my youth increased, grew stronger on me;
> That still pursues me, and, though once recovered,
> In scorn of reason, and, what's more, religion,
> Again seeks to betray me.

As the play advances, Vitelli becomes something more than a true Christian who has repented his first lapse and resisted further tempta-

tion; encouraged by Francisco, he aspires to martyrdom for the
Faith.

> What punishment
> Soe'er I undergo, I am still a Christian!

he cries in Act III, scene v, after his intrigue with Donusa has been
discovered and he has been seized by her guardians; and in Act IV,
scene iii, in prison he reveals his ambition to Francisco:

> I grant, to have mastered
> The rebel appetite of flesh and blood,
> Was far above my strength; and still owe for it
> To that great Power that lent it: but when, I
> Shall make't apparent the grim looks of Death
> Affright me not, and that I can put off
> The fond desire of life (that, like a garment,
> Covers and clothes our frailty), hastening to
> My martyrdom, as to a heavenly banquet,
> To which I was a choice invited guest;
> Then you may boldly say, you did not plough,
> Or trust the barren and ungrateful sands
> With the fruitful grain of your religious counsels.

With eloquent and burning faith he continues;

> I would now
> Pluck out that wicked tongue, that hath blasphemed
> The great Omnipotency, at whose nod
> The fabric of the world shakes. Dare you bring
> Your juggling prophet in comparison with
> That most inscrutable and infinite Essence,
> That made this All, and comprehends his work!—
> The place is too profane to mention Him
> Whose only name is sacred.

It is not impossible that Massinger meant a *double entente* in the last
two lines—the prison at Tunis and the stage on which the Act of
May 27th, 1606, 'to Restraine Abuses of Players' had made it an
indictable offence 'jestingly or prophanely [to] speake or use the
holy Name of God or of Christ Jesus or of the Holy Ghoste or of the
Trinitie; which are not to be spoken but with feare and reverence'.
And it is also possible that, so far from Massinger regarding this as a
restriction, he may have reverently acquiesced in its propriety.

After *The Renegado* the play in which the religious strand is most
obvious is *The Maid of Honour*. In this play, however, notwithstanding the elevated symbolic interpretation of Camiola's renunciation of the world which has been suggested by Chelli,[1] I cannot but

---

[1] *Drame*, pp. 332–335.

feel that a great deal of the religious element is part and parcel of,
is indeed demanded by the exigencies of, the drama of surprise.
Much of the story seems to centre on the lack of serious regard which
Bertoldo, the hero, has for his vows as a Knight of Malta. When, in
Act I, scene ii, Camiola refuses to marry him, after describing the
difference in their rank which is a barrier to their marriage, she goes
on to say,

> . . . the stronger bar,
> Religion, stops our entrance: you are, sir,
> A knight of Malta, by your order bound
> To a single life; you cannot marry me;
> And, I assure myself, you are too noble
> To seek me, though my frailty should consent,
> In a base path.

To this Bertoldo protests,

> A dispensation, lady,
> Will easily absolve me;

And The Maid of Honour rounds on him with,

> O take heed, sir!
> When what is vowed to heaven is dispensed with,
> To serve our ends on earth, a curse must follow,
> And not a blessing.

Bertoldo acquiesces in her 'determinate sentence' and goes off to
fight against the Duchess of Sienna and relieve the besieged Duke of
Urbin. However, he is defeated and taken prisoner by the Duchess's
general, Gonzago, a fellow Knight of Malta. When the latter
recognises his captive we learn of another way in which Bertoldo has
broken his vows:

> The brave Bertoldo!
> A brother of our order! By Saint John,
> Our holy patron, I am more amazed,
> Nay, thunderstruck with thy apostasy,
> And precipice from the most solemn vows
> Made unto heaven, when this, the glorious badge
> Of our Redeemer, was conferred upon thee
> By the great master, than if I had seen
> A reprobate Jew, an atheist, Turk, or Tartar,
> Baptized in our religion.[1]

And Gonzago goes on:

> Fellow-soldiers,
> Behold this man, and, taught by his example,
> Know that 'tis safer far to play with lightning:

[1] II. v.

> Than trifle in things sacred. In my rage (*Weeps*)
> I shed these at the funeral of his virtue,
> Faith, and Religion.

Then, for his crime in taking arms against a woman, he tears the cross of St John from Bertoldo's breast.

This is, however, almost all we hear of Bertoldo's vows. The religious bar to their marriage, about which Camiola had been so adamant in Act I, scene ii, has seemingly ceased to trouble her by Act III, scene iii, when, on hearing of her suitor's captivity, she arranges to ransom him on condition that he takes an oath to marry her on his return to Sicily. Certainly she does not mention the religious bar to their marriage, although she deals very fully with her original first objection, namely, that difference in their rank which has been levelled out by the miserable state to which his imprisonment and the anger of his ruler have brought him. Nor does she make any comment in Act V, scene ii, when the Duchess Aurelia, having resigned her claim to Bertoldo, hands him over to her, saying,

> The dispensation procured by me,
> Freeing Bertoldo from his vow, makes way
> To your embraces.[1]

The reason for the neglect of this theme in the latter part of the play is, of course, that the matter of Bertoldo's religious vows is not really Massinger's main concern but merely provides an excuse for his favourite theme of the conflict between reason and the passions, in this case in a woman, in Camiola, the woman who gives the play its title. It is she who is the main focus of our interest. It is she who, when in Act I, scene ii, Bertoldo is announced, exclaims,

> Camiola, if ever, now be constant:
> This is, indeed, a suitor, whose sweet presence,
> Courtship, and loving language, would have staggered
> The chaste Penelope; and, to increase
> The wonder, did not modesty forbid it,
> I should ask that from him he sues to me for:
> And yet my reason, like a tyrant, tells me
> I must nor give nor take it;

and who, when he leaves her, sobs,

> How soon my sun is set, he being absent,
> Never to rise again! What a fierce battle
> Is fought between my passions!

---

[1] This dispensation is mentioned in Act IV, scene iv, where Aurelia says, 'A dispensation shall meet with us'. The Duchess seems to be partial to dispensations, since, earlier in Act V, scene ii, she has suggested that the solemn contract between Bertoldo and Camiola may be dispensed with.

It is she who succumbs to these passions and, ignoring Bertoldo's religious obligations, resolves to marry him. It is she to whom Bertoldo is unfaithful; who is able to discern clearly the flaw in his character, that inconstancy which had made him unfaithful to her in much the same way as he had been heedless of his religious vows, and it is she who weeps for him:

> When good men pursue
> The path marked out by virtue, the blest saints
> With joy look on it, and seraphic angels
> Clap their celestial wings in heavenly plaudits,
> To see a scene of grace so well presented,
> The fiends, and men made up of envy, mourning.
> Whereas now, on the contrary, as far
> As their divinity can partake of passion,
> With me they weep, beholding a fair temple,
> Built in Bertoldo's loyalty, turned to ashes
> By the flames of his inconstancy, the damned
> Rejoicing in the object.[1]

When the full force of Bertoldo's disloyalty touches her pride, she cries, still very much under the influence of her passions,

> You, perhaps,
> Expect now I should seek recovery
> Of what I have lost, by tears, and with bent knees
> Beg his compassion. No; my towering virtue,
> From the assurance of my merit, scorns
> To stoop so low. I'll take a nobler course,
> And, confident in the justice of my cause,
> The king his brother, and new mistress, judges,
> Ravish him from her arms. . . .
> He shall be, then, against his will, my husband.[2]

It is she who lessons Bertoldo, restores him to 'the path marked out by virtue', and who, having done this, surrenders herself in an escape from her passions into the hands of the Church. Of course, Bertoldo is not an insignificant character. But the play is Camiola's: it is not his play. There is almost no conflict in his mind and he worries little about his own moral shortcomings. He is aware that he has broken his vows in going to war against a woman and is in abject misery in his imprisonment; he has a momentary qualm about breaking his word to Camiola, a qualm that is immediately suppressed by his ambition to gain a crown; and in the end he is chastened and returns to his holy brotherhood. That is all. The breaking

[1] v. i.   [2] v. i.

of his religious vows not only means little to him, it seems to mean little to Camiola either, since she can so easily ignore it. It is largely, in fact, little more than a piquant ingredient of a typical 'surprise' plot, and is treated with comparative inconsequence by Massinger almost as a light matter. His censure is never more than implied.

Nevertheless, this matter of the breaking of religious vows does have a contribution to make towards Massinger's end which demonstrates the triumph of virtue. As in *The Renegado* and elsewhere, this end is an assertion of the supremacy of the good, the religious, the Christian, way of life.

The second religious strand in the play is a quite blatant 'turn' of the drama of surprise. And in this case it really is a surprise. This is Camiola's suddenly announced decision to renounce the world, divide up her property, and enter a convent. The first indication of this comes at the end of Act V, scene i, only some twenty-five lines after the militant speech of hers which I have last quoted:

> I will . . . attire myself
> Like a virgin bride; and something I will do,
> That shall deserve men's praise, and wonder too.

Camiola has certainly taken her resolve a little too quickly for probability. It must be remarked, however, that this would not be at all apparent to the audience in a theatre. The foolish Signior Sylli imagines that she is going to marry him: the audience, on the other hand, imagines that she is at last going to marry Bertoldo. In the source[1] she refuses to marry Bertoldo and resolves to live chaste for ever after, but such an ending is not enough for Massinger. Almost to the last he deceives us: Bertoldo's iniquities have been made public; Aurelia has surrendered him, as we might well think, to Camiola's embrace; and when a priest, Father Paulo, appears it is presumably to perform the marriage ceremony. But there is no marriage. In a rhyming jingle (strangely reminiscent of an inferior version of *Il Penseroso*) the priest receives her for the Church. That Massinger should invent such an incident is not to be wondered at since it is a sudden and surprising turn of events which accords well with the drama of surprise, however ludicrous it might appear to us today. But it also accords well with Massinger's seriousness of purpose, a heavy underlining at the end of what could well be a lighter play, which tells us that while one way out, one way of life, may be pleasant, there is only one way that is right, in this case and for

---

[1] Painter, II, p. 32, after Boccaccio, *De Mulieribus Claris*, CIII.

Camiola, the life of religious contemplation. It is after the priest has ended his stern harangue that Massinger himself seems to peep out, endowing Camiola's words with something of his own conviction and devotion:

> This is the marriage! this the port to which
> My vows must steer me! Fill my spreading sails
> With the pure wind of your devotions for me,
> That I may touch the secure haven, where
> Eternal happiness keeps her residence,
> Temptations to frailty never entering!
> I am dead to the world, and thus dispose
> Of what I leave behind me.

This is almost the only truly religious note in the play together with the grave religious resolution of the intrigue which is so typical of Massinger's work as a whole. Yet this ending, together with the few quotations I have made from earlier in the play, are sufficient to demonstrate clearly the prominence in *The Maid of Honour* of religious issues, however little we may catch a glimpse of Massinger's own religious convictions. He does, however, as is always his way, make his message clear in the concluding motto:

> She well deserves
> Her name, The Maid of Honour! May she stand,
> To all posterity, a fair example
> For noble maids to imitate! Since to live
> In wealth and pleasure's common, but to part with
> Such poisoned baits is rare.

Outside the two plays just discussed, *The Renegado* and *The Maid of Honour*, Massinger does not put religion in the forefront of any play. That does not mean that it is not strongly operative. On the contrary, Massinger is never beyond its gravitational pull. Not only does he scatter pious sayings and phrases, 'divine maxims, scorning comparison with moral precepts',[1] throughout them, but he sees life always with the grave regard of a deeply religious and sincere Christian. His Christianity rules his morality, social, marital, and sexual, and determines the lines of all his thinking on politics and kingship.

It was Gifford who first opened the question of Massinger's personal faith and declared that 'A close and repeated perusal of Massinger's work has convinced me that he was a Catholic: *The Virgin Martyr*, *The Renegado*, *The Maid of Honour*, exhibit innumerable

---

[1] *The Renegado*, I. i.

proofs of it; to say nothing of those casual intimations which are scattered over his remaining dramas.'[1] In his opinion Massinger may have been converted to Roman Catholicism while he was at Oxford; and thus, the surmise goes on, he lost the patronage of Pembroke. As discussed at the beginning of this book,[2] it is not clear why Gifford made Oxford the locus; conversions could and did occur anywhere, as for example Ben Jonson's in prison. Secondly, there is no evidence that Massinger ever lost the patronage of Pembroke, or indeed that he ever had it, or enjoyed any from anybody until he began to dedicate plays to patrons, including Philip, Earl of Montgomery and Robert, Earl of Carnarvon, both of the Herbert clan. On the other hand, Gifford's general statement as to the Roman-Catholic colouring of the plays deserves the most careful consideration. Gifford was a first-rate editor by the standards of his time and an acute student of the older dramatists he edited. The results of 'close and repeated perusal' by such a man are not to be lightly set aside. By 'innumerable proofs' in *The Virgin Martyr*, *The Renegado*, and *The Maid of Honour* and 'casual intimations' elsewhere he does not of course mean overt declarations. In the nature of the case, a Roman Catholic (alleged) writing for a pretty precarious living, for theatrical companies that knew on which side their bread was buttered, for an audience overwhelmingly Protestant, under the eyes of a very watchful Master of the Revels, to say nothing of higher authorities in Church and State—in the nature of such a case manifestos of Romanism were impossible. What are to be looked for are rather accidental or unguarded hints and clues which are cumulatively impressive.

The first person after Gifford to have much to say on the matter was Hartley Coleridge.[3] He took his text from Gifford without acknowledgement and likewise his biographical facts, such as they were; but he comes down hard on Gifford's suggestion of Massinger's Roman Catholicism. It would be interesting to know if Hartley Coleridge had ever heard his father on the subject. At any rate, what he has to say is more vigorous than illuminating.

Since Hartley Coleridge's time, most of the students of Massinger have made some reference to his possible Roman Catholicism, but rather inconclusively. The most recent of them, Professors Boyle, Koeppel, Chelli, and Cruickshank leave the matter still open for want of any positive external evidence. If Koeppel is impressed by

---

[1] Introduction, p. xliv.   [2] Chap. I, pp. 49–51.
[3] His edition of the plays was first published in 1839 (it actually appeared in 1840. *See* Bibliography).

the 'marked predilection for the religious observances of the papal church'[1] and by Massinger's departure from his source for *The Maid of Honour* in order to make his saintly Camiola decide on the discovery of her lover's faithlessness to take the veil, Chelli comes down on the whole on the negative side. 'Autant il est difficile,' he says, 'de prouver chez lui une conversion formelle, autant il est aisé de concilier des sympathies romaines avec l'adhésion générale à l'Église établie d'Angleterre.'[2]

As a further contribution to the argument, there is evidence available from a play which has not been discussed in this connexion before, *The City Madam*. It seems highly significant that in this play on life and manners in contemporary London Massinger should have introduced many Roman Catholic features or details. Such features or details can perhaps be largely explained away in plays set in Italy or Bohemia or France as part of the local colour, which, apart from the religious persuasion of the countries, Massinger did undoubtedly try to suggest.[3] But this explanation can hardly be given for *The City Madam*. Surely it was very unusual and highly atypical for a London merchant in the time of James I to be a Roman Catholic. Yet Sir John Frugal undoubtedly is. So is his hypocritical brother Luke, and so are his wife and daughters. In Act III, scene ii, we are told that Luke Frugal

> is much given
> To his devotion.
> And takes time to mumble
> A paternoster to himself;

and that Sir John Frugal

> is retired into a monastery
> Where he is resolved to end his days.

Lord Lacy

> . . . saw him take post for Dover, and the wind
> Sitting so fair, by this he's safe at Calais,
> And ere long will be at Louvain.

Louvain, be it noted, one of the chief seminaries for the despatch of Jesuit priests to England and a centre to which many English

---

[1] *CHEL*, VI, p. 150.
[2] *Drame*, p. 337.
[3] To take only one example, *The Renegado*, the Oriental and Mohammedan colouring, as well as certain suggestions for the story, were taken from a study of contemporary travel accounts by Lavender, Sandys, and Knolles. *See* Professor W. G. Rice, *The Sources of Massinger's 'The Renegado'*, *PQ*, XI, 1932.

Catholics fled![1] And Luke Frugal avows that the money which has suddenly been entrusted to him is

> A curse I cannot thank you for; and, much less,
> Rejoice in that tranquillity of mind
> My brother's vow must purchase. I have made
> A dear exchange with him: he now enjoys
> My peace and poverty, the trouble of
> His wealth conferred on me.

Perhaps we are not entitled to say that Luke's undertaking in the next scene to convert three American Indians (really Sir John Frugal, Sir Maurice Lacy, and Mr. Plenty in disguise) is a more Roman Catholic than Anglican activity, even though at the time the Roman Church was much more vigorous in proselytising the heathen. But Luke's rejoicing over his apparent success in life has several phrases that would come oddly from a Protestant:

> Continue this felicity, not gained
> By vows to saints above, and much less purchased
> By thriving industry; nor fallen upon me
> As a reward to piety, and religion,
> Or service to my country: I owe all
> This to dissimulation, and the shape
> I wore of goodness. Let my brother number
> His beads devoutly, and believe his alms
> To beggars, his compassion to his debtors,
> Will wing his better part, disrobed of flesh,
> To soar above the firmament.[2]

And Lady Frugal's penitent address to her husband's portrait later in the same scene is that of a Roman Catholic wife to a Roman Catholic husband:

> My kind husband,
> (Blessed in my misery) from the monastery
> To which my disobedience confined thee,
> With thy soul's eye, which distance cannot hinder,
> Look on my penitence. O, that I could
> Call back time past! Thy holy vow dispensed,
> With what humility would I observe
> My long-neglected duty!

[1] Canon David Mathew says (*The Age of Charles I*, 1951, p. 135): 'It was a simple matter for members of such families [i.e. recusants] to enter the English convents in France and the Low Countries. There was a recognised, if illegal line of travel'; and in a footnote on the same page he quotes two examples culled from the State Papers of 1633 and 1634 of men accused of transporting across the sea to Dunkirk people who were making for Louvain.   [2] v. iii.

Massinger was accustomed, as I have noted, to give some local colour in his other plays; and, it must be remarked, there is nothing savouring of popery in the other play set in contemporary England, *A New Way to Pay Old Debts*. However, in *The City Madam* Massinger has gone out of his way to misrepresent the local circumstances. If, in some hypothetical source, the story was set in a Roman Catholic milieu, say in Italy or in Spain, there is no reason why Massinger, in transposing the plot, should not have taken more pains to make it accord better with the actualities of Protestant London. But, in fact, there is no known source for *The City Madam*, and the discovery of a source in a work by a Roman Catholic would not suffice to explain Massinger's handling of it. In any case, Massinger at other times took such liberties as he pleased with his sources.

Two of these deserve some notice in the present connection. The first, *The Maid of Honour*, has already been referred to in Koeppel's notice of Massinger's gratuitous departure from the source (a *novella*, after Boccaccio, in Painter's *Palace of Pleasure*) in making his heroine renounce the world and take the veil. The setting in Sicily and in Sienna, which is taken over from Painter, makes this appropriate enough. But the fact that Bertoldo is a Knight of Malta and the moral issues depending thereon, as well as the device of making Camiola enter a nunnery at the end of the play, are introduced by Massinger. In particular, the whole tone of the passage in which Camiola renounces the world and, as in many other plays by Massinger, much of the phraseology, referring as it so often does to saints, guardian angels, the penitential system, purgatory, and so on,[1] can hardly be attributed to one who was not definitely sympathetic with, if not committed to, the Roman Catholic habitude. Here, as elsewhere, 'Out of the abundance of the heart the mouth speaketh.'[2]

The second play is *The Renegado*, the source of which is Cervantes's play, *Los Baños de Argel*. Massinger has made Cervantes's Spaniards into Italians, Venetians in fact; but of course he has kept them Roman Catholics.

Now, it has been argued that Massinger has in this play betrayed an ignorance as to a Roman Catholic fact which an actual Romanist today could hardly make. That is to say, his Francisco is at once a Jesuit and a Bishop. As Chelli puts it, 'il nous représente un jesuite

[1] Some examples of Massinger's characters using such phrases to be found in *The City Madam* are II. iii: 'Though saints and angels were their physicians;' and v. iii: '. . . not gained by vows to saints above'; and for some of the multitudinous examples in other plays, see: *Duke of Milan*, II. iii; *Unnatural Combat*, III. iii, v. i, and v. iii; *Maid of Honour*, v. i; *Picture*, I. i (three examples); *Guardian*, II. v; *Believe As You List*, IV. ii; and *Bashful Lover*, II. iv, III. iii, and IV. i.

[2] *Matthew* xii. 3.

évêque, ou habillé en évêque: deux choses également monstrueuses'.[1]
The stage direction for Francisco's entrance in Act IV, scene i, is

Enter Francisco in a cope, like a Bishop.

It should be noted that this particular vestment is of some importance
in the plot, and so the direction is more likely to have been introduced
by Massinger than by the playhouse bookkeeper. For the renegade
Grimaldi had committed sacrilege in St. Mark's in Venice (before
the play's action begins) while Francisco had been celebrating mass
in these very robes. When Francisco enters in them, the repentant
Grimaldi kneels and confesses:

> In this reverend habit,
> All that I am turned into eyes, I look on
> A deed of mine so fiend-like, that repentance,
> Though with my tears I taught the sea new tides,
> Can never wash off: all my thefts, my rapes,
> Are venial trespasses, compared to what
> I offered to that shape, and in a place too,
> Where I stood bound to kneel to't.

And Francisco himself refers to the vestments in his reply:

> 'Tis forgiven:
> I with his tongue, whom, in these sacred vestments,
> With impure hands thou didst offend, pronounce it.

Now, one might point out that the stage direction '*in a cope, like a
Bishop*' does not say that he is a bishop, and in any case is only a
direction for the actor and producer. Not one in ten, probably not
one in a hundred, of Massinger's audience had ever seen Mass
celebrated, by bishop or priest. All that they did have was a hazy
notion that Roman Catholic clergy celebrated in gorgeous vestments,[2]
and all that was needed to provide them with an impressive stage-
picture was 'a cope, like a Bishop's'. In addition, however, one might
point out, in direct contradiction to Chelli, that a Jesuit Bishop is
not, after all, such a 'chose monstrueuse'. Sir James Fitzjames
Stephen points out in his essay on the founders of the Jesuit order[3]
that '. . . every Jesuit was to bind himself to reject all secular or
ecclesiastical dignities, except such as the society itself might have to
bestow. But it was provided that if the Pope should constrain any

---

[1] *Drame*, pp. 329–330.
[2] Whereas in the Anglican Church, from Archbishop Parker's *Advertisement* of 1566 to
secure uniformity in the matter of clerical robes (confirmed by the canons of 1603 under
Archbishop Whitgift), the vestments were much simpler. Except in cathedrals and collegiate churches the surplice was the only vestment in use; and soon even in the cathedrals
and collegiate churches the permissive cope was added only on occasions of high ceremony.
[3] *Essays in Ecclesiastical Biography*, London, 1849, Vol. I, p. 180.

member to accept a bishopric, he would, in that capacity, give heed to the advice of his General.' The Pope, then, could constrain a Jesuit to accept a bishopric—though it must be admitted that such an event has never been common. Massinger may have been aware of this fact and not at all ignorant of Roman Catholic practice. Still the evidence is inconclusive, and it is open to question whether the cope is merely a piece of playhouse mummery induced by Massinger's ignorance or whether he really did know that under some circumstances a Jesuit could also be a bishop.

Much more evidential are certain features not in the source: the undeniable sympathy with persons governed by Roman Catholic motives and outlook and with the appropriate devotional practice; the making of Francisco a Jesuit, in Massinger's day a particularly odious kind of Romanist; the scene of the conversion and baptism of Donusa; and the discussion of the lawfulness and efficacy of lay baptism.[1]

Chelli's own conclusion, if conclusion it can be called, is as follows:

'Autant il est difficile de prouver chez lui une conversion formelle, autant il est aisé de concilier des sympathies romaines avec l'adhésion générale à l'Eglise établie d'Angleterre. D'abord, il exista de tout temps, au sein de l'anglicanisme, une tendance vers le mysticisme ritualiste, en même temps que cette impulsion inverse du côté du calvinisme plus strict et plus froid. Laud, Charles Ier lui-même, ne furent-ils pas soupçonnés d'affinités papistes? L'époque de Massinger est celle aussi de G. Herbert et de Nicholas Ferrar. Les trente-neuf articles souffrirent les interprétations les plus diverses.'[2]

This seems to me to be very much an opinion *ab extra*, the opinion of a foreigner who has not caught the English religious idiom. The reference to the different interpretations put on the Thirty-Nine Articles and the reading of seventeenth-century Anglicanism are coloured by a knowledge of Tractarianism and *Tract XC*. Massinger is fond of ritual all right—not merely associated with religious observance, but also with the formalities of polite intercourse. But what he shows as regards religious ritual is not at all ritualistic mysticism. There is nothing mystical about his religion. It is, on the contrary, declaratory, practical, defined. His mind, one can say quite definitely, is non-mystical. The impression of Roman Catholicism which it conveys is not as elusive as Chelli's words suggest: it comes on the one hand from a ready and frequent resort to the terminology of Roman Catholic usage and on the other from the

---

[1] The remarks on lay baptism were perhaps suggested to Massinger by another Cervantes' passage, *Don Quixote*, I, chap. xxxvii.　　　[2] *Drame*, p. 337.

way of presenting Roman Catholic characters in action. All this is quite different from the true ritualistic mysticism of Nicholas Farrar or from the centrally Anglican devotion of George Herbert, and quite different from what led the ultra-Protestant to apply 'Catholic' and 'papist' opprobriously to Charles I and Laud. It is rather the familiarity and sympathy with Roman Catholicism of one speaking from inside the Roman fold.

As for the Anglican establishment, Massinger provides no hint of his attitude. It would be quite unreasonable to read anything into the slight sketch of the compliant Parson Willdo, Overreach's chaplain in *A New Way to Pay Old Debts*. Again, Massinger's plays are singularly free from attacks on Puritans, either those within the Church of England or the Presbyterians and others outside. No Puritan himself, he never satirises and only occasionally even mentions them.[1] Even in defending the stage and actors in *The Roman Actor*, he keeps Paris much more to apology than to attack on detractors (whom, if he had attacked them, his audience would have understood to be Puritan theatrophobes). It was common form in other dramatists to present Puritans as canting hypocrites. But Massinger's chief hypocrite, Luke Frugal, is in fact a Roman Catholic.

While I have inclined more to the view that Massinger had Roman Catholic sympathies, probably to the degree of being a Romanist, the question is still arguable. What does seem to emerge quite clearly from the plays is that, Anglican or Roman Catholic, Massinger had a respectful tolerance in matters of faith rare in his century. He was never polemical or satirical or flippant where religion was concerned. He respected piety, devotion, and sincerity; he abhorred impiety, blasphemy, and sham.

★

Massinger's relation to Stoicism is the most interesting, as well as the most involved, aspect of his thought. But a full investigation of this would move far beyond the confines of this book and must, of necessity, form part of a much wider study of the philosophic, as distinct from the purely dramatic, implications of sixteenth- and seventeenth-century Senecanism. It is only possible, therefore, to indicate here certain lines of approach which may be of use to future workers in this field.

[1] The only examples I can find occur in *Renegado*, I. i, *Unnatural Combat*, III. i, *Duke of Milan*, I. i, *A New Way to Pay Old Debts*, I. i.

I would approach Massinger's relation to Stoicism through what I venture to call his ethical psychology. As I have pointed out, both in this and in previous chapters, the tension between the reason and the passions profoundly interested him. In fact, methodical man that he was, he largely built his characterisation on it and his plotting round it. Moreover, incidental references or allusions to it are continually cropping up. It colours his conception of the relationship between the sexes on the one hand and his conception of the ideal ruler on the other. And everywhere, in regard to sex or love, politics and rule, and religion, the paramount importance of the reason is expressed or assumed. Massinger's characters (at least all those he respects, and some of the others as well) are reasoners more or less at odds with passions.

The dichotomy in the soul which so impressed him, or something like it, is of course implicit in St. Paul's confession and cry:

> For the good that I would I do not: but the evil which I would not, that I do. . . . I see another law in my members, warring against the law of my mind, and bringing me into captivity to the law of sin which is in my members.[1]

And it might be regarded as a diffusive commonplace in practical ethics. But Massinger held his belief in it much more deliberately, and he was scholarly moralist enough to be aware, in some measure at least, of its ancient source in Stoicism.[2]

He owed, however, much more than his psychological principles to Stoicism, and it is a debt that is constantly apparent. Many of the cardinal principles of Stoicism are implicit in his plays, and there are numerous places in which he quotes its dogma with evident approval. A brief, though necessarily oversimplified, statement of a few of these principles, other than the Stoic view of the mind, will perhaps best show, when compared with the aspects of his thought which I have discussed earlier in this chapter, the full extent of Massinger's debt. According to the Stoic view, the universe is governed by one good and wise God who exercises a moral government. Human beings must raise their minds to comprehend this government by universal law and must enter into the views of a Creator who, divinely just, regards all interests equally. The interests of the whole world are infinitely greater than those of a single created being. Good exists in the world, and consequently also evil, and man is free to choose

---

[1] *Romans* vii. 19 and 23.

[2] There were anticipations in Aristotle's *Nichomachean Ethics* and *De Anima* and in the Socratic–Platonic conception of the tripartite soul allegorised in the *Phaedrus* as the charioteer and his two horses.

between them. Man has contact with the Deity through the higher, more intellectual, part of his nature, and his endeavour ought to be to advance constantly in virtue. The pains which are met with in life are an evil, but with the aid of the discipline of the will, they may be triumphed over. There are, in addition, numerous associated ideas, all of which we likewise meet in Massinger: the universal brotherhood of mankind is stressed and kindness to slaves is encouraged; the ideal 'Wise Man' is praised and the duties of active citizenship are urged upon all men; the four virtues, Prudence, Justice, Fortitude, and Temperance, are continually praised, with Justice, as the social virtue, placed above the rest[1]; morality is based on piety, on duty to God, and the idea of obligatory Duty in general is inculcated. Even Massinger's 'feminism' is found to have its antecedent in Seneca.[2]

I have here presented, in their simplest form, merely some of the facets of Stoic thought, some of which are most obvious in Massinger. It is in these, more generalised, respects that his debt to Stoicism and the consistency of his adherence to its doctrine are most clear. Mere approving quotation of Stoic dogma is, of course, no more than a seventeenth-century dramatic commonplace,[3] but the underlying Stoic fabric of such otherwise widely differing plays as, for example, *Believe As You List* and *The Bondman* cannot be ignored.

It is obvious that the Stoic ethic is, of all classical thought, the feature most easily reconcilable with Christianity. As R. M. Gummere says, '. . . Stoicism was the porch to Christianity. Then, as now, it was the thought-force that lay nearest to our inspirational religion.'[4] In a sense, that is, by an unfortunate and inevitable concatenation of events, in which Paul of Tarsus, the director of the Christian ethic, played no small part, Christianity and Stoicism became inextricably interwoven and intermingled.

Thus it comes about that it is difficult to decide how much of Massinger's Stoic cast of thought has come to him direct and how much is that diluted Christianised Stoicism that was rapidly coming into distillation in the sixteenth and early seventeenth centuries.[5] The

---

[1] See in particular, Cicero, *De Officiis*.

[2] 'Feminism, that most modern of all modern topics, offers the most fruitful field for Seneca's reform ideas.' R. M. Gummere, *Seneca the Philosopher and his Modern Message*, London, 1922, p. 72.

[3] Massinger always quotes Stoic dogma with approval, explicit or implicit—sometimes in extensive passages. In this connexion see particularly the opening of Act IV, scene iii, of *The Maid of Honour* and the dying speeches of Rusticus and Sura in *The Roman Actor*, III. ii.   [4] *Op. cit.*, p. 54.

[5] It must be remembered, however, that many Stoic tenets now accepted as Christian commonplaces would not have been so accepted at the beginning of the seventeenth century.

matter is one for argument, of course, but almost certainly his Stoicism came to him direct and, as is only natural in a dramatist writing at that time, from Seneca.

The history of dramatic Senecanism and its appeal to the Elizabethan taste need not be rehearsed here. Seneca was Latin, not Greek. He could even be quoted in the original[1] with a fair chance of being understood, even in the public theatre. His linguistic bravura appealed to the Elizabethan love of declamation and bombast. Moreover, since governmental restrictions imposed a serious handicap on dramatists in forbidding them to deal seriously with religion,[2] they largely resorted to Senecan Stoicism as a substitute and tragic makeweight. What the dramatic followers of Seneca got, from Seneca himself (both in the original or in translation) and from a multitude of secondary sources, was, to put the count briefly: more of an artistic conscience, a standard of dignity and dramatic decorum, a feeling for the tragic mood, the more appropriate vehicle of blank verse, the weight of philosophical or gnomic reflection and aphorism, an elaboration of descriptive expatiation, abundance of classical allusion, the crime-and-revenge motif, the ghost and his accessories, sensational and melodramatic—not to say abnormal— horrors and thrills, and strong passions and the accompanying rhetoric and rant.

It was into this dramatic tradition which had absorbed Senecan Stoicism—which held it in suspension, as it were—that Massinger came. He breathed the Senecan aroma in the very air of the theatre. All the same, it seems plain to a reader of the plays that Massinger, like Chapman in his later tragedies,[3] was not content merely with the tradition: he took to Stoicism also afresh and on his own because of something in it congenial to himself, fusing it easily with his naturally austere Christian ethic and using it for much more than $\delta\iota\acute{\alpha}\nu\omicron\iota\alpha$ and ethical comment. It is this preoccupation in his plays with Stoic ideas, posing Stoic problems and giving Stoic answers, that goes a long way towards giving a Latin colouring to his ethic and impressing a classical seal upon his thought.

The classical quiddity in his thought-pattern is of course not something unique in his period. Most of his contemporaries in the quality were after all still giving expression in serious drama to 'that vein of talent which Shakespeare has christened "Ercles vein" '.[4] But more

---

[1] Hieronimo in *The Spanish Tragedy*, III, xiii, enters with Seneca's plays in his hand (cf. Massinger's *The Maid of Honour*, IV. iii).

[2] Cf. E. K. Chambers, *The Elizabethan Stage*, I, pp. 276, 303.

[3] See J. W. Wieler, *George Chapman—The Effect of Stoicism upon his Tragedies*, New York, 1949, for a particularly illuminating study in this field.

[4] H. W. Garrod, *The Profession of Poetry*, Oxford, 1929, p. 227.

than most (Ben Jonson, who was the best classical scholar among the dramatists, Chapman the second best, and probably also Marston, being the only exceptions), Massinger seems to have studied things Roman, republican history and the Romano-Stoic attitude in particular, and to have infused something of the stern Roman mood into his own work. This spirit is not a mere matter of allusion and reference, plentiful as both are.[1] As a matter of fact, though not a few of the allusions and references are sufficiently out-of-the-way to show Massinger as moving freely about the field, the general tendency is rather to the more banal and demonetised kind. It is much more significant that what Massinger borrowed from the authors he read was the idea, the thought behind the statement; very much in the same way as he borrowed an idea or sentiment from Shakespeare and in doing so deprived it of its emotional quality by reclothing it in grey, abstract words.[2] So an interesting light is cast on the nature of Massinger's mind and his concern with abstract ideas more than emotions by the fact that, whereas other dramatists like Webster and Marston seized on the outward symbols of Seneca, he extracted little of the features that go to make up what is known as theatrical Senecanism (though he has some of its horrors) and peered behind the melodrama at the thought-content. To put it another way: instead of being merely buttressed with Senecanism, his plays are erected, from their very foundations, upon a skeleton of Stoicism.

It is not surprising that they are so. Stoicism, at least on its ethical side, was bound to appeal to Massinger, since it was meant to be a lofty but practical workaday philosophy of life, combining an ethical idealism with a regard for the world of affairs. Seneca's thought in particular, whether it came to him direct from the Latin or from the intellectual climate of his day and Renaissance writers, appealed to him, as it had appealed to hundreds of distinguished thinkers from Petrarch onwards, to say nothing of those before, because of its practical common sense, a commodity of which Massinger had a considerable store.

That he had some slight knowledge of Greek may be possible.[3] Whether it was enough to read Epictetus and Marcus Aurelius in the original scarcely matters. Both were available in the bilingual (Greek-Latin) editions of the sixteenth and seventeenth centuries, and he had no need except laziness or haste to resort to such English translations as there were—the *Manual* of Epictetus in the version of

---

[1] Chelli has made a long and comprehensive collection and has supplied the sources. *Collaboration*, pp. 187–213.

[2] See below, pp. 203–210.

[3] See Cruickshank, *Philip Massinger*, Appendix II.

James Sandford (1567), and of John Healey (1610, 1616, and 1636). It is, however, much more probable that it was Seneca in the original to whom Massinger resorted for ethical hint and maxim. Thomas Lodge's *Works of Lucius Annaeus Seneca, Both Morall and Naturall*, with a life of Seneca by Lipsius, was at hand from 1614 and was reprinted in 1620 and 1632 (there can be no question but that Massinger knew this work very well indeed), in addition to the translations of the plays, and a few other translations of separate works, if Massinger wanted to take the ready and easy way.[1]

Whatever may be the debt to Stoicism, Massinger shows no attraction to the ethics—and as I have all along implied, ethics, not metaphysics, was his philosophical concern—of either Plato or Aristotle. That Plato should have no appeal excites no surprise. The mind of Massinger was completely unmystical, if not indeed anti-mystical. And though a neo-neo-Platonism was in the Renaissance air, the rhapsodies of Ficino, the speculations of Bruno, and the Platonised Christianity of Spenser's *Hymns* could not have been to his severely practical taste.

But Aristotle is practical enough in his ethical teaching. Moreover, a very much mediated and scholastic Aristotelianism was still deeply entrenched in the Universities. By the early 1600's, however, the hold of Aristotle on the human mind was here and there weakening; although, to be sure, while his authority in certain fields (for example, metaphysics and physics) was losing its effect, his authority in poetics and rhetoric was only beginning, so far as the modern world is concerned, and, of course, his authority in logic remained unchallenged. Naturally Massinger could not have escaped at Oxford from the academic Aristotelianism which a few years before had annoyed Bacon within the sister university. But apart from what of Aristotelian origin in the ethical field was warp and woof of Western thought, so interfused as not to be separable and therefore so much a common factor as to have no special interest in a study of Massinger's mind, he mentions Aristotle only twice, both times as a logician[2]: but on anything like the conscious level of indebtedness as regards ethics Massinger owes little to his teaching. He pays little or no regard, for instance, to the peculiarly Aristotelian concept of virtue, and rarely deals with such important Aristotelian themes as Courage, Liberality, Magnificence, Reputation, Gentleness, or

---

[1] See *CBEL*, i, p. 807, for works by Robert Whittington, Arthur Golding, and Sir Ralph Freeman.

[2] *The Emperor of the East*, II. i, in which the logical element of the Greek national temperament, in the person of Aristotle, is rejected by Theophilus; and *The Unnatural Combat*, IV. ii, where Belgarde, Massinger's metaphysical Captain, is conducting an academic disputation in the street.

Friendliness. Of course, such elements of Aristotelian thought as had passed into Stoicism are represented. Massinger's view of Justice, for example, is of the practical Stoic virtue, far removed from the somewhat rarefied δικαιοσύνη of Aristotle, let alone that of Plato. Similarly, the Aristotelian doctrine of the golden mean is reduced to the more limited Stoic idea of Temperance. The very phrase, 'golden mean', occurs only once, and then in a context that shows that Massinger is resorting to a cliché.[1]

Enough has been said to demonstrate Massinger's intense preoccupation with moral problems as they affect human conduct. It is this fundamental gravity, as much as the absence of competition from other dramatists, which made him the leading figure in the theatre of the late 1620's. The Jacobean–Caroline period was, after all, a serious age. As Professor F. P. Wilson has said:

> Readers whose knowledge of Elizabethan and Jacobean literature is confined to anthologies of poetry—the sonnet, the erotic poem, the pastoral, the secular lyric—may be surprised at the statement that the main preoccupations of Elizabethans and Jacobeans alike were with religion, theological controversy, and what may be called compendiously if loosely moral philosophy; yet it was so. What distinguishes the Jacobean age from the Elizabethan is its more exact, more searching, more detailed enquiry into moral and political questions and its interest in the analysis of the mysteries and perturbations of the human mind.[2]

It was to this very interest in his age that Massinger's plays appealed; and I would venture to suggest that this feature of his work is the one which retains most interest for the student today.

★

As might be expected of a moralist with an expressed intention to 'reform the modern vices', Massinger was also something of a satirist. Not that a satiric purpose governs any of his plays as such a purpose rules the bitter comedies of Ben Jonson. The satiric in them is limited to incidental comments and occasional extra-dramatic passages of some length. In these he does allow himself a kind of Malvolio

---

[1] *Great Duke of Florence*, I. i:
      'Happy the golden mean! Had I been born
      In a poor sordid cottage, not nursed up
      With expectation to command a court,
      I might, like such of your condition, sweetest,
      Have ta'en a safe and middle course . . .'

[2] *Elizabethan and Jacobean* (Alexander Lectures in English, 1943), Oxford, 1945, pp. 19–20.

smile. Otherwise he is too much in earnest to treat the human tragedy or tragi-comedy any way but seriously. No doubt a case might be made out for describing some of his type characters, especially the more single and homogeneous ones, whether with or without ticket-names, as satiric or semi-satiric. But it seems true that characterisation by types in Massinger is more a dramaturgic method than an act of moral condemnation. His characters are at least trying to be real people, and they occupy a middle place between Jonson's farcical 'humours' or the 'characters' of Hall and Earle and the well-rounded *vraisemblances* of Shakespeare. In short, they incline more towards the Shavian or the Dickensian than to the Jonsonian.[1]

It is convenient to notice here that there are certain recurring themes which never fail to rouse his ire or contempt. The contemporary state of England and her unpreparedness for war is a frequent subject. It comes, by analogy, into Timoleon's long arraignment of the supine state of Syracuse in Act I, scene iii, of *The Bondman* and in many of the passages aimed at Buckingham to which I have already referred in this chapter.[2] The theme is sometimes, as in Cleora's speeches in Act I, scene iii, of *The Bondman* and Bertoldo's in Act I, scene i, of *The Maid of Honour*, coupled with a fervent patriotic outburst. Again the debauched state of the court in which the play happens to be set (but which all the audience would understand to represent the court at Westminster), its nepotism and favouritism, its prodigally expensive masques, and its courtiers' extravagances, especially in dress, are often lashed, as in *The Duke of Milan*, Act II, scene i, and Act IV, scene i, *The Renegado*, Act II, scene i, and Act III, scene iv, *The Maid of Honour*, Act III, scene iii, *The Picture*, Act II, scene ii, and *The Great Duke of Florence*, Act I, scene i, and Act III, scene ii. On the other hand, Massinger introduces satire of country life in Act II, scene ii, of *The City Madam*, and the relation between the city and the court is satirically presented in Act IV, scene iii, of *The Parliament of Love*.

There was one subject on which Massinger grew particularly heated. So much indeed does indignation sound in his lines on this theme that, even although it may be dismissed as a commonplace of seventeenth-century drama, one is inclined to surmise that he was speaking with the bitter memory of an unhappy personal experience. This is his frequent denunciation of the treatment meted out to the ex-Serviceman. It makes up practically the whole of the interpolation, as it might be called, of Belgarde in *The Unnatural Combat*,

---

[1] As perhaps might be expected, Massinger was one of Dickens's favourite dramatists.
[2] See above, pp. 173–174.

including his set speeches, almost in the manner of an academic exercise, in Act III, scene iii. The subject is taken up again from the same point of view in Act III, scene i, of *The Duke of Milan*. But perhaps the best display by Massinger on this theme is the long speech of Eubulus in Act II, scene ii, of *The Picture*:

> What wise man,
> That, with judicious eyes, looks on a soldier,
> But must confess that fortune's swing is more
> O'er that profession, than all kinds else
> Of life pursued by man? They, in a state,
> Are but as surgeons to wounded men,
> E'en desperate in their hopes: while pain and anguish
> Make them blaspheme, and call in vain for death,
> Their wives and children kiss the surgeon's knees,
> Promise him mountains, if his saving hand
> Restore the tortured wretch to former strength:
> And when grim Death, by Aesculapius' art,
> Is frighted from the house, and health appears
> In sanguine colours on the sick man's face,
> All is forgot; and, asking his reward,
> He's paid with curses, often receives wounds
> From him whose wounds he cured: so soldiers,
> Though of more worth and use, meet the same fate,
> As it is too apparent. I have observed,
> When horrid Mars, the touch of whose rough hand
> With palsies shakes a kingdom, hath put on
> His dreadful helmet, and with terror fills
> The place where he, like an unwelcome guest,
> Resolves to revel, how the lords of her, like
> The tradesman, merchant, and litigious pleader,
> And such-like scarabs bred in the dung of peace,
> In hope of their protection, humbly offer
> Their daughters to their beds, heirs to their service,
> And wash with tears their sweat, their dust, their scars:
> But when those clouds of war, that menaced
> A bloody deluge to the affrighted state,
> Are, by their breath, dispersed, and overblown,
> And famine, blood, and death, Bellona's pages,
> Whipt from the quiet continent to Thrace;
> Soldiers, that, like the foolish hedge-sparrow,
> To their own ruin, hatch this cuckoo, peace,
> Are straight thought burthensome; since want of means,
> Growing from want of action, breeds contempt:
> And that, the worst of ills, falls to their lot,
> Their service, with the danger, soon forgot.

There is truth in the remark of Professor Cruickshank, at least if it be taken as referring to the more self-expressive passages in the plays, that 'Honest indignation is perhaps the emotion which he [Massinger] handles best. The uncontrollable anger which meanness and unworthiness provoke expresses itself in lofty language'.[1] This honest indignation, manly as it is, inclines to the solemn and for that reason perhaps takes from Massinger's talent as a satirist. By giving rein to his anger, he throws away that most formidable weapon in the armoury of the satirist, the rapier of cool and bitter incisiveness of which Pope is such a masterly wielder. Indignation and denunciation are not enough for satire, that most simulating and dissimulating of the literary kinds. I feel that Massinger was both too honest and too single-minded (not to mention too unsubtle in mind), and perhaps too humane, to be a really telling satirist. He disliked without disguise and he condemned without qualification— no more. He lacked the wit and still more the humour, the poise, the assumption of cool contempt, the command of detached and damaging ridicule without which the sophisticated art of satire is too like mere invective.

★

In the course of this chapter I have spoken at some length of Massinger's morality and moral intention. I do not, however, want to leave the impression that the plays belong to a species of dramatic sermon. They are very far from that, heavily larded as they are with moralising.

Professor Cruickshank tried both to sum up and to dismiss the matter when he said, 'Massinger, in his grasp of stagecraft, his flexible metre, his desire in the sphere of ethics to exploit both vice and virtue, is typical of an age which had much culture, but which, without being exactly corrupt, lacked moral fibre.'[2] Into this pantechnicon sentence the author has crammed somewhat unrelated ideas. It is difficult to see why the 'grasp of stagecraft' and the 'flexible metre' are 'typical of an age which lacked moral fibre'. Be that as it may, the sentence, even without these phrases, requires elucidation, though hardly the sophisticated elucidation it receives from Mr. T. S. Eliot.[3] According to Professor Cruickshank, Massinger wanted to exploit both vice and virtue. With this (so far as I understand it) I disagree. I feel that Professor Cruickshank should have contented

---

[1] *Philip Massinger*, pp. 34–35.   [2] *Ibid.*, p. 29.
[3] Throughout a review of Professor Cruickshank's book, printed in *Selected Essays*, London, 1932.

himself with saying that many things in Massinger's plays reflect the taste of his time and that much in his plays to which we take moral exception or which we find morally unpalatable can be excused on the score of the public for whom he wrote. It was an audience demanding that its plays should be liberally spiced with sexual 'danger', sexual obliquity, ambiguity, and pregnancy; an audience which 'sought from tragedy, not its proper satisfaction, but every kind of satisfaction'[1]; an audience largely of the court and its hangers-on, all drawn more to dalliance in the antechamber than to danger on the battlefield (a preference which Massinger was never slow to point out); an audience which enjoyed the thrill of virtue tempted and got an equal excitement from its triumph or its fall. As Coleridge said, speaking of the typical plays of this period, love 'in Massinger, and Beaumont and Fletcher . . . really is on both sides little better than sheer animal desire. There is scarcely a suitor in all their plays, whose *abilities* are not discussed by the lady or her waiting-woman.'[2] There is, however, a very marked difference between Massinger on the one hand and Beaumont and Fletcher on the other. They have a lubricity probably greater than the average of their audience—an even more slippery ethic: they presented rather what the audience tended to and would liked to have indulged, but were inhibited from. But Massinger had something of the Puritan in him, at once fascinated by sin and censorious of it. He shared the interest of his audience; but he recommended a more excellent way. As Professor Cruickshank says (and here I cannot but agree with him), 'unlike some of his literary contemporaries, Massinger wishes to show Virtue triumphant and Vice beaten. Vice is never glorified in his pages, or condoned.'[3] Or as S. R. Gardiner puts it, 'He never descends to paint immoral intention as virtuous because it does not succeed in converting itself into vicious act.'[4] There is nothing of the essential immorality of Fletcher or perversion of moral standards of Ford.

He never forgot, however, even in his most moralistic vein, that he was writing plays. Had he written in a constantly sermonising strain his work would not have gained the favour it did both in the public theatres and at Court. He dramatised his morality as much as Ibsen or Strindberg did theirs, if without the subtlety that they owed as much to their later age as to their peculiar geniuses.

---

[1] H. W. Garrod (after Aristotle), *The Profession of Poetry*, Oxford, 1929, p. 232.
[2] *Table-Talk and Omniana*, Oxford Edn., p. 232.
[3] *P.M.*, p. 34.   [4] Op. cit., p. 495.

Chapter Six

STYLE

The development of poetry during the seventeenth century is marked by what T. S. Eliot has called a 'dissociation of sensibility'.[1] If we prefer a less obscure interpretation[2] then we can content ourselves by saying that there was a fall in the poetic temperature, a decline from the intensity of poetic mood which distinguishes the Elizabethan–Jacobean creative peak. It is very difficult to break away from such generalisations; but when we come down to consider specific matters of style, the words a poet uses (diction) and the way in which he arranges these words (syntax), it is possible to particularise certain features in which the shift away from the Elizabethan–Jacobean poetic method can be more clearly seen, features symptomatic of a falling-off in poetic tension and intensity. It is those features in particular that I propose to examine in Massinger's style, by comparing and contrasting his work with that of earlier writers, especially Shakespeare.

For Massinger can be usefully compared only with Shakespeare. Only such a comparison can at one and the same time characterise the seventeenth-century poetic change and establish certain objective criteria for Massinger's style to aid in the disentanglement of his hand in collaborated plays. Everyone knows Shakespeare: few know Fletcher, Field or Daborne. In any case, comparison with Fletcher, whose style is as completely different from Massinger's as may be imagined, would be useless if not impossible. Few nowadays care to know the exact line in a scene at which one collaborator left off and another commenced, but once the characteristics of Massinger's style are established, a glance at the page should reveal whether he or, say, Fletcher wrote it. Comparison with Chapman, the Jacobean playwright who most closely approaches Massinger stylistically, would also be of little use since the two were not collaborators.

Indeed, the comparison of Massinger with Shakespeare is particularly significant. As I have noted before,[3] Massinger's work

---

[1] Cf. his *Selected Essays*, in particular the essays entitled *Philip Massinger* and *The Metaphysical Poets*.

[2] The phrase, Mr. Eliot tells us ('Milton', *Proc. Brit. Acad.*, xxxiii, p. 7), is one of the 'two or three phrases' of his coinage 'which have had a success in the world astonishing to their author'. The most interesting examination of the phrase is F. W. Bateson's 'Dissociation of Sensibility' in *Essays in Criticism* for July, 1951 (Vol. 1, No. 3, p. 302).

[3] See above, Chap. I, p. 53.

belongs both in spirit and by subject-matter to the romantic school of Shakespeare and Fletcher (though, to be sure, its moralistic aim and serious intention owe something to the contrasting school of Ben Jonson). In his plays, as in those of Webster, Tourneur, Fletcher, and others, there are, however, constant echoes and reminiscences of Shakespeare, of a different kind.

As for the reminiscences, by which I mean imitations of plot, motif, or incident, they occur more or less unmistakably in nearly every play. As they do not concern Massinger's stylistic relation to Shakespeare, I need mention here only a few of the more striking. The story of *The Duke of Milan*, for example, in which a husband is convinced of the adultery of his innocent wife by a man whom he trusts but who is in reality an enemy waiting for an opportunity of revenge, is a sort of *traduction raisonnée* of *Othello*, with an attempt in it to supply the traitor with an unequivocal motive. In *The Fatal Dowry* a new, and not unsuccessful, twist is given to a similar plot by creating a situation in which a loyal and disinterested friend, not an enemy this time, has the unpleasant task of persuading a husband that he is indeed married to an adulteress. In *A New Way to Pay Old Debts* there are striking correspondences to *The Merchant of Venice*; the extortioner, Overreach, closely resembles Shylock; the stolen marriage between Margaret Overreach and young Allworth is exactly parallel to that between Jessica and Lorenzo; and Lady Allworth, Lord Lovell, and Wellborn may be likened to Portia, Antonio, and Bassanio. Many other instances of similarity in situation could be quoted: the scenes in the forest in *The Guardian* recall *As You Like It* and *A Midsummer Night's Dream*; Beaupré's passing the night as the mistress of her own husband in *The Parliament of Love* recalls the similar device in *All's Well That Ends Well* and *Measure for Measure*; and, as an example of a lesser reminiscence, Sir Giles Overreach in *A New Way to Pay Old Debts* is carried away to 'some dark room' like Malvolio in *Twelfth Night*.

There are, however, even more striking echoes; that is to say, verbal or phrasal recalls and parallels in thought and image. They are so common as to be one of the Massingerian stigmata and lead us to the inevitable conclusion that Massinger must have been a very close student indeed of Shakespeare's work, either as presented on the stage or as read in the quartos and First Folio. These echoes are of varying degrees of clarity, as it were, but frequently they border on direct quotation. And they vary in another way, from echoes of mere turns of phrase, which in themselves make no contribution to the thought, all the way to transfers of Shakespearian διάνοια.

Professor Cruickshank has given[1] a selection of Shakespearian echoes in Massinger, chosen at random from his plays. But I feel that, as a complete list is out of the question, it might be more revealing to present in the first instance the more obvious examples (not all) in one play. I have chosen as a representative play for this purpose *The Duke of Milan*. When this play was actually written is not known; but there is much internal evidence for 1620–1621.[2] In any case, as it was published for the first time in 1623, the knowledge it displays of a familiarity with Shakespeare could hardly have come from a last-minute reading of the First Folio.

In the first scene of the play Graccho, Julio, and Giovanni enter drinking in celebration of the Duchess's birthday. In the course of the conversation, which is reminiscent of such alcoholic occasions in Shakespeare as those in *1 Henry IV*, *Twelfth Night*, and especially *Othello*, because both here and in *The Duke of Milan* the occasions are festal,[3] Graccho declares:

> It is capital treason (*i.e. to be found sober*).
> Or, if you mitigate it, let such pay
> Forty crowns to the poor: but give a pension
> To all the magistrates you find singing catches,
> Or their wives dancing; for the courtiers reeling,
> And the duke himself, I dare not say distempered,
> But kind, and in his tottering chair carousing,
> They do the country service . . .
>   We've nought else to think on.
> And so, dear friends, copartners in my travails,
> Drink hard; and let the health run through the city,
> Until it reel again, and with me cry,
> Long live the duchess!

And a few lines later he adds:

>   Your lord, by his patent,
> Stands bound to take his rouse.

It can hardly be doubted that when Massinger wrote these lines he had in mind quite naturally Hamlet's contemptuous description of the revelry at Elsinore:

> The king doth wake tonight and takes his rouse,
> Keeps wassail and the swagg'ring upspring reels.[4]

Another slighter parallel to *Hamlet* occurs in Act I, scene iii, when the

---

[1] *Philip Massinger*, pp. 78–80, and Appendix IV.
[2] See T. W. Baldwin's edition, Lancaster, Pa., 1918.
[3] *Othello* was first published in 1622. *Twelfth Night* did not appear in print before the First Folio of 1623.   [4] *Hamlet*, i. iii.

birthday celebrations are once again the topic of conversation. 'There's a masque,' says the Third Gentleman, adding a question that repeats Claudius's suspicious query:

> Have you heard what's the invention?

In the same scene the Duke abruptly ends the birthday celebrations on hearing the news of the military disaster by saying,

> Silence that harsh music;
> 'Tis now unseasonable: a tolling bell,
> As a sad harbinger to tell me, that
> This pampered lump of flesh must feast the worms,
> Is fitter for me.

These lines, besides a possible subsidiary echo of Donne's famous passage in the *Devotions upon Emergent Occasions*,[1] recall Orsino's order in *Twelfth Night*:

> Enough! no more:
> 'Tis not so sweet now as it was before;

and may owe something as well to Northumberland's,

> Yet the first bringer of unwelcome news
> Hath but a losing office, and his tongue
> Sounds ever after as a sullen bell,
> Remembered knolling a departing friend;

in *2 Henry IV*.[2] The word 'pampered' in the Massinger passage occurs elsewhere in *2 Henry IV* where it is quoted as a catchword from Tamburlaine.[3]

Rather more positive proof that *2 Henry IV*, however different it might be thematically, was floating in Massinger's mind when he was engaged on *The Duke of Milan* is provided by the Emperor Charles's exoneration of Sforza:

> Thou didst not borrow of vice her indirect,
> Crooked, and abject means.[4]

The Shakespeare suggestion is in King Henry's speech to Prince Hal in Act IV, scene v, of *2 Henry IV*:

> God knows, my son,
> By what by-paths and indirect crook'd ways
> I met this crown.

---

[1] *The Bell* (*Oxford Book of English Prose*, No. 116). The 'bell' and 'worm' figures are, of course, constantly recurring in Donne (cf. in particular, *Donne's Last Sermon*, Pearsall Smith, *Donne's Sermons*, 1920, No. 155). [2] I. i.

[3] *2 Henry IV*, II. iv: 'And hollow pampered jades of Asia'. Cf. *Tamburlaine*, line 3980: 'Holla, ye pampered jades of Asia'. [4] III. i.

A closer imitation than anything yet cited is found in Act II, scene i, of the play. The Duke's mother and sister are baiting his very much indulged and adored wife during his absence at the Emperor's court. An open quarrel develops, and in the course of it the following phrases are bandied about:

'For you, puppet ——' . . .
'What of me, pine-tree?' . . .
    '. . . Little you are, I grant,
And have as little worth, but much less wit;' . . .
    '. . . O that I could reach you!
The little one you scorn so, with her nails
Would tear your painted face, and scratch those eyes out.
    '. . . Where are you,
You modicum, you dwarf!' . . .
'Here, giantess, here.'

The interchange is clearly imitated from the quarrel of Hermia and Helena in Act III, scene ii, of *A Midsummer Night's Dream*:

'Fie, fie! you counterfeit, you puppet you!'
'Puppet! why, so: ay, that way goes the game.
Now I perceive that she hath made compare
Between our statures: she hath urged her height; . .
How low am I, thou painted maypole? speak;
How low am I? I am not yet so low
But that my nails can reach unto thine eyes.' . . .
    '. . . Get you gone, you dwarf;
You minimus, of hindering knot-grass made;
You bead, you acorn!'

I would note in particular Massinger's repetition of Shakespeare's 'dwarf' and 'puppet' and his substitution of 'pine-tree' and 'modicum' for Shakespeare's 'maypole' and 'minimus', to say nothing of his referring, like Shakespeare, to 'scratching eyes' and a 'painted face'.

Other Shakespearian echoes in the play are much slighter. Thus, 'She's walking in the gallery,' in Act III, scene ii, seems to recall the lobby Hamlet frequented; 'Stands prepared for either fortune' in Act III, scene i, recalls Hamlet's description of the man 'who is not passion's slave'[1]; the use of the verb 'mewed up' in Act IV, scene iii, has a Shakespearian ring about it[2]; 'let my head answer it if I offend' in the same scene recalls Polonius's 'Take this from this, if this be

---

[1] But see below, p. 245, for a closer parallel to this *Hamlet* passage taken from *The Bondman*, iii. iii. Cf. also *Believe As You List*, i. i.
[2] Cf. *The Taming of the Shrew*, i. i. 187, and *K. John*, iv. ii. 57.

otherwise'; Graccho's 'plummet that may sound his deepest counsels' in Act IV, scene i, recalls faintly Prospero's farewell to his book; and editors have been so influenced by Shakespeare as always to print Massinger's 'discourse or reason' in Act III, scene ii, as 'discourse of reason'.[1] Among other echoes of *Hamlet* which may be found in the play are 'fright the wicked or confirm the good' in Act I, scene iii, and ''Tis wormwood, and it works' and 'creatures wanting reason' in Act II, scene i.

I have given only such striking correspondences to Shakespeare as I have detected in one representative play by Massinger. I know that there are others, and I assume that a Shakespearian with a better verbal memory than I have would find still more.

But the subject of Massinger's Shakespearian correspondences demands further consideration. Their number is one thing. But what about their origin? How far were they consciously recalled? It is clear, to begin with, that Massinger knew Shakespeare's plays well. So well, indeed, that he could not have escaped involuntary recalls even if he had wanted to, any more than Hazlitt could. The very nature of many of the echoes pretty well precludes the possibility of conscious recall. They are mere turns of insignificant phrase—phrases which though peculiarly Shakespearian and not merely Elizabethan–Jacobean common form, are nevertheless little or no more than expletive, or, if more, quite fragmentary. Such phrases are not the least revealing. On the other hand, there are plenty of echoes of Shakespeare which, if Massinger himself did not realise he was making them, his audience certainly would. Such, for example, is:

> I once observed,
> In a tragedy of ours, in which a murder
> Was acted to the life, a guilty hearer
> Forced by the terror of a wounded conscience
> To make discovery of that which torture
> Could not wring from him.[2]

But the assumption is, however, that in this and similar cases Massinger knew quite well what he was about. Indeed, it could scarcely be otherwise. Often, of course, the situation with which he was dealing had a certain similarity to another in Shakespeare and so helped the recall. But perhaps more often the contexts in Shakespeare and Massinger are quite different and the reasons for his echoing of this or that passage must remain obscure—a matter of Massinger's now irrecoverable private associations. That Massinger had seen many or

---

[1] For a further note on this, see Professor Baldwin's Edition, p. 162.
[2] *The Roman Actor*, II. i. See below, p. 244.

all of Shakespeare's plays acted, perhaps many times, may be taken for granted; and in days when memories were better than they are today and when to assist their memories men, especially men with literary interests, were in the habit of jotting down memoranda from sermons and plays and familiar conversation, a man of the theatre like Massinger must have accumulated Shakespeareana. Massinger, however, as we have already seen, was nothing if not methodical, and it is certain that he was a reader of such published plays of Shakespeare as he could get hold of, and that sometimes at least he seems to have been working from a Shakespeare text. In this connexion it is interesting to notice that in *The Duke of Milan* there are at least two notable 'borrowings' from writers other than Shakespeare, one from Jonson's *Catiline* and one from Tourneur's *Revenger's Tragedy*, and the balance of probability is that they were made from the published texts of the plays.[1]

However Massinger did sometimes indulge in patently memorial rearrangement, and the way in which he managed this memorial rearrangement on an apparently conscious level while other half-conscious recalls floated into his mind can be illustrated from *The Emperor of the East*. It is a play in which an uxorious husband falls into jealousy. As Massinger approached the motif of jealousy he inevitably remembered *Othello*. The first sign is Theodosius's,

> Methinks I find Paulinus on her lips;[2]

with its nearly verbatim repetition of Othello's

> I found not Cassio's kisses on her lips.[3]

---

[1] *Duke of Milan*, II. i:

> 'For with this arm I'll swim through seas of blood,
> Or make a bridge, arched with the bones of men.'

Cf. *Catiline*, III. ii:

> 'I would not go through open doors, but break 'em
> Swim to my ends through blood; or build a bridge
> of carcases.'

Duke of Milan, v. ii:

> 'and good angels
> Clap their celestial wings to give it plaudits.'

Cf. *Revenger's Tragedy*, II. i:

> 'O angels, clap your wings upon the skies,
> And give this virgin crystal plaudits.'

Cf. also *Maid of Honour*, v. i:

> 'seraphic angels
> Clap their celestial wings in heavenly plaudits.'

[2] IV. v.   [3] *Othello*, v. ii.

Then, in Act V, scene ii, the jealous husband exclaims:

> Can I call back yesterday, with all their aids
> That bow unto my sceptre? or restore
> My mind to that tranquillity and peace
> It then enjoyed?—Can I make Eudocia chaste,
> Or vile Paulinus honest?

It is impossible to doubt that these lines in the given situation were inspired by Iago's

> Not poppy, nor mandragora,
> Nor all the drowsy syrups of the world,
> Shall ever med'cine thee to that sweet sleep
> Which thou ow'dst yesterday;[1]

and blended with the recurring motif of 'honesty' which we find in *Othello*.[2] But the suggestion from Iago's speech has been fused with another from Othello's cry fifteen lines on:

> O, now for ever
> Farewell the tranquil mind; farewell content.

And it has also, by some unconscious operation of Massinger's mind, been blended with another exclamation from *Richard II*:

> O, call back yesterday, bid time return.[3]

It will be seen from this that the process has not been one of single and straightforward borrowing from Shakespeare, since several threads, two of them, very naturally in the circumstances, from a play dealing with jealousy, have been intertwined. Another echo from *Othello* comes in Act V, scene iii, only a hundred lines later:

> Her greater light as it dimmed mine, I practised
> To have it quite put out;

though Massinger supplies a different emotional context.

All the other plays of Massinger would exemplify just as well as *The Duke of Milan* or *The Emperor of the East* his indebtedness to Shakespeare—an indebtedness greater than that of any other dramatist with the possible exception of Webster. But a full exploration of the subject would justify another study devoted to it alone. I have myself counted over seventy really important reminiscences of Shakespearian passages in the fifteen plays Massinger wrote alone, to say nothing of a multitude of others less striking. These correspondences, it must be remembered, are only those which were immediately

---

[1] *Othello*, III. iii.
[2] For a detailed treatment of the use of this word in *Othello*, see William Empson, *The Structure of Complex Words*, London, 1951.
[3] *Richard II*, III. ii.

obvious in the course of what has been a study of Massinger for a broader purpose than to track him down in Shakespeare's pages.

Undoubtedly there must be many more than either I myself or the recent editors of Massinger have noted. The important thing to note, in this chapter on Massinger's style, is that on an average every play of Massinger's contains at least five resounding echoes from Shakespeare and that such a Shakespearian habitude constitutes a stylistic idiosyncrasy.

The plays of which he shows certain knowledge are: *A Midsummer Night's Dream, As You Like It, The Merchant of Venice, Measure for Measure, Twelfth Night, Much Ado About Nothing, All's Well That Ends Well, Romeo and Juliet, The Taming of the Shrew, Two Gentleman of Verona, Henry IV, Henry V, Henry VI, Richard II, Richard III, Macbeth, King Lear, Julius Caesar, Antony and Cleopatra, Coriolanus*, as well as *Henry VIII*. But the two plays which, to judge by the number of times they are echoed, were Massinger's favourites, are *Hamlet* and *Othello*. Something like 40 per cent of the echoes derive from them.[1] The reasons for these preferences are not far to seek: *Hamlet* was, then as now, probably the best known play by Shakespeare on the stage; and the husband-wife relationship and the motif of jealousy and alleged infidelity of *Othello* would be enough to give it a special place in Massinger's esteem.[2]

★

So far I have concerned myself with Massinger's debts to Shakespeare both for their own interest and as affording a basis for the discussion of Massinger's style in relation to his master. There is, however, another feature which is not altogether unrelated to his imitation of Shakespeare. This might be described as Massinger's imitation of Massinger. Just as he took good things from Shakespeare, so he economically repeated himself. Or at least he had a large store of Massingerian clichés.

The recurrence of favourite words, and the repetition of phrases, sentences, and ideas in Massinger is so frequent as to constitute an abnormality. Shakespeare, of course, seems to have an inexhaustible supply of words and ideas; and the mark of his style is variety and

---

[1] In case it should be objected that the high percentage is due to a closer knowledge of these two plays, I would add that an examination of the reminiscences given by Professor Cruickshank gives an almost identical result.

[2] And not only in Massinger's esteem. As Professor H. W. Wells says (*Elizabethan and Jacobean Playwrights*, New York, 1939, p. 61), 'the romantic narrative, the aristocratic setting, ... the portrait of physical passion represented in *Othello* much attracted the Cavalier mind. Beaumont and Fletcher, Ford, Massinger, and Shirley ... imitate this play far more often than any other work by the master dramatist'.

perpetually specific aptness. While Massinger is not wanting in aptness, his thoughts move within a more conventional orbit and his expression of them runs to the rhetorical cliché. If it is perhaps unfair to contrast him with Shakespeare in his plenitude, it is not so to measure him against, say, Fletcher or Shirley or Ford; and when this is done, one comes away with the impression that Massinger's style was much less flexible and much more reduplicating than perhaps any of his contemporaries. His style was more appliqué than organic; and the recurrence of counters is merely one of the consequences. Just how pervasive and constant this self-repetitiveness is can be realised from the list Miss E. W. Bryne has compiled from a single play, *The Maid of Honour*, of phrases and expressions which Massinger had already used in earlier plays or was to repeat in later ones. This list, with the parallels alongside in another column, runs to thirty pages of close print.[1]

Many of Massinger's repetitions are of favourite words and phrases. Thus the unusual word *apostata* occurs thrice in both *The Virgin Martyr*[2] and *Believe As You List*,[3] and twice each in *The Unnatural Combat*[4] and *The Renegado*[5]; and the corresponding abstract *apostasy* figures in *The Bashful Lover*[6] and *The Maid of Honour*.[7] Another word, rare at the time (especially in a figurative sense), is *embryon*. It is found at least five times in Massinger, always in a figurative use, the plays being: *Believe As You List*,[8] *The Bashful Lover*,[9] *The Great Duke of Florence*,[10] *The Guardian*,[11] and *The Picture*.[12]

Other favourite expressions are: *nil ultra*,[13] *frontless impudence*,[14] *starcrossed*,[15] *phoenix*,[16] *sail-stretched wings*,[17] *to wash an Ethiop*,[18] and a whole host of references to *angels* (especially *guardian angels*) and *saints*.[19]

---

[1] Printed in her edition of *The Maid of Honour*, London, 1927.
[2] III. i; IV. iii, and v. ii. (All Massinger scenes.) [3] II. ii (twice), and v. i.
[4] I. i (twice). [5] I. i, and IV. iii. [6] III. iii.
[7] II. v. The word is not used at all by Shakespeare. [8] I. ii.
[9] IV. i. [10] III. i. [11] II. iii.
[12] II. ii. Cf. also *Thierry and Theodoret*, II. iii, and *The Double Marriage*, v. iii.
[13] *Bashful Lover*, I. i; *Guardian*, v. iv; *Maid of Honour*, IV. iii; *Parliament of Love*, III. iii; *Renegado*, IV, iii; *Unnatural Combat*, II. iii; and *New Way to Pay Old Debts*, IV. i. Cf. also *The Prophetess*, IV. vi.
[14] *Believe As You List*, IV. iv; *Duke of Milan*, II. i; *Guardian*, IV. i; *Parliament of Love*, v. i; *Unnatural Combat*, v. i. Cf. also *Cupid's Revenge*, II. ii; Jonson's *Volpone*, IV. v; and Chapman's *Odyssey*, I. 425.
[15] *Believe As You List*, IV. ii; *Emperor of the East*, v. i; *Great Duke of Florence*, v. iii; also in the poem *Sero Sed Serio*, line 6 (Gifford, iv, p. 596). Cf. also *Romeo and Juliet*, Prologue.
[16] *Emperor of the East*, I. ii; *Picture*, I. ii; *Great Duke of Florence*, III. i; *Maid of Honour*, IV. iii, and v. ii; *Parliament of Love*, v. ii; and *Unnatural Combat*, II. iii. Cf. also *The False One*, II. i; *Henry VIII*, v. v; and Fletcher's *Valentinian*, I. i; I. ii, and III. i.
[17] *Believe As You List*, III. iii; *Bondman*, I. iii; *Unnatural Combat*, I. i. Cf. also *The Prophetess*, II. iii, and see Gifford's footnote, vol. i, p. 141.
[18] *Bondman*, v. iii; *Parliament of Love*, II. ii; *Roman Actor*. III. ii. Cf. also *The False One*, I. ii; Fletcher's *The Woman's Prize*, III. ii, and Beaumont's *Love's Cure*, II. ii.
[19] There are over sixty references to *angels* alone in the plays.

To come now to repeated thought and images. Again and again when a battle is toward Massinger makes one of the characters use the same image to suggest doubt as to the outcome:

> And, it being in suspense, on whose fair tent
> Winged Victory will make her glorious stand.[1]

> Till plumed Victory
> Had made her constant stand upon their helmets.[2]

> . . . it continuing doubtful
> Upon whose tent plumed Victory would take
> Her glorious stand.[3]

> . . . plumed Victory
> Would make her glorious stand upon my tent.[4]

Along with this list may be taken the following in which also Victory is imagined as winged:

> . . . plumed Victory
> Is truly painted with a cheerful look.[5]

> . . . to hug the mistress,
> He doted on, plumed Victory.[6]

> And Victory sit ever on your sword![7]

> But Victory still sits upon your sword.[8]

The examples of the same image in *The False One*:

> The sword . . . which, in civil wars,
> Appoints the tent on which winged Victory
> Shall make her certain stand;[9]

and *The Prophetess*:

> Winged Victory shall take stand on thy tent;[10]

are in themselves good indications that the passages in these collaborations with Fletcher were written by Massinger.

To exemplify further Massinger's self-repetitions of thoughts and images without attempting anything like completeness, I choose three other apparently favourite ideas. The first is the unsavoury one in *The Duke of Milan*:

> These sponges, that suck up a kingdom's fat,
> Battening like scarabs in the dung of peace;[11]

---

[1] *Duke of Milan*, I. i. [2] *Unnatural Combat*, II. i. [3] *Picture*, II. ii.
[4] *Maid of Honour*, I, ii. [5] *Bondman*, III. iv. [6] *Parliament of Love*, III. iii.
[7] *Parliament of Love*, I. v. [8] *Parliament of Love*, IV. ii. [9] I. i.
[10] II. ii. [11] III. i.

so closely repeated in *The Picture*:

> The tradesman, merchant, and litigious pleader,
> And such like scarabs bred in the dung of peace.[1]

The second appears in very similar terms in *The Duke of Milan*[2]:

> There are so many ways to let out life,
> I would not live for one short minute his;[3]

and *The Parliament of Love*:

> There are a thousand doors to let out life;
> You keep not guard of all;[4]

and again in *A Very Woman*, which, although in the first place written by Fletcher, was extensively revised by Massinger:

> Death hath a thousand doors to let out life,
> I shall find one.[5]

The third idea occurs in no less than four plays:

> With your continued wishes, strive to imp
> New feathers to the broken wings of time;[6]

> Could I imp feathers to the wings of time;[7]

> Imp feathers to the broken wings of time;[8]

> Your too much sufferance imps the broken feathers
> Which carry her to this proud height.[9]

These and similar evidences of Massinger's frequent resort to his conscious and unconscious memory of Shakespeare and of the tendency of his mind to run to favourite clichés afford valuable secondary clues to Massinger's share in certain plays in which he only collaborated or which he revised. As such they have been used by those whose chief aim was the detection of Massinger's hand or that of another (Fletcher, Field, Dekker, Daborne, or others) and its disengagement.

But their interest here is the light they throw on the nature and temper of Massinger's mind in relation to his style. We should therefore be justified in coming to the conclusion that a man with such

---

[1] II. ii.
[2] Though the source is in a remarkable passage in *The Duchess of Malfi*, IV. ii:

> 'I know death hath ten thousand several doors
> For men to take their exits.'

[3] I. iii.   [4] IV. ii.   [5] V. i.
[6] *Renegado*, V. viii.   [7] *Roman Actor*, V. ii.
[8] *Great Duke of Florence*, I. i.
[9] *Emperor of the East*, III. ii. The phrase 'imp feathers', drawn from falconry, appears in the Prologue (which may be by Massinger) to *The Little French Lawyer*. Shakespeare uses a similar expression in *Richard II*, II. i. (292): 'Imp out our drooping country's broken wing.'

habitudes or mannerisms exhibits a curious rigidity of mind, a tendency to think in what I have called clichés and counters, and to choose very often the line of least resistance in expressing an idea. Such a tendency, of course, manifests itself in Massinger in other ways, as, for example, in the frequency with which he expresses a moral idea in a moralistic tag and in his irritating gift for stating the obvious.

Massinger's rigidity, however, is not that of the lazy mind. His style exhibits, on the contrary, a kind of dogged and painstaking muscularity, as does his work in other respects as well. Its inelasticity is that of the man temperamentally humourless, lacking in the warm fire of the sensuous imagination and sicklied o'er with the pale cast of convention and abstraction. His mind is deficient in that enterprising enthusiasm and intense energy which is required for the poetic effort and for the unpredictable power of poetry

To haunt, to startle, and waylay.

Naturally such a man, conscientious rather than inventive, scrupulous to the degree of pedantry, was likely to fall into set ways of expression and to repeat what he himself, or another, had said well before. The more so with Massinger, since his situations, characters, motifs, and points of view are all recurring. His self-repetitions and his echoes and borrowings from Shakespeare (and how wan and drooping these become when transplanted) or others, were, in the same way as his characters, extracted from the pigeon-holes where they had lain awaiting use and re-use. They are, of course, symptomatic of the falling-off from the Elizabethan–Jacobean exuberance already mentioned.

I have already remarked briefly, without going further, on one very important feature of Massinger's style, namely, the tendency to periodic, suspended, and parenthetic syntaxis. It is a feature which has received little attention, certainly far less than it deserves, from the students of all our major poets. When I spoke of this marked feature of Massinger's style in the chapter on his stagecraft[1] I was for the time being concerned with the elocutionary demands made on the actors in his plays and the corresponding difficulties of the audience in following such involved sentences. On the other hand, when I referred to the same involution in the chapter on his characterisation,[2] I was particularly interested in the question of the verisimili-

[1] Chap. III, p. 99.   [2] Chap. IV, p. 139.

tude of the dialogue or, rather, of its lack of verisimilitude. It is now the occasion to examine this tendency more specifically as a syntactical phenomenon.

When we read a play by Massinger, even in a modernised text with all the aids that modern logical or grammatical punctuation affords, we are struck by the over-all slowness of our reading and by the number of times we stumble or are forced to pause. On retracing our steps, perhaps by going back to the beginning of the sentence, sometimes by having also to cast our eyes back a speech or two, and re-reading the knotted and labyrinthine sentences, we do get the meaning, if not immediately, then by a little in the way of general analysis. Here are some examples, chosen more or less at random from a much longer list, of the passages which have given most trouble to disentangle:

> Can he tax me,
> That have received some worldly trifles from him,
> For being ungrateful; when he, that first tasted,
> And hath so long enjoyed, your sweet embraces,
> In which all blessings that our frail condition
> Is capable of, are wholly comprehended,
> As cloyed with happiness, contemns the giver
> Of his felicity; and, as he reached not
> The masterpiece of mischief which he aims at,
> Unless he pay those favours he stands bound to,
> With fell and deadly hate![1]

> I, that have read
> The copious volumes of all women's falsehood,
> Commented on by the heart-breaking groans
> Of abused lovers; all the doubts washed off
> With fruitless tears, the spider's cobweb veil
> Of arguments alleged in their defence
> Blown off with sighs of desperate men, and they
> Appearing in their full deformity;
> Know that some other hath displanted me,
> With her dishonour.[2]

> How I have loved, and how much I have suffered,
> And with what pleasure undergone the burthen
> Of my ambitious hopes, (in aiming at
> The glad possession of a happiness,
> The abstract of all goodness in mankind
> Can at no part deserve) with my confession
> Of mine own wants, is all that can plead for me.[3]

---

[1] *The Duke of Milan*, ii. i.   [2] *Renegado*, iii. i.   [3] *Bondman*, v. iii.

Who brings Gonzago's head, or take him prisoner,
(Which I incline to rather, that he may
Be sensible of those tortures, which I vow
To inflict upon him for denial of
His daughter to our bed) shall have a blank,
With our hand and signet made authentical,
In which he may write down himself, what wealth
Or honours he desires.[1]

                  Imperious Love,
As at thy ever-flaming altars Iphis,
Thy never-tired votary, hath presented,
With scalding tears, whole hecatombs of sighs,
Preferring thy power and thy Paphian mother's
Before the Thunderer's, Neptune's or Pluto's
(That, after Saturn, did divide the world,
And had the sway of things, yet were compelled
By thy inevitable shafts to yield,
And fight under thy ensigns) be auspicious
To this last trial of my sacrifice
Of love and service![2]

                I, [that] have stood
The shock of fierce temptations, stopped mine ears
Against all Syren notes lust ever sung,
To draw my bark of chastity (that with wonder
Hath kept a constant and an honoured course)
Into the gulf of a deserved ill-fame,
Now fall unpitied; and, in a moment,
With mine own hands, dig up a grave to bury
The monumental heap of all my years,
Employed in noble actions.[3]

But when I . . . heard her say,
               . . . all favours
That should preserve her in her innocence,
By lust inverted to be used as bawds;
I could not but in duty (though I know
That the relation kills in you all hope
Of peace hereafter, and in me 'twill show
Both base and poor to rise up her accuser)
Freely discover it.[4]

It may be said that the meaning never actually fails to yield itself.
For it is characteristic of Massinger that he is painfully anxious to

---

[1] *Bashful Lover*, II. v.   [2] *Roman Actor*, III. iii.
[3] *The Renegado*, I. iii. See Gifford's footnote, vol. ii, p. 148.
[4] *The Duke of Milan*, IV. iii.

supply every verbal counter with pedantic fullness. He has no short-
cuts to his meaning—'no mitigation or remorse of voice'. Like the
Prologue to *The Mousetrap*, he 'cannot keep counsel; he tells all'.
What gives us pause is not the ambiguities and condensations, the
metaphors dissolving into metaphors, the implications and meanings between the lines, the imaginative daring and the emotional
overtones which at once fascinate and baffle us (and the commenta-
tors) in Shakespeare. Nor are there the verbal and textual corrup-
tions which produce the Shakespearian cruces. The grammar is correct and the constructions intact, barring frequent ellipses. That is,
every sentence says what it means to say and says it with a regard for
verbal usage and grammatical and syntactical orthodoxy. Nevertheless, sentences may be correct without being good, and accurate
without being idiomatic. As Blair says: ' . . . be the subject what it
will, if the sentences be constructed in a clumsy, perplexed, or feeble
manner, it is impossible that a work, composed of such sentences, can
be read with pleasure, or even with profit'.[1] Such Massinger's sentences too often are. They do indeed tend to 'be constructed in a
clumsy, perplexed, or feeble manner'; at least, if 'feeble' in this context be interpreted as meaning 'labouring and overburdened'. They
are not 'feeble' in the sense of 'lacking muscularity'. But it is a muscularity without grace or ease. His sentences do not possess that great
advantage of the periodic form which, as Genung says, 'lies in the
fact that it keeps up and concentrates the reader's attention'.[2] On
the contrary, 'the number and intricacy of the suspensive details are
a draft on the reader's interpreting power'.[3] How much more difficult, then, for an audience in the theatre. In some kinds of poetry,
and particularly in poetry to be read, the poet may take large liberties, trusting his subtleties and complexities to a reader who can turn
back the page. But that was certainly not what Massinger was trying
to provide. Nor was it Shakespeare's kind. Admittedly, Shakespeare's style can be very difficult. As Matthew Arnold said,

> his gift of expression . . . leads him astray, degenerating sometimes into
> a fondness for curiosity of expression, into an irritability of fancy, which
> seems to make it impossible for him to say a thing plainly, even when
> the press of the action demands the very directest language, or its level
> character the very simplest. Mr. Hallam . . . has had the courage . . .
> to remark how extremely and faultily difficult Shakespeare's language
> often is. It is so: you may find main scenes in some of his greatest

---

[1] Hugh Blair, *Lectures on Rhetoric and Belles-Lettres*, London, 1837, p. 131.
[2] J. F. Genung, *The Working Principles of Rhetoric*, New York, 1900, p. 350.
[3] Ibid., p. 351.

tragedies, *King Lear* for example, where the language is so artificial, so curiously tortured, and so difficult, that every speech has to be read two or three times before its meaning can be comprehended. This over-curiousness of expression is indeed but the excessive employment of a wonderful gift—of the power of saying a thing in a happier way than any other man; nevertheless, it is carried so far that one understands what M. Guizot meant when he said that Shakespeare appears in his language to have tried all styles except that of simplicity.[1]

But it is to be noticed in the first place that these opinions of Arnold, Hallam, and Guizot are separated by more than two hundred years from Shakespeare's idiom, by the Great Divide which is 'dissociation of sensibility', and in Guizot's case by a difference of native language. Secondly, what these three critics of Shakespeare's style are speaking about (as, indeed, are most critics when they speak about 'style'—Coleridge not excepted) is his diction, phraseology, and imagery. They are not concerned with his syntax. And however difficult Shakespeare's style may be by reason of the diction, phraseology, and imagery, it is always a speakable style in a strictly elocutionary sense. The thought-elements of it come in an order that is faithful to that of unpremeditated utterance. It observes familiar and colloquial syntax; it runs to principal clauses or their phrasal equivalents, to loose and accumulative rather than to periodic sentences, and to simple constructions; and it resorts little to suspensions, parentheses, and inversions—or, at least, only to such as have a colloquial sanction. It should perhaps be added that, whereas Massinger's style is all-but-invariable for every character and every purpose, Shakespeare's is infinitely and sinuously adjustable.

Before proceeding further, we should perhaps try to discriminate between the terms (1) *period* or *periodic sentence*; (2) *suspension*; and (3) *parenthesis*. These three rhetorical phenomena overlap and blend. Nevertheless, they can be analytically discriminated.

The *period* is a simple or a complex sentence in which the principal clause is not complete until the last word (or, not to be too rigorous, until practically the last word). Periodicity in the rhetorical sense, then, is and can only be manifested in and by a total sentence. Its opposite is the loose sentence, which reaches a completeness of statement long before its end, but goes on to add phrases or clauses. Compound sentences, by their very nature, are loose in this sense; but simple and complex may likewise be loose. A period need not display suspension or parenthesis. Thus a sentence, made up of a string of

---

[1] Preface to *Poems*, 1853, from *English Critical Essays: XIX Century* (World's Classics), Oxford, 1916, pp. 369–370.

preliminary hypotheses and concluding with an apodosis as the principal clause, is a period. And the presence of suspension or parenthesis does not by any means necessarily produce a period. It is, however, fair to say that the suspension of the total sense which is inherent in the period tends to attract to it a fair amount of rhetorical suspension.

A *suspension* is a hold-up or interposition between words in close grammatical relationship, as, for example, between a subject and its verb, a verb and its object, a preposition and its noun, and so on. In a strict interpretation any such intervention is a suspension. But in practice the term is generally reserved for such gaps as are considerable and truly suspensive. It should be noted that the interrupting matter is not subtractable without loss to the sentence as a *Gestalt*; it is integral to the sentence, and requires a grammatical adjustment of the rest of the sentence. It is of such suspensions that Blair is speaking in this passage: 'When a circumstance is interposed in the middle of a sentence, it sometimes requires attention how to place it, so as to divest it of all ambiguity.'[1]

A *parenthesis* is akin to a suspension in so far as it interrupts. But for one thing it does not generally intervene between words in close grammatical relationship; it comes rather at the internal joins of a sentence, between phrasal groups or between clauses. Secondly (and this is its chief differentia), a parenthesis is like a footnote comment or marginalium slipped into the text. It has, as it were, its own grammatical independence and may indeed itself be a complete sentence. It can be dropped without loss to the sentence to which it is parasitic. Blair's rules for the preserving of sentence-unity include the recommendation 'to keep clear of all parentheses . . . for the most part, their effect is extremely bad; being a sort of wheel within wheels; sentences in the midst of sentences; the perplexed method of disposing of some thought which a writer wants art to introduce in its proper place'.[2]

It is true that it might be difficult in many cases to decide whether an interruption is a suspension or a parenthesis. But I have advanced a notional difference which is also real enough for most purposes.

That these devices have their uses is undeniable; and that they can be used to help the reader is as certain. But there are limits beyond which they cannot be carried except at the cost of defeating their own end. Moreover, they are, especially the period, more

[1] *Lectures*, p. 133. For suspension in general, see Genung, op. cit., pp. 279–287.
[2] Ibid., p. 140.

appropriate to prose than to poetry, and to prose for reading not for oral delivery at that. Their psychological temperature is below the blood-heat of poetry. They imply a prospectiveness of mind and a cool detachment from the subject that are foreign to poetry.

All three of these devices, the period, the suspension, and the parenthesis, are amply illustrated in the passages I have quoted from Massinger's plays. Massinger has no hesitation in burdening both the actor and the hearer, not to mention the reader, with a mass of preparatory and subordinate matter before he releases them by completing a principal clause. His periods run to as much as thirteen or fourteen lines and eighty or ninety words. They are made the more involved by suspension after suspension (very often interrupting the subject, either of a subordinate clause or of the principal clause, by, as in one example I have given, as many as eleven lines) and by parentheses, and parentheses within parentheses, and parentheses within suspensions. Certainly it may be said without hesitation that no dramatist of his age (with the possible exception of Chapman) comes near Massinger in syntactical complexity.

At the risk of tediousness but because the fact is important, it is worth illustrating the involuting habit still further by examples arbitrarily drawn from the first scenes of the last acts of some of the plays. Each of the sentences quoted comes quite early in the scene, and, indeed, some of them are the opening sentences:

> Why, couldst thou think, Eugenia, that rewards,
> Graces, or favours, though strewed thick upon me
> Could ever bribe me to forget mine honour?[1]

> Were his honours
> And glories centupled, as I must confess,
> Leosthenes is most worthy, yet I will not,
> However I may counsel, force affection.[2]

> Should I spare cost, or not wear cheerful looks
> Upon my wedding day, it were ominous,
> And showed I did repent it; which I dare not,
> It being a marriage, howsoever sad
> In the first ceremonies that confirm it,
> That will for ever arm me against fears,
> Repentance, doubts, or jealousies, and bring
> Perpetual comforts, peace of mind, and quiet
> To the glad couple.[3]

---

[1] *The Duke of Milan.*   [2] *The Bondman.*   [3] *The Renegado.*

The relation
That you have made me, Stephanos, of these late
Strange passions in Caesar, much amaze me.[1]

    Yet take heed,
Take heed, lord Philanax, that, for private spleen,
Or any false-conceived grudge against me,
(Since in one thought of wrong to you I am
Sincerely innocent) you do not that
My royal master must in justice punish,
If you pass to your own heart through mine,
The murder, as it will come out, discovered.[2]

    A desire too
Of the recovery of our own, kept from us
With strong hand, by his violent persecutor,
Titus Flaminius, when he was at Carthage,
Urged us to seek redress.[3]

This devil, whose priest I am, and by him made
A deep magician (for I can do wonders)
Appeared to me in Virginia, and commanded,
With many stripes, for that's his cruel custom,
I should provide, on pain of his fierce wrath,
Against the next great sacrifice, at which
We, grovelling on our faces, fall before him,
Two Christian virgins, that with their pure blood,
Might dye his horrid altars; and a third,
In his hate to such embraces as are lawful,
As an oblation unto Hecate,
And wanton lust, her favourite.[4]

    But how, Iolante,
You that have spent your past days, slumbering in
The down of quiet, can endure the hardness
And rough condition of our present being,
Does much disturb me.[5]

You need not doubt, sir, were not peace proclaimed
And celebrated with a general joy,
The high displeasure of the Mantuan duke,
Raised on just grounds, not jealous suppositions,
The saving of our lives (which, next to heaven,
To you alone is proper) would force mercy
For an offence, though capital.[6]

[1] *The Roman Actor.*   [2] *The Emperor of the East.*   [3] *Believe As You List.*
[4] *The City Madam.*   [5] *The Guardian.*   [6] *The Bashful Lover.*

As regards these particular examples, it cannot of course be maintained that they are all manifestations of an absolute vicious-ness of style, either through unintelligibility, unwieldiness or inelegance; however relatively inappropriate they may be as a feature of an idiom that was intended to be a poetic-dramatic approximation to the speech that men do use. Nevertheless, it is worth while to point out that of the sixteen examples of single sentences I have given,[1] three are very difficult to grasp without analysis or resolution by means of simpler equivalents; five others require at least close and unremitting attention; three of the rest are awkward; and almost all of them, besides being more or less clumsy, could have been more naturally and better expressed in a looser order.

I have referred more than once already, in this chapter and elsewhere, to the unsuitability of Massinger's style for the stage. It is worthwhile before leaving the subject to give further point to my remarks. In evaluating any dramatist his theatrical effectiveness is, properly understood, the prime consideration. He may have many other virtues, but if he fails theatrically he is a poor dramatist. The theatre is the final court of appeal. No doubt theatrical effectiveness is a resulting complex of many factors. But one of them, and not the least important, is the mechanism through which the others must act; that is to say, the dialogue. If it is clogged and contorted, if it cannot say much in little, if it constantly employs sledgehammers to crack nuts, if it labours to bring forth a mouse, if it tries to untie Gordian knots instead of slicing through them with the razor of wit, then it is not only bad in itself but obstructive for all the rest.[2]

Herein lies Massinger's greatest stylistic weakness. For, were his periods faultlessly turned and of impeccable clarity and precision (as they decidedly are not), they would still not be, except for certain very limited uses in set speeches, a vehicle, flexible, appropriate, or even valid, for dramatic dialogue. The periodic style, complex, concentrated, and highly organised, has great advantages for the writer of certain kinds of prose. Without it, Sir Thomas Browne could not accomplish his musical incantations; Jeremy Taylor and Burke, their emotional intellection; Gibbon, the economic manipulation of details and comments; or Pater, his sinuous and seductive subtlety. But the periodic is a cumbrous instrument for the poet, especially the poet-dramatist. When it is used as the staple of dramatic dialogue, it is too slow, too ponderous, too considered, and too inflexible to give

---

[1] On pages 215, 216 and above.
[2] *A New Way to Pay Old Debts*, perhaps because of its contemporary setting, has in general racier dialogue than the other plays. This is one, but only one, of the factors which have contributed towards its survival on the stage.

that heightened echo of human speech at which poetic drama aims. Human beings on the spur of the moment just do not speak in periods, the less and less so the more and more they are caught up by passion and feeling; and the dramatist who makes his characters speak so, all of them with insignificant exceptions, is defeating his own end more thoroughly than by lapses in *vraisemblance*, plot, or characterisation. Awkwardnesses in plot are not very apparent in a performance, especially if the producer knows his business. And the personality of the actor can carry off unreal characterisation. But there is no escape from the syntax of the dialogue.

Of course, in the circumstances of heightened emotion or feeling which are the frequent concern of the poetic dramatist, especially a dramatist like Massinger of cloak-and-dagger romance, we could not endure the incoherences with which real people confront a crisis; and the less emotional passages likewise demand something more than the *sermo pedestris* of unpremeditated speech with its long-windedness, solecisms, inconsistencies, corrections and second thoughts, pauses, illogicalities, truncations, half-thoughts and oral shorthand, ejaculations, and anacolutha. The dialogue of poetic drama has to be intensified and raised above a level imitation of life. With Coleridge, we can adduce as a reason 'the high spiritual instinct of the human being impelling us to seek unity by harmonious adjustment, and thus establishing the principle, that *all* the parts of an organised whole must be assimilated to the more *important* and *essential* parts.'[1] Nevertheless, there are ways *and* ways of harmonising a heightened imitation of human speech with a heightened imitation of human action and life. And Massinger's is not the right way. A dialogue made up in effect of set speeches, for which each sentence in all its elaborate subordination has been carefully thought out, is not the way to deal with the difficulty. Massinger's characters always speak the same parlance: the voice is the voice of Cleora, or Donusa, or Sophia, or Grimaldi, or Sforza, or Wellborn; but the syntax is the syntax of Massinger. So, in fact, is everything in the dialogue. The style is invariable and the characters have learned to speak parrot-fashion. Whether Massinger might have achieved a more adaptable style if he could have been released from the Procrustean bed of his own syntax is doubtful. But certainly his syntax, second nature as it had become, constricted every speech and stereotyped the utterance of every character.

The other dramatists of Massinger's generation and the generation before had also to find modes of dialogue for poetic drama. Naturally

[1] *Biographia Literaria* (ed. Shawcross), II, p. 56.

there are as many solutions as there are dramatists. But none of them, with the partial exception of Chapman, resorted for a basis to what was a Ciceronian, literary-*prose* style, as Massinger did. They knew instinctively, if not consciously, that 'there are . . . modes of expression, a *construction*, and an *order* of sentences, which are in their fit and natural place in a serious prose composition, but would be disproportionate and heterogeneous in metrical poetry'.[1] The basis of their dialogue, so far as syntax at least is concerned, is the loose and cumulative sentence-structure of colloquial speech. This remains their syntactical basis, however much the broken and wasteful idiom is displaced by a more consecutive and purposive one.

★

I hope by now to have established a first precise and valid ground for a comparison of the style of Massinger with that of Shakespeare. It is this fundamental difference in respect of syntax—something which seems simple and not important at the first glance, but which is on the contrary of far-reaching significance.

It is easy enough to establish the broad difference. But for a number of reasons it is difficult to apply to it the statistical methods which can be used, with due caution, in the matter of versification. The readiest statistical line would be to count the number of principal clauses in, say, half-a-dozen scenes of some length from the same number of plays by Shakespeare, to express the result as a percentage, and to set it against the result of a similar investigation of Massinger's sentences. The comparison would be extremely laborious; the percentages arrived at would, in the nature of the case, only approximate to scientific accuracy; and the cold inhumanity of such statistics would add not one jot or tittle to our true understanding of either Shakespeare or Massinger. Such pedantical numbers can, like Humpty-Dumpty's words, be interpreted to mean what one chooses them to mean, and the temptation is always to make them add up to 'a nice knock-down argument'.

I have, however, examined closely seven typical and well-known passages from Shakespeare[2] not too far removed in subject matter

---

[1] *Biographia Literaria* (ed. Shawcross), II, p. 49.
[2] *Macbeth*, v. v. 17–28 ('She should have died hereafter').
Henry V, iii. i. 1–9 ('Once more unto the breach').
Julius Caesar, iii. ii. 73–80 ('Friends, Romans, countrymen').
The Merchant of Venice, iv. i. 183–196 ('The quality of mercy is not strained').
The Tempest, iv. i. 148–158 ('Our revels now are ended').
Othello, v. ii. 1–22 ('It is the cause').
Richard II, iii. ii. 155–170 ('For God's sake, let us sit upon the ground').

and emotional tone (reflective, expository, argumentative, or exhortatory) from the equally typical passages I have chosen from Massinger. The matter in these passages is expressed in quite brief thought-units or rhetorical-units, following each other in a sequence of straightforward simplicity. The statements drop down one after the other like pearls on a string. It is true that Shakespeare has a fair number of ellipses and inversions. But if some of the ellipses might set a grammarian problems in general analysis, they seldom give the ordinary reader or hearer, especially one with the slightest familiarity with Elizabethan–Jacobean idiom, any trouble; and his inversions for special effect or emphasis (not *metri causa*) are not of the forced and non-colloquial kind. On the whole, Shakespeare's sentences (and by no means all that is said is said in sentences) are short. Whether they are short or long, they are for the most part syntactically uncomplicated. They tend to be simple in the technical sense, or compound and made up of co-ordinate principal clauses, or complex only to a minor degree of subordination. They are generally loose, with a complete statement achieved quite early in their progress; and subordinate matter, in clauses or in phrases, usually comes after rather than before the principal clauses and allows other full closes to the sense. Thus, in short, Shakespeare has an inherent simplicity of sentence-structure with the spontaneity of life, and an order which is dictated by natural logic or, if I may use the term, *psychologic*, an order in which the ideas would occur to a speaker and could be communicated to a hearer according to the long-established conventions of colloquial English syntax. But I may be thus far statistical in support of it: in the 90 lines which I have examined from Shakespeare's plays, there are no less than 76 principal statements, the majority of which are in the form of principal clauses and the remainder in the form of independent phrases; in the same 90 lines there are only five suspensions (one of them formed by a brief parenthesis) three of which are less than four words long; there are only four clauses which are subordinate to subordinate clauses; and there are only five subordinate clauses which precede their principal clauses, and these are all, as might perhaps be expected, conditional adverbial clauses.

A diagrammatic lay-out of typical Shakespearian sentences will make their syntactical simplicity even more apparent.[1] The scheme which I use has three columns, the first for principal clauses (or

---

[1] Such are the vagaries of publication that this diagrammatic scheme was conceived several years before the appearance of a somewhat similar scheme in Harry Levin's *The Overreacher, A Study of Christopher Marlowe*, London, 1954.

statements), the second for subordinate clauses (or statements), and
the third for clauses which are subordinate to subordinate clauses.
The clauses are written in rectangles of single rules (clauses broken
by suspension in broken rectangles the sides of which are linked by
dotted lines); and the lines joining the nearest angle of rectangle and
rectangle represent the delivery line, not the syntactical relationship,
of the sentences. Parenthetic, as distinct from subordinate, matter
is put in one or other of the columns for subordinate matter, but in
rectangles whose sides consist of double rules. I have added in square
brackets [ ] such words and phrases as seemed necessary to complete
shortened or elliptical constructions. The sentences as thus analysed
have to be read in a downward zigzag. Thus the sentence:

> If I quench thee, thou flaming minister,
> I can again thy former light restore,
> Should I repent me;

can be represented thus:

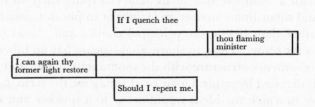

That first example, though really simple enough, is in fact more complicated than most. Only occasionally does Shakespeare make an
excursion into the third column, to speak in diagrammatic terms:

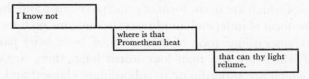

And that structure is hardly what could be called complicated. As a
rule Shakespeare's sentences have an even simpler shape, however:

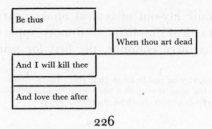

226

More often than not we get a succession of principal statements, connected by conjunctions, or appositionally, or by counterparting:

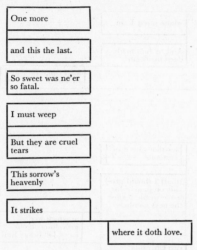

As for Shakespeare's suspensions, they are of the briefest and simplest sort. For example, such Shakespearian suspensions as:

>These our actors
>*As I foretold you*, were all spirits;

and,

>The evil *that men do* lives after them;

can be represented simply thus:

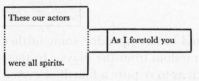

As soon as we turn to Massinger, we are faced with sentences of great diagrammatic complexity. Diagrams follow for two of his sentences which I have already quoted. The first shows a lengthy suspension in what is really a comparatively short sentence:

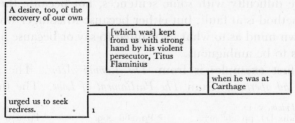

[1] *Believe As You List*, v. i.

227

The second shows how the complexities increase with the length:

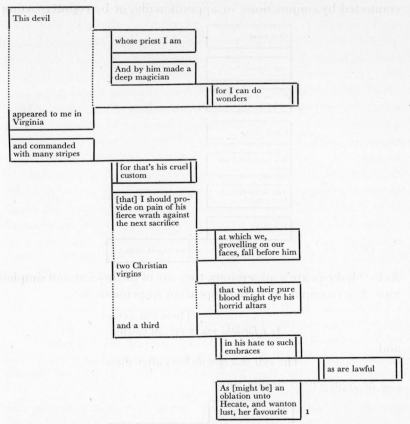

This devil

whose priest I am

And by him made a deep magician

for I can do wonders

appeared to me in Virginia

and commanded with many stripes

for that's his cruel custom

[that] I should provide on pain of his fierce wrath against the next sacrifice

at which we, grovelling on our faces, fall before him

two Christian virgins

that with their pure blood might dye his horrid altars

and a third

in his hate to such embraces

as are lawful

As [might be] an oblation unto Hecate, and wanton lust, her favourite   1

I have relegated to an appendix[2] some further examples, selected pretty much at random from the plays. In these the degree of subordination is such as to require a fourth or even a fifth column in the diagrammatic layout. Once more, I have thought it advisable, in dealing with interpolated matter, to supply such pronouns and verbs as the sense demands in association with certain very long participial phrases. Even with such additional mechanism, I have had considerable difficulty with some sentences, not because the diagrammatic method is at fault, but either because Massinger was not clear in his own mind as to what he wanted to say or because he says it so badly as to be ambiguous.

The first example[3] is from *The Roman Actor*. The second[4] is selected *ad aperturam* from *The Parliament of Love*. The third[5] is the

[1] *City Madam*, v. i.
[2] Appendix III, pp. 268–272.   [3] Pp. 268–269.   [4] Pp. 270–271.
[5] P. 272.

very first sentence that met my eye on opening *The Unnatural Combat* at random. It is an uncompleted sentence spoken by Theocrine in Act V, scene i. I shall not declare that she could never have completed it; but I very much doubt whether anyone could understand it at one hearing or any reader analyse it satisfactorily. As will be seen, Massinger never reaches the second principal clause of his compound-complex sentence. He is tied up in subordination and subordination to subordination, and subordination to subordination to subordination . . ., in suspensions and suspensions doubly or trebly suspended, and in parentheses, themselves involving subordination or suspension. Such a sentence is worse than Coleridge's worst, which, when he sighed for Southey's terseness and crispness, he likened to 'Surinam toads with young ones sprouting and hanging about them as they go'.[1] Another remark of Coleridge on poetic style in general is here apt: 'The great thing in poetry is, *quocunque modo*, to effect a unity of impression upon the whole; and a too great fullness and profusion of points in the parts will prevent this'.[2] Massinger is indeed guilty of a too great fullness of syntactical morticing and profusion of interlocking points.

The diagrammatic analysis of Massinger's sentences could be continued indefinitely to lend weight to the case, were that needed. But I scarcely think that it is or that anyone giving a glance or two through a few pages of Massinger's plays will say that the case has been overstated. It should be added that in the 84 lines of Massinger's verse that have been analysed (above and in Appendix III) there are only 25 principal clauses, no less than 19 suspensions, and 10 parentheses (three of them within suspensions), all of considerable, and some of great length. Thus, as compared with Shakespeare,[3] Massinger has only about one-third as many principal clauses and four times the number (much more than four times the amount) of suspensions; and his sentences tend to be from three to four times as long.

★

The length of Massinger's sentences leads on to the length of the speeches he assigns to his characters. The average has been computed by Professor Baldwin to be 3·54 lines.[4] At first sight this may not seem out-of-the-ordinary. But in fact we shall realise that it is really quite long, when we take into account how great a proportion

[1] *Saintsbury, History of Criticism*, Vol. III, London, 1900–1904, p. 218, note.
[2] *Table Talk and Omniana*, p. 256.
[3] See above, p. 225.
[4] In the statistical table in his edition of *The Duke of Milan*, Lancaster, Pa., 1918.

of any play, even a play in verse, is of necessity taken up with brief
questions and answers, asides, interjections, exclamations, and trivial
interchanges between character and character. A comparison of the
speech-length average of Massinger with that of any of his contemporaries will be a further corrective. By a count I have made
specially for this purpose I got the following figures: Webster's
Duchess of Malfi: 2·8 lines; Beaumont and Fletcher's *Philaster*: 3·0
lines; Shakespeare's *Coriolanus*: 3·04 lines, and *Macbeth*: 3·22 lines;
and Heywood's *A Woman Killed with Kindness*: 3·49 lines. Undoubtedly
the ordinary reader of the plays, ignorant of these statistics, must get
the impression that Massinger's characters, especially the more important, are longer in the wind than the more important characters
of other dramatists.[1] Massinger himself seemed aware of this in the
more or less set speeches and tried to disguise the length of them by
artificial breaks at which the bystanders give voice in comment.[2]

It is of course difficult to particularise about the shorter speeches
or to treat them in the same way as the longer speeches with which I
have been dealing in so much of this chapter: short speeches in
sentence-form are made in much the same way by all dramatists and
offer less variety. I should like, however, to make one or two general
observations about Massinger's shorter speeches, in addition to the
already-noted fact that he has fewer than other playwrights of his
age. The first point is that Massinger prefers his characters to speak
complete sentences: phrases without finite verbs are rare as separate
speeches, and single word speeches are rarer still. Even when he is
writing what he means to be a lively interchange of sallies, he makes
nearly every speech a sentence fully-dressed:

Olympia. I offered myself twice, and yet the churl
   Would not salute me.
Corisca.   Let him kiss his drum!
   I'll save my lips, I rest on it.
Olympia.   He thinks women
   No part of the republic.
Corisca.   He shall find
   We are a commonwealth.
Cleon.   The less your honour.[3]

---

[1] Most important of all in creating this impression is, however, the length of individual
sentences. Long sentences and periodic and suspensive structure tend to go hand in hand.
From my own observation (though I have not investigated the matter exhaustively) I
should say that Shakespeare in his last plays tends to use longer sentences (with a corresponding increase in periodicity and suspension) and to give longer speeches to his
characters irrespective of their importance. Ben Jonson, on the other hand, whose
characters as a whole tend to speak at great length, uses fairly short sentences in the
comedies—although perhaps significantly, he uses more complex sentences in the two
Roman tragedies.

[2] See above, Chap. III, p. 104.   [3] *The Bondman*, I. iii.

Perigot. 'Twas prince-like entertainment.
Chamont. You o'erprize it.
Dinant. Your cheerful looks made every dish a feast,
And 'tis that crowns a welcome.
Lamira. For my part,
I hold society and honest mirth
The greatest blessing of a civil life.[1]

These passages, which could be infinitely supplemented, show Massinger's partiality for ending a speech and beginning the next somewhere within the line. He is always, be it noticed, careful to complete each line metrically. Again, two consecutive brief speeches are often made one grammatically;[2] that is, they are either linked by conjunctions or the second speaker catches up and completes a sentence that the first had begun:

Clarindore. It is their pride.
Bellisant. Or your unworthiness.[3]

Vitelli. You shall see me act
This last scene to the life.
Francisco. And though now fall,
Rise a blessed martyr.[4]

Asambeg. How he eyes her!
Mustapha. As if he would look through her.
Asambeg. His eyes flame too,
As threatening violence.[5]

Timagoras. 'Twas a deed
Deserving rather trophies than reproof.
Leosthenes. And will be still remembered to your honour
If you forsake not us.[6]

Olympia. Were he a courtier
I've sweetmeat in my closet shall content him,
Be his palate ne'er so curious.
Corisca. And, if need be,
I have a couch and a banqueting-house in my orchard,
Where many a man of honour has not scorned
To spend an afternoon.[7]

---

[1] *The Parliament of Love,* III. i.   [2] Cf. above, Chap. III, pp. 103–104.
[3] *The Parliament of Love,* I. v.   [4] *The Renegado,* v. i.
[5] Ibid., IV. iii.   [6] *The Bondman,* I. iii.   [7] Ibid., I. iii.

Though long suspensions and parentheses are impossible in briefer sentences, Massinger has short ones even there; and in them he tends to his usual periodic structure.

★

The results of this investigation into Massinger's sentence-structure may be briefly summed up as follows: Massinger uses with a high frequency long sentences of a predominantly periodic kind with involved subordination and many suspensions and parentheses to the detriment of the clarity and the ruin of the colloquial naturalness. That this type of sentence and this syntactical involution, though not of course new in English prose, constitute in Massinger a departure from the dramatic verse-idiom of his fellow-dramatists has been underlined and illustrated by a comparison with Shakespeare's practice; and I have maintained that such a syntax is not suited to dramatic purposes in English, or, for that matter, in any (at least any uninflected) language.

Certain conclusions remain to be drawn, in all fairness, from Massinger's practice in this matter. The first is an amplification of ideas as to Massinger's personality that we have already suggested. The mind which chooses to express itself (in Massinger's case there can be no question of *his* expressing his characters) in periodic and involved sentences displays a logical and methodical turn, a necessity to get everything cut-and-dried, a vein of pedantry. It is an inelastic mind as likely to adopt and adhere to certain principles and attitudes and points of view as to fall into the syntactical habitude in question. The periodic and involved sentence is a work of deliberation; and its mould, like a gyroscopic pilot, always tends to bring things back to a predetermined course. It acts as a snaffle upon a mind which, if it could have expressed itself in a loose, aggregative sentence, would have felt free to pause, or alter, or entirely change its direction. After all we have learned about Massinger's mind from other manifestations of its operation, it seems natural that he should have deliberately chosen his peculiar manner of expression.

That he did so deliberately is my second conclusion. No English writer, however he may have been biased, like Massinger, by a classical and largely rhetorical education, expresses himself in involved periods because he cannot help it; though of course there will come a time when after long practice such a manner will become second nature. That is to imply that at some stage the practitioner of periodic involution makes a conscious choice. The Ciceronian period, (if we may adopt the term as a convenient label), is not native to English, however important a part it has played in the development of English prose. The native tradition in prose,

> . . . going back to mediaeval times, is based on the simple colloquial or aggregative sentence, with sprawling members, loosely connected by temporal and co-ordinating conjunctions, unemphatic in effect. It uses the simplest kind of amplification—cataloguing, the heaping of synonyms, words of similar meaning, or phrases of similar construction; for oral ornament it employs alliteration and synonymous word-pairs;[1]

and

> The Ciceronian manner of writing in comprehensive periods requires an implicated style. . . ; but such a style is dependent upon a complex suspended syntax which imposes the greatest difficulties upon an uninflected language.[2]

Period involution is, in fact, a deliberately chosen and artificial mode of expression.

> The loose mode of structure is the early and natural way of writing; the periodic is later and the result of art. . . . Basically, the period is not a form of thought . . . but a form of composition or expression, an arrangement of words.[3]

Now, this is not the place to go at any length into the problematic history of English prose at the beginning of the seventeenth century. It is extremely debatable territory, a stamping-ground for some protagonists and a lists for others; it would be a rash person who ventured far into such country without a formidable battery of theories and counter-theories about the sundry *isms* (Euphuism, Gongorism, Marinism, Ciceronianism, anti-Ciceronianism, Senecanism, Taciteanism, Atticism, Laconicism, Asianism, Isocraticism, and so on) which beset this battlefield.[4] Who shall decide when critics disagree diametrically, for example, on Milton, Professor Williamson rating him as a Ciceronian[5] and Professor Highet as an anti-Ciceronian?[6]

Massinger has not hitherto figured in discussions of prose style, for

---

[1] George Williamson, *The Senecan Amble*, London, 1951, p. 26 (after G. P. Krapp, *The Rise of English Literary Prose*, 1915).
[2] Ibid., p. 55.   [3] Ibid., p. 44.
[4] In this respect, see particularly Williamson, op. cit.; various articles by Professor Morris W. Croll, such as *Attic Prose in the Seventeenth Century (Studies in Philol.*, 18 (1921), 2, pp. 79–128), *Muret and the History of Attic Prose*, (*PMLA*, 39 (1924), pp. 254–309), and, *The Baroque Style in Prose (Studies in English Philology . . . in honour of Frederick Klaeber* ed. Malone and Rund, Minneapolis, 1929); various articles by Professor R. F. Jones, repr. in *The Seventeenth Century*, (Stanford, Cal., 1951); and Gilbert Highet, *The Classical Tradition*, London, 1949, Chap. 18.
[5] *The Senecan Amble*, pp. 209–211.   [6] *The Classical Tradition*, p. 325.

the good reason that the amount of his prose is negligible. Nevertheless, his employment of the Ciceronian period links him to contemporary views regarding prose style. It may be broadly said that, while there were many prose stylists in practice, as many as there were prose writers, those who were conscious shapers of their styles thought of themselves as either Ciceronian or anti-Ciceronian; and the anti-Ciceronians generally set up, as their Latin rival to Cicero, Seneca.

As I have suggested in another chapter, Massinger was stoically inclined and drew largely on Seneca for his moral philosophy. One may, then, perhaps express a little surprise that he does not display in his style, to any extent at least, the stylistic features commonly associated with Stoicism and in particular with Seneca—the curt, pointed sentence, with its epigrammatism, its antithetic edge, and its economy and memorableness. If he had known, as is not at all improbable, the *Manductio ad Stoicam Philosophiam* of Justus Lipsius, published in 1604 (when Massinger was presumably still at Oxford) and widely disseminated soon after publication, he could not have failed to note the anti-Ciceronian, pro-Senecan strictures on style contained therein.[1]

It must be remembered, however, that although the periodic structure or Ciceronianism is necessarily a deliberate choice, it was not in the earlier seventeenth century such a self-conscious innovation as was Senecanism. That is to say that, while its opponents from the time of Erasmus's *Ciceronianus*[2] and more particularly its opponents in Massinger's own day, such men as Ben Jonson[3] and Bacon,[4] knew exactly what they objected to and were extremely self-conscious in their studied Senecanism, those authors who were Ciceronian in practice (Hooker, Raleigh, Sidney, North, Camden, Hakluyt, and so on) were not at all quick to spring to a theoretical justification or counter-attack. The reason is simply that they did not feel the need to do so. Ciceronianism had got in on the ground storey of Renaissance education; the schoolmasters and the dons who did not model their own and their pupils' latinity on Cicero were quite exceptional.

Massinger could hardly be in theatrical circles in London without encountering Ben Jonson *in propria persona* and hearing his innovating

---

[1] Cf. Williamson, op. cit., 111.

[2] 1528. See also Vives, *De Tradendis Disciplinis* (trans. Foster Watson, *Vives on Education*, 1913) and Ramus. For early English anti-Ciceronian pronouncements, see John Jewell, *Oratio contra Rhetoricam* (c. 1548), and Gabriel Harvey, *Ciceronianus* (1577).

[3] In *Discoveries* and elsewhere.

[4] Who attacked the Ciceronians in the first edition of *The Advancement of Learning* (1605) —though of course, as exemplified in the successive editions of the *Essays*, he moved gradually away from the extremist Senecan position until in the edition of 1623 (*De Augmentis*) he is attacking it too.

views on style. Yet in spite of this (or perhaps even because of this) the conservative Massinger chose to write in the English equivalent of the style he had been brought up in. In general, then, his style (though not, of course, absolutely Ciceronian, since poetic drama never could be) is basically a periodic one, 'the clauses of which are suspended on the voice of the speaker till the whole is completed by the last clause'.[1] With his preference for the long sentence he is diffuse and non-epigrammatic rather than curt and pointed. He ignores the balance and antithesis which marks the Euphuistic development of Ciceronianism in the Senecan direction. And he strives after fullness and completeness ('clarity' would be a misleading word in connection with a style that so taxes the attention), rather than a somewhat cryptic wit. If Lyly and Bacon have the smallest amount of subordinate matter amongst English writers since the Renaissance,[2] Massinger must be among those who have the most. As we have already seen, no contemporary dramatist rivals him in this. It was, says Professor Williamson, 'the abuse of sub-dependence that made sixteenth- and seventeenth-century periods heavy, and the influence of Ciceronian Latin provoked the excess of subordination'.[3] It might have been of Massinger that Sir William Cornwallis was writing when he said,

> How shall a man hope to come to an end of their works, when he cannot with two breathes saile through a period, and is sometimes gravelled in a parenthesis?[4]

Later writers in the seventeenth century, who were working towards that purgation and pruning of prose which the Royal Society desiderated and which produced the easy elegance of Dryden, Temple, and Addison, might have been more severe. Here is Hobbes on the contrast between what is suitable for oral delivery and what is allowable in matter for reading:

> For words that pass away (as in public orations they must) without pause, ought to be understood with ease, and are lost else: though words that remain in writing for the reader to meditate on, ought rather to be pithy and full.[5]

Here is Fuller's account of the Ciceronian periods of Hooker:

> His style was long and pithy, driving on a whole flock of several

---

[1] St. Augustine, *De Doctrina Christiana*, IV, 7, 11.
[2] R. R. Aurner, *The History of Certain Aspects of the English Sentence*, PQ, 2, 1923, pp. 187–208, and *Caxton and the English Sentence*, Wisconsin Studies in Lang. and Lit., No. 18, 1923, p. 50. *See* Williamson, op. cit., pp. 39–40.
[3] Op. cit., p. 107, note 3.   [4] In his essay, *Of Vanity* (1601).
[5] *English Works*, ed. Molesworth, London, 1843, vol. viii, p. xxxi.

clauses before he came to the close of a sentence. So that when the copiousness of his style met not with proportionate capacity in his auditors, it was unjustly censured for perplexed, tedious, and obscure.[1]

And here Bishop Burnet on the periodic style for sermons which, like plays, have to be taken in by the ear:

> All long *Periods*, such as carry two or three different Thoughts in them, must be avoided; for few Hearers can follow or apprehend these.[2]

If a periodic and involved style is generally unsuitable for dramatic dialogue, it is made still more so when coupled with a blank verse that has too much freedom and too little discipline. Marlowe is one of the more periodically given of the dramatists; but his variety of blank verse saved him:

> Nature, that fram'd us of four elements
> Warring within our breasts for regiment,
> Doth teach us all to have aspiring minds:
> Our souls, whose faculties can comprehend
> The wondrous architecture of the world,
> And measure every wandering planet's course,
> Still climbing after knowledge infinite,
> And always moving as the restless spheres,
> Will us to wear ourselves, and never rest,
> Until we reach the ripest fruit of all,
> That perfect bliss and sole felicity,
> The sweet fruition of an earthly crown.[3]

Here the corsetting is provided by a line-by-line or end-stopped versification: the mechanism of the verse prevents subordination, suspension, and involution from getting out of hand. Massinger, however, came after the drumming decasyllabon had been loosened and stretched by much exercise at the hands of many practitioners, notably Shakespeare, and Beaumont and Fletcher. Although Massinger's blank verse is remarkably regular in the number and placing of the stresses in the line and in the number of syllables, with a lower percentage of hypermetric syllables than was becoming normal in the rapid disintegration of blank verse after 1601, it is far from being end-stopped. His lines spill over one into the other endlessly and according to no determinable laws of ear or mind. He puts his rests as far as possible within the line: phrases, clauses, sentences, and speeches generally begin and end there at a widely variable caesura.

---

[1] *Church History of Britain*, ed. Nichols, III, p. 141.
[2] *A Discourse of the Pastoral Care*, London, 1692, p. 108.
[3] *Tamburlaine*, I, 869.

Massinger is, in fact, a palmary example of that sort of seventeenth-century poet of whom Bishop Atterbury wrote:

> . . . their verses ran all into one another; and hung together, through-out a whole copy. . . . There was no distinction of parts, no regular stops, nothing for the ear to rest upon; but, as soon as the copy began, down it went, like a larum, incessantly, and the reader was sure to be out of breath, before he got to the end of it.[1]

From such a versification he got no help in disciplining and limiting his periods.

But it is very doubtful if he would have desired any such helpful restriction. With him verse has no emotive quality, no dramatic power, no poetic value in itself. This, I maintain, in spite of Cole-ridge's assertion that Massinger's blank verse is 'perhaps . . . even still nobler' than the 'very masterly and individual' blank verse of Ben Jonson.[2] It is merely the vehicle prescribed by an unwritten law of the seventeenth-century theatre for serious romantic plays. As such it had in his hands to bend and adjust itself to the complexity of his sentences. His periodic thought had the right-of-way and the prior claim. It is reasonable to assume that if the serious drama in prose had existed in Massinger's day, alongside blank-verse drama, he would have used prose.

That could never be said of Milton, however syntactically complex he too may be. The Miltonic verse is always essential, never acci-dental. The potency of the Miltonic magic lies as much in the in-cantatory character of the verse as in anything else. I do not say that Milton's blank verse is particularly dramatic or very suitable for dialogue. But then, except in *Comus*, it was not used by him for stage-dialogue. The speeches in *Paradise Lost* and *Paradise Regained* are epical and for reading, and it was likewise only for reading that Milton wrote *Samson Agonistes*. Nevertheless, just because Milton is a metrical master and realises to the full the value and beauty of verse, he can make complicated syntax more acceptable than Massinger can to both reader and hearer.

There is indeed one virtue which Massinger's style owes largely to its periodic structure. That is its dignity and eloquence. 'Stateli-ness,' says Demetrius, 'is . . . produced by adopting a rounded period.'[3] And Massinger must have valued himself on his eloquence because he so often provides opportunities for its display in set speeches, forensic, deliberative, and epideictic, not to mention the

---

[1] Preface to Waller's *Poems*, 1690.
[2] *Table-Talk and Omniana*, Oxford Edn., 1917, p. 295.
[3] *On Style*, 45 (Everyman Edn., p. 212).

numerous scenes of pleading and expostulation with which his plays are punctuated. Indeed, it might be said that Massinger's dramaturgy is largely determined by his desire to function as continuously as possible as a rhetorician. While I admit that the result of this desire, coupled with his periodicity and involution in general, is to spread a uniform, and, let it be admitted, monotonous eloquence everywhere and with even hand among practically every character; and while such a pompous idiom is often incongruously out-of-place in recording the lighter moments of life; yet there can be no doubt that it lends a peculiar and impressive gravity elsewhere.

The most unqualified praise of Massinger on this score is perhaps Nathan Drake's. He speaks of Massinger's 'spirit of commanding *eloquence*, a dignity and force of thought, which, while they approach the precincts of sublimity, and indicate great depth and clearness of intellect, show, by the nervous elegance of language in which they are clothed, a combination and comprehension of talent of very unfrequent occurrence'.[1] One is prepared to admit, with modified rapture, most of this tribute, boggling principally at the reference to 'nervous elegance of language' and questioning whether a 'clearness of intellect' that does not command clearness of expression is of much use.

A much later judgement by Whipple, though uncomplimentary to Massinger the poet, attributes to him as a rhetorician certain qualities, only some of which I would concede: 'Massinger's style, though it does not evince a single great quality of the poet, has always charmed English readers by its dignity, flexibility, eloquence, clearness, and ease'.[2] Against this, place Mrs. Browning's words on Massinger: 'He is too ostentatiously strong for flexibility, and too heavy for rapidity'.[3] His 'ease' is as conspicuous by its absence as are his elegance and his clarity.

★

The characteristics of Massinger's diction and the way in which it differs from the diction of his dramatic predecessors and contemporaries can be fairly easily appreciated without recourse to any highly complex terminology. My difficulty will not be so much in expressing the quality of Massinger's diction as in trying to adduce reasons for that quality.

In respect of the quality of the diction, then, every reader of

---

[1] *Shakespeare and His Times*, 1817, II, p. 561.
[2] E. W. Whipple, *The Literature of the Age of Elizabeth*, p. 182.
[3] *The Book of the Poets*.

Massinger will at once be aware that he is in a different world from that which he moved in when reading Marlowe, Greene, Kyd, Shakespeare, Webster, Tourneur, Dekker, Beaumont, and even Jonson and Fletcher. He is in a world from which sense perceptions have been to a large extent extracted and the vivid, graphic, or otherwise sense-stimulating image has been largely banished. The colourless and non-sensuous aridity will be the more apparent if Massinger has been approached, as he should be if he is to be set in his proper context in a century of change, through the 'gaudy, blabbing, and remorseful' poetry of the Elizabethans than if he is gone back to from the drabber verse of the Augustans. Accordingly, I propose, as I have already done with Massinger's syntax, to examine his diction with constant reference to and comparison with that of Shakespeare.

As quick a way as any to get at the quality of Massinger's diction is to make a list from any randomly-chosen passage (in Massinger the random is always the typical) from any of the plays of the words which carry the weight of the sense, that is, all those presentive[1] words (nouns, adjectives, verbs, and adverbs) which have more than a merely grammatical or symbolic[2] function. It will be as well to keep nouns and their associated adjectives together and also such groups of words as form a unity. This may seem a naive, or even clumsy method of dealing with such fragile matter as diction provides—rather like dismantling a watch with a sledgehammer—but notwithstanding the Cambridge school, there are as yet no instruments devised for the dissection of diction, and we have to fall back upon the brutal and effective method of tearing the words apart one from the other.

The first list is compiled from the last 70 lines of Act IV, scene iii, of *The Duke of Milan*, the scene in which Sforza murders his wife Marcelia:

> monster—walking tree of jealousy—dreamer—horned beast—commandment—allowance—basely used—virtues—labours—services—cares—to please—suspicious—unthankful—blush—mine own trumpet—barbarous course—seal of shame—impudence—ugly—whore—blood—honest blush—intent . . . act (sexual)—dishonour—deserv'st—common lecher—chief minion—chosen favourite—wooed (adj.) Francisco—wretch—dead—by my hand—bloodier villain—wondered—love—

---

[1] 'The Presentive [words] are those which present an object to the memory or to the imagination; or in brief, which present any conception to the mind.' John Earle, *The Philology of the English Tongue*, Oxford, 1871, p. 195.

[2] 'The Symbolic words are those which by themselves present no meaning to the mind, and which depend for their intelligibility on a relation to some presentive word or words' ibid., p. 195.

object (sb.)—killed—profess—loved—thousand queens—rivals—to thy teeth—dares—dares—jealous fool—murderer—mischief—justice—fooled into my grave—grieve—slain—innocent—suffer—innocent—lives —vile creature—justify—falsehood—whorish flatteries—tempted—stale—bawd—property—wantonness—took horse—ports—abused—undone—death—obey—tempted—tempter—to win—warrant you signed—death—believe—believe—innocent—contemned—upon his knees—tears—beseech—reveal—soft-hearted fool—judging—true penitence—won—unkindness—sentenced¦—guilty—seeming anger—heaven forgive—sweet soul—beauteous prison (body)—motion—grief stopped the organ of his speech—body—physicians—heart-strings.

It is possible to analyse this list in different ways. We could, in the first place, imagine it a list prepared by someone else from a passage we had not ourselves read. Then from a reading of the list alone we should quite easily gather something about the passage from which it is extracted. From the number of words like *suspicion, shame, dishonour, villainy, impudence,* and so on, commonly associated with a self-regarding or egotistical and unsympathetic diathesis; from the terms of denunciation; from those of sexual connotation; and from words referring to death, crime, punishment, repentance, and impenitence, we could deduce that the total passage almost certainly dealt with an unhappy situation involving indignation, recrimination, and the infliction after a moral judgement of a punishment that bordered on or descended to the violent and flagitious. This amounts to no more than saying that the author has apparently expressed what he wanted to express. For it would be impossible to present an accusation, a crescendo of indignation, a murder, and a remorseful revulsion without the use of such words as are used.

On the other hand, what we must also examine in the list is not the bare denotations of the words but their quality, and since the list has been compiled from what purports to be a passage of poetry, that overplus of significance, implication and imaginative potency which ought to raise the passage above the level and temperature of common speech.

Whenever we do this, we are sadly disappointed. There is indeed little to suggest that the list comes from a passage of poetry at all. And this prosaicness is only confirmed when, putting aside the mere list of words for a moment, we examine the passage as a whole. There is in it no heightened simile, no imagination-releasing comparison or image, and no more of the metaphorical than might be used in making a purchase or in any of the more everyday conversational exchanges. To return to the words: the terms of abuse (*monster, chief minion, chosen favourite, wretch, bloodier villain, jealous fool, vile creature*) are commonplace; and equally so are those relating to sexuality (*horned beast, whore, act, common lecher, whorish, stale, bawd, property*), death (*dead, killed, murderer, grave, slain, death*), and the body (*blush, blood, by my hand, to thy teeth, upon his knees, tears, organ of his speech, body, heart-strings*). They are like coins that have been worn flat—

'tis something; nothing;
'Twas mine, 'tis his, and has been slave to thousands.

They have almost no freshness of power over and above their conventionally delimited meaning. Moreover, they beget in the mind no image that is not so conventional as to have lost all virtue. There is no appeal to the senses of sight or sound, no recall of smell or taste, no sense of touch, no stimulus of the muscular sense. Nor is there any incantatory onomatopoeic effect. In short, the words are grey and devitalised and the lines present a smooth and textureless surface. Though the context is a scene of violent agitation and physical action, the words themselves have nothing physical about them. They are no more than words descriptive of mental or moral states or processes of the most generalised sort, and colourless terms for mental or moral attributes, qualities, and relationships. Thus, 62 out of the 102 words in the list are just such words denoting abstract qualities or non-physical processes, as, for example, *jealousy, commandment, virtues, services, labours, shame, impudence, falsehood, justice, penitence, innocent, anger, mischief, grieve, wantonness, dishonour, dare,* and so on.

There is in fact only one phrase in the whole passage with the slightest spark of life or vitality in it. Thus the metaphor *walking tree of jealousy* is an unusual term of abuse. But even so, with its recall of the Biblical 'I saw men as trees walking',[1] it hardly seems to be a very apt description for a jealous man, even if we are to understand by a rather forced interpretation that Sforza had as many horns or antlers as a tree has branches.

So we have dipped our net into Massinger's diction with results that are revealing but hardly as regards a high poetic freshness and cutting-edge.

To underline the conventionality of it, let us make another list taken from a similar or parallel passage in Shakespeare, Act V, scene ii, of *Othello* down to line 71, in which the mind of the hero is in a tumult of tender anguish and stern resolve:

cause—cause—soul—name (vb.)—chaste stars—cause—shed blood—
scar (vb.)—whiter skin than snow—smooth as monumental alabaster—

[1] *St. Mark* viii. 24.

die—betray—light—light—quench—flaming minister—former light
restore—repent—put out thy light—cunning'st pattern of excelling
nature—Promethean heat—light relume—plucked—the rose—vital
growth—wither—smell (vb.)—tree—balmy breath—persuade Justice
to break her sword—dead—kill—love—the last—so sweet—so fatal—
weep—cruel tears—this sorrow's heavenly—sorrow strikes—doth love—
wakes — bed — prayed — bethink — unreconciled — heaven — grace
—solicit—brief—walk—kill—unprepared spirit—heaven forfend—kill
thy soul—killing—heaven have mercy—Amen—heart—kill—fear (vb.)
—fatal—eyes roll—fear (vb.)—guiltiness—I feel I fear—sins—loves—
bear (vb.)—diest—death—unnatural—kills—loving—gnaw your nether
lip—bloody passion—frame—portents—hope (vb.)—hope (vb.)—
point (vb.)—peace—still—loved—life—soul—sweet soul—perjury—
death-bed—to die—confess—sin—deny each article—oath—choke—
strong conception—groan (vb.)—to die—Lord—mercy—Amen—
mercy—offend—general warranty of heaven—love—token—perjured
—stone my heart—murder—sacrifice—used (sexual)—unlawfully—
mouth is stopped.

An analysis of this passage in detail would be almost impossible.
But some (necessarily brief) analytic suggestions may be of interest.
In the first place, the words are more profoundly integrated and
more psycho-emotively interrelated than those in the list from *The
Duke of Milan*. The ideas and images come in associated clusters.
Thus *blood* and *scar* suggest skin. Desdemona's skin is white and
smooth, and the idea of whiteness leads to *light* and *flame*. Othello's
purpose easily gives these words a secondary significance, that of the
flame of life which he is about to quench. But Desdemona's beauty
is still before him, and this beauty, together with the physical motion
which the action of quenching a light suggests, still dominated by
his awareness of how he is about to destroy life, brings him (not
Shakespeare speaking *through* Othello but *as* Othello, a living
human being who is not Shakespeare) to the idea of plucking a
rose. The rose in its turn suggests growth and living fragrance—
both its own and Desdemona's 'balmy breath'—as contrasted with
death.

This momentary picking-up of merely one thread in the first
fifteen lines of the *Othello* scene must seem, I am aware, in the very
nature of the great poetry of whose pattern this thread is only a tiny
part, presumptuous, perfunctory, and casual. But the very act of
admitting that such treatment is merely scratching at the surface of
the top layer of Shakespeare's multi-stratumed meaning, will suffice
to show a close-packed significance which is quite unlike anything
we can find anywhere in Massinger. Such a passage cannot be

analysed: it can only be experienced. And it yields a meaning on infinitely-receding planes, a meaning in depth, as contrasted with the immediately apparent meaning of the passage from *The Duke of Milan*.

However, unlike Massinger's words, which do little more than express a bare meaning, Shakespeare's manage also to convey a *feeling*, and to reproduce in us much of the actual physical, emotional, and spiritual experience of the hero. Almost every presentive word in the passage is strong and echoing and is so by virtue of the poetic and imaginative intensity and absolute singularity. Language, instead of being so many dead counters, is vibrant with life and un-expected but inevitable aptness. And this it is, not only (though of course mainly) by the total imaginative-dramatic texture they build up, but by their mere power as isolated words and phrases. They express life and its sense-experience and its emotions and its spiritual alacrity. *Justice breaking her sword* is an image, a picture which deepens and quickens the meaning and emotional significance of the statement. The sense of sight is awake to *whiter skin than snow* and both sight and touch to *smooth as monumental alabaster*. The verbs are not inert but such as make an imaginative impact on the senses and suggest physical activity: *scar, smell, gnaw, roll, weep, strike, sacrifice, groan, relume, wither*. In addition, the words in the Shakespeare passage which refer to things spiritual (*mercy, sin, spirit, Amen, oath, confess, grace, heaven*, and so on) are, because of the way in which they are associated with and integrated into the human experience of worship, very different from Massinger's generalised abstractions (*honesty, jealousy, honour, innocence, mischief, justice, falsehood, wantonness, temptation, anger, belief, unkindness, grief*) which do not come out of a vital experience at all but out of a moralistic detachment and the pages of books. Simile, personification—all the figures of speech—occur in Shakespeare as in the intense language of real passion, and the amount of metaphor is impossible to estimate since practically the whole of the opening of the speech is metaphorical—meta-phorical, too, in an untranslatable way. The thought is metaphor and the metaphor is thought.

The two passages I have contrasted with regard to their poetical quality handle a similar situation. But they do not, as it were, overlap. Massinger has avoided, or at least not given anything more than a general parallel: there are no verbal or phrasal approxima-tions to Shakespeare. On the other hand, it is possible to exhibit the same contrast in quality by a shorter parallel in which Massinger is actually competing against Shakespeare in a rewording of him.

The Massinger quotation is from Act II, scene i, of *The Roman Actor*:

> I once observed,
> In a tragedy of ours, in which a murder
> Was acted to the life, a guilty hearer,
> Forced by the terror of a wounded conscience,
> To make discovery of that which torture
> Could not wring from him.

And the Shakespearian original is in Act II, scene ii, of *Hamlet*:

> I have heard
> That guilty creatures sitting at a play
> Have by the very cunning of the scene
> Been struck so to the soul that presently
> They have proclaimed their malefactions.

Now of course Massinger has, to borrow the slang phrase, cashed in on the Shakespearian quality: he is living on the Shakespearian capital. But he does not add to it. Here are the words and phrases of the two dramatists set down side by side:

Hamlet		*The Roman Actor*
I have heard	:	I once observed
play	:	tragedy
have by the very cunning of	:	in which a murder was acted to
the scene	:	the life
guilty creatures	:	a guilty hearer
been struck so to the soul	:	forced by the terror of a wounded
	:	conscience
they have proclaimed	:	to make discovery
their malefactions	:	that which torture could not wring
	:	from him

Obviously Massinger's version is diffuser and greyer. He employs 40 words to Shakespeare's 31; and they include 9 disyllables against Shakespeare's 6, and two trisyllables against Shakespeare's one.[1] And the quality is weaker. *I once observed* is weaker than *I have heard*; *guilty hearer* than *guilty creature*; *forced by the terror of a wounded conscience* than *struck so to the soul*; *make discovery* than *proclaimed*; and *that which torture could not wring from him* is a feeble periphrasis, almost a pointless euphemism, for *malefactions*.

At first sight this second example has revealed a difference in

---

[1] Although Shakespeare's *presently*, with its weak final syllable is not so lengthy as either of Massinger's trisyllables. A singularly fine effect is given by the weight of Hamlet's polysyllabic *malefactions* coming at the end of the statement, as contrasted with the monosyllabic weakness and anticlimax of Massinger's *could not wring from him*.

quality which is not quite the same as that which was shown by the comparison between the passages from *The Duke of Milan* and *Othello*. It has indeed shown as before a diffuseness and a flaccidity in Massinger which is all the more obvious because of the close parallel in ideas: it has, like a photograph of a photograph, less 'contrast' and a more compressed tonal range. But that is not the same as a difference in sensuous impact. The reason is that Massinger is in the second example, as I have said, 'translating' a Shakespearian statement into other words. It is therefore less typical of Massinger. Comparison is in fact more impressive when Massinger is originating and expressing in his own characteristic manner ideas that can be more or less paralleled in Shakespeare or are perhaps drawn from Shakespeare but without the verbal and phrasal echoes. This is the method Mr. Eliot used when he first pointed out the essential difference between Massinger's and Shakespeare's diction.[1]

> Can I call back yesterday, with all their aids
> That bow unto my sceptre? or restore
> My mind to that tranquillity and peace
> It then enjoyed?[2]

is a sensuously pallid recollection of

> Not poppy, nor mandragora,
> Nor all the drowsy syrups of the world
> Shall ever medicine thee to that sweet sleep
> Which thou owd'st yesterday.[3]

As Mr. Eliot says of this parallel, 'Massinger's is a general rhetorical question, the language just and pure, but colourless. Shakespeare's has particular significance; and the adjective "drowsy" and the verb "medicine" infuse a precise vigour'.[4] In Massinger virtue has gone out of the expression. The same may be said of,

> Happy are those,
> That knowing, in their births, they are subject to
> Uncertain change, are still prepared, and armed
> For either fortune;[5]

as compared with

> A man that fortune's buffets and rewards
> Hath ta'en with equal thanks; and bless'd are those
> Whose blood and judgment are so well commingled
> That they are not a pipe for fortune's finger
> To sound what stop she please.[6]

[1] *Philip Massinger*, 1920; cf. *Selected Essays.*
[2] *Emperor of the East*, v. ii.   [3] *Othello*, III. iii. 331.
[4] *Selected Essays*, p. 207.   [5] *Bondman*, III. iii.   [6] *Hamlet*, III. ii.

Yet perhaps the diffuseness and watering-down seen in Massinger's direct and almost direct translation from Shakespeare, is really the same thing as the filming-over of the hue of life and the diminished sensuous vitality of which I spoke before. Both are indicative of a talent which is not 'immediately at the tips of the senses'.[1] In the case of his direct translations Massinger is not expressing something he has experienced himself but is merely repeating the words of another. In the case of his own original statement, as in *The Duke of Milan* passage, Massinger may be expressing something he has experienced himself (or, to be more precise, the re-creation of Sforza's experience in himself), but he is expressing it in a way which indicates that it is recollected, or rather generalised, in tranquillity; that is to say, while he is writing his characters' speeches he is not himself experiencing the sensations and emotions fully-rounded characters like Shakespeare's are experiencing and which Shakespeare himself must have experienced in his writing, but is standing, as it were, at one remove from reality and writing *about* his characters rather than *as* his characters. In both cases, in direct translation and in original statement, what is missing from the expression is life itself. This shows itself in what the characters say. Shakespeare's characters (Othello, for example) speak for themselves and live and breathe as human beings, experiencing emotions and responding to sensory stimuli as do real human beings. Massinger's characters, on the other hand, do not seem to feel at all, however much they may talk about such feelings as grief, pain, jealousy, love, or anger. They do not use words which express directly any of these feelings, sensations, or emotions, but content themselves with a generalised description of them.

The differences between Massinger and Shakespeare as regards their diction might be summed up briefly in general terms as follows: where Shakespeare is precise, Massinger is vague; where Shakespeare is tense, Massinger is slack; where Shakespeare is terse, Massinger is diffuse; and where Shakespeare is concentrated, Massinger is dilute. That is the crux of the matter. In Massinger the high degree of condensation, the packed significance and suggestiveness, we know from Shakespeare and expect from many of his lesser brethren, is gone, and the effect of his verse upon the reader or audience is of a considerably reduced impact. We can, in fact, apply to him (and with more justice) what Garrick said of Dr. Johnson: 'All that he writes comes from his head. Shakespeare, when he sat down to write, dipped his pen in his heart.'[2] That

[1] T. S. Eliot, op. cit., p. 210.   [2] Margaret Barton, *Garrick*, London, 1948, p. 204.

which comes from the head is organised, rationalised, and, in order that all its parts may be seen clearly, is often thinly spread: that which comes from the heart is poured out undiluted, and though it is perhaps to be apprehended rather than comprehended, it speaks to us more directly. The lack in Massinger is a lack of just this sort of concentrated directness, this unifying totality of experience, which we find in Shakespeare.

It is, of course, impossible to describe adequately what is lacking in Massinger's diction by any quotation from Massinger. I can only direct the reader to Massinger's verse itself taken as a whole, and in particular to the lack in it of words with sensuous connotations or overtones. To take only one small example: in the first scenes of the first acts of eight of the plays (*The Great Duke of Florence*, *The Bondman*, *The Renegado*, *The Roman Actor*, *The City Madam*, *The Guardian*, *The Bashful Lover*, and *The Emperor of the East*) there are only four occasions on which Massinger uses words which call up, however faintly, the impression of some colour. Thus, in *The Great Duke of Florence* we have 'golden mean', a phrase which (to me, at least) has only the faintest tinge of the colour of gold; in *The Renegado* we have 'a green apron', an object Massinger refers to merely to show his knowledge of the Muslim sacred colour; and in *The Guardian* we have 'the roses frighted from your cheeks' and 'my tenants' nut-brown daughters', both uses of colour words so conventional as to be almost completely unevocative. The monochromatic rendering of the world of which this is only a sample contrasts strangely with Shakespeare's panchromatic presentation.

This, however, indicates merely one way in which an examination of the poetic quality of Massinger's verse can be conducted, by comparing the words in isolation in certain passages and in their specific parallels in Shakespeare. I should like now to continue the examination of Massinger's style more discursively, though still with an eye to comparison with Shakespeare.

Let us begin with Giovanni, the young hero of *The Great Duke of Florence*, declaring his love for the first time to Lidia:

> O Lidia,
> Of maids the honour, and your sex's glory!
> It is not fear to die, but to lose you,
> That brings this fever on me. I will now
> Discover to you, that which, till this minute,
> I durst not trust the air with. Ere you knew
> What power the magic of your beauty had,
> I was enchanted by it, liked, and loved it,

> My fondness still increasing with my years;
> And, flattered by false hopes, I did attend
> Some blessed opportunity to move
> The duke with his consent to make you mine:
> But now, such is my star-crossed destiny,
> When he beholds you as you are, he cannot
> Deny himself the happiness to enjoy you.
> And I as well in reason may entreat him
> To give away his crown, as to part from
> A jewel of more value, such as you are.[1]

This is artificiality indeed, but not the sparkling, jewelled artificiality of the early Shakespeare, the artificiality which enchants by a shimmering illusion of life, which for all its legerdemain is shot through and through with life and sense. Massinger's is an artificiality approaching the factitious and the listless. The young lover who speaks is described at the very beginning of the play[2] as having a 'sharp wit and pregnant apprehension':

> All that he speaks being with such grace delivered,
> That it makes perfect harmony.

We have to take Massinger's word for that. Certainly, his use of 'star-crossed', adopted from the prologue to *Romeo and Juliet*, bears out the assertion that he makes use

> Of what's read to him, but 'tis straight digested,
> And truly made his own.

Yet one wonders whether if Romeo had spoken with such pedestrian ardour to Juliet the Capulets would ever have lost her.

Next take a passage from the play of Massinger's which has the most of passionate excitement in it, *The Unnatural Combat*. Here is Malefort confronted with the ghosts of his dead wife and son:

> Ha! is't fancy?
> Or hath hell heard me, and makes proof if I
> Dare stand the trial? Yes, I do; and now
> I view these apparitions, I feel
> I once did know the substances. For what come you?
> Are your aerial forms deprived of language,
> And so denied to tell me, that by signs
> You bid me ask here of myself? 'Tis so:
> And there is something here makes answer for you.
> You come to lance my seared-up conscience; yes,
> And to instruct me, that those thunderbolts,
> That hurled me headlong from the height of glory,

---

[1] v. iii.　　[2] i. i.

Wealth, honours, worldly happiness, were forged
Upon the anvil of my impious wrongs,
And cruelty to you! I do confess it;
And that my lust compelling me to make way
For a second wife, I poisoned thee; and that
The cause (which to the world is undiscovered)
That forced thee to shake off thy filial duty
To me, thy father, had its spring and source
From thy impatience, to know thy mother,
That with all duty and obedience served me
(For now with horror I acknowledge it)
Removed unjustly: yet, thou being my son,
Wert not a competent judge marked out by heaven
For her revenge, which thy falling by
My weaker hand confirmed.—'Tis granted by thee.
Can any penance expiate my guilt,
Or can repentance save me?—

　　　　　　　　　　　They are vanished![1]

The situation bears a general resemblance to others in *Julius Caesar*, *Hamlet*, and *Macbeth*. But how utterly different! This is a spurious supernaturalism and as spurious an encounter with it. Massinger's apparitions come, 'use various gestures' like mute puppets, and then disappear. They are attended with no mystery or awe. They shake no gory locks: they wave with no courteous action to a more removed ground: they neither speak cryptic warning of a Philippi nor

　　　　　　　a tale unfold whose lightest word
　　Would harrow up the soul.

Malefort encounters them as he would any physically substantial character and is inspired with no 'thoughts beyond the reaches of our souls'. After a (very cool) doubt as to the reality of the apparitions and a query as to their coming which compares weakly indeed with Hamlet's awe-struck and awe-inspiring

　　Angels and ministers of grace defend us!
　　Be thou a spirit of health or goblin damned,
　　Bring with thee airs from heaven or blasts from hell,
　　Be thy intents wicked or charitable . . .[2]

—after a weak beginning, Malefort proceeds to a speech of such businesslike discourse as was never, outside laboratories for the investigation of paranormal psychology and E.S.P., addressed to disembodied spirits. Whereas Malefort asks 'For what come you?' in a question that has no spread beyond the immediate situation, Hamlet

[1] v. ii.　　　　[2] *Hamlet*, i. iv.

takes us by his adjuration behind and beyond the situation and makes us see another scene which, although itself outside the play, casts an illuminating flash on it:

> but tell
> Why thy canonized bones, hearsed in death,
> Have burst their cerements; why the sepulchre,
> Wherein we saw thee quietly inurned,
> Hath op'd his ponderous and marble jaws,
> To cast thee up again.[1]

As a result Malefort communicates scarcely a ripple to us, whose response to the supernatural is conditioned as indirectly by its impact on him as directly by its impact on us. He presents us with a problem to disentangle, a problem of generalised words, unbedded in psycho-physical reality, and of elaborately suspended syntax. The words, figures, and images are not linked by any sort of 'unified sensibility'. And, it might be added, our puzzlement is made the more complete by our being given in this speech the only answer we ever receive to one of the enigmas of the play—why did Malefort and his son quarrel?

Examples of this inferiority in poetic quality in Massinger could be doubled and redoubled. The important thing to notice is that this is not only an inferiority to Shakespeare, though I have chosen Shakespeare as an example of the supreme in poetic quality of expression, but it is also an almost absolute lack of poetical quality, a lack of what, in Keats's words,[2] we must term the 'poetical character'. Little more remains to be said on the subject.

I have, however, not yet mentioned Massinger's use of figures of speech. Indeed, he uses them sparingly—and then only in the most ordinary and everyday way. The most important of these figures is metaphor. Now, it would of course be untrue to say that Massinger never uses metaphor, though he uses it seldom. For it might be said that just as any use of language is elliptical, so it is metaphorical. Language, or at least expression, is inevitably metaphorical—from the covert to the overt, from the dead[3] to the living.

Shakespeare's use of metaphor is rarely conscious and deliberate. Yet he is one of the most richly, variously, and vitally metaphorical writers in the world's literature. And surely Aristotle is right in saying that: 'Much the most important thing is to be able to use metaphors, for this is the one thing that cannot be learned from others; and it is also a mark of genius, since a good metaphor implies

---

[1] *Hamlet*, i. iv.   [2] See above, Chap. IV, p. 136.
[3] Which, however, as H. W. Fowler says (*A Dictionary of Modern English Usage*, p. 349), may be at times galvanised into activity again.

an intuitive perception of the similarity in dissimilarity.'[1] I would underline Aristotle's *intuitive*. For that is what characterises Shakespeare in his metaphors. He does not, except rarely and for particular reasons of appropriateness to a speaker and his momentary occasion, take thought about his metaphors. They are his willing and absolute slaves crowding to do his service—to carry his ideas. But even that does not convey adequately what I want to say. It is rather that the whole language in Shakespeare's hands is charged with the most potent metaphorical electricity and magnetism; and the words which are all but inert by comparison in others' hands combine and recombine like the most stubborn elements in the electro-magnetic intensity of the sun. Shakespeare's style is a shot-silk texture of metaphor. Metaphor dissolves into metaphor. As soon as a metaphor has, like a note or chord in music, contributed its iota, it ceases to be. There is no metaphorical economy, no eking out a limited supply. 'A cistern contains,' says Blake: 'a fountain overflows.' And Shakespeare is a never-failing fountain.

On the other hand, Massinger is a much more conscious, deliberate and parsimonious user of metaphor. He does not use it with the intuitive spontaneity of the genius, but with the precise pedantry of the rather literally-minded student of rhetoric. He says to himself, 'Go to, I will here bring in a metaphor.' His metaphors, therefore, tend either to give the impression of verbal appliqué work and of something not absorbed into the speech or to swell out and take charge of what is being said, the completion and elaborate carrying-out of the metaphor becoming an end in itself rather than a means to an end.

Here is a passage which demonstrates the first, or unassimilated use. Sanazarro, in Act I, scene ii, of *The Great Duke of Florence*, has brought news of a sea-victory to Duke Cozimo. Cozimo exclaims:

> Still my nightingale,
> That with sweet accents dost assure me, that
> My spring of happiness comes fast upon me!
> Embrace me boldly.

And a few lines later the Duke says, still speaking of Sanazarro;

> we have not
> Received into our bosom and our grace
> A glorious lazy drone, grown fat with feeding
> On others' toil, but an industrious bee,
> That crops the sweet flowers of our enemies
> And every happy evening returns
> Loaden with wax and honey to our hive.

[1] *The Rhetoric*, III, x.

Both those metaphors are patently 'stuck on' as ornamentation.
Sanazarro is first of all a nightingale and then an 'industrious bee';
and in any case a bee, industrious or otherwise, in his bosom would
create an effect upon the Duke very different from that Massinger is
wishing to express.[1] The metaphors here are both inappropriate and,
if not dead or moribund, at least dormant, and, given no life by
Massinger, spring from no life in Cozimo's speech.

The second of the two metaphors I have quoted is quite long, but
has not yet swollen quite enough to appear of more importance than
its context. Here, to demonstrate the second faulty use of metaphor
by Massinger, is a passage from Act III, scene i, of *A New Way to
Pay Old Debts* showing the inflated metaphor—the usurping cuckoo-
in-the-nest: Young Allworth is describing Margaret Overreach to his
master, Lord Lovell:

> *Allworth.* Were you to encounter with a single foe,
>   The victory were certain; but to stand
>   The charge of two such potent enemies,
>   At once assaulting you, as wealth and beauty,
>   And those too seconded with power, is odds
>   Too great for Hercules.
> *Lovell.*   Speak your doubts and fears,
>   Since you will nourish them, in plainer language,
>   That I may understand them.
> *Allworth.*   What's your will,
>   Though I lend arms against myself, (provided
>   They may advantage you) must be obeyed.
>   My much-loved lord, were Margaret only fair,
>   The cannon of her more than earthly form,
>   Though mounted high, commanding all beneath it,
>   And rammed with bullets of her sparkling eyes,
>   Of all the bulwarks that defend your senses
>   Could batter none, but that which guards your sight.
>   But when the well-tuned accents of her tongue
>   Make music to you, and with numerous sounds
>   Assault your hearing (such as if Ulysses
>   Now lived again, howe'er he stood the Syrens,
>   Could not resist), the combat must grow doubtful
>   Between your reason and rebellious passions.
>   Add this too; when you feel her touch, and breath
>   Like a soft western wind, when it glides o'er
>   Arabia, creating gums and spices;
>   And in the van, the nectar of her lips,

---

[1] 'A bee in a bosom' in this particular context is almost an example of what Fowler
calls (*Modern English Usage*, p. 350) a 'battle of dead metaphors'.

Which you must taste, bring the battalia on,
Well armed, and strongly lined with her discourse,
And knowing manners, to give entertainment;—
Hippolytus himself would leave Diana,
To follow such a Venus.

Lovell.   Love hath made you
Poetical, Allworth.

One may take leave to doubt Lord Lovell's last remark, and, having
regard to Allworth's syntax, question whether he has indeed expressed
his doubts and fears 'in plainer language'. Be that as it may, the
extended metaphor from warfare that is my concern at the moment
is laboriously excogitated and tediously drawn-out. Stale as it is,
Massinger doubtless thought it an appropriate one to introduce in
a conversation between a man of military experience and a would-be
soldier. But that is just the trouble. It has been dragged in. And
like the periodic syntax it has been imposed *ab extra*.

What I have said about Massinger's use of metaphor applies with
equal vigour to his use of simile, with the added comment that, since
a simile of more than minimum content always has the air of being
deliberately inserted as a sort of poetical grace-note or parenthetical
embellishment, its defects tend to be even more apparent.

[He] breaks through all law-nets, made to curb ill men,
As they were cobwebs;[1]

is a simile that is allowable since it is both appropriate and brief.
More often than not, however, Massinger's similes are not brief.
They tend, that is to say, like the second type of metaphor
described above, towards the inflated. Here is an example of two
such similes occurring in the space of a few lines from Act V, scene
iii, of *The Bondman*:

But if that pure desires, not blended with
Foul thoughts, that, like a river, keeps his course,
Retaining still the clearness of the spring
From whence it took beginning, may be thought
Worthy acceptance; then I dare rise up,
And tell this gay man to his teeth, I never
Durst doubt her constancy, that, like a rock,
Beats off temptations, as that mocks the fury
Of the proud waves.

The most important flaw in Massinger's use of figures of speech,
however, is that when he uses them he sprinkles them indiscriminately through his speeches, not only unassimilated, as already

[1] *New Way to Pay Old Debts*, II. ii.

suggested, but also quite unrelated one with the other. Thus we might note that in the long metaphorical passage previously quoted from *A New Way to Pay Old Debts*[1] there are two lengthy similes introduced, either of which might be quite pleasant in itself, but which are singularly inappropriate when set in the midst of the sustained military imagery of the rest of the statement. Similarly, the passage quoted above from *The Bondman* continues:

> nor, from my jealous fears,
> Question that goodness to which, as an altar
> Of all perfection, he that truly loved
> Should rather bring a sacrifice of service,
> Than raze it with the engines of suspicion:
> Of which, when he can wash an Aethiop white,
> Leosthenes may hope to free himself;
> But, till then, never.

The barbola-work effect which results from applying on top of a statement a collection of improperly articulated and quite unrelated figures of speech of different types is shown in these lines from Act V, scene viii, of *The Renegado*:

> Excuse me, Mustapha, though this night to me
> Appear as tedious as that treble one
> Was to the world, when Jove on fair Alcimena
> Begot Alcides. Were you to encounter
> Those ravishing pleasures, which the slow-paced hours
> (To me they are such) bar me from, you would
> With your continued wishes, strive to imp
> New feathers to the broken wings of time,
> And chide the amorous sun, for too long dalliance
> In Thetis' watery bosom.

Far from being exceptional, this rag-bag method of throwing figures together is Massinger's almost invariable practice, and is still another indication of his lack of investing his work with emotion.

It may be thought that there is little so far to commend in Massinger as a poetic stylist; and perhaps we should in fairness ask whether Massinger's poetry is all bad, whether there are not indeed occasions upon which he rises above the level of involved and colourless mediocrity I have illustrated at considerable length. The answer to this question will be a somewhat qualified one.

When he does manage to produce verses with some fire and warmth in them is when he himself happens to be deeply moved by the particular idea and sentiments expressed. This does not mean, how-

[1] P. 252

ever, that the passages ring quite true. If Massinger himself is moved, the character is not. Or rather, the character's identity is forgotten and Massinger speaks to us directly—a bad flaw in a dramatist attempting an approach to an imitation of life. Such passages are set speeches and many of them have the air of being complete poems or tirades written by Massinger separately from the play in which they appear, and introduced by him *ex gratia* to 'make the gruel thick and slab'. I have already given several specimens of this extra-dramatic matter when speaking of Massinger's satire.[1] But perhaps I may give here other examples of the kind of thing I mean. The first is spoken by Lady Allworth to her stepson in *A New Way to Pay Old Debts*. There is no pretence here that the sentiments are those of the speaker: they are offered as a father's charge to his son, not given directly, as surely such a charge would be, but indirectly by the stepmother to whom they had been entrusted:

These were your father's words: 'If e'er my son
Follow the war, tell him it is a school,
Where all the principles tending to honour
Are taught, if truly followed: but for such
As repair thither, as a place in which
They do presume they may with license practise
Their lusts and riots, they shall never merit
The noble name of soldiers. To dare boldly
In a fair cause, and, for their country's safety,
To run upon the cannon's mouth undaunted;
To obey their leaders, and shun mutinies;
To bear with patience the winter's cold,
And summer's scorching heat, and not to faint,
When plenty of provision fails, with hunger;
Are the essential parts make up a soldier,
Not swearing, dice, or drinking.[2]

The fact is that Massinger himself was very much the militarist, the soldier's advocate, and the panegyrist of martial courage and bearing; and he made opportunities to express such sentiments.

The second example is from a speech of Bertoldo in *The Maid of Honour* to rouse the sluggish Sicilians to warlike ire. The rest of the speech has a dramatic relevance; but the following lines could be quite easily detached from the context without harming the dramatic flow or purpose in the least:

If examples
May move you more than arguments, look on England,
The empress of the European isles,

[1] Above, Chap. V, pp. 197 ff.   [2] I. ii.

And unto whom alone ours yields precedence:
When did she flourish so, as when she was
The mistress of the ocean, her navies
Putting a girdle round about the world?
When the Iberian quaked, her worthies named;
And the fair flower-de-luce grew pale, set by
The red rose and the white? Let not our armour
Hung up, or our unrigged armada, make us
Ridiculous to the late poor snakes our neighbours,
Warmed in our bosoms, and to whom again
We may be terrible; while we spend our hours
Without variety, confined to drink,
Dice, cards, or whores. Rouse us, sir, from the sleep
Of idleness, and redeem our mortgaged honours.[1]

It is Massinger the patriotic Englishman who has displaced Bertoldo for the time being.

Still more obviously inset and interrupting to the action is the 'lively rhodomontade', as Gifford calls it,[2] of Durazzo's description of country sports in *The Guardian*, almost the only passage on nature and its wild life in Massinger:

> In the afternoon,
> For we will have variety of delights,
> We'll to the field again, no game shall rise
> But we'll be ready for't: if a hare, my greyhounds
> Shall make a course; for the pie or jay, a sparhawk
> Flies from the fist; the crow so near pursued,
> Shall be compelled to seek protection under
> Our horses' bellies; a hearn put from her siege,
> And a pistol shot off in her breach, shall mount
> So high, that, to your view, she'll seem to soar
> Above the middle region of the air:
> A cast of haggard falcons, by me manned,
> Eyeing the prey at first, appears as if
> They did turn tail; but with their labouring wings
> Getting above her, with a thought their pinions
> Cleaving the purer element, make in,
> And by turns bind with her; the frighted fowl,
> Lying at her defence upon her back,
> With her dreadful beak awhile defers her death,
> But by degrees forced down, we part the fray,
> And feast upon her. . . . Then, for an evening flight,
> A tiercel gentle, which I call, my masters,
> As he were sent a messenger to the moon,

---

[1] *The Maid of Honour*, i. i.   [2] Vol. iv, p. 142.

In such a place flies, as he seems to say,
See me, or see me not! the partridge sprung,
He makes his stoop; but wanting breath, is forced
To cancelier; then, with such speed as if
He carried lightning in his wings, he strikes
The trembling bird, who even in death appears
Proud to be made his quarry.[1]

In these and a few other passages, Massinger pleases us by expressing with a certain extra vigour a sentiment that came from his own heart or a first-hand physical experience. The trouble is that, like a new patch on old clothes, they show up the overall drabness of their contexts. Besides, all told they are rare; and such as there are, are generally powerful, even eloquent, expressions of one of Massinger's intellectual or moral conclusions and convictions rather than of his response to some experience lived and felt in blood and bone.

★

At the beginning of this chapter I expressed the opinion that Massinger's stylistic idiosyncrasy is an illustration of the so-called 'dissociation of sensibility' which is now pretty generally accepted as a true diagnosis of the change that spread like a sclerosis in seventeenth-century poetry.

As to the diction and imagery, the case for placing Massinger in the long succession leading to the aridity and lack of sensuous and emotional content of much eighteenth-century diction is self-evident, and has been so ever since Mr. Eliot first broached the subject. Indeed, in the colourlessness of his poetry in general, Massinger has the air of being, instead of almost contemporaneous with Shakespeare, removed in time by almost a century from him.

It is true, of course, that Massinger displays an innate lack of that sensory awareness so noticeable in Shakespeare. Shakespeare was, after all, as Dryden tells us, 'the man who of all modern, and perhaps ancient poets, had the largest and most comprehensive soul. All the images of nature were still present to him, and he drew them, not laboriously, but luckily; when he describes any thing, you more than see it, you feel it too.'[2] Shakespeare makes us feel; perhaps luckily, as Dryden suggests, but certainly because he too could feel as well as build the lofty rhyme. With Massinger we do not ever know whether he felt or not, so devoid of the sense-element and so imbued with intellectual abstraction is his diction. No 'pure and eloquent

[1] I. i.   [2] *Essay of Dramatic Poesy*, ed. Arnold, Rev. Edn., 1939, p. 67.

blood' speaks in his verse, and none could suggest that, like Shakespeare's, his 'body thought'. But we must remember that Shakespeare himself (though, to be sure, he never lost his capacity for feeling and expressing feeling) was profoundly influenced in his last plays by changing conditions of theatrical production and a changing attitude in his audience, and that these changes had become still more complete by the time of Massinger's greatest output. In addition, we must remember that, whereas Shakespeare came to manhood in the optimistic and exuberant Elizabethan years, Massinger developed in the pessimistic and more reserved times of James, when the political shadows were beginning to lengthen and thought was coming to concentrate with increasing gravity and seriousness on moral, philosophical, and social topics. I would myself consider these last influences as paramount, acting, as they did in Massinger's case, upon a mind already inclined to be over-serious. It is not, then, that Massinger cannot feel. Such a failing is a manifest impossibility in a human being. Rather, I would say, he does not choose to feel, since his interest, and consequently his ability, are not, as in Shakespeare, centred upon the human soul as it is and on man living, breathing, feeling, and suffering, but upon the outward appearance of man as a social animal, acting according to some idealised code of conduct, upon what man should be rather than what man is. It must be recognised also, that what we have found in Massinger's diction is already present, though not to the same extent, in his master, Fletcher, and that it was the Fletcher-Massinger *genre* of romantic tragi-comedy that was picked up and developed at the Restoration after the hiatus caused in production by the closing of the theatres.

The one circumstance whose pressure no author can resist is that of the state of the language which prevails at the time in which he is writing. And one development of language is sufficient to account both for the phenomena of Massinger's diction and for the phenomena of eighteenth-century so-called 'poetic diction'. This development was clearly appreciated by Macaulay, when, writing a hundred years before Mr. Eliot, he summed up the reasons for the change in seventeenth-century poetry and provided an analysis of the situation which, albeit incomplete, has not since been superseded, even although it has perhaps been forgotten or overlooked. According to Macaulay's view, imagination is at its greatest potency in the primitive mind. At this stage the mind is not able to give expression to its imagination in poetry since it possesses no language adequate for the purpose and cannot clothe its imaginative experience in words. As the mind develops (argues Macaulay) its 'reasoning powers are improved at the expense of the imagination', but it reaches a point of equilibrium where it possesses both an adequate language and a residue of the primitive potency of imagination which, taken together, are sufficient to produce a poetry that is truly great—that is, creative, imaginative, poetry. In time, Reason and its handmaid, Language, develop still further and the power of the imagination declines. Then the poetry which is produced is what Macaulay calls 'critical poetry', dominated by reason at the expense of the imagination. Can this, I wonder, be what Mr. Eliot means when he says that 'a feeling for language ... outstripped ... a feeling for things'?[1] Here, at any rate, is Macaulay's statement of his case; much more naive than Mr. Eliot's perhaps, but as much to be respected:

> In process of time, the instruments [i.e. words] by which the imagination works are brought to perfection. Men have not more imagination than their rude ancestors. We strongly suspect that they have much less. But they produce better works of imagination. Thus, up to a certain period, the diminution of the poetical powers is far more than compensated by the improvement of all the appliances and means of which these powers stand in need. Then comes the short period of splendid and consummate excellence. And then, from causes against which it is vain to struggle, poetry begins to decline. The progress of language, which was at first favourable, becomes fatal to it, and instead of compensating for the decay of the imagination, accelerates that decay, and renders it more obvious. . . . At first it calls up a world of glorious illusions; but, when it becomes too copious, it altogether destroys the visual power.
>
> As the development of the mind proceeds, symbols, instead of being employed to convey images, are substituted for them. Civilised men think as they trade, not in kind, but by means of a circulating medium. In these circumstances, the sciences improve rapidly, and criticism among the rest; but poetry, in the highest sense of the word, disappears. Then comes the dotage of the fine arts, a second childhood, as feeble as the former, and far more hopeless. This is the age of critical poetry, of poetry by courtesy, of poetry to which the memory, the judgement, and the wit contribute far more than the imagination.[2]

Although, of course, Macaulay's statement is surprisingly wrong in that it allows no room for a revival of poetry at any time in the history of a civilisation, it remains a substantially correct statement of what did actually happen in seventeenth-century poetry. By

[1] *Selected Essays*, p. 209.
[2] An essay entitled *John Dryden* in *The Edinburgh Review*, January, 1828 (repr. *The Miscellaneous Writings and Speeches of Lord Macaulay*, London, 1900, p. 113).

reason of a complex of as yet unexplained causes (though certainly the rationalistic-scientific wave of the Renaissance had something to do with it) there took place in our poetry a split between Intellect and Feeling. This split showed itself chiefly in the diction and the imagery, in that the intellectual content of words began to outweigh their sensuous, and consequently to a great extent their emotional, potencies. The denotations of words asserted themselves and claimed the first place in the poet's attention; and yet the style as a medium of stimulus and suggestiveness became less, instead of more, alive. Not only were the words more or less divorced from sensuous and emotive purposes and chosen rather for the simple meaning they conveyed than for their sensuously evocative 'inscape', but the direct expression of Feeling was ousted by the more oblique workings of the abstracting and generalising Intellect. The net result of this was that many poets (though not all by any means) tended to express themselves in generalisations; to lose force inasmuch as their work delivered a reduced emotional impact; to convey their meanings more prosaically and clearly, perhaps more logically,[1] but certainly less imaginatively and concretely; and to lose the condensation and highly-compressed and image-provoking texture of, say, Shakespeare, Marlowe, and Webster. The whole complexion and hue of poetry became drier and greyer; clichés of general and vague import, instead of specific and vital *ad hoc* phraseology, became a feature of writing; poets wrote of life's ciphers, not life itself—prose concepts, instead of poetic images; and their phrases had the savour of prose rather than of poetry.

Ever since Mr. Eliot first used the phrase 'dissociation of sensibility' to describe this change in poetry it has been generally accepted that Massinger is a prime example of a writer deeply affected by it in respect of diction. But it seems clear also (as has not been remarked before) that the matter of syntax is not unrelated to this subject. I would not, of course, affirm that the tendency towards syntactical complexity which we have uncovered in Massinger appears in the final product of the seventeenth-century 'change'. Nevertheless it had its part to play in the process. In Milton, for example, and in some of the eighteenth-century blank verse writers who followed him, the same tendency is present; and in the final event, the couplet discipline, itself an intellectual form or imposition upon natural order, is in certain respects a reaction against, or an endeavour to reform, just such stylistic aberration. The two extremes, the curt couplet and the sprawling period, are part of the

[1] But see above, p. 232.

same process of intellectual sophistication, just as in the development of prose the Senecan and Ciceronian extremes are manifestations of the same tendency towards intellection. After the process was completed, the couplet emerged dominant, but this is not to discount syntactical complexity as one of the 'growing pains' (or perhaps 'arthritic twinges' describes it better) poetry had to experience to reach this state. The two features are involved in the same process.

It will thus be plain from what has been adduced that Massinger's syntax, especially his propensity towards involution, relates itself to this process. His syntax is much more a product of Intellect than of Feeling, or, to use his own terms, it springs much more from Reason than from Passion.[1] It is, in short, part of the same process of intellection which abstracted sensuous significance from his diction, and takes the form of his thinking too much both about what he wishes to say and about how he is to say it. That is, the things said are too intellectually excogitated and the saying of them is too ratiocinatively considered. As a result, the speech of his characters lacks immediacy and spontaneity: it has been put into their mouths rather than appearing as an unpremeditated response or product of themselves. The author steps between us and the characters. Or, to put it more precisely, an involved intellectual process has come between the author's vision of life and his presentation of it; between, if you like, his first intuition and his final expression. This intrusion of the intellect between the feeling and the expression, to such an extent as to subdue rather than merely to transmute the former, is what I understand Mr. Eliot to mean by 'dissociation of sensibility'. And my contention is that it occurs as much when the organising intellect changes the order of natural *psychologic* (loose and processional) into the logic of the periodic style (ordered and articulated, but withal sophisticated), as when it changes the diction and imagery, which were Mr. Eliot's area of attention, from the particularised, concrete, and sensuous into the generalised, abstract, and emasculated.

Perhaps Mr. Eliot himself best described in *The Hollow Men* what happened:

> Between the idea
> And the reality
> Between the motion
> And the act
> Falls the Shadow . . .
>
> Between the conception
> And the creation

[1] Though, of course, his intellectual processes were not of the finest.

Between the emotion
And the response
Falls the Shadow.

★

For the sake of completeness, in a discussion of Massinger's style, mention must be made of two mannerisms in which he frequently indulges, mannerisms which, while they are not of any particular significance, are typical and may on occasion be used in determining the authorship of certain passages in collaborated plays.

The first is Massinger's liking for appositional phrases. Here are some examples:

> Patience, the beggar's virtue,
> Shall find no harbour here.[1]

> The fury of the many-headed monster,
> The giddy multitude.[2]

> the parent of security,
> Long-absent peace.[3]

> A wooden dish, the beggar's plate.[4]

> my prayers,
> The beggar's satisfaction.[5]

> pity,
> The poor man's orisons.[6]

> profuseness of expense, the parent
> Of wretched poverty, her fatal daughter.[7]

> The beggar's cure, patience.[8]

The fact that so many of these examples refer to poverty and beggars, while one further indication of Massinger's Plautine habit of repeating himself, may be no more than a coincidence. In form, however, they are typical, and might be described as a sort of condensed moral aphorism—indeed, the nearest that Massinger ever gets to condensation and terseness of phrase.

The second, and very individual mannerism, is the habit he has of reduplicating a word, as in the following examples:

> My pride, my pride. . . .[9]

---

[1] *New Way to Pay Old Debts*, v. i. [2] *Unnatural Combat*, iii. ii.
[3] *Bashful Lover*, iv. iii. [4] Ibid., iii. iii. [5] *City Madam*, i. i.
[6] Ibid., iv. iii. [7] Ibid., ii. iii. [8] *Renegado*, ii. v.
[9] *Guardian*, iii. vi.

> You are wide,
> Wide the whole region.[1]

> but, if lessened, then,
> Then my poor heart-strings crack.[2]

> thus, thus I pierce it.[3]
> For 'tis a deed of night, of night, Francisco.[4]

> my wife, my wife, Pescara,
> Being absent, I am dead.[5]

To show how such a mannerism can be of value as contributory evidence of authorship here are three examples from Massinger scenes in *The Virgin Martyr*:

> Oh, mine own,
> Mine own dear lord [6]

> tell her I have worn,
> In all the battles I have fought, her figure,
> Her figure in my heart.[7]

> but take heed,
> Take heed, my lord.[8]

As will be seen, the repetition of the phrase, occurring as it does so often between one line and the next, is usually no more than a device for filling out the metre, not for dramatic or rhetorical effect. Fletcher, who also has a trick of repeating phrases, does so in a slightly more elaborate way that indicates that he on the other hand is striving after some particular pathetic or dramatic effect:

> But through the world, the wide world, thus to wander,
> The wretched world alone, no comfort with me;[9]

an example which also exhibits Fletcher's tendency to alliteration, a tendency almost completely absent in Massinger.

★

The features of Massinger's versification, while they are chiefly of interest in disengaging his hand from that of other writers, may be summarised very briefly as follows:

(i) Regarded purely on a numerical basis, Massinger constructs his verses very regularly; that is, he has the correct number of syllables and stresses in each line, according to a fairly rigid iambic pattern.

---

[1] *City Madam*, III. ii. [2] *Roman Actor*, II. i. [3] *Renegado*, v. vii.
[4] *Duke of Milan*, I. iii. [5] Ibid., III. i. [6] I. i.
[7] I. i. [8] v. ii.
[9] Fletcher, *Women Pleased*. Quoted by Oliphant, *Engl. Studien.*, XIV.

(ii)   He makes a large use of run-on lines—about 40% as compared with Fletcher's 15–20%.[1]

(iii) As compared with Fletcher's combination of the double-stressed ending and the end-stopped line (a combination found in no other Elizabethan-Jacobean author) Massinger has, together with his run-on lines, many light and weak endings; that is, he often ends his lines with words that cannot be grammatically separated from the next line. Unlike Fletcher, he rarely accents the hypermetric or eleventh syllable.

(iv)   The pauses in his lines are very freely distributed.

(v)   The number of his speeches which end in the middle of a line is sometimes as high as 80%, whereas a similar percentage of Fletcher's speeches finish at the end of a line.[2] Massinger always completes his metrical line with the opening of the next speech.

(vi)   He rarely uses rhyme, except at a scene or act ending.[3]

(vii) He rarely uses prose.[4]

(viii) His verse is smoother and 'flatter' than Fletcher's; that is, its metrical pattern is not so apparent.

There are, however, certain respects in which a poet's versification is of interest in a consideration of his style. These respects tend to resolve themselves into an examination of the efficiency with which the verse acts as a conductor of the style. Viewed from this angle, Massinger's verse is an extremely efficient channel, offering a very low resistance to the matter it has to transmit. It flows easily. The linkage of the run-on lines carries the weight of the subordination lightly, really too lightly, and slips easily from the pen of one who, as Chelli says, 'révèle une oreille qui aime à enchaîner les mètres par le sens'.[5] But this, as I have suggested before, is its great fault. The function of versification is indeed to act as a medium for the style, but it must at the same time set bounds to the style, keeping it within its channel, and exercising a unifying restraint upon, and applying an artistic mould or form to, the material. Otherwise there is little purpose to verse at all—apart from the muttered undertone provided by the regular metre. It is this controlling and unifying capacity that is lacking in Massinger's verse. In fact, the slack rhythms and lack of restraint of his verse approach very close to those of prose.

---

[1] Baldwin's Edition of *The Duke of Milan*, and Boyle, *Engl. Studien.*, V.
[2] Oliphant, loc. cit.   [3] See above, Chap. III, p. 82.
[4] Examples occur in *City Madam*, II. ii; *Renegado*, I. iii; *Bashful Lover*, III. iii (Gothrio); and *Emperor of the East*, IV. iv.   [5] *Drame*, p. 119.

Here, for example, is a passage from Massinger:

If you think them unworthy to taste of these cates you feed on or wear such costly garments, will you grant them the privilege and prerogative of great minds which you were born to? Honour won in war and to be styled preservers of their country are titles fit for free and generous spirits and not for bondmen. Had I been born a man and such never-dying glories made the prize to bold heroic courage by Diana, I would not to my brother, nay, my father, be bribed to part with the least piece of honour I should gain in this action.

There is almost nothing in this passage, written out as prose, to indic-ate that it is really verse—Massinger's 'verse'. In fact, it is part of Cleora's speech in Act I, scene iii, of *The Bondman*.

Here is another example:

> How much I must acknowledge myself bound
> For your so many and extraordinary favours
> Conferred upon me, as far as is in my power,
> Posterity shall notice. I, myself,
> Were most unworthy of such noble friends,
> If I should not, with heart-felt thankfulness,
> Profess and own them.

In this case I have written, with the minimum of addition,[1] the first two sentences of the prose Dedicatory Epistle to *The Roman Actor* as if they were verse. One accustomed to Massinger's verse could not be blamed if he accepted these lines as true coin.

The truth of the matter is, as Coleridge said, that '. . . in Mas-singer the style is differenced, but differenced in the smallest degree possible, from animated conversation by the vein of poetry'.[2] His verse, according to Professor Morris, 'would make good rhythmical prose';[3] and Fleay speaks of the 'Massinger weak line, which often is as hard to distinguish from measured prose as the iambics of Dickens or Musaeus are from *Thalaba* or *Queen Mab* verse'.[4] And even Pro-fessor Cruickshank, always ready to spring to Massinger's defence, admits that his style 'is constantly on the border-line of prose'; and adds that 'Massinger thought in blank verse because he was a dramatist rather than because he was a poet'.[5] Mr. Harley Gran-ville-Barker, discussing the decline of blank verse at the time of Massinger and Shirley, although he is inclined to forgive what he

---

[1] Comparison with the original will show I have added two words (*must*, line 1; *myself*, line 4), deleted two words (*it*, line 3; *rake*, line 4), and changed *all* to *heartfelt* (line 6).
[2] *Table Talk*, p. 212.
[3] *On the Date and Composition of 'The Old Law'*, PMLA, XVII, 1902, p. 28.
[4] *Chronicle History*, p. 256.   [5] *Philip Massinger*, p. 34.

calls 'the loose freedoms of the metre', touches the crux of the matter when he says; 'What was wrong was the lack of compelling emotion. As it was not poetry it should not have been framed in verse at all. The discipline of prose would have been fitter'.[1]

Massinger, in short, is not a poet. Only rarely is there any 'compelling emotion' behind his work. His periodic structure is a prose-form. His ideas are prose-concepts, springing not from Feeling but from Intellect, and 'prose is,' as Professor Highet remarks, above all 'the language of the intellect'.[2] Perhaps, then, it is only natural that his verse also should be attached by the merest threads to the implement that Shakespeare and Marlowe and the greatest poets have used. 'Tout ce qui n'est point vers est prose.' And we can imagine Massinger exclaiming with Monsieur Jourdain, 'Par ma foi! Il y a plus de quarante ans que je dis de la prose sans que j'en susse rien'.

[1] *On Dramatic Method* (The Clark Lectures, 1930), London, 1931, p. 64.
[2] *The Classical Tradition*, p. 322.

APPENDIX I

The following is a list of plays with which Massinger's name can be definitely linked (from internal evidence of style) as a collaborator.[1]

Date	Play	Collaborator
About 1613	The Bloody Brother	Fletcher, Field, and Daborne[2]
Late 1617	Thierry and Theodoret	Fletcher and Field
Before 1619	The Knight of Malta	Fletcher and Field
1617 or 1618	The Queen of Corinth	Fletcher and Field
Aug. 1619	Sir John van Olden Barnavel	Fletcher
About 1619	The Custom of the Country	Fletcher
About 1619	The Fatal Dowry	Field[3]
1619–20	The Little French Lawyer	Fletcher
About 1620	The False One	Fletcher
Before 1622	The Beggar's Bush	Fletcher[4]
May 1622	The Prophetess	Fletcher
Oct. 1622	The Spanish Curate	Fletcher

APPENDIX II

The following list is of plays with which Massinger may be associated as a reviser:[1]

King Henry VIII. Possibly Shakespeare and Fletcher revised by M. (?)[5]
The Virgin Martyr. Dekker and (possibly) another, revised by M. 1620. (M.: i, iii. i and ii, v. ii.)
The Laws of Candy. Beaumont revised by M. ca. 1620. (M.: i and v.)
The Sea Voyage. Fletcher lightly revised by M. (lic. 1622).
Love's Cure. Beaumont revised by M. mid-1620's. (Possibly some touches of Fletcher as well).
The Fair Maid of the Inn. Fletcher very extensively revised by M. and Rowley (January 1626).
The Lover's Progress. Fletcher extensively rewritten by M.
A Very Woman. Fletcher extensively revised by M. (lic. 1634).
The Coxcomb. Beaumont and Fletcher revised by M. (ca. 1636).
The Elder Brother. Fletcher revised by M. (1637).
The Double Marriage. Fletcher revised by M. (after Fletcher's death).

There seems to be no reason for associating Massinger with any of the following plays:

The Captain, Cupid's Revenge, The Honest Man's Fortune, Love's Pilgrimage, Two Noble Kinsmen, The Faithful Friends, The Island Princess, The Old Law, or *A Cure for a Cuckold.*

[1] Compiled from evidence presented by Chelli in his *Collaboration.*
[2] Possibly the play mentioned in the Tripartite Letter.
[3] The only play in the list definitely associated with Massinger during his lifetime.
[4] Possibly revised by a later hand.
[5] In my opinion, Massinger's hand can be demonstrated in *The Winter's Tale* (e.g. III. ii).

APPENDIX III

On the following pages are given random examples of Massinger's syntax diagrammatically analysed. These examples have already been discussed in Chapter VI (pages 228–229).

Example I: *The Roman Actor*, I, iii.

If I free not myself

and [if I free not] in myself the rest of my profession from these false imputations

and I prove

that they make that a libel

which the poet writ for comedy.

[and which was] so acted too

It is but justice

that we undergo the heaviest censure.

Are you on the stage

you talk so boldly ?

EXAMPLE I (*continued*)

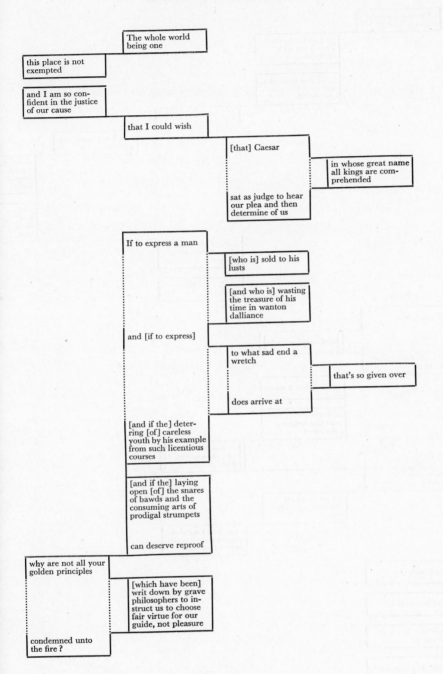

The whole world being one

this place is not exempted

and I am so confident in the justice of our cause

that I could wish

[that] Caesar

in whose great name all kings are comprehended

sat as judge to hear our plea and then determine of us

If to express a man

[who is] sold to his lusts

[and who is] wasting the treasure of his time in wanton dalliance

and [if to express]

to what sad end a wretch

that's so given over

does arrive at

[and if the] deterring [of] careless youth by his example from such licentious courses

[and if the] laying open [of] the snares of bawds and the consuming arts of prodigal strumpets

can deserve reproof

why are not all your golden principles

[which have been] writ down by grave philosophers to instruct us to choose fair virtue for our guide, not pleasure

condemned unto the fire ?

Example II: *The Parliament of Love,* III, ii.

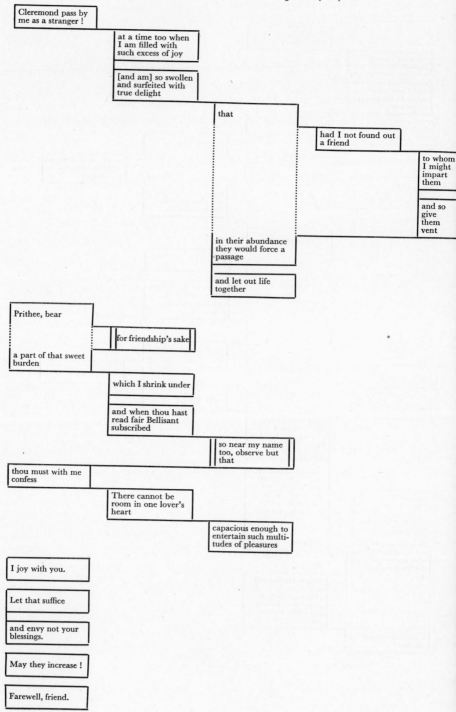

EXAMPLE II *(continued)*

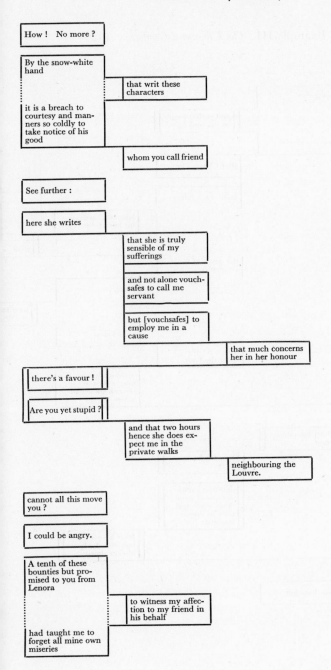

How !   No more ?

By the snow-white hand

that writ these characters

it is a breach to courtesy and manners so coldly to take notice of his good

whom you call friend

See further :

here she writes

that she is truly sensible of my sufferings

and not alone vouchsafes to call me servant

but [vouchsafes] to employ me in a cause

that much concerns her in her honour

there's a favour !

Are you yet stupid ?

and that two hours hence she does expect me in the private walks

neighbouring the Louvre.

cannot all this move you ?

I could be angry.

A tenth of these bounties but promised to you from Lenora

to witness my affection to my friend in his behalf

had taught me to forget all mine own miseries

Example III: *The Unnatural Combat*, v, i.

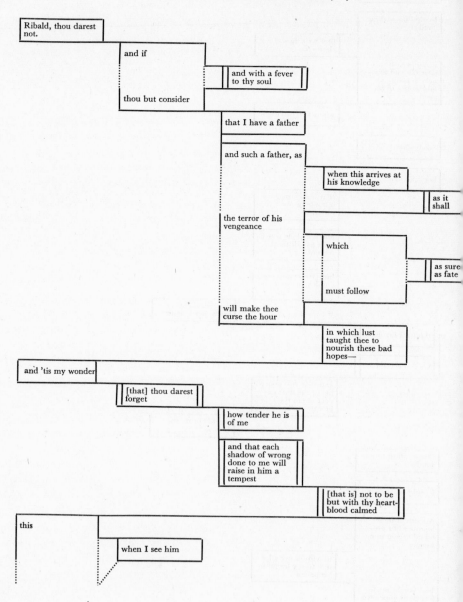

ABBREVIATIONS

For quotation from Massinger's plays I have used W. Gifford's *The Plays of Philip Massinger*, Second Edition (1813) (abbr. *Gifford*), and for quotation from *Believe As You List*, which does not appear in Gifford, I have used the text given in Francis Cunningham's *The Plays of Philip Massinger* (1871) (abbr. *Cunningham*). Other abbreviations used are as follows (for fuller particulars, see *Bibliography*):

BCED	F. G. Fleay: *Biographical Chronical of the English Drama*, 2 vols., 1891.
Bentley	G. E. Bentley: *The Jacobean and Caroline Stage*, 2 vols., 1941.
Bywater	I. Bywater: *Aristotle on the Art of Poetry*, 1929.
CBEL	*The Cambridge Bibliography of English Literature*, 4 vols., 1940.
CHEL	*The Cambridge History of English Literature*, 15 vols., 1932 Edition.
Collaboration	M. Chelli: *Étude sur la Collaboration de Massinger avec Fletcher et son Groupe*, 1926.
Drame	M. Chelli: *Le Drame de Massinger*, 1924.
E.K.C.	E. K. Chambers: *The Elizabethan Stage*, 4 vols., 1923.
H. Coleridge	*The Dramatic Works of Massinger and Ford*, Introduction by Hartley Coleridge, 1839.
Herbert	*The Dramatic Records of Sir Henry Herbert*, Ed. J. Q. Adams, 1917.
Monck Mason	*The Dramatick Works of Philip Massinger*, Ed. J. Monck Mason, 4 vols., 1779. (For Thos. Davies' *Short Essay on the Life and Writings of Massinger*.)
Philip Massinger	A. H. Cruickshank: *Philip Massinger*, 1920.
Raysor: Misc. Crit.	*Coleridge's Miscellaneous Criticism*, Ed. T. M. Raysor, 1936.

Titles of periodicals, etc., are abbreviated. The following are those most commonly used:

MLN	*Modern Language Notes*
MLR	*Modern Language Review*
PMLA	*Proceedings of the Modern Language Association*
PQ	*The Philological Quarterly*
RES	*The Review of English Studies*
TLS	*The Times Literary Supplement*

BIBLIOGRAPHY

The following is a list of those works, editions, articles, and other sources which have been used most frequently in the preparation of this book. For a comprehensive Bibliography of Massinger, the reader is referred to:

TANNENBAUM, S. A. *Philip Massinger: A Concise Bibliography* (Elizabethan Bibliographies, 4) New York, 1938

I. COLLECTED EDITIONS

The Dramatic Works of Philip Massinger, Ed. T. Coxeter, 4 vols, London, 1761

The Dramatick Works of Philip Massinger, Ed. J. Monck Mason, 4 vols, London, 1779. (Includes T. Davies' *Short Essay on the Life and Writings of Massinger*)

The Plays of Philip Massinger, Ed. W. Gifford, 4 vols, London, 1813. (2nd Edition)[1]

The Dramatic Works of Massinger and Ford, Ed. H. Coleridge, London, 1839–40. (Moxon's Dramatic Library)

The Plays of Philip Massinger, Ed. F. Cunningham, London, 1871[2]

II. SELECTIONS

The Best Plays of the Old Dramatists: Philip Massinger, Ed. A. Symons, 2 vols, London, 1887–9. (Mermaid Series, 4–5)

III. SEPARATE EDITIONS OF UNCOLLABORATED PLAYS

Believe As You List, Ed. T. C. Croker (Percy Soc. 27), London, 1849
    Tudor Facsimile Texts, London, 1907
    Ed. R. A. Sherman (Masterpieces of Eng. Drama. 5), New York, 1912
    Ed. C. J. Sisson (Malone Society Reprint 1927), Oxford, 1928

The Bondman, Ed. B. T. Spencer, Princeton, 1932

The City Madam, Ed. Rudolf Kirk (Princeton Studies in English, 10), Princeton, 1934

The Duke of Milan, Ed. T. W. Baldwin, Lancaster, Pa., 1918

The Great Duke of Florence, Ed. Janet M. Stochholm, Baltimore, 1933

The Maid of Honour, Ed. Eva A. W. Bryne, London, 1927

A New Way to Pay Old Debts, Ed. C. B. Wheeler, (in *Six Plays by Contemporaries of Shakespeare*), Oxford (World's Classics), 1915
    Ed. G. Stronach (Temple Dramatists), London, 1923
    Ed. A. H. Cruickshank, Oxford, 1926
    Ed. F. E. Schelling (in *Typical Elizabethan Plays*), 1926
    Ed. M. St. Clare Byrne, London, 1950

The Parliament of Love, Ed. Kathleen M. Lea (Malone Society Reprint, 1928), Oxford, 1929

The Roman Actor, Ed. W. L. Sandidge (Princeton Studies in English, 4), Princeton, 1929

The Unnatural Combat, Ed. R. S. Telfer (Princeton Studies in English, 7), Princeton, 1932

---

[1] This is the edition I have used throughout the text for quotations from all the plays, except *Believe As You List*. The First Edition was published in 1805.

[2] This is a reprint of Gifford's text with the addition of *Believe As You List*. All quotations from this play are given as in this edition.

IV. BIOGRAPHY, CRITICISM, ETC.

ALEXANDER, PETER. *A Shakespeare Primer*, London, 1951

ARBER, EDWARD. *Transcript of the Registers of the Company of Stationers, 1554–1640*, London, 1875–94, 5 vols

ARISTOTLE. *Aristotle on the Art of Poetry*, A revised text by Ingram Bywater, Oxford, 1929

AUBREY, JOHN. *Brief Lives*, Ed. A. Clark, 2 vols, Oxford, 1898
Natural History of Wiltshire, Ed. J. Britton, 2 vols., London, 1847

BALL, R. H. *Massinger and the House of Pembroke* (*MLN*, XLVI, 1931)
The Amazing Career of Sir Giles Overreach, London, 1939

BARNOUW, A. J. *De Tragedie van Johann van Oldenbarnevelt*, Amsterdam, 1922

BARTON, MARGARET. *Garrick*, London, 1948

BASSE, WILLIAM. *The Poetical Works of William Basse*, Ed. R. W. Bond, London, 1893

BATESON, F. W. *Contributions to a Dictionary of Critical Terms. II. 'Dissociation of Sensibility'* [*Essays in Criticism*, I, 3 (July, 1951)], Oxford, 1951
(Editor) *The Cambridge Bibliography of English Literature*, 4 vols., Cambridge, 1940

BEAUMONT, FRANCIS (and FLETCHER, JOHN). *Works*, Ed. A. Dyce, 11 vols., London, 1843–6
Works: Variorum Edition, Ed. A. H. Bullen, London, 4 vols., 1904–12 (uncompleted)

BECK, C. *Philip Massinger 'The Fatal Dowry'*, Einleitung zu einer neuen Ausgabe, Bayreuth, 1906

BENNETT, H. S. *Shakespeare's Audience* (Annual Shakespeare Lecture, British Academy 1944), Proceedings of the British Academy, XXX, London, 1944

BENTLEY, G. E. *The Jacobean and Caroline Stage*, 2 vols., Oxford, 1941

BETHELL, S. L. *The Cultural Revolution of the 17th Century*, London, 1951

BLAIR, HUGH. *Lectures on Rhetoric and Belles-Lettres*, London, 1837

BOAS, F. S. *An Introduction to Stuart Drama*, Oxford, 1946

BOYLE, R. *On Beaumont, Fletcher, and Massinger*, (*Engl. Studien*, V, 1882; VI–X, 1884–7)
Philip Massinger (article in *Dictionary of National Biography*).

BRADBROOK, M. C. *Themes and Conventions of Elizabethan Tragedy*, Cambridge, 1935

BRODRICK, G. C. *Memorials of Merton College* (Oxford Historical Society Publications), Oxford, 1885

BROOKE, C. F. T. *Shakespeare Apocrypha*, Oxford, 1918
The Tudor Drama, New York, 1911

Calendar of State Papers, Domestic, for the Reign of Elizabeth

CAMPBELL, LILY B. *Shakespeare's Tragic Heroes: Slaves of Passion*, Cambridge, 1930

CAPES, W. W. *Stoicism*, (Ancient Philosophies for Modern Readers), London, 1880

CHAMBERS, E. K. *The Elizabethan Stage*, 4 vols., Oxford, 1923

CHELLI, MAURICE. *Le Drame de Massinger*, Lyons, 1924
Étude sur la Collaboration de Massinger avec Fletcher et son Groupe, Paris, 1926

COKAINE, SIR ASTON. *Small Poems of Divers Sorts*, London, 1658

COLERIDGE, S. T. *Biographia Literaria*, Ed. J. Shawcross, 2 vols., Oxford, 1907
Coleridge's Miscellaneous Criticism, Ed. T. M. Raysor, London, 1936
Table Talk and Omniana (O.U.P. Edn.), London, 1917

COLLIER, J. P. *Memoirs of Edward Alleyn*, Shakespeare Society, 1841
The History of English Poetry of the Time of Shakespeare and Annals of the Stage to the Restoration, 3 vols., London, 1879

COURTHOPE, W. J. *History of English Poetry*, 6 vols., London, 1895–1910

CRAIG, HARDIN. *The Enchanted Glass*, Oxford, 1950

CREIZENACH, W. *Die Schauspiele der Englischen Komödianten*, (Deutsche Nat. Litt. Bd. 23), Berlin and Stuttgart, 1889
The English Drama in the Age of Shakespeare, London, 1916

CRUICKSHANK, A. H. *Philip Massinger*, Oxford, 1920
Massinger and 'The Two Noble Kinsmen', Oxford, 1922

DASENT, J. R. *Acts of the Privy Council of England, 1542–1604*, Ed. J. R. D., 32 vols., London, 1890–1907

DAVIES, J. S. *The Tropenell Cartulary: the contents of an old Wiltshire Muniment Chest*, 2 vols., Devizes, 1908

DAVIES, THOMAS. *Some Account of the Life and Writings of Philip Massinger, 1789*, (see in Monck Mason's Edition, 1779)

DEMETRIUS. *On Style* (Everyman's Library, 901, Ed. T. A. Moxon), London, 1934

DRAKE, NATHAN. *Shakespeare and His Times*, 2 vols., London, 1817

DRYDEN, JOHN. *The Essays of John Dryden*, Ed. W. P. Ker, 2 vols., Oxford, 1900

EARLE, JOHN. *The Philology of the English Tongue*, Oxford, 1871

EBSWORTH, J. W. *Choyce Drollery*, (Reprint of 1st Edition, 1656), Ed. J. W. E., London, 1876. (See also in Shakespeare Society Papers, III, 1847)

ECCLES, MARK. Letter in *TLS.*, 16 July 1931

ELIOT, T. S. *Philip Massinger* (in *The Sacred Wood*, 1920)
Selected Essays: 1917–1932, London, 1932

ELLIS-FERMOR, U. M. *The Jacobean Drama*, London, 1936

FLEAY, F. G. *Shakespeare Manual*, London, 1878
On the Chronology of the plays of Beaumont, Fletcher and Massinger, (*Englische Studien*, IX, 886)
Chronicle History of the London Stage, 1559–1642, London, 1890
Biographical Chronical of the English Drama, 2 vols., London, 1891

FOSTER, JOSEPH. *Alumni Oxoniensis, 1500–1714*, 4 vols., Oxford, 1891–2

FOWLER, H. W. *A Dictionary of Modern English Usage*, Oxford, 1926

FRIJLINCK, W. P. *The Tragedy of Sir John van Olden Barnavelt*, Ed. from the MS by W. P. F., Amsterdam, 1922[1]

FURNIVALL, F. J. *A Couple of Protests*, (*Anglia*, II, 504, 1879)

GARDINER, S. R. *The Political Element in Massinger* (*Contemporary Review*, Aug., 1876). Reprinted from the Transactions of the New Shakespeare Society, I, 1875–6)

GARROD, R. W. *Massinger* (in *The Profession of Poetry*, Oxford, 1929)

GENEST, J. *Some Account of the English Stage from the Restoration in 1660 to 1830*, 10 vols., Bath, 1832

GENUNG, J. F. *The Working Principles of Rhetoric*, New York, 1900

GERHARDT, E. P. *Massingers 'The Duke of Milan' und seine Quellen*, Halle, 1902

GIBSON, STRICKLAND. *A Bibliography of Francis Kirkman*, (Oxford Bibliographical Society New Series I, Fasc. ii, 1947) Oxford, 1949

GOSSE, EDMUND. *From Shakespeare to Pope*, Cambridge, 1885

GRANVILLE-BARKER, H. *On Dramatic Method* (Clark Lectures, 1930), London, 1931

---

[1] The copy of this in the Honours English Library of the University of Edinburgh has belonged at one time to Professor A. H. Cruickshank and contains many pencilled notes by him, chiefly as regards the authorship of various parts of the play.

The Great Assises holden in Parnassus by Apollo and his Assessors: 1645. (Luttrell Reprints No. 6, Introduction by H. Macdonald, Oxford, 1948)

GREG, W. W. *Henslowe's Diary,* 1904
Henslowe Papers, 1907
The Bakings of Betsy (*Library,* 3rd Series, II, 1911)
Autograph Corrections in 'The Duke of Milan' (*Library,* IV, 1923)
More Massinger Corrections (*Library,* V, 1924)
Dramatic Documents from the Elizabethan Playhouses, 2 vols., Oxford, 1931.

GUMMERE, R. M. *Seneca the Philosopher and His Modern Message* (Our Debt to Greece and Rome, 16), London, 1922,

HALLAM, HENRY. *Introduction to the Literature of Europe,* vol. 3, London, 1839

HALLIDAY, F. E. *Shakespeare and His Critics,* London, 1949

HATCHER, O. L. *Fletcher's Habits of Dramatic Collaboration* (*Anglia,* XXXIII, 219)

HAZLITT, WILLIAM. *Lectures on the Dramatic Literature of the Age of Elizabeth* (Bohn Edition), London, 1897
New Writings by William Hazlett: Second Series. Collected by P. P. Howe, London, 1927

HECKMANN, T. *Massingers 'The Renegado' und seine Spanischen Quellen,* Halle, 1905

HEMMINGE, WILLIAM. *Elegy on Randolph's Finger,* Oxford, 1923

HERBERT, SIR H. *The Dramatic Records of Sir Henry Herbert,* Ed. J. Q. Adams (Cornell Studies in English, 3), Yale, 1917

HERZ, G. *Englische Schauspieler und englisches Schauspiel* (Theatergeschichtliche Forschungen, XVIII), Hamburg und Leipzig, 1903

HIGHET, GILBERT. *The Classical Tradition,* Oxford, 1949

Historical MSS Comm. *Calendar of the MSS belonging to the Marquis of Salisbury,* 1883–1915

HOARE, SIR R. C. *History of Modern Wiltshire: Salisbury and Old Sarum,* 1843

HUNTER, SIR M. *Act and Scene-Division in the Plays of Shakespeare* (*RES,* II, 7, July 1926)

JOHNSON, SAMUEL. *Preface to Shakespeare,* 1765 (*Johnson on Shakespeare,* Ed. Sir W. Raleigh, London, 1916)

JONES, F. L. *An Experiment with Massinger's Verse* (*PMLA,* XLVII, 1932)

JONES, R. F. *The Seventeenth Century,* Stanford, California, 1951

JONSON, BEN. *Works,* Ed. C. H. Herford and P. Simpson, 10 vols., Oxford, 1925–50
The Poems of Ben Jonson, Ed. B. H. Newdigate, Oxford, 1936

JOSEPH, B. L. *How the Elizabethans Acted Shakespeare* (*Listener,* 5 January, 1950)
Elizabethan Acting, London, 1951

JUMP, J. D. *Rollo, Duke of Normandy,* Ed. J. D. J. (Liverpool English Texts and Studies), London, 1948

KEATS, JOHN. *Letters,* Ed. Sir S. Colvin, London, 1925

KNIGHTS, L. C. *Drama and Society in the Age of Jonson,* London, 1937

KOEPPEL, E. *Quellen-Studien zu den Dramen George Chapmans, Philip Massingers, und John Fords* (*QF,* LXXXII, 1897) (Reprinted Münchener Beiträge, XI)
Philip Massinger (*CHEL,* Vol. VI)

LAMB, CHARLES. *Specimens of English Dramatic Poets,* 1808 (Bohn Edition, 1854)

LANGBAINE, GERARD. *An Account of the English Dramatick Poets,* Oxford, 1691. Copy in British Museum—C.28.g.1.—contains MS notes by W. Oldys)

Lansdowne MSS (British Museum), Nos. 63 and 67

LAWRENCE, W. J. *The Renegado* (*TLS,* 24 October, 1929, late 17th-century adaptation in MS)

Massinger's Punctuation (*Criterion*, XI, 1932) (Reprinted in *Those Nut-Cracking Elizabethans*, London, 1935)

LOCKERT, C. L. *The Fatal Dowry* (Massinger and Field), an edition by C. L. L., Lancaster, Pa., 1918

London Magazine, or *The Gentleman's Monthly Intelligencer*, Vol. XXI (4 August, 1762)

London's Lamentable Estate, in any great Visitation, MS poem of 206 lines on plague of 1625, signed 'Ph. M.' (Bodleian MS Rawl. poet. 61)

LOVEJOY, ARTHUR. *The Great Chain of Being*, Cambridge, Mass., 1936

LOWELL, J. R. *Massinger and Ford* (in *Latest Literary Essays and Addresses*, 1891)

LUCAS, F. L. *Seneca and Elizabethan Tragedy*, Cambridge, 1922

MAKKINK, H. J. *Philip Massinger and John Fletcher*, A comparison, Rotterdam, 1927

MALONE, E. *The Plays and Poems of William Shakespeare*, Ed. J. Boswell, 21 vols., 1821 (Vol. III includes Chalmers' *Account of the English Stage*)

MATHEW, DAVID. *The Jacobean Age*, London, 1938
The Social Structure in Caroline England, Oxford, 1948
The Age of Charles I, London, 1951

MAXWELL, BALDWIN. *Studies in Beaumont, Fletcher, and Massinger*, New York, 1939

MEISSNER, J. *Die Englischen Komödianten zur Zeit Shakespeares in Oesterreich* (Beiträge Geschichte der deutschen Litteratur, No. IV), Wien, 1884. (See Jahrbuch der deutschen Shakespeare Gesellschaft, XIX)

MESSINGER, G. W. *New England Historical and Genealogical Register and Antiquarian Journal*, XIV, 75–6, Boston, 1860

MORRIS, E. C. *On the Date and Composition of 'The Old Law'* (*PMLA*, XVII, 1902)

MURRAY, J. T. *English Dramatic Companies, 1558–1642*, 2 vols., Boston and New York, 1910

MACAULAY, G. C. *Beaumont and Fletcher* (*CHEL*, Vol. VI)

MACAULAY, LORD. *John Dryden* (in *Edinburgh Review*, January 1828) (Reprinted in *The Miscellaneous Writings and Speeches of Lord Macaulay*, London, 1900)

McILWRAITH, A. K. *The Virgin's Character*, Reprint of MS poem signed 'P. M.' (*RES*, IV, 1928, 64–8)
RES, IV, 1928, 326–7 (on identification of 'W. B.')
Did Massinger Revise 'The Emperor of the East'? (*RES*, V, 1929)
Some Bibliographical Notes on Massinger (*Library*, XI, 1930)
On the Date of 'A New Way to Pay Old Debts' (*MLR*, XXVIII, 1933)
RES, IX, 1933, October (On dating of *Unnatural Combat*)

McMANAWAY, J. G. *Philip Massinger and the Restoration Drama.*

NEVILL, E. R. *The Chrysom Book of St Thomas, New Sarum* (Wiltshire Notes and Queries, VI, 1908–10, 304)

NICOLL, ALLARDYCE. *The Theory of Drama*, London, 1931

Notes and Queries. I, iii, 52; I, x, 206; II, vi, 229; III, i, 188; IV, xii, 449; V, i, 335; V, x, 465; VIII, viii, 93; X, vi, 248

OLIPHANT, E. H. C. *The Works of Beaumont and Fletcher* (*Englische Studien*, XIV–XVI, 1890–2)
Shakespeare's Plays: an Examination (*MLR*. III–IV, 1908–9)
The Plays of Beaumont and Fletcher, New Haven, 1927
The Plays of Beaumont and Fletcher, Some additional notes (*PQ*, IX, 1930)

Oxford. *Register of the University of Oxford, 1571–1622* (4 parts), Ed. A. Clark, Oxford, 1887–9

PAINTER, WILLIAM. *The Palace of Pleasure*, Ed. J. Jacobs, 3 vols., London, 1890

PHELAN, J. *The Life of Philip Massinger* (*Anglia*, II–III), 1879–80

PHILLIMORE, W. P. W. *Wiltshire Parish Registers: Marriages*, Ed. by W. P. W. P., and others (Phillimore's Parish Register Series), 14 vols., 1905–

PUGH, R. B., *Calender of Antrobus Deeds before 1625*, (Wiltshire Archaeological and Natural History Society, Records Branch, 3) Devizes, 1947

RAEBEL, K. *Massingers Drama 'The Maid of Honour' in seinem Verhältnis zu Painter's 'Palace of Pleasure'*, Halle, 1901

RICE, W. G. *The Sources of Massinger's 'The Renegado' (PQ, XI, 1932)*

RISTINE, F. H. *English Tragi-comedy: Its Origin and History*, New York, 1910

SADLER, J. *Extracts and Notes on Wiltshire Documents and Genealogy* (unpublished) The Museum, Devizes
The Sadler Papers (unpublished), The Museum, Devizes

SAINTSBURY, GEORGE. *A History of English Prosody*, Vol. II, London, 1908

SCHELLING, F. E. *Elizabethan Drama 1558–1642*, Boston and New York, 1908

SCHÜCKING, L. L. *The Baroque Character of the Elizabethan Tragic Hero* (Annual Shakespeare Lecture of British Academy, 19) Proceedings of the British Academy, XXIV, London, 1938

SENECA. *Seneca His Tenne Tragedies translated into English, Edited by Thomas Newton Anno 1581*, With an introduction by T. S. Eliot (Tudor Translations, 2nd series, 11–12) London, 1927

SHANDS, H. A. *Massingers 'The Great Duke of Florence' und seine Quellen*, Halle, 1902

SHEAVYN, PHOEBE. *The Literary Profession in the Elizabethan Age*, Manchester, 1909

SISSON, C. J. *Bibliographical Aspects of Some Stuart Dramatic Manuscripts (RES, I, 4 1925)* (See also under *Believe As You List*)

SMITH, G. G. *Ben Jonson* (Englishmen of Letters), London, 1919

SPENCER, B. T. *Philip Massinger*, (in *Seventeenth Century Studies*, Ed. R. Shaefer, Princeton, 1933)

SPINGARN, J. E. *Critical Essays of the Seventeenth Century*, 3 vols, 1908

SPRAGUE, A. C. *Beaumont and Fletcher on the Restoration Stage*, Cambridge, Mass., 1926

STENIER, A. *Massinger's 'The Picture', Bandello, and Hungary (MLN, XLVI, 1931)*

STEPHEN, SIR J. F. *Essays in Ecclesiastical Biography*, 2 vols, London, 1849

STEPHEN, SIR L. *Philip Massinger* (Hours in A Library, II) 1899

STEWART, J. I. M. *Character and Motive in Shakespeare*, London, 1949

STOCKS, J. L. *Aristotelianism* (Our Debt to Greece and Rome, No. 20), London, 1925

STOKES, ETHEL. *Abstracts of Inquisitiones Post Mortem . . . Edward III* (Wiltshire Archaeological and Natural History Society), London, 1914

SWINBURNE, A. C. *Philip Massinger* (Fortnightly Review, July 1889) (Reprinted in *Contemporaries of Shakespeare*, 1919)

SYKES, H. D. *Sidelights on Elizabethan Drama*, London, 1924

TANNENBAUM, S. A. *Corrections to the Text of 'Believe As You List' (PMLA, September 1927)*

THOMPSON, E. N. S. *Elizabethan Dramatic Collaboration (Englische Studien, XL, 1909)*

THORNDIKE, A. H. *The Influence of Beaumont and Fletcher on Shakespeare*, Worcester, Mass., 1901
Tragedy, New York, 1908
Shakespeare's Theater, New York, 1916

THORN-DRURY, G. *A Little Ark*, London, 1921

Times Literary Supplement: Philip Massinger, 1583–1640, Anonymous article on the occasion of the tercentenary of Massinger's death in the Issue dated 16 March, 1940. (But see also Clifford Leech, 23 March, 1940)

WALLIS, L. B. *Fletcher, Beaumont, and Company*, 1947

WANN, L. *The Collaboration of Beaumont, Fletcher, and Massinger* (in *Shakespeare Studies* by Department of English of the University of Wisconsin, Madison, 1916)

WARD, SIR A. W. *A History of English Dramatic Literature*, 3 vols, London, 1899

WELLS, H. W. *Elizabethan and Jacobean Playwrights*, 1939

WIELER, J. W. *George Chapman—the effect of Stoicism upon his Tragedies*, New York, 1949

WILLIAMSON, GEORGE. *The Senecan Amble*, London, 1951

WILSON, F. P. *Library*, VII, 1926, 199. (Mention of MS of *London's Lamentable Estate*, see above)
  Elizabethan and Jacobean (Alexander Lectures in English, 1943), Oxford, 1945

WILSON, J. DOVER. *Act and Scene-Divisions in the Plays of Shakespeare: A Rejoinder to Sir Mark Hunter* (*RES*, III, 1927)
  The New Cambridge Shakespeare: Critical Introductions to those plays in this series issued under Professor Dover Wilson's editorship

Wiltshire Notes and Queries } published by the Wiltshire Archaeological and
Wiltshire Archaeological Magazine} Natural History Society, The Museum, Devizes

Wit and Fancy in a Maze, etc., An anonymous mock-romance, London, 1656

WOOD, ANTHONY À. *Athenae Oxoniensis*, Ed. P. Bliss, 4 vols, London, 1813–20

WURZBACH, W. VON. *Philip Massinger*, Shakespeare Jahrbuch, XXXV–XXXVI, 1899–1900

INDEX

Major references to the dramatist and his work will be found arranged under Main-Headings, viz. *Characters*, *Massinger*, and *Plays*

Abstract nouns, 241
Act- and scene-divisions, 57
Act-endings, 82
Adultery, 160
Allusion, contemporary, 172 ff.
Anglicanism, 190–1
Appositional phrases, 262
Aristotle, 125, 136, 196–7, 251
Arnold, Matthew, 217–18
Asides, 86–92
    length of, 86–7, 88, 90–1, 92
    number of, 86
    Shakespeare's, 87
    two types of, 87–90
Atterbury, Francis, 237
Aubrey, John, 24, 46, 48–9, 50
Augustine, St., 235
Aurner, R. R., 235

Bacon, Sir Francis, 234, 235
Bagnall, William, 43
Baldwin, T. W., 31 note 1, 86, 229
Basse, William, 43
Bawdy, in heroines' speech, 115
Beaumont, Francis, 55, 107–8, 236
Beaumont and Fletcher, 1647 Folio, 27
Bibliography, 274–80
    Biography, criticism, etc., 275–80
    Collected Editions, 274
    Selections, 274
    Separate Editions, 274
Blair, Hugh, 217, 219
Blake, William, 251
Bradbrook, Muriel C., 106
Browne, William, 42–3
Browning, Elizabeth Barrett, 238
Bryne, Eva W., 211
Buckingham, George Villiers, 1st Duke of, 23, 173–4
Burnet, Gilbert, 236

Carnarvon, Robert Dormer, 1st Earl of, 50, 185
Casting, 100–2
Chambers, Sir E. K., 11
Chapman, George, 195, 202
Characterisation, flaws in, 135–41
    type-characterisation, 106–8, 121–2, 131
Characters
    Adorni, 120; Beaumelle, 114; Bellisant, 116–17; Bertoldo, 179–84; Camiola, 115, 116, 179–84; Charalois, 110, 112; Cleora, 115, 118; Domitian, 128, 166, 167–9; Donusa, 177–8; Luke Frugal, 125–6; Malefort, 126–8; Marcelia, 115, 154–5; Overreach, 122–5, 126–7; Romont, 120; Sforza, 109; Vitelli, 177–9

Characters–*cont.*
    Change of direction in, 136–8
    Comic characters, 130–1
    Credibility of, 136–8
    Criminal characters, 121–9
    Individuality of, 131
    Jaloux, 108–12
    Man of passion, 109–12, 113
    Man of virtue, 119–20
    Minor characters, 120–1
    Woman of passion, 112–15
    Woman of virtue, 114–19
Charles I, 174–6
Chastity, 115–18, 160
Chelli, Maurice, viii, 11, 55, 108, 111, 115, 132, 140, 147, 149, 166, 167, 179, 186, 189, 190, 195, 264, 267
Chorus, 96–7, 98
Ciceronianism, 232 ff., 261
Classicism, 195–6
Clavell, John, 36
Climaxes, 57–8
Climaxes, Act IV, 68–70
Cokaine, Aston, 20, 26–7, 45–6, 48–9, 50
Coleridge, Hartley, vii, 10, 11, 185
Coleridge, S. T., 135, 136, 165, 201, 223, 224, 229, 237, 265
Collaboration, 24 ff., 267
Commentation, 98–100
Companies, theatrical, 28 ff.
Cornwallis, Sir William, 235
Couplet discipline, 260–1
Couplet-endings, 82–3
Coxeter, Thomas, 54
Craig, Hardin, 137
Crowd-scenes, 95–6
Cruickshank, A. H., v, 55, 126, 135, 137, 138, 200, 201, 204, 265, 276 note 1
Cunningham, Francis, 10

Daborne, Robert, 15–16
Davies, Thomas, 4, 41, 42
Debate in dialogue, 139–40
Dekker, Thomas, 28
Demetrius, 237
Description, 'scenic-descriptive', 83–4, 256–7
    'sense-descriptive', 84, 241, 245–6
Dialogue, character-differentiation in, 139–141
    distribution of, 101–2, 103–5
    style of, 94 ff., 222–4
Diction, 238 ff., 257–60
Didacticism, 142 ff.
Dignity of Massinger's style, 237–8
'Discovery', 79
'Dissociation of sensibility', 202, 257–62
Donne, George, 26, 45

Printed in Great Britain by Thomas Nelson and Sons Ltd, Edinburgh